EMPLOYEE OWNERSHIP

EMPLOYEE OWNERSHIP

Revolution or Ripoff?

Joseph Raphael Blasi

1817

HARPER BUSINESS

A Division of Harper & Row Publishers, New York

Grand Rapids, Philadelphia, St. Louis, San Francisco
London, Singapore, Sydney, Tokyo, Toronto

International Standard Book Number: 0–88730–065–0 (cloth)
0–88730–443–5 (paper)

Library of Congress Catalog Card Number: 87–35402

Printed in the United States of America

Library of Congress Cataloging-in-Publication Data

Blasi, Joseph R.
    Employee ownership: revolution or ripoff? / Joseph Raphael Blasi.
        p.   cm.
    Includes index.
    ISBN 0–88730–065–0 (cloth)
    ISBN 0–88730–443–5 (paper)
    1. Employee ownership—United States. 2. Profit-sharing—United States. 3. Industrial relations—United States. I. Title.
HD5660.U5B569   1988
388.6—dc19

87–35402
CIP

90 91 92 93 HC 9 8 7 6 5 4 3 2 1

CONTENTS

ACKNOWLEDGMENTS

The title of this book is inspired by the April 15, 1985, Business Week cover story of the same name by John Hoerr, with Gelvin Stevenson, James R. Norman, and Pete Engardio. That article helped to raise many of the serious questions with which this book is concerned, and the title is used with the permission of Mr. Hoerr and Business Week Editor-in-Chief Stephen B. Shepard. This book is dedicated to my parents, Angelo and Jean Blasi, and my sister, Tina Blasi, who gave me unbelievable support during the time it was being written and whose love and devotion know no bounds.

The idea for the book initially grew out of a paper written for the Industrial Relations Research Association at the behest of David Bloom, professor of economics at Columbia University, and the constant encouragement of Philip N. Warburg, both of whom are close friends and comrades in ideas. While my colleague at Harvard, David helped plan the book and find a publisher and he monitored its progress at every turn. Philip's impact on my career and ideas has been seminal. I wish to thank the entire Warburg family and their foundation, Bydale, for significant support of my research over a decade. Jerry Frug of the Harvard Law School pushed me to include an analysis of the law in detail. My colleagues William Foote Whyte of Cornell University and Corey Rosen and Karen Young of the National Center for Employee Ownership shared the many stages of my public policy, personal, and intellectual involvement with the book, and each has contributed much time in reviewing manuscripts and aiding me in other ways.

Douglas Kruse of Harvard's Department of Economics worked for me as a researcher and painstakingly assembled materials, prepared memoranda on key questions, and exposed weaknesses in my arguments. The research and the writing simply could not have taken place without him. I owe special thanks to the team at Ballinger. Marjorie

Richman, my editor, believed in the book and steered it through multiple drafts with uncommon dedication. Barbara Roth guided the actual editing with exquisite patience. The manuscript editor, Sarah St. Onge, deserves a special note of thanks for actually making this a readable book after months of careful work. She made a habit of challenging me on many fronts, and her impact cannot be exaggerated. Carol Franco, the president of Ballinger, gave the project the benefit of the exceptional commitment of her whole staff and resource base.

This book has been at least ten years in the making. It pulls together research, case studies, policy experience, theory, and practice that span many settings: a decade of lecturing at Harvard University and learning the unique interdisciplinary approach of the Social Studies Department; five years as an advisor on employee ownership and participation in the U.S. House of Representatives with Congressman Peter H. Kostmayer (D-Pa.); many years of research and writing on Israel's system of worker-owned kibbutzim and unique labor movement in the context of Harvard's Project for Kibbutz Studies.

In 1984 I began a study group on worker ownership and participation in business at Harvard, which brought together scholars and business, government, and labor leaders to discuss the implications of emerging laws, cases, and trends in this area. Through the study group, several of us began to initiate research and refine these ideas and discuss them at monthly public forums. I am indebted to the Harman Program at the Kennedy School of Government, which helped me to convene many of these meetings and contributed its own perspective on these issues; Michael Maccoby and Harvey Brooks of that program were particularly generous with their support.

Many students who participated in the study group wrote senior and doctoral theses that contributed to my thinking, especially Steven Bloom who also read this manuscript, Adam Blumenthal, Gail Sokoloff, Ken Hahn, Perry Mehrling, Steven Dostart, Pretta Bansal, Megan Campbell, Douglas Kruse, Wendy Coleman, Paul Edelman, Scott Androes, Amy Tighe, and David Finegold.

The study group's final research project was a documentation of labor-management cooperation at Eastern Airlines, funded by the U.S. Department of Labor as a joint Harvard/Brigham Young University project, the conclusions of which will be published by the U.S. Department of Labor Publications Division. My involvement in the Eastern study had a profound impact on the conclusions advanced in this book, and I view it as a companion volume. That project would not have succeeded without the leadership and hard work of Beverly Smaby and the cooperation of Chris Meek, both my colleagues and friends, and Catherine Barnes and Pretta Bansal. It was made possible through the initial cooperation of Jack Johnson, former senior vice president at Eastern and now director of the U.S. Federal Mediation and Conciliation Service, Charles Bryan of the International Association of Machinists, and Randy Barber of the Center for Economic Organizing.

This book was written while I was a visiting researcher at the Harvard Business School. I acknowledge the graciousness of George Cabot Lodge and Paul Lawrence of the Human Resources Management Group. George Lodge's ideological leadership significantly influenced my findings and he also provided practical support when the study group convened sessions at the Business School faculty club over the many years we have been associated.

In 1985 I began my continuing service on the faculty of Harvard's Trade Union Program, the spring sessions of which sparked crucial debates between various trade union leaders and employee ownership and participation actors whom I invited to conduct seminars. Professor James Medoff, program chairman, and Linda Kaboolian, executive director, continue to help make this program possible. Harvard's Social Studies Department enthusiastically supported my activities over many years and was particularly generous the year this book was written. I would like to thank the chairman, Professor David Landes; the head tutor, Judy N. Vichniac; Professor Rick Hunt; and Professor Michael Donnelly, this last for his quiet support over the years; along with the former chairman of Princeton's Institute for Advanced Studies, Michael Walzer, as well as Jan Bedau and Lucy White. The final editing of the book took place at the California Polytechnic School of Business during the summer and fall of 1987, and I am indebted to the following individuals for extending to me their goodwill and allowing me to accomplish this task with an appropriate teaching and travel schedule: Dean Ken Walters; Associate Dean Zaf Iqbal; former department heads Allan Baillie and Rolf Rogers; department head David Beach; Professor Abraham Shani; Joyce Coe; and Malcolm Wilson, academic vice president of the university.

Several other organizations figured prominently in my work in this area: the National Center for Employee Ownership, with its excellent resources; David Ellerman, Chris Mackin, and Steve Dawson at the Industrial Cooperative Association; Howard Samuel and Richard Prosten at the Industrial Union Department of the AFL-CIO, who gave me an opportunity to meet with the national presidents on these matters; Pat Grasso at the U.S. General Accounting Office, who provided access to their studies; Senator Russell Long, Jeff Gates, and Jack Curtis, formerly of the Senate Finance Committee; the Work in America Institute, which catalyzed the focus on public corporations; former CEO Robert Loughhead and Chuck Cronin of the Weirton Steel Corporation; Jared Kaplan of Keck, Mahin, & Cate; Ray Schmitt of Congressional Research Service; Laithe Wilson and Michael Quarrey of NCEO; Suzanne Kempel (Hilles Library) and Nano Dickson (Baker Library) of Harvard University; David Binns of the ESOP Association of America; Sherman Kreiner of the Philadelphia Association for Cooperative Enterprise; Sev Bruyn and Charles Derber of the Social Economy Program at Boston College; and Robert McKersie and Tom Kochan of the Industrial Relations Section of the Sloan School at MIT, who gave their helpful insights on the overall trends in U.S. labor relations.

I would also like to thank a number of individuals whose kindness and generosity influenced me greatly: the members of the Auburn House Association in especial; Lakshmi Reddy Bloom; Menachem Rosner; Edward Mitchell; Chip Brewer; Keith Bradley; Ben Fischer; Kirsten Wever; Michael Quarrey; Chuck Leddon of CSX Corporation; Innaki Gorrono and Maria Jesus Zabaleta of the Caja Laboral Popular; Malon Wilkus; Susan Sklar; Avraham Yassour; Benjamin Beit-Hallahmi; Lucy Jones; Norman Kurland; Susan Bruce; Ron Ludwig; Richard Wakefield; Phil Stone; Jerome Weiman; Yehuda Paz; Seymour Melman; Yehuda Don; Don Oliver, Kathy Cahill, Dana Gibson, Jim and Cheryl Keen; Louis and Patricia Kelso; Heidi Larson; Peggy Schnorr; Elisha Frank; Nancy Yahanda; Alex Drier; Wally Cook; Nathan Glazer; Mike Kearney; Wallace Gonzalez, Sr.; Wallace Gonzalez, Jr.; David Myers; Jay Jones; and Evelyn Haralampu, who advised me on the technical and legal chapters.

I take full responsiblity for any errors.

INTRODUCTION

We are witnessing the most significant attempt in recent history to expand worker ownership in American society. For nearly fifteen years, employee ownership and participation have been heralded as a premier form of labor-management cooperation as well as the solution to America's lagging competitiveness. The most popular method for fostering worker ownership in individual firms is the Employee Stock Ownership Plan, or ESOP. Quite simply, an ESOP is a means by which employees can own stock in the companies where they work. It is a form of worker ownership and participation designed for taxpaying corporations and encouraged by federal law.

REVOLUTION OR RIPOFF?

Is employee ownership a revolution or a ripoff? It is a ripoff when it uses public tax expenditures to serve the interests of highly paid employees alone or to entrench existing management. It is a cheat when it denies employees voting rights on their stock and severely limits the rights and responsibilities to which owners are traditionally entitled. It is a disappointment when the meager amount of stock involved or the promise of stock only upon retirement undercuts a worker's sense of identification with the company. It is a poor incentive when it is not combined with short-term profit sharing that allows immediate participation in the success of the company. It becomes the pied piper of competitiveness when advocates claim that employees' owning "a piece of the action" automatically improves corporate economic performance.

On the other hand, employee ownership could be considered revolutionary in terms of the commitment it can create among various work groups within an organization. It can elicit the American version of

Japanese loyalty. It can go beyond wages and incentives to forge a joint sense of partnership by establishing a longer-term identification between the worker and the company.

To transform the conflict-ridden American labor-management system requires a shift in ideologies among all the players, as George Lodge of the Harvard Business School has forcefully argued.[1] Now, both management and labor are firmly committed to outmoded images of the corporation that undermine the entrepreneurial thrust of the best side of American capitalism. In this tradition, managers feel entitled to royal rewards, while workers expect to be cared and provided for by a corporation whose inner workings they do not attempt to understand. Under these conditions, labor-management relations will remain mired in conflict and distrust.

For employee ownership to constitute a true revolution in labor-management relations, it must be accompanied by substantial involvement of workers in their companies. Without labor-management cooperation in practical problem solving, workers purchase equity in their companies only to experience frustration and disillusionment later. Employee ownership can topple the feudal monolith if it becomes part of a broader plan that links reward with performance. It can serve as a sign that management considers workers deserving of responsibility and worthy of entrepreneurial involvement in their companies.

A major shortcoming shared by management books, consultants, and scholars is the tendency to focus on only one of four elements that can supposedly revive the corporation: employee ownership, profit sharing, labor-management cooperation, and work redesign. However, as I shall demonstrate, it is only when the four are applied *in concert* that we can begin to realize the goal of workplace reform.

The nexus of cultural change in a company is labor-management cooperation; no element of status, prerogative, or rank should interfere with whatever must be done to identify and solve problems and to improve productivity and competitiveness. Such cooperation depends on far-reaching changes in attitudes and behaviors, which can be achieved only through education and resocialization of managers and workers, organized and unorganized alike. Employee ownership may promote a special relationship between employee and company that increases their commitment to resolving problems, and profit sharing may provide the short-term rewards of such problem solving, but in the end people are motivated by contributing to creative solutions that bear results and make exciting use of their skills.

The intellectual ripoff of employee ownership is based on the belief that profit sharing and stock ownership *cause* success. However, when employee ownership provides limited equity but retains the outdated notions about worker motivation, compensation, work design, and the roles of labor and management, it only recreates the system it was intended to replace. No amount of employee ownership or profit sharing will disguise the fundamental weakness of work tasks that are inefficiently organized or designed in such a way that they minimize the autonomy and interest of the employee. As Jesus said in the gospels, new wine poured into old wineskins can only take on the taste of the old.

Political leaders have relied on the ESOP's federal tax incentives to counteract the concentration of wealth that has long dominated American capitalism. In fact, employee ownership has broadened wealth only minimally in the last fifteen years, since most of the tax expenditures in effect subsidized Fortune 1000 corporations whose tax-credit ESOPs generally benefitted highly compensated employees. Today, in 1988, there are fewer than 2,000 majority employee-owned companies in the United States, although recent events suggest that their numbers may burgeon in the years to come.

Federal policies have always been the major determinant of worker investments in U.S. industry. Since governmental initiatives set the basic rules and regulations of the structure and rights of worker ownership, the ESOP represents an important test case of how the state seeks to connect work, ownership, and participation in American society. That relationship will be explored in this book as we examine how the ESOP has evolved since its emergence a decade and a half ago.

At present, the employee-ownership movement carries a perverse anti-worker bias. It has discounted the rights and responsibilities of rank-and-file workers. The law facilitates the exclusion of unionized workers from employee-ownership plans. Unions, reacting with suspicion to employee ownership, have generally not attempted to shape its formulation in Congress, to encourage it as a form of labor organization, to endorse it as a political program, or to support locals and unorganized workers in employee-ownership initiatives. As this book goes to press, the AFL-CIO Executive Council has issued a thoughtful and detailed employee-ownership policy, but more remains to be done.

Inherent in employee ownership's current ideology is the naive assumption that workers who become owners will metamorphose into well-behaved capitalists who no longer need an autonomous voice in the corporation. This distorted realization of a concept that was intended primarily to benefit workers is responsible for much of the cynicism with which organized labor and many unorganized workers have responded to employee ownership. It is a regrettable reaction given that opinion polls have revealed widespread support from the American public for the principle of employee ownership.

If a truly vibrant "people's capitalism" is to form the economic foundation of a political democracy in the United States, employee ownership must transcend its legacy as an intellectual and political ripoff--a legacy it will be forced to inherit if its champions continue to tout it as the answer to *the* frustrations of managers seeking to motivate, to the despair of unions in decline, and to the hopelessness of leaders struggling to reinvigorate a waning competitive system. When combined with genuine labor-management cooperation and a flexible approach to compensation, however, employee ownership is an important part of the answer. It is to the history and roots of employee ownership's pitfalls and to the tremendous potential that awaits genuine work reform that we now turn our attention.

Chapter 1

The Birth of the ESOP

The 3,000 employees of W. L. Gore & Associates of Newark, Delaware, largely own their company through an employee stock ownership plan. No Gore facility has more than 200 employees. They are all encouraged to take initiative and interact freely with any member of the company without regard to traditional hierarchy in order to develop new projects. Diverse applications of the fabric Gore-Tex® have made the company immensely profitable, and all employees share in this through two profit-sharing plans.[1]

Although Hallmark Cards, Inc., of Kansas City, Missouri, is largely owned by the Hall family, employees own about one-third of the company through a profit-sharing plan that invests much of its assets in Hallmark stock. In 1983 the company put $32 million— about 11 percent of the employees' total annual salaries—into the fund. As part of its "family" philosophy, the company has instituted a no-layoff policy and strives to provide a creative yet secure environment for artists.[2]

Lincoln Electric in Cleveland, Ohio, has an extensive system of gainsharing that ties all or part of its employees' pay to productivity or financial performance rather than to a fixed wage. Each employee receives an annual bonus, which has averaged 100 percent of their annual salary in recent years. Through a stock-purchase plan, any employee with more than one year of service can buy stock at book value, and over 40 percent of Lincoln's stock is owned by about 75 percent of the workforce. Since it instituted the plan, Lincoln Electric has reported substantial increases in productivity with three times fewer supervisors than comparable firms.[3]

Federal Express of Memphis, Tennessee, is a people-oriented company that emphasizes excellence in service and fair treatment of its 30,000 employees. Like many publicly held companies, Federal Express has several plans that provide ownership to employees. The company pays top wages and has a profit-sharing plan, an ESOP, an employee stock-purchase plan for all workers, and a stock-option plan for managers.[4]

F or employee ownership to play a significant role in restructuring American business, extensive public dialogue and debate must determine what form it should take and how it should be coordinated with a broader reform of the corporation.

Signs of ferment already abound. For the purposes of this book, I have estimated that 8 million workers, comprising 7 percent of the private-sector workforce, are participating in employee-ownership plans with assets of about $19 billion in 7,500 companies, about 1,500 of which are majority or fully employee owned. Yet, in September 1987 alone, three major transformations of ownership have altered the ESOP landscape: Hospital Corporation of American sold 104 general hospitals to an employee-owned company for $2.1 billion; Avis Rent-a-Car sold its entire national system to its employees for $750 million; and the December 14, 1987 issue of *Business Week* reports four recent cases where takeover bids were initiated by trade unions and totalled over $5 billion. These and other anticipated ESOP transactions in large corporations may foretell a dramatic increase in employee-ownership participants, assets, and companies.[5]

Employee Stock Ownership Plans

Throughout this book, the term ESOP will be used to refer to all types of ESOPs. There are three main types: the nonleveraged ESOP, the leveraged ESOP, and the tax-credit ESOP (the TRASOP and the PAYSOP).

The Nonleveraged ESOP

This form of the ESOP creates worker ownership from cash or stock the employer has on hand, although it can later become leveraged. The company contributes stock or cash to buy stock to a trust that buys worker shares. When the worker retires or otherwise leaves the firm, any shares that have been vested must be redeemed with cash.

The Leveraged ESOP

Often called the Kelso-ESOP, this variation is based on federally subsidized producer credit. It establishes worker ownership with money the company or the ESOP borrows to invest in company stock for workers. The corporation guarantees that it will make periodic payments to the worker-ownership trust to amortize the loan. The relationship is symbiotic—the trust uses the borrowed funds to buy stock in the corporation, which in turn gets to use the capital for its own purposes. Because company contributions to a worker-ownership trust are deductible within certain limits, the amounts attributable to repaying both the interest and the principal of this loan are tax deductible. Indebtedness is paid with pretax dollars.

The Tax-Credit ESOP

The TRASOP (or Tax Reduction Act stock ownership plan), later the PAYSOP (or payroll-based stock ownership plan), generally accounts for a small percentage of employee ownership in large publicly held companies. When they establish these plans, firms get a dollar-for-dollar tax credit, the upper limit of which is related to their annual capital investment (in the TRASOP) or payroll (in the PAYSOP). They cannot use debt financing to purchase stock for workers. The Chicago law firm of Keck, Mahin and Cate described the PAYSOP this way in its promotional literature: "Through the use of a PAYSOP, a company may compel the government to purchase employer stock for cash and give the stock back to its employees."[6]

Common Characteristics

Employee-ownership trusts are set up with approval from the Internal Revenue Service. Company contributions to the trust—of stock, cash, or even real estate—are exempt from federal income tax, and the trustees of the ESOP invest these chiefly in company stock. In all three cases, when the company contributes stock or cash to buy stock to the employee stock ownership trust, the company actually retains the use of the capital until the worker leaves or retires. This is quite different from other benefit plans, where in most cases the worker-investment trust purposely invests outside the company. Companies can deduct their contributions to these ESOP trusts from pretax corporate income, and the trust does not pay tax on its profit on investments. For employees, this is deferred compensation on which they do not pay tax until it is distributed to them, usually at retirement.

A company or an ESOP can go to the credit markets to borrow the funds to purchase worker ownership with substantial tax incentives. No other benefit plans can leverage credit for worker ownership or for direct benefits. Federal law has in fact provided the ESOP with the richest tax incentives ever through laws passed from 1974 to 1986 (see Appendix A).

Perhaps most notably, the ESOP is designed to invest primarily in employer securities and does not have to diversify its investments. An ESOP can hold more than 10 percent of its assets in the stock of the employer corporation. Generally, other types of employee-benefit plans, with the exception of some specially designated profit-sharing plans, cannot do this.

The ESOP's unique structure eliminates some critical barriers to broadened ownership. Acknowledging that most workers do not have the savings to buy stock in their companies or to start up new employee-owned firms even if they so desired, it offers instead the option of credit to purchase worker equity. It provides a way to establish employee ownership in closely held firms whose stock is not traded on a public exchange. Finally, companies, unions, and workers themselves can use employee stock ownership to accomplish a wide array of corporate activities (see Appendix B).

As of 1987, it is estimated that only about 7,000 to 8,000 U.S. companies have employee stock ownership plans, with approximately 8 million worker participants. About 1,000 to 1,500 of these companies are 51 to 100 percent owned by their workers, who probably number around 1 million. Perhaps as many as another million workers are in firms that are 20 to 50 percent employee owned. About 100 to 150 ESOP firms are the result of worker buyouts of failing companies or successful subsidiaries of large concerns.[7]

Since they are built around stock, ESOPs can be established only in publicly or privately held corporations that issue stock. These account for about 40 percent of the country's business ownership, approximately 90 percent of its employment and sales, and the lion's share of its productive capacity. In addition, ESOPs can be installed usefully only where taxes are paid, and about 56 percent of all corporations do not even pay taxes. Theoretically, then, the ESOP can affect at most less than a quarter of the ownership in the country and still reach almost half the workforce The corporate form of ownership truly dominates the American economy. Changes in ownership and participation in this sector will affect business as a whole.

Why Employee Ownership?

The concept of and support for employee ownership have their roots in a variety of social, political, and economic ideologies that stretch across party lines. Consider, for example, Ronald Reagan's comments:

Our Founding Fathers well understood that concentrated power is the enemy of liberty and the rights of man. They knew that the American experiment in individual liberty, free enterprise and republican self-government could succeed only if power was widely distributed. And since in any society social and political power flow from economic power, they saw that wealth and property would have to be widely distributed among the people of the country. The truth of this insight is immediately apparent. Could there be anything resembling a free enterprise economy, if wealth and property were concentrated in the hands of a few, while the greatest majority owned little more than the shirts on their backs? Could there be anything but widespread misery, where a privileged few controlled a nation's wealth, while millions labored for a pittance, and millions more were desperate for want of employment? It should be clear to everyone that the nation's steadfast policy should afford every American of working age a realistic opportunity to acquire the ownership and control of some meaningful form of property in a growing national economy.

And compare with that Hubert Humphrey's viewpoint:

Capital, and the question of who owns it and therefore reaps the benefit of its productiveness, is an extremely important issue that is complementary to the issue of full employment . . . . I see these as the twin pillars of our economy: Full employment of our labor resources and widespread ownership of our capital resources. Such twin pillars would go a long way in providing a firm underlying support for future economic growth that would be equitably shared.

Indeed, employee ownership is widely believed to be one of many useful responses to the challenges of increased economic competition.[8]

In 1975 the Peter Hart Organization asked a national sample of citizens whether they would rather work in a firm owned by outside investors, by the employees, or by the government. Sixty-six percent wished to work for a firm owned by its employees. A 1980 Gallup/Chamber of Commerce poll found that 84 percent of the population said they would work harder and do a better job if they were involved in decisions related to their work.[9] Furthermore, a 1982 New York Stock Exchange survey of managers in corporations with 500 or more employees showed that 82 percent considered participative management to be a promising approach for business enterprises, while 78 percent of the managers gave the programs in their experience good marks for improving productivity and lowering costs.[10]

Despite this substantial unanimity, which is consistent across different racial and income groups, political parties, and geographical regions, little careful thought has been given to exactly what form employee ownership should take. What do worker ownership and participation mean to men and women who do not work for corporations, such as the self-employed, employees of the government, members of the armed services, employees of nonprofit organizations, and so forth? If worker equity were widespread, would it be equally good for society as a whole, for business, and for workers, or would it require the sacrifice of power and resources by some for the benefit of others? Does employee ownership involve real changes for workers, unions, entrepreneurs, owners, and managers, or will its influence be purely superficial? Do we find worker participation where we find worker ownership? Does ownership cause the individual worker to change his or her attitudes or behavior? Finally, what will be the impact on the performance of the firm, the economy, and the individual worker? Is employee ownership good in itself or is its potentially positive impact what interests us? And who is to decide?

Different groups, although in agreement about the essential validity of employee ownership, have different answers to these questions. The popular, scholarly, and legislative discussion about ESOPs can be reduced to five major claims. Taken together they predict a certain impact of ESOPs on power, prestige, and resources in corporations and in society as a whole. First, the ethical claim is that employee ownership and participation will lead to a society based on justice, equality, democracy, and respect for the person. Second, the legal claim is that ESOPs have real political potential in modern American society and that legislative intervention can make the innovation work by setting proper goals, creating a workable instrument, and establishing an appropriate ideology for worker ownership. Third, the psychological claim is that ownership makes workers more committed to their jobs, their companies, and their work performance. Fourth, the economic claim says that a firm with employee ownership will be more profitable and productive than a comparable firm in the same industry, all other things being equal, and suggests that ESOPs can promote flexible systems of compensation to deal with an uncertain economic climate. Regarding the economy at large, it says that new forms of corporate finance can meaningfully change the patterns of ownership in the economy and encourage new capital formation. Finally, the sociological claim is that labor and management will be more cooperative under employee ownership.

Senator Russell Long (D-La.) has been the main architect of ESOP law, although his initiatives easily attracted widespread support on both sides of Capitol Hill. Investment banker and lawyer Louis Kelso supplied Long with an analysis of capitalism and ownership. Long and Kelso are not carbon copies of each other, nor was either man able to dictate entirely the resultant body of law. Indeed, Kelso's broader views about how the economy works are anathema to many economists, but his initial insights about the relationship between work and ownership made practical sense to legislators and their influence cannot be ignored.

Briefly, Kelso noted that, although corporations create new capital every year, the state has so constructed the system of financing this new capital investment that ownership stays concentrated. Most corporations invest mainly past profits and debt to create new capital—as the Federal Reserve Board found to be the case from 1955 to 1985—and this benefits existing shareholders. Generally, less than 5 percent of the new capital is issued in new shares. Over 95 percent goes to the existing shareholders, who already control most of America's corporate wealth.[11]

Kelso felt that the structure of wealth creation was wrongly rigged. In his view, capital investment often pays for itself no matter who owns it, especially in the large corporations that can justify large capital expenditures and show a projection of future profits. His solution was to recommend an alternative construction. His Financed Capitalist Plan was straightforward: (1) Require corporations to pay out all their earnings as dividends except those necessary for general operations; (2) Require corporations to obtain new capital by issuing new stock instead of using current earnings or debt; (3) Eliminate or drastically reduce the corporate income tax so that more money can go to individuals; (4) Have the federal government change the system of credit so that families with little or no capital can get credit to buy stock, which will be held in escrow until dividends pay for it; (5) Create a new government agency to guarantee bank loans to individuals for the acquisition of stock.

This plan did not depend on employment; the new capitalists did not have to work in the corporations where they owned stock. And it was based on the capital growth of the largest and most successful corporations in the country, who would have to present feasibility studies showing that their new capital items would pay for themselves out of future earnings within a reasonable number of years, which is exactly what they do now when they finance new capital acquisitions through loans or even retained earnings. This far-reaching plan was never adopted, but the ESOP was designed to achieve some of its goals.[12]

In Search of Employee Ownership

The fact remains, however, that most employee ownership stems from benefit plans. After World War I Congress was looking for ways to help industry attract and hold workers. The Revenue Act of 1921 gave the first tax-favored status to stock-bonus and profit-sharing plans; five years later, the same status was accorded pension plans. Even so, in 1939 there were only 659 such plans of all types in the United States. During World War II, however, government wage and price controls prompted employers and unions to develop jointly various types of plans in order to retain and compensate workers without causing inflation. In 1947 the Supreme Court upheld a National Labor Relations Board ruling requiring employers to bargain in good faith about the terms of retirement-benefit plans. Plans numbered about 25,000 by 1954, just over 100,000 by 1964, and over 400,000 in 1974, just after Congress passed the Employee Retirement Income Security Act, which more carefully defined and regulated the various approaches to worker investment and retirement security. A surge in the development of retirement plans followed this law. In 1986 there were about one million worker-investment plans in the country. A U.S. company is not required to establish a retirement plan, but if it does it must abide by federal regulations. Organized labor had a major part in the proliferation of retirement plans.[13]

Defined-benefit pension plans and defined-contribution pension plans essentially allow workers to set up tax-sheltered investment trusts with their own and/or company contributions. Later, the workers benefit from the investment performance of these trusts. To encourage the employer to contribute, the earnings on these investments, as well as the contributions themselves, are not subject to corporate tax.

In the defined-benefit plan, the company is required by law to contribute enough funds to allow the trust to generate sufficient assets to pay a predefined benefit, which is insured by the Pension Benefits Guarantee Corporation. With such a plan, it is not always possible to predict what the capital requirements for employee benefits will be over time. In the defined-contribution plan, the company commits only to making certain contributions to the plan; the employee benefit depends solely on the investment performance of these contributions. This tax-exempt trust, like all retirement-plan trusts, is regulated by the Internal Revenue Service and the Department of Labor. Each account is credited with its share of investment return over time, including any increases or decreases in the market value of the underlying investments. These plans are often referred to as capital-accumulation plans because that is what they allow workers to do. In addition to ESOPs, they include *profit-sharing plans*, which base the contribution on profit—although they are no longer required to do so under the 1986 tax law—and distribute cash to workers in cash plans or invest profits in a trust in deferred plans; *stock-bonus plans*, which distribute stock to workers and do not base the contribution on profit; *money-purchase pension plans*, where the company makes fixed contributions not based on profit; *thrift* or *savings plans*, where employees contribute a predetermined portion of earnings to an investment account, and the employer matches these contributions; and *401(k) plans*, where employees channel part of their salary before income taxes to an investment trust.

Defined-contribution plans are not insured by the Pension Benefits Guarantee Corporation. They are also a fairly recent phenomenon. There were only thirty-nine profit-sharing plans in 1939. By 1956 there were about 2,000 defined-contribution plans, most of which were profit-sharing plans. They then began to increase rapidly through the sixties and seventies as new types of plans were introduced. Defined-contribution plans are cheaper, easier, more predictable in costs, and simpler for companies to administer.[14]

The more expensive defined-benefit plan is found in medium and large companies, while the defined-contribution plan is more common in smaller firms. Instead of increasing the benefit levels of defined-benefit pension plans—widely viewed as one of the great outcomes of labor organizing since the fifties—many companies are supplementing or even replacing such plans with defined-contribution plans. Data indicate that 60 percent of workers in defined-contribution plans are in companies with defined-benefit pension plans.[15] Four-fifths of the Fortune 500 firms sponsor at least one defined-contribution plan along with their defined-benefit plan, commonly a deferred profit-sharing plan, a 401(k) plan, or an ESOP, in that order of frequency.[16] This new preference for benefit plans that have fewer fixed obligations, even for sharing capital accumulation in a way that is tied to performance, seems to be part of a larger move away from the fixed-wage system, as discussed by Martin Weitzman in his book, *The Share Economy.*[17] The shift is happening differently than Weitzman envisions it, however—in essence, a capital role for labor is emerging in the country, defined by the policies the government has constructed to regulate these various investment plans.

Worker Ownership of Their Own Firms

One can argue that worker ownership of stock in any company is worthwhile and works toward a general broadening of wealth in this country. However, more relevant for our purposes is the amount of ownership by workers of the firms where they work. Table 1–1 summarizes the distribution in the United States of various types of worker ownership of corporate stock. For now, we will concentrate on benefit plans other than the ESOP.

Through Defined-Benefit Plans. Federal law prohibits defined-benefit plans from putting more than 10 percent of their assets in employer stock; this ensures that risk can be shared among a number of investment vehicles. Currently, no figures are available on how many defined-benefit plans own stock in their own companies, but the maximum investment could be no more than $65 billion.[18] If investment managers invest in employer stock at the same rate they invest in all stock—43 percent of all assets in corporate- and union-sponsored plans in 1985—total defined-benefit plan investment in employer stock is more likely $28 billion. Indeed, the evidence suggests that defined-benefit pension plans are investing far less in their own company's stock: the figure is only about $4.3 billion (see Table 1–1).[19]

Through Defined-Contribution Plans. Capital-accumulation plans depend on investment performance for their success, so companies and workers have generally avoided massive investment in their own firms. In addition, employees generally do not seem to have the savings to invest in such plans: Nearly seven-tenths of the participants in defined-contribution plans had their benefits wholly financed by the employer. But a slight trend toward investment in employer stock is discernible. Figures for participation of U.S. employees in various defined-contribution plans are based on the most recent (1985) Department of Labor national survey of establishments employing more than 50, 100, or 250 employees, depending on the industry. Twenty-four percent of all employees in such firms were in employee stock ownership plans, although this number fell to 2 percent when the tax-credit ESOP was excluded.[20] It is estimated that the total assets of defined-contribution plans held as worker ownership of the stock of employer companies is about $45 billion or about 2.1 percent of all corporate equity (see Table 1–1).

Table 1–1.   Types of Corporate Employee Ownership and Assets in the United States.[a]

Total stock outstanding in 1983	100.00%	$2,151.5	trillion
Worker ownership of employer and nonemployer stock through pension funds of all kinds[a]	18.4	395.87	billion
Worker ownership of employer company stock in pension and other arrangements	3.87	83.26	billion
In private pension plans:			
Defined-benefit plans	.2	4.3	billion
Defined-contribution plans, excluding ESOPs (mostly profit-sharing plans)	2.1	45.18	billion
Deferred profit-sharing plans (included in above entry)	1.2	25.82	billion
ESOPs	.87	18.72	billion
Total	3.17	68.2	billion
In other arrangements:			
Stock-purchase plans	.7	15.06	billion
Stock-option plans		not available[b]	
Producer cooperatives		insignificant	
Total	.7	15.06	billion
Worker ownership of nonemployer company stock through pension plans	15.23	327.67	billion

a. Stock-purchase plans are not figured into this total, which does not include forms of worker ownership other than pension plans.

b. This is likely a sizable figure, and the equity most probably belongs mainly to highly paid employees.

Source: Calculations from selected public and private data sources. Based on computations from Douglas Kruse, Harvard University Department of Economics. ESOP data from U.S. General Accounting Office figures.

Profit-sharing plans are the predominant form of defined-contribution plan. In 1983 they accounted for about 350,000, or over 60 percent of all defined-contribution plans. An average 22,000 new plans have been established per year throughout the eighties. Eighteen percent of employees in 1985 had profit-sharing plans, while cash plans covered 1 percent of all employees, with 3 percent in combination plans in medium to large firms. Deferred plans covered 14 percent of all employees—indeed, they have accounted for half of all the retirement plans established since the passage of ERISA in 1974. Until the 1986 tax reform act, deferred profit-sharing plans were tax-exempt trusts with the employers' contributions based on the company's profit. They are more prevalent than plans that give a cash share of profits directly to workers.

Nonetheless, although it is widespread—especially in smaller companies—there is little evidence that profit sharing involves much worker ownership of their own firms. A number of very large companies invest about 40 to 100 percent of their profit-sharing plans' assets in their own stock, yet this still does not add up to much. Best estimates are that the plans account for the greater part of the $25 billion, or 1.2 percent of the corporate equity that is probably held by all defined-contribution plans (see Table 1–1).[21]

Thrift (or savings) plans involve payroll-based employee savings with company contributions directly related to the amount saved by the worker. Just over one-fourth of all employees in medium and large firms participated in such plans, which were more prevalent among white-collar workers (36 percent versus 17 percent of blue-collar workers). The plans allow for the employee to choose from a set of investment alternatives. There are less than 10,000 such plans in the country; obviously they tend to be concentrated in some very large firms, some of which have put together sizable portfolios of worker investments. Forty-one percent of the plans require that the company's contribution be invested in company stock, effectively turning those contributions into a stock bonus. Among nine different alternatives for worker investment, 54 percent of the plans include stock in the employer company. The Labor Department study found that, nationwide, companies usually required the participants to invest half of the company's contribution in employer stock.[22]

These plans have not spread throughout the economy or had a substantial impact—they are based mainly on savings, which most employees do not possess in abundance, and they tend to exclude hourly workers, who constitute the bulk of the workforce.

401(k) (or salary-reduction) plans came into being in 1978, when Congress allowed employees to make contributions to these plans from their paychecks before income taxes but after social security taxes. Companies can match these contributions. This favorable tax treatment has led to the conversion of many thrift plans to 401(k) plans. One survey showed that 73 percent of a sample of major U.S. companies had 401(k) plans and suggested that they were becoming an increasingly dominant form of defined-contribution plan. Thirty-seven percent of all white-collar employees and 14 percent of all blue-collar employees are eligible to participate in such plans, although some studies indicate that only a third of those who are eligible actually participate.

There are currently no estimates available on investment in company stock by 401(k) plans as a whole. One survey indicated that 51 percent of 401(k) plans had an investment option for company stock. Also, 16 percent of all employees in salary-reduction plans had their contributions invested through profit-sharing plans, and 68 percent through thrift plans, both of which use employer stock. There is evidence that the workers who actually participate are those with higher incomes.[23]

Stock-bonus plans provide benefits without a cash outlay. The company contributes stock, often its own, to the tax-exempt trust. The plans are not, however, required to own stock in their own companies. Stock-bonus plans are the most unpopular type of defined-contribution plan; excluding ESOPs, which are a special kind of stock-bonus plan, they probably number fewer than 1,000, or less than a third of a percent of all defined-contribution plans. Only 1 percent of all employees in medium to large firms were in these plans.[24]

Through Direct Stock-Purchase Plans. Stock-purchase plans encourage direct employee ownership of stock through voluntary purchase. They are not supported by extensive tax incentives, although a 1984 Hewitt Associates study suggested that, of the 40 percent of Fortune Directory companies with such plans, as many as a quarter enjoy some tax advantages under Section 423 of the Internal Revenue Code, as long as the plan is offered to virtually all employees.[25] Sponsoring corporations often make no contribution other than to offer stock at a discount price and provide a payroll-deduction mechanism and reduced brokerage fees.

In 1983 one out of three American shareholders, or about 12 million people, were participating in such plans. Over 10 million individuals reported to the New York Stock Exchange that they first acquired stock this way. For five million of these individuals—about 12 percent of all shareholders—this is the only stock they own. Evidently, despite the popularity and state support of stock ownership through various retirement benefit plans, direct stock ownership plans remain the more common approach to employee ownership. The vast majority of these plans, however—almost 90 percent—own less than 5 percent of their companies' stock. Yet, although company stock owned by employees through these plans amounts to only about 0.7 percent of all stock held by households, and figures for both stock-purchase and stock-option plans indicate participation by only 3 percent of all employees in medium to large firms nationally, direct stock-purchase arrangements have created a substantial amount of employee ownership even though they have fewer tax incentives than the other plans discussed.[26]

Stock-option plans, which tend to be strongly management oriented, are the major means of putting stock into employee hands according to New York Stock Exchange estimates. The Internal Revenue Act of 1964 provided some favorable tax treatment for these plans—called incentive stock-option plans—for both companies and employees, although they have come in and out of U.S. tax law over the last three decades. When Congress reinstated these plans in 1981, it acknowledged the value of employee equity, saying they "will provide an important incentive device for corporations to attract new management and to retain the service of executives who might otherwise leave, by providing an opportunity to acquire an interest in the business." No estimates are available of how much employer stock is held through stock-option plans.[27]

Through Closely Held Companies, Proprietorships, and Partnerships. Workers can own stock in their companies by founding or buying into closely held companies, organized joint-stock companies, partnerships, or proprietorships, using their own capital or funds borrowed on the credit market. Existing owners can also take on employees as partners by trading stock for wages or offering part of the business in return for other specified goods, services, or agreements. Lack of credit, lack of government encouragement through tax incentives, and lack of interest probably explain why there is not much evidence of this phenomenon in the United States outside of producer cooperatives. Sizable participation in ownership and decisionmaking may occur in small family businesses.

Through Producer Cooperatives. Workers can start producer cooperatives or worker cooperatives, which are by definition owned and governed mainly by worker-members. From 1835 to 1934, historians have recorded only 595 firms of this type in the United States.[28] The author's estimate is that there are currently 1,000 producer cooperatives in the country, most quite small and representing an insignificant amount of equity ownership.[29] Detailed figures are not available.

The Spread of Worker Ownership

In his 1976 book, *The Unseen Revolution*, economist-philosopher Peter Drucker postulated that the United States was becoming a "socialistic" country because employees owned 25 percent of public corporate stock through pension funds. He further stated that this "pension-fund socialism" was incomplete, since workers are not aware of their investment nor can they control its management, although such pensions do create a certain worker independence. Drucker also noted that the pension-fund investment philosophy put forth by GM President Charles Wilson in the fifties opposed investing in the workers' own companies.[30]

U.S. workers now own $1.5 trillion dollars in pension assets. About 35 percent of these assets are in public employee pension funds, covering over 75 percent of state and local employees. About 45 percent are in defined-benefit pension plans covering about 41 million workers, and the remainder are in defined-contribution pension plans covering about 27 million workers.[31] All of these retirement mechanisms involve substantial and varied employee ownership.

Obviously, public employees currently have no opportunity to own governmental facilities, but their funds do own stock in companies, typically invested via the public stock market. Public pension funds controlled 3.9 percent of corporate stock in 1983, about the same amount held by foreign investors. Private pension funds controlled 14.5 percent of the assets of public companies in the same year. With total stock outstanding in public companies at $2.15 trillion in 1981, these plans own about $396 billion.[32] As Figure 1–1 shows, this institutional ownership of American corporations has been growing substantially since the fifties.

Figure 1–1.   Institutional Ownership of American Corporations: Historical Evolution.[a]

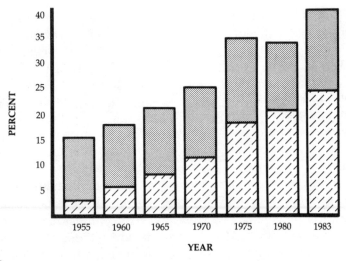

YEAR

Portion of corporate ownership attributable to pension funds.

Portion of corporate ownership attributable to non-pension institutional investors.

a. Based on ownership of publicly traded companies.

Source: Chart used with permission of the editorial staff, *Labor and Investments*, AFL-CIO, Industrial Union Department, Washington, D.C.

But corporate stocks represent only about 40 percent of pension assets. Drucker predicted that pension control of corporations would reach 50 percent, if not 60 percent, of all corporate stock equity by 1985 and exceed two-thirds by the turn of the century. He called this development the "revolution that no one noticed." Perhaps it never happened.

Table 1–1 plainly demonstrates that the notion that workers own America through their pension funds is exaggerated. These plans do not invest exclusively in corporate stock, let alone employer stock, and indirect worker holdings of assets do not necessarily mean worker ownership or control of corporations.

Very few employees start their own companies and share ownership among the workers. This type of worker entrepreneurship is therefore insignificant. Workers are mainly becoming owners in the context of existing ownership situations. Outside of these various plans, employee ownership has had little effect on the concentration of resources in this country. While 68.1 percent of total corporate equity was held by individual households in 1983, close to 60 percent of this was in the hands of the top 1 percent of the population and close to 90 percent was in the hands of the richest 10 percent of households.[33] Direct employee stock-purchase and -option plans account for a good deal of worker ownership in the employer's firm, despite the absence of any comprehensive government encouragement, but overall this type of private worker initiative does little to broaden stock ownership. Most of the remaining stock ownership has resulted from intentional plans, such as tax-favored defined-contribution plans.

For a number of reasons, this ownership generally contributes to the concentration of wealth. Many employees simply do not or cannot participate in a number of these plans. Employees with salaries over $20,000 a year are far more likely to be in a retirement plan of some type, even those with state tax incentives, and benefits are usually based on earnings and integrated with Social Security. As a result, two to three times the beneficial share ownership is distributed to the employees who already own almost two to five times more corporate stock.[34] When all the possible employee-ownership arrangements of a large sample of companies were reviewed, the New York Stock Exchange found that management-oriented stock-option plans were the dominant form.[35]

A serious program to spread worker ownership in American industry would indeed be radical, given the current insignificant and slow accumulation of capital by workers of all types—but especially low and moderately paid employees—in their own firms. And yet only such an effort could correct for the fact that more highly paid workers generally accumulate the most stock under conventional programs and that the top 10 percent of the population essentially controls individual stock ownership.

The Conceptual Model for ESOP Legislation

Both Kelso and Long likened the ESOP to an "industrial" Homestead Act, and this comparison has also been made by President Reagan. Yet Yale political scientist Robert Dahl believes that the 1862 Homestead Act's contribution to farm ownership has been generally overrated, accounting for only 600,000 out of an increase of nearly 4 million farms and 80 million out of an increase of 430 million acres in total farmland between 1860 and 1900, and for little beyond 1900.[36] A number of other laws have also expanded ownership in the United States, but the tradition of state interference in ownership distribution in this country has been more in keeping with the modest reality of the Homestead Act than with its apocryphal history.

More notable has been the state's massive influence on corporations' retained earnings through variations in the business tax rate since 1950, when accelerated depreciation was introduced. This has been responsible for 35 to 67 percent of the cash flow of American corporations from 1955 to 1985. Reduced business taxes since the fifties and income-tax loopholes for the super-rich have greatly contributed to the concentration of ownership (for Federal Reserve data on this period see Appendix C, Table C–1).[37]

In 1953 the Internal Revenue Service published a ruling allowing corporations to use profit-sharing or stock-bonus plans to borrow money for investment in company stock. Thus appeared the distinctive feature of the Employee Stock Ownership Plan: the use of financial leverage to allow employees to buy stock in their own companies without putting up any of their own money.[38] Based on this ruling, Louis Kelso set up the first ESOP at Peninsula Newspapers, Inc., in California.

From 1973 to 1987 Congress, with Russell Long in the vanguard, addressed employee stock ownership plans in over fifteen separate laws. During this entire period, the conceptual model behind the legislation has remained consistent, judging from all relevant public documents.[39] According to this model, employee ownership should and would broaden and expand ownership; encourage capital formation and innovative corporate finance; improve labor-management relations, productivity, and profitability in firms; help the economy accommodate developments in technology, the spread of transfer payments, and inflation; and create an economic democracy.

Broadened Ownership

The basic argument in favor of broadening wealth was to be repeated many times. The holdings of wealth, especially corporate stock, are highly concentrated; the ESOP could create beneficial equity ownership for workers in their own companies with no reduction in pay or benefits or surrender of any other rights. This was the central topic of Long's maiden speech to the Senate on December 11, 1973, in which he also discussed how much employee ownership should be attained in any one company: "The financing technique must be so designed as to build significant capital ownership in the worker over a reasonable working lifetime."[40]

Following a number of hearings and floor speeches on ESOPs, Long's proposal mandating a federal study of a possible ESOP for Conrail became law on January 2, 1974.[41] The core of the ESOP, the provision allowing companies to deduct contributions of stock or cash to a workers' trust from their corporate income for tax purposes, became law on September 2, 1974, without substantial hearings.[42]

According to this law, the amount of worker ownership that can be established in any particular year is constrained by limiting a company's deductions for contributions to a worker trust to 15 to 25 percent of the participating workers' annual compensation, with liberal carryover rules. Only the employer can initiate a trust. In nonleveraged ESOPs, companies rely heavily on the deduction to offset their contributions, while in leveraged ESOPs, the tax advantages exist only when the annual payments to a commercial lender for credit to buy stock match the deduction limits.[43] The TRASOP/PAYSOP limits ownership to a small percentage of capital or payroll. Because the nonleveraged and leveraged ESOPs essentially provide tax incentives to establish worker ownership that is later paid for out of future corporate earnings, we refer to them as the classic ESOPs. The tax-credit ESOP is really a complete government grant to buy stock for workers and has little connection to the philosophy behind employee ownership.

On January 14, 1975, Congressman William Frenzel (D-Ill.) proposed in the Accelerated Capital Formation Act that deduction limits be lifted for contributions to a leveraged ESOP designed to use debt to acquire stock. He also proposed that ESOPs have the characteristics of charitable trusts to encourage affluent taxpayers to set up worker-owned firms. Neither measure passed.[44]

The first detailed congressional hearings on ESOPs took place under the auspices of the Joint Economic Committee on December 11–12, 1975. The chairman of the committee, Hubert H. Humphrey (D-Minn.), only noted that the committee would be "examining some of the broader implications of expanding the ownership of stock by employees through the ESOP." But Senator Jacob Javits (R-N.Y.) was clearly excited, saying that properly developed employee ownership could "improve the financial condition of working Americans and at the same time improve the productivity of American industry."[45]

Problems were raised by several witnesses at the hearings. The under secretary of the treasury, Charls Walker, disagreed that ownership in companies where employees worked was the best method to broaden wealth:

It is important also that the tax inducement for broadening the base of stock ownership be neutral in the identification of taxpayers who can benefit from the inducement. Thus, the tax benefit should not be limited to taxpayers who are employees of employers having qualified ESOPs. The benefit should be extended to all taxpayers who are employees of corporate employers who do not have qualified plans; self-employed individuals; employees of governmental units, nonprofit corporations, and noncorporate enterprises which do not have a qualified ESOP; and members of the Armed Forces.[46]

Hans Brems, a professor of economics at the University of Illinois, questioned whether ESOPs could ever control substantial amounts of corporate stock, since corporations could have such irregular schedules of contribution to their plans. He also noted that one-quarter of all physical capital stock in the United States is owned by noncorporations, partnerships, and proprietorships, to which ESOPs have no access.

Subsequently, the staff of the Joint Economic Committee prepared a study entitled *Broadening the Ownership of New Capital: ESOPs and Other Alternatives*, which confirmed that wealth holding was extremely concentrated in the United States. While it recognized that corporate stock was a major component of wealth, it suggested that the use of corporate equity as a whole in the economy had to be increased to achieve the goal of broadening the wealth. The committee pinpointed a number of concerns about ESOPs that remained valid for the next decade and a half: structural problems making them less attractive than other financing techniques in certain situations, particularly among publicly held companies; the lack of employee involvement in governance; and the nature of the incentive that was supposed to increase productivity.[47]

An attempt was made in 1978 to expand the TRASOP credit to 2 percent of an employer's investment and the PAYSOP credit to 1 percent of an employer's payroll. In the same year Senator Mike Gravel (D-Alaska) proposed in *S. 3291* that the deduction limits for ESOPs be increased to 50 percent of payroll. Neither effort was successful. Senator Long was impatient with this progress, correctly noting that "companies with significant employee ownership where employees own a substantial percentage of the stock still continue to be the exception rather than the rule."[48]

Only in the late seventies did key developments in employee ownership emerge, with ESOP initiatives in worker buyouts, Chrysler, and
small business. On February 15, 1979, Congressman Peter H.
Kostmayer (D-Pa.) was joined by Congressmen Stanley Lundine (D-
N.Y.) and Matthew McHugh (D-N.Y.) in proposing special Department
of Commerce loans and technical assistance to worker groups to help
them save troubled plants through majority worker ownership. Hearings on the bills in both the House and Senate and extensive treatment
in the press of the legislation and actual cases of worker buyouts
prompted general interest in majority worker ownership. Plant shutdowns in many members' districts led to increased support for the idea
in both houses of Congress.[49]

In 1979 Congress passed the Chrysler Corporation Loan Guarantee
Act, providing that about $162 million of the government's $1.5 billion
in loan guarantees to the company would be used for mandatory contributions to a newly formed ESOP to purchase new shares of stock, thus
creating 20- to 25-percent worker ownership of that company.[50]

In 1980 the Small Business Development Act—introduced by Senator Donald W. Stewart (D-Ala.) and Congressman Kostmayer—would
favor majority employee ownership by tying certain SBA loan guarantees to a 51-percent stake held by at least 51 percent of the workers. The
hearings on this bill, which became law on May 1, 1980, demonstrated
that significant potential for majority worker ownership existed in small
closely held companies where owners wished to retire and had no
acceptable successor arrangement. Most conservative small-business
associations sent representatives who strongly endorsed the idea of
worker ownership.

One major obstacle to increased worker ownership was the incentive
for small businesspeople without successors to sell their companies to
larger firms on retirement. Congressman Kostmayer and Senator Long
introduced landmark legislation in this period that allowed a small businessperson who sold more than 30 percent of his or her firm to the
employees to be excused from capital-gains taxes if he or she rolled over
the proceeds of the sale into stock in another American corporation.
This proposal subsequently became law in the 1984 tax bill, and it is a
major reason for the spread of employee ownership in small business.[51]

In 1981 Senator Long succeeded in raising the deduction limits in
the Economic Recovery Tax Act so that companies with nonleveraged
ESOPs could deduct up to 25 percent of compensation with fewer com-
plications and those with leveraged ESOPs could deduct 25 percent of

payroll for contributions used to pay principal, with unlimited deductions for contributions used to pay interest. Senator Long's hopes that "the deduction limitation should be based solely on the company's capacity to service the debt" would never be realized because of opposition by the Department of the Treasury.[52]

Capital Formation and Corporate Finance

In Long's view, ESOPs would create new wealth, rather than redistribute existing wealth. Productive wealth was expected to increase by $2 to $4 trillion by the end of the century, and the ESOP was intended to spread this broadly by providing workers credit to enter the capitalistic system. Central to Long's concept of employee ownership was that workers would not have to put up their own money. He believed that middle- and low-income white- and blue-collar employees and managers just could not save their way to significant capital ownership. The plan would be designed to work in both closely held and publicly traded companies, so that various ownership forms would be opened up.[53]

According to the theory, companies installing ESOPs would issue new stock to sell to their plans, rather than redeal existing stock. Where would this new wealth come from? Long explained:

In no sense is this a "gift" of productive capital to employees; rather the capital is paid for out of future earnings that the new capital itself generates. As the already rich know so well, the new capital's productiveness generally pays for itself. The ESOP participants, however, also "earn" their ownership interest in the company through the ESOP's vesting schedule—which generally allocates stock to employees' accounts based on a combination of length of service and relative compensation.[54]

The anticipated productiveness of ESOP capital was crucial. Through it, Long bound the ownership-broadening ideology of the ESOP to a beneficial impact on the firm. The tax subsidy to ESOP firms was simply an incentive for existing owners to share equity. It involved a distribution of tax dollars purely as an initial investment. The economic performance of the ESOP firm would both make up for the tax subsidy and retire any loans used to buy the worker equity in the first place. On April 17, 1979, Dickson C. Buxton, chairman of the board of the frontline ESOP investment bank, Kelso and Company, confirmed this position:

Dear Senator Long,
Results are in from twenty-two corporations . . . carefully selected to reflect a cross-section of our ESOP company clients by sales volume, number of employ-

ees, and type of industry . . . . This survey shows that your initial thoughts are correct: ESOPs are not a revenue drain on the Treasury—they help offset deficits, they don't create them! . . . Key conclusions (average ESOP life 3.3 years): 1. Federal taxes paid—112 percent increase; 2. Productivity per employee—38 percent increase; 3. Total sales—67 percent increase; 4. Corporate profits—125 percent increase; 5. Number of people employed—30 percent increase . . . . The ESOPs also created tax-sheltered capital for these companies to use in increasing employment opportunity—and this saves our government money and reduces transfer payments . . . . There are still thousands more companies in our country large and stable enough to adopt ESOPs.[55]

The promise of improved economic performance with the ESOP was not incidental to the program—it was the justification for it.

Another central goal of the legislation was to develop a new technique of corporate finance. The Senate Report on the the 1975 law calls corporate finance the key element of the ESOP, and other official interpretations of the laws second this claim. Senator Long called the ESOP "a socially improved technique of corporate finance that also serves as a new type of employee benefit."[56] Section 401(a) of the Internal Revenue Code, however, states explicitly that ESOPs must be for the exclusive and general benefit of participating employees—the corporate finance uses are intended to be incidental.

The deductibility of interest in the tax system encourages corporations to use debt rather than equity to finance a substantial portion of their capital needs. With this method, no new ownership is created. The other principal source of funds is income generated internally through retained earnings, the investment tax credit, and depreciation reserves. The Federal Reserve reported that corporate equities accounted for only 0.89 percent of the total funds raised by nonfinancial sectors during 1979 and only 3.7 percent of new capital for all of the 1970s.[57] (For a complete review, see Appendix C, Table C–1.) The ESOP would, in theory, reverse this process by surpassing the deductibility of interest with the deductibility of principal and interest (the leveraged ESOP), by stealing some of the fire of the investment tax credit (through the TRASOP and PAYSOP), and by offering a wide variety of tax and corporate financing incentives to push companies and individuals toward the use of the public or private equity market.

Labor-Management Relations

Russell Long's faith in the ESOP as a route to new harmony between labor and management was absolute:

Each worker will be put in a position where his own efforts towards cost mini-mization and increased production will directly influence the value [of the] capital estate which he acquires during his working lifetime. I would anticipate that strikes and slowdowns, antiquated work rules, featherbedding, resistance to automation, and unreasonable wage demands—all seemingly insoluble problems up to now—will eventually disappear as workers come to realize how these activities not only work against the interests of consumers as a whole but against their own individual interests.[58]

Elsewhere, he claims that "management's search for a way out of the class conflict era of labor-management relations would take a new and brighter turn through the use of ESOP financing, [and its energy would] be united with that of employees in revitalizing the private enterprise system generally, while building economic security into all employees."[59] He was in accord with economist John Bates Clark, who predicted that the ESOP would result in "productive property owned in undivided shares by laboring men, contention over the division of products replaced by general fraternity."[60] In a letter to his colleagues on November 5, 1975, Senator Mark O. Hatfield (R-Oreg.) said that building a property stake into the system would create a unity of inter-est and a strike-immune economy.[61] Senator Charles H. Percy (R-Ill.) backed up these claims with an example from his executive experience at the Bell and Howell Company, and even the Treasury Department's Walker did not deny the potential benefits in industrial relations.[62]

Ownership alone was supposed to effect this transformation. A form of sharing, common interest, and common communication, it would simply lead to greater worker commitment. President Carter's special counselor on Inflation, Robert Strauss, stated, "In noneconomic terms, my experience as a lawyer, businessman and in public life absolutely convinces me that people perform better if they have a piece of the action."[63] Deeply suspicious of this ostensibly pro-worker concept that presupposed an end to adversarial unionism, organized labor did not share this conviction. (No representatives of organized labor testified in the major 1975, 1978, or 1979 hearings.) But management and workers in ESOP companies in general usually develop some new expectations about participation; at the very least, they feel that ownership involve-ment will somehow improve the company and labor-management rela-tions.

There is no suggestion whatsoever that the framers, especially Sena-tor Long, thought that any change in management bureaucracy or hier-archy would be necessary. Indeed, the consistent legislative formulation of ESOPs as a method of corporate finance that serves as an employee benefit quite neatly defines the tool in terms of the expectations. The ESOP would work because "U.S. business corporations have always needed but heretofore never had a way to raise the incomes of employees without raising corporate costs." It would work because business needs worker participation "and of course employee stock ownership tends to bring that about."[64]

While this optimistic view of the ESOP's effect on labor-management relations dominated the hearings, the speeches, and the structure of the law itself, several objections to it were raised. On the very first day of the major hearings, Senator Javits pointedly raised the role issue. He said such plans should be voluntarily negotiated and administered by both labor and management and that it was premature to endorse any one model of employee ownership as the road to future success. He singled out the Kelso plan and said that he was "as yet unable to perceive how workers suddenly can become more productive upon the receipt of stock by an encumbered trust in which they have no voting right and no financial relationship."[65]

Consultants for the U.S. Railway Association appearing at the hearings argued aggressively that the ability to motivate that the framers attributed to the ESOP did not exist. A year later, in 1976, the Joint Economic Committee staff study of ESOPs definitively recommended that employees in every ESOP at the minimum elect an advisory committee to protect and represent their interests more effectively. The same year Javits and Humphrey introduced a proposal (*S. 3300*) to the Senate to address the legitimate concerns of labor. Their plan was to make employee ownership an integral element of collective bargaining and to interest unions in negotiating about it. They proposed joint trusteeship by the employer and the union of the employee-ownership trust under Section 302 of the Taft-Hartley Act.[66] This bill went nowhere, and these arguments never resurfaced. The view that divorced ownership from governance endured.

Economic Performance

A 1980 report to the Senate Finance Committee by the Comptroller General of the United States and a 1986 report by the U.S. General Accounting Office to Senator Russell Long affirm that the objective of improved economic performance was central to the legislative program. Even the cautious Jacob Javits opened the 1975 hearings with a strong statement of his belief that, if labor's role could be ironed out, improved productivity would result. Ownership would give workers an incentive to minimize costs, a possibility of profit sharing, and a reason not to oppose technology. Long saw the railroad experiment as a test of the ESOP's influence on economic performance. When the U.S. Railway Association brought evidence to disprove the claim, he still did not change his mind, nor did anyone else in Congress appear to doubt that ownership would improve productivity.

Even some economists who were otherwise bitterly critical of ESOPs as a national program and Louis Kelso's theories in particular admitted that the productivity expectation made sense. But motivational expert Saul Gellerman steadfastly maintained that improved productivity would come only from changing the relationship between labor and management and the workplace itself, not from improperly structured packets of distant ownership.

In 1976, the Joint Economic Committee study noted that ESOPs might enhance motivation and increase productivity. At the 1978 hearings of the Senate Finance Committee, Senator Long said that a number of executives from ESOP companies "were unanimous in their feelings that by providing employees with an ownership interest in their employer and a common goal of profitability with their employer, they have greatly increased the motivation and productivity of these employees."[67]

By the late seventies studies appeared that seemed to support this argument. Kelso and Company purported to find that ESOPs led to improved economic performance in their 1979 survey. Subsequently, an expanded version of this survey was adopted and referred to as a Senate Finance Committee study. A Department of Commerce study, commissioned by the Economic Development Administration, would be used to strengthen the developing psychology of ownership and cited again in 1979, at hearings on the Small Business Employee Ownership Act and in a Senate Small Business Committee report on the federal government's role in encouraging employee ownership. Long emphasized the study's finding that successful economic performance was related to the amount of employee ownership.[68] Subsequent Senate documents continued to cite research on the successful economic performance of ESOP companies.

It is now clear that these studies improperly measured productivity and ascribed results to employee ownership that had other more complex causes. Kelso and Long had often been criticized for not backing up their claims with econometric studies—it is ironic that when they cited social science research to support their positions, it proved to be unreliable.[69]

Economic Democracy

Behind the development of the ESOP was the concept of the "second income," based on Kelso's theory that capital was increasingly dominant in its responsibility for productivity, and labor increasingly less so. In this scenario, if citizens must rely solely on labor power for their income, they are not depending on the true source of economic growth and future wealth. Long believed that technology would become so efficient that it would displace workers. If, on the other hand, they owned the means of production, they could retain some form of income while accommodating technological innovation.[70]

Long argued that, as capitalism became more efficient, ownership would become concentrated, and the market system would break down. Technological unemployment would place the bulk of wealth in the hands of a few, who, "however, could consume only a small portion of the gross national product." He was restating Marx's notion that capitalism would undo itself by exploiting workers so much that they would not be prosperous enough to support the marketplace.[71] Long wanted to break Keynes's "more or less permanent social structure" by giving individual citizens access to ownership of the newly emerging capital instruments. The dividends, appreciation in value, and redemption of this ownership in later life would essentially provide every citizen with a second income, which would eliminate workers' enormous alienation and resistance to technological improvements, while preserving these workers as necessary consumers in the capitalist system.

As the conservative wave struck America in 1980, Long closely associated the idea of the second income with the goal of reducing transfer payments (welfare, food stamps, unemployment, etc.). He suggested that broadened ownership of capital instruments would ultimately replace the need for ever-larger publicly funded employment programs and transfer payments. Citing National Bureau of Economic Research reports that the majority of American families considered their most important "wealth" to be their Social Security pension, Long claimed that the best way to reduce government spending over the long term was to reduce the need for it.[72]

Like Kelso, Long attributed inflation to concentrated ownership. Keynes's response to the permanent social structure of the distribution of ownership and reduced demand was to put more purchasing power in the hands of remaining consumers. Yet this, according to Long, was a primary catalyst of inflation, while the growth of transfer payments and public-sector employment signaled incipient socialism. Long was searching for a logically consistent theory of capitalism that would determine how taxes were written, how corporations were organized, and how welfare was designed. Long never used the term "economic democracy," but he was unquestionably proposing a modification of the American political tradition that would limit property rights to protect democracy. With the 1984 amendment to the Deficit Reduction Act that allows banks to deduct 50 percent of their interest income on loans to ESOPs, Long began to accomplish this goal through the tax system.[73]

A Need for Inquiry

The actual law that emerged between 1973 and 1987 did not necessarily correspond to the conceptual model. There are a number of reasons for this—the law was fairly sparse and did not go into theories but rather designed structures and regulations. Also, while Senator Russell Long , his staff assistants on the Senate Finance Committee, and colleagues in the House and Senate dominated the law-writing process, other voices had their say as well. The Labor Department and the IRS wrote regulations governing the law; the administration sometimes entered the picture. ESOP law usually emerged tucked into minor sections of the huge, technically complicated tax acts that appeared at the end of each year. They were drafted by the Senate Finance Committee, fought over in long conferences with the House of Representatives, modified after both houses of Congress passed their respective versions. Compromise and horse-trading were inevitable.

An impartial analysis of the ESOP, its inception, and its evolution after its first decade of experience does not exist.[74] The view of enthusiasts is quite simple: Years of work have gone into putting federal laws on the books; no one is really ethically against the idea of employee ownership; public discourse should focus on refining the tool and telling of successes. As one ESOP lawyer has said, "The bus is built. We lawyers are only bus drivers. It's not useful to ask questions about how the bus was constructed."[75] Social scientists have been far more cautious, wondering whether the relations between labor and management really are transformed in ESOP firms and if work is organized in a more innovative way. Economists ask cynically why employee ownership and participation have not taken over the economy if they really do improve profits and productivity. Some policy thinkers question whether the benefits of ESOPs have justified the estimated $15 + billion in taxes lost to the federal treasury from 1973 to 1987. Others correctly point out that the ESOP is just one form of employee ownership—perhaps the motives are correct but the tool is wrong.

The crucial questions, however, are: what has the ESOP done to power, resources, and prestige inside companies? How has the work environment been affected? What is the best way to understand what has happened?

To answer these questions, we will examine each of the legislative claims about the ESOP to determine whether they were borne out in practice. Chapter 2 looks closely at the structure of the ESOP, the actual instrument, and considers the possible uses designed into its legal mechanisms. Chapter 3 turns to capital formation, the root from which ESOPs spring, describing, too, the variety of corporate finance uses to which ESOPs been put. Chapter 4 details the amount of employee ownership resulting from ESOPs—is an economic democracy in the making? Chapter 5 examines the rights and responsibilities of worker-owners in ESOPs, key issues raised by John Hoerr in his pathbreaking *Business Week* article, "ESOPs: Revolution or Ripoff?" after which this book is named. Chapter 6 establishes how the ideology at the root of ESOP law determines these rights and responsibilities. Chapter 7 studies changes in labor-management cooperation, and the attendant effects on productivity and profitability. Chapter 8 discusses the actual and projected outcomes in the national economy. The final chapter summarizes the evidence and closes with a policy section that suggests how to modify the existing program.

CHAPTER 2

The ESOP'S Moving Parts

Seymour Specialty Steel of Seymour, Connecticut, emerged as a 100-percent worker-owned firm in a divestiture from National Distillers that was organized by the Industrial Cooperative Association of Somerville, Massachusetts. Over two hundred workers took a 10-percent wage cut to help finance the leveraged-ESOP buyout. Workers have full voting rights on their stock in the privately held company and elect the board of directors on a one-person/one-vote basis. Newly appointed management and the United Auto Workers union local have established labor-management committees dealing with productivity, quality control, and new product development.[1]

Galaxy Manufacturing (a pseudonym) is a New England firm with a company union and 500 employees. Its ESOP held 52 percent of the company's stock, and managers purchased the remaining 48 percent. Employees had no say in the original decision to purchase the company. The employees' stock, distributed according to salary, was non-voting, and management appointed the ESOP trustees. Other than a new sign reading "Owners' Washroom" on the appropriate door, little was done to involve the employees in their company. One day, management announced that the firm, including all the ESOP stock, had been sold.[2]

American Recreation Centers of Sacramento, California, operates bowling centers and manages real estate. One of the first ESOPs established, the plan holds 25 percent of the company's shares and includes both full- and part-time workers. The publicly held firm has also devised a number of incentive and profit-sharing plans to motivate the 800 workers to act like owners.[3]

In 1985 the management of Scott and Fetzer, the owner of World Book Encyclopedia and Kirby Vacuum Cleaners, proposed a leveraged buyout of the company. Workers would pay $44.39 a share for 41 percent of the firm, management and the investment banking firm Kelso and Company would pay $4 to $7 a share for 29 percent, and GE Credit would purchase the remainder for $1.50 a share. Excess assets from terminated pension plans would be used to finance the deal. The Amalgamated Clothing and Textile Workers Union and the U.S. Department of Labor suggested that the stock prices and the division of control were unfair; after attempts at compromise, the transaction was abandoned.[4]

As these examples illustrate, there is no single model for employee-owned companies. The ESOP is like a machine: It has its basic functions and then it has a variety of moving parts that can be custom designed to produce a more specialized end product. Like any machine, the ESOP has a default, a minimum function to which it will revert if left to itself. But what are its moving parts? What are their possible arrangements?

All firms adopting ESOPs must decide how worker ownership will be made available, which workers are eligible, how ownership will be allocated to them, when they get the rights of ownership, how the ownership will ultimately be distributed or paid out as cash, how ownership will be represented in the company, whether there will be dividends and if so their size, and a host of other issues critical to the definition of the employee-owned entity. There is also the question of what kind of set-up the law itself encourages.[5] Most of the moving parts are guided by the general laws on pensions plans, which also apply to ESOPs.

Congress has worked with the ESOP continually since the early seventies. Generally, the law has addressed a variety of problems simultaneously, and the new Tax Reform Act of 1986 has contributed its share of changes as well. One set of laws has defined the main ESOP tax-incentives, which are continuously modified—what made little sense in terms of employee ownership one year ago may now be eminently practical. Other laws deal mainly with the structure of employee ownership inside the firm. Yet another set has tried to ensure government support for ESOPs through its main agencies or economic policies.[6] Finally, through the years Congress has suggested or mandated employee ownership as a solution to specific problems: The proposed Conrail ESOP is one example, as is the more dramatic Chrysler ESOP. Generally, the state has governed employee ownership through such responses to special circumstances, although administrative fiat or policy changes may eventually replace congressional legislation as the primary source of the state's influence.

Table 2–1 outlines the development of ESOP law, and the reader should review it thoroughly, along with Appendices A and B.

Table 2–1. The Evolution of the ESOP as an Instrument of Employee Ownership.[a]

Regional Rail Reorganization Act of 1973. Public Law 93–236. This early act mandated a study of the use of ESOPs to reorganize several northeastern railroads
into what became Conrail. Conrail later did develop an ESOP, although this
study recommended against the use of one at that time.

Employee Retirement Income Security Act (ERISA) of 1974. Public Law 93–406. This
major attempt to define and protect the rights of workers participating in various retirement plans authorized the central ESOP mechanism: the use of credit
to buy employee stock and the subsequent tax deductions of principal and
interest on a loan used to purchase employee stock ownership. Many of the
ERISA rules on vesting, allocation, and other aspects of employee-benefit plans
apply to ESOPs, which were however exempted from certain limitations
imposed on other plans: ESOPs can invest more than 10 percent of their assets
in employer securities without demonstrating that the investments are sound
and do not have to diversify their investments to avoid risk. This law led to the
ongoing development of leveraged and nonleveraged ESOPs.

Trade Act of 1974. Public Law 93–618. As part of establishing a Commerce Department loan and loan-guarantee program for companies in communities
adversely affected by foreign trade, this law gives preference to companies that
contribute 25 percent of such a loan's principal to an ESOP.

Tax Reduction Act of 1975. Public Law 94–12. As part of increasing the investment
tax credit from 7 to 10 percent, this law established the first of the tax-credit
ESOPs (TRASOP), which allowed companies to claim an additional percent of
investment credit if the funds were used to purchase stock for employees
through an ESOP. In 1981, it was replaced by the PAYSOP, which was then
repealed in 1986.

Tax Reform Act of 1976. Public Law 94–455. This law extended TRASOPs through
1980 and allowed employers to claim an additional 1/2-percent investment tax
credit, provided employees contributed to the ESOP an amount equal to the
additional 1/2 percent from their own funds. Companies were also allowed to
reimburse themselves partially for the costs of establishing a TRASOP. The
House-Senate Conference Report for this law included a strong congressional
statement supporting ESOPs and criticizing proposed regulations on ESOPs by
the Department of Labor and the Internal Revenue Service. The report also
clarified that ESOPs were not to be considered conventional retirement plans in
view of the special purposes for which Congress had created them.

Revenue Act of 1978. Public Law 95–600. This law extended the TRASOP through
1983. It required limited voting rights on certain major issues for workers in all
ESOPs and in other plans with more than 10 percent of their assets in employer
securities; all publicly traded companies had to allow workers to vote their stock
fully. It also required companies to offer workers a put option (i.e., the workers
would have a right to demand cash for their securities) on leveraged ESOP

stock that is not publicly traded. It authorized the General Stock Ownership Corporation until 1984 to encourage general equity ownership among the residents of a political unit.

Regional Rail Reorganization Act Amendments of 1978. Public Law 95–565. This law required that 15 percent of Conrail be owned by the workers through an ESOP as a condition of a congressional contribution of new funds to the railroad.

U.S. Railway Association—1979 Appropriation Authorization. Public Law 95–611. This law authorized an additional $2 million in loans to the Delaware and Hudson Railroad, provided it adopted an ESOP.

Technical Corrections Act of 1979. Public Law 96–222. This law clarified how a TRASOP could qualify for the extra 1/2-percent investment tax credit and confirmed the IRS's definition of the leveraged ESOP.

The Chrysler Loan Guarantee Act of 1979. Public Law 96–185. In return for a loan guarantee of not more than $1.5 billion, this law required Chrysler to establish an ESOP and contribute to it $162.5 million—or about 1 percent of the loan guarantee—over four years, to establish about 25-percent worker ownership of the company. In 1986 Chrysler workers sold back most of their stock to the company, indicating that both Chrysler and the union viewed employee ownership only as a temporary part of the company's revival.

Milwaukee Railroad Restructuring Act of 1980. Public Law 96–101. This law required establishment of an ESOP in return for federal financial assistance for the railroad.

ESOP Improvements Act of 1980. This law again extended the TRASOP investment tax credit and made a number of technical amendments to existing ESOP legislation.

The Small Business Development Act of 1980. This law amended Small Business Administration rules in order to make loan guarantees available to companies with employee ownership of different kinds, including ESOPs. (Previously, the Small Business Administration's rules for loans to these companies had often made such assistance impossible.) It also specified that workers should have broader voting rights and be involved in deciding the structure of the employee-owned company.

Northeast Rail Service Act of 1981. This law authorized the sale of Conrail to the private sector, but directed the Department of Transportation to give priority to a worker purchase should no other bidder make an acceptable offer for the railroad as a unit. Conrail went public in 1987, although its workers retained a substantial equity stake of 15 percent.[b]

Economic Recovery Tax Act (ERTA) of 1981. Public Law 97–34. This law replaced the TRASOP with the PAYSOP, which based the tax credit on 0.5 percent of payroll for 1983 to 1984 and 0.75 percent of payroll for 1985 to 1987 (the tax-credit ESOP was repealed altogether in 1986). It amended the rules on leveraged ESOPs, permitting an annual corporate tax deduction of 25 percent of payroll without the necessity of combining a stock-bonus plan with a money-purchase pension plan, which was the only way to achieve such a large deduction under previous law. Contributions to a leveraged ESOP to repay interest on a worker equity loan were no longer included in the percentage-of-pay corporate-deduction limitation. Also, as long as a corporation did not allocate more than one-third of the worker equity to certain large stockholders or highly compensated employees in any year, contributions to the ESOP intended to pay loan interest and forfeitures of stock of departing employees were no longer subject to the limits on how much stock could be allocated annually to a worker. The "put option" (under which the corporation must redeem stock for cash at fair market value within sixty days after it is distributed) was broadened to all ESOPs. Also, companies whose stock was entirely or substantially employee owned were allowed to require departing employees to take cash instead of stock so the firm would be owned only by current employees.

Tax Equity and Fiscal Responsibility Act of 1982. This bill changed all employee-benefit plans that were "top heavy"—that is, where more than 60 percent of account balances went to "key" employees. Such plans were required to vest all employees more quickly and to follow certain rules so that more benefits would go to other employees. The act limited any company's deductions when it had more than one qualified plan and lowered the dollar limit of annual contributions to a worker's account from $47,475 to $30,000.

Trade Adjustment Assistance Act Amendments of 1983. Amending the Trade Act of 1975, these amendments provided that, in granting loans and loan guarantees to firms adversely affected by foreign competition, preference would be given to companies that financed at least 25 percent of such assistance through an ESOP.

Deficit Reduction Act of 1984. Public Law 98–369. This law included five primary changes to tax incentives for ESOPs. If a business owner sold at least 30 percent of the company to an ESOP or worker co-op, he or she would be excused from capital-gains taxes if the proceeds of the sale were invested in another American company within twelve months (referred to as a rollover). Capital-gains taxes would not be payable until the new stock was sold. Dividends on stock held in an ESOP became deductible if they were paid directly to workers. This law accelerated the rate at which generally successful small businesses could convert to worker ownership. Banks, insurance companies, or other commercial lenders could deduct up to 50 percent of their interest income on loans to ESOP companies that used the credit to finance worker equity, which facilitated cheaper credit when employee ownership was used in leveraged buyouts (LBOs). ESOPs or worker co-ops could assume the estate-tax liability of a business estate in return for a stock contribution worth at least as much as the tax liability. Finally, the PAYSOP was frozen at 0.5 percent through 1987, and, as noted, it expired on December 31, 1986.

Tax Reform Act of 1986. The new tax act affected the general tax situation, tax incentives, and structure of ESOPs, as well as requirements for all employee-benefit plans affecting ESOPs.[c]

1. General Tax Situation. The special tax treatment for long-term capital gains has been eliminated, so capital-gains income on sales of stock to an ESOP by an individual are taxable at 28 percent, unless the proceeds are rolled over into stock of another corporation, as noted above (this may change for 1988). Under the previous law, the top tax rate on capital gains was 20 percent. The special tax treatment for long-term capital gains has been part of the tax code since 1921. Opponents of this change in the 1986 tax law charge that it will discourage investment and entrepreneurship. However, it does increase federal support for owners to sell their businesses to their employees, since the 1984 provision excusing such ownership from capital-gains taxes under certain conditions involves more tax savings, given the new law. Many entrepreneurs say the single most important incentive for people who start new companies, venture capitalists, and new executives in these companies is the different treatment of earned income and capital gains. The preferential treatment of capital gains that still exists with ESOPs when such people sell at least 30 percent of their start-up companies to their employees makes employee ownership a way to preserve these incentives. The new maximum corporate tax of 34 percent, rather than 46 percent, decreases the value of all deductions, including ESOP deductions. The tax-credit ESOP (PAYSOP) was repealed.

2. Tax Incentives. Until 1991, there is a 50-percent exclusion on estate taxes when stock is sold to an ESOP. This provision has caused substantial controversy—because of a loophole not intended by legislators, it could all but eliminate estate taxes and end up costing the government $20 billion in revenue over five years. As the law was written, the estate of anyone who has purchased the stock of an ESOP company in the open market can sell that stock to the company's ESOP and avoid paying taxes. A person's estate could buy large amounts of a company's stock after the person's death and sell it to the company's ESOP to eliminate all estate-tax liability. The tax incentive was really intended for owners of controlling interests in closely held companies who wanted to turn over part of that control to the employees after death, but it began to be used as a tax-avoidance scheme in publicly traded corporations. The loophole has been closed by the IRS—the deceased person must own the securities directly at the time of death and after the sale the securities must be allocated to participants in the ESOP. Further retroactive legislation would prohibit the deduction for securities that are publicly traded, limit the tax benefit to $750,000 per estate, and prevent stock transfers to people shortly before their deaths.[d] Mutual funds can now extend credit to ESOPs and deduct their interest income from their taxable income. Through 1988 ESOPs are excused from the 10-percent tax on excess-asset reversions from terminated employee-benefit plans if the excess assets are rolled over into an ESOP. In order to promote the use of ESOPs in stock buybacks and other transactions, a corporation can take a tax deduction for corporate borrowing coordinated with the contribution of stock to a nonleveraged ESOP as long as the stock is allocated to employees all in the same year. The corporation will have seven years to pay back the loan. Also, dividends can now be paid to workers' accounts (rather then to workers directly) and still be deducted by the corporation if they are used to pay for

principal and interest on a loan to buy worker equity. Lenders can deduct their interest income on loans for the acquisition of employer securities made after May 23, 1984, which are refinanced for a seven-year period. These provisions make ESOPs a beneficial way for publicly traded companies to perform stock buybacks. The new law limits a corporation's ability to use a net operating-loss carryforward and certain tax credits following a significant (i.e., more than 50-percent) ownership change, but exempts ESOPs from this rule.

3. Structure of ESOPs. ESOPs must have a regular independent outside valuation of the worth of their shares. Stock-bonus plans of all types must now agree to repurchase the shares of departing employees. In order to give more financial security to older employees, at age 55 employees who have been in an ESOP for ten years can take 25 percent of their assets or demand three diversified investment options other than employer securities for this amount. This increases to 50 percent at age 60 and applies to stock acquired after December 31, 1986. The law affirms that employees in closely held companies must be able to vote their allocated shares on issues related to the merger, consolidation, recapitalization, reclassification, liquidation, dissolution, or sale of the firm. Companies with a one-person/one-vote arrangement are not bound by these rules. Voting rights for the ESOPs of certain closely held newspaper publishers are eliminated. The definition of a highly compensated employee has been changed. This is relevant when no more than a third of the employer's contributions in any year can go to officers, 10-percent shareholders, or highly compensated employees. An ESOP must now permit the distribution of worker equity to employees who separate from service before normal retirement age. The act has imposed new requirements on the timing of stock distributions and accelerated benefit-commencement dates. It has also clarified the put-option requirements applicable to distributed shares of employer stock not readily tradeable on an established market and included other additional technical amendments.

4. Requirements for Employee-Benefit Plans Affecting ESOPs, Effective Beginning in 1989. Plans must cover at least fifty employees or, if the company employs less than fifty people, at least 40 percent of all employees. The definition of a highly compensated employee is tightened. Also, while union employees can still be excluded from a plan (as long as they can bargain for inclusion), along with part-time, temporary, new, or under-21-year-old employees, new rules make the plans somewhat more inclusionary. Plans must now include at least 70 percent of all non-highly compensated employees, or the percentage of non-highly compensated employees must be at least 70 percent of the percentage of highly compensated employees, or the plan must include a fair cross-section of employees and the average benefit given to non-highly compensated employees as a percentage of their compensation must be at least 70 percent of the benefits given to highly compensated employees as a percentage of compensation. ESOPs are exempted for three years from the 10-percent additional income tax on certain early withdrawals prior to age 59 1/2 that is imposed on all qualified employee-benefit plans. Ten- or fifteen-year vesting is reduced to five to seven years. Individuals over 59 1/2 who get distributions from plans can only average this income over the next five instead of ten years. Contributions

to profit-sharing plans no longer need depend on profits, which blurs the distinction between them and all capital-accumulation plans.

a. Laws that have been repealed are noted.
b. "Conrail Offering Raises Record $1.65 Billion," Wall Street Journal, March 26, 1987.
c. Congressional Record, September 18, 1986, pp. 7704–5, 7708–9, 7713–20, 7725, 7744, 7823.
d. See National Center for Employee Ownership, "Estate Tax Issue to be Resolved," Employee Ownership 7, no. 2 (March/April 1987): 3.

Source: Adapted from Jeffrey Gates, Synopsis of ESOP-Related Legislation (1973–1984) (Washington, D.C.: Senate Finance Committee, 1985).

Internal Workings and Structure

ESOPs have many moving parts. They are not simple, direct vehicles of worker ownership or worker participation in governance. The nonleveraged ESOP, the leveraged ESOP, and the tax-credit ESOP (TRASOP/PAYSOP) share some features, yet each enjoys its own peculiarities. Generally, however, ESOPs do abide by the rules for all defined-contribution employee-benefit plans.

It is useful to remember that the employee shoulders the risk of the trust's variable market performance in a defined-contribution plan—the exact benefit is impossible to predict. The worker's account includes the employer's original contribution, increases or decreases in the underlying market value of that investment, and income on the investment, such as dividends that are not paid out in cash to the worker but are retained in the trust. In addition, the value of the accounts of workers who have left the plan before acquiring rights to their benefits may be redistributed to the accounts of all workers.

The Amount of Ownership

The ultimate decision to set up an ESOP belongs exclusively to the management of a corporation.[7] Any subgroup of employees can start the process, but existing owners, management, or stockholders must agree to sell them stock. In various transfers of ownership, such as spinoffs of successful subsidiaries or buyouts of failing firms, employees will often make the first move. Workers may also take part in hostile or friendly takeovers of closely held or publicly traded companies by creating shell corporations with leveraged ESOPs. In fact, recently American Capital Strategies, Inc., of Bethesda, Maryland, has been created as an investment banking firm for labor. It proposes to add capital strategies to labor's collective-bargaining strategies and hopes to aid organized and unorganized labor to use the ESOP to develop an activist strategy toward mergers, acquisitions, and leveraged buyouts, usually orchestrated by management.[8]

Ceilings and Limitations. In every ESOP, the company contributes cash or stock to a workers' trust (the Employee Stock Ownership Trust or ESOT). Several ceilings that are an integral part of the ESOP mechanism determine the actual extent of employee ownership.

In the leveraged ESOP the amount of the company contribution is defined by the annual debt obligation of the trust and the annual tax-deductible maximum of 25 percent of the pay of ESOP participants. There is an unlimited deduction for corporate contributions to the workers' trust that are applied to the payment of interest on the loan that made the worker ownership possible. A company getting credit to establish worker ownership—and using the retained capital for its business operations—will be careful to match its annual debt obligation (of principal) to its tax-deduction limit. Obviously, the commitment to specific loan payments obligates the company to a set annual amount of worker ownership.[9]

Tax deductions for contributions to other defined-contribution plans cannot exceed 15 percent of pay—the 25-percent limit for the classic leveraged ESOP is especially high. In addition, if contributions surpass the 25-percent limit in any one year, the deduction can be carried over to succeeding years in which the tax deduction is not entirely used up.

In the nonleveraged ESOP, the annual contribution can be any amount up to 15 percent of the participants' pay. When contributions are below that limit, the unused deduction can be carried forward to a deductible limit of 25 percent of pay in any one year. When contributions to the worker trust exceed that limit, these, too, can be carried forward to succeeding years as long as the 25-percent annual limit is respected. These carryover provisions have been somewhat changed in the 1986 tax law. The law allows a money-purchase pension plan to be combined with a stock-bonus plan so that a nonleveraged ESOP can receive contributions of up to 25 percent of pay. Some nonleveraged ESOPs make provisions for leveraged transactions in their plan documents. (Throughout this book, especially when referring to General Accounting Office surveys, these will be called leverageable ESOPs.)

In the TRASOP, a corporation received tax credits based on a percentage of its qualifying capital expenditures; in the PAYSOP, the credit was figured on a percentage of the compensation of participating employees. The unused tax credit could be carried forward or back for fifteen years. Even though the TRASOP/PAYSOP was repealed in 1986, companies may still carry forward some of the tax benefits.

Each type of ESOP produces different amounts of employee ownership. The tax-credit ESOP generally produced very little annually, based as it was on a tiny percent of a company's capital investment or payroll. The leveraged ESOP, depending on credit arrangements and the company's actual need for capital, can result in significant ownership. The nonleveraged ESOP will generally hold smaller amounts, although very profitable companies or those that wish to shift a lot of equity to employees can also produce substantial employee ownership.

The Evidence on ESOP Contributions. The variations in the amount, certainty, and continuity of company contributions are important in analyzing the impact of ESOPs on employees. Indeed, the National Center for Employee Ownership has found that the size of the contribution is the most valuable predictor of positive employee attitudes toward their plans.[10]

Contributions in tax-credit plans were set by law. Thus, the PAYSOP contribution could be up to 0.5 percent of the payroll of participating employees annually. The median benefit for a typical PAYSOP participant was $125 in 1983. Given the insignificance of this contribution, it probably meant little to most workers. It is difficult to establish the continuity of contributions in tax-credit ESOPs because they underwent changes every few years and uncertainty surrounded their future at every juncture. The certainty of the contribution was impossible to predict in a TRASOP company and possible to predict in a PAYSOP company, although again the size of the contribution most likely made this inconsequential.[11]

In the nonleveraged ESOP, there is more worker equity and less certainty. In both leveraged and nonleveraged versions, companies cannot contribute more than 15 percent or 25 percent of compensation, according to the ceiling set by the state. However, in nonleveraged ESOPs, contributions are usually completely variable and indefinite unless a money-purchase pension format is used in which the annual contribution must be defined. Otherwise, management is free to decide on all three aspects and may continue or discontinue contributions at will.

In a pure, or trust-financed, leveraged ESOP, where the ESOP borrows the money, the amount is determined by how much the company contributes to the ESOP to allow it to offset principal and interest payments on the loan for worker stock and perhaps for dividends. Contributions are thus definite and continuous until the loan is paid off. In a company-financed leveraged ESOP, a company has essentially established a nonleveraged ESOP with money it has borrowed itself. Neither the continuity, certainty, nor size of the contribution to the ESOP is completely assured—the company makes no guarantees but decides annually what amount, related to the loan to the company, to contribute. Because the loan is to the company rather than to the ESOP, management is not locked in to establishing a certain amount of employee ownership each year. But since the company may have initiated this ESOP because no other tax deductions were open to it, contributions will likely match the loan installments.

A study by the College of Law at the University of Iowa found that 43 percent of the companies surveyed contributed more than 10 percent of compensation to their plans and 23 percent contributed at the 15-percent limit. Contributions were insignificant in about a third of the firms. The study also revealed that smaller private companies tended to contribute more than larger publicly held firms and confirmed that the higher the company contributions, the more worker ownership of company stock existed in the ESOT.[12] The thirty-five companies studied by the National Center for Employee Ownership contributed an average 8.17 percent of their covered payroll to their ESOPs each year. Six contributed 10.1 to 13 percent and only three contributed 25 percent.[13] This information on company contributions plainly establishes that the presence of employee ownership in a company does not necessarily correspond to a definite commitment from management to increase the employee ownership every year or to sell a specific amount of employee ownership in any particular year. It will be useful to recall this later when we analyze the effects of ownership on employee motivation.

Eligibility

Employee ownership is not open to every employee.[14] The present law defines who can participate in an ESOP, supposedly ensuring that a significant percentage or a fair cross-section of a company's workforce will be eligible for benefits. Yet the specifics of the law permit companies to eliminate many workers from the running.

Legal Exclusions. A plan can completely exclude members of a collective-bargaining unit as long as the union has the option to bargain directly for employee ownership on behalf of its members (only the possibility must exist; no actual discussion need take place). Workers under 21, workers who have put in less than 1,000 hours of service in a year or have been with the company for less than a year, and foreign nationals can also be excluded. If a plan vests employees 100 percent immediately—as tax-credit ESOPs do—it can exclude workers who have not completed three years of service. A worker cannot be excluded for being too old but can be refused entry if he or she is within five years of the ESOP's normal retirement age at the time of hiring. A worker who has a break in service for 500 hours—or even less, if specified—can be dropped from the plan. Under certain circumstances, a worker who has completed more than 500 but less than 1,000 hours of service in a year may be denied his or her share in the employer contribution or any forfeitures during that year. Indeed, the IRS has ruled that a worker not employed on the last day of the plan year may be denied any allocation even if he or she had more than 1,000 hours of service that same year. A worker who declines to make mandatory contributions to the plan may be excluded from receiving any employer contribution for that period.

Discrimination. Once eligibility is defined, the plan must meet one of three tests to be sure it does not discriminate in favor of key members, namely, company officers, major shareholders, or employees defined as highly compensated in the recent tax law.[15] Until the recent tax reforms, a plan was considered nondiscriminatory if it included 70 percent or more of all workers or 80 percent of all eligible workers if only 70 percent were eligible (for a total of 56 percent). Nonresident aliens, members of an excluded collective-bargaining unit, and workers not meeting the minimum age and service requirements were excluded before this test was applied. The new tax law tightens the requirements, but does not alter the basic engine of discrimination in ESOPs. If the plan did not satisfy the requirements of the first test, it could still pass muster if it covered a fair cross-section of the workforce. There was no explicit definition of "fair cross-section" in the law, but, generally, if a plan covered employees over a wide salary range, it would be approved as long as it was not heavily weighted in favor of highly compensated workers. As with the first test, many workers could be excluded from the plan before this test was applied. For the tax-credit ESOP (TRASOP/PAYSOP), the test was even more flexible: A minimum of only 50 percent of eligible workers had to be included, and the total amount any one worker received could not exceed 2 percent of his or her compensation for that year.

Research on Excluded Workers. In the end, then, an ESOP can exclude large numbers of workers, favor more highly paid workers, and still be considered nondiscriminatory.[16] Table 2–2 reports on the percentage of total employees participating in the different types of ESOPs based on a study by the U.S. General Accounting Office. Half of the companies with ESOPs excluded a third of their employees. While this may be legal, the question remains whether it is useful if the country wishes to use its tax revenues to encourage a beneficial and workable type of employee ownership.

Table 2–2 cites median statistics, showing only the amount of inclusion and exclusion practiced by half the firms surveyed, which suggests that there may be many companies, such as Federal Distillers, discussed at the beginning of Chapter 5, that exclude a much larger number of employees. Tax-credit ESOPs tend to exclude even greater numbers of workers (see Table 5–3) and through a strange coincidence of the rules the law has made it easier for them to do so. Because the law mandated 100-percent vesting immediately for these ESOPs, they were conveniently allowed to exclude employees who had not completed three years of service. Given that a sizable number of employees change jobs before three years, this is yet another area where the law strengthened tax-credit ESOPs' exclusivity during the eleven years they were on the books.

Table 2–2. Median Percent of Total Employees Participating in ESOPs.[a]

Tax-credit	62.8
Leveraged	72.7
Nonleveraged	73.9
Other	78.7
Total participants	70.6
Total excluded	29.4

a. These are figures for the median—50 percent of all ESOPs. Other research suggests that the other 50 percent excludes far more employees.

Source: U.S. General Accounting Office, Employee Stock Ownership Plans: Interim Report on a Survey and Related Economic Trends (Washington, D.C.: U.S. General Accounting Office, February 1986), p. 33.

A 1981 survey of 229 ESOPs in the *Journal of Corporation Law* is even more revealing. It found that 45 percent of the ESOPs covered more than three-quarters of the company's workforce, but that 29 percent covered less than half of the workforce. The number of workers included diminished as the size of the companies increased.[17] The GAO figures, then, seem to have obscured the substantial definition of workers out of employee ownership in many firms. But, as the examples at the beginning of this chapter illustrate, inclusion has little to do with the total amount of stock controlled by workers, nor does it guarantee a respectable share in the ownership. The *Journal of Corporation Law* survey has been the only ESOP study that has measured the actual percentage of worker equity allocated to the accounts of salaried versus nonsalaried workers. In brief, one-third of the ESOPs had 100 percent of their assets and another 40 percent had 51 to 99 percent in the accounts of salaried workers. Apparently, what the law makes possible in theory is exactly what results in practice.

Many employee-ownership proponents have reacted to these findings by claiming that most ESOPs include all employees who meet age and service rules unless the union is excluded. Indeed, one prominent ESOP lawyer contends that union membership accounts for most of the exclusions. These assertions were tested by examining 2,181 ESOPs of all kinds that reported complete employment data to the IRS in 1984. The results, summarized in Table 2–3, shed light on why different groups of workers are excluded from ESOPs, so that policymakers can understand what causes this exclusion.[18]

Table 2–3. Actual Number of Excluded Employees and Reasons for Exclusion for 2,181 ESOPs in 1984.

	Number	Percentage
Total employment	17,572,793	100.0
Total employee participants in ESOPs	8,311,329	47.3
Total employees excluded from ESOPs	9,261,464	52.7
Excluded because of minimum age and service requirements	2,620,560	14.9
Excluded as ineligible	3,150,333	17.9
Excluded as union members or foreign workers	3,490,571	19.9

Source: Internal Revenue Service Computer Tapes, 1984, computed by Douglas Kruse, Harvard University Department of Economics.

Some managers certainly do not want union members in employee-ownership plans, and if the wage structures of salaried and hourly workers are similar, it becomes that much easier for a company to include a fair cross-section of workers of all salary classes while effectively redlining unionized workers. And, as Table 2–3 shows, members of collective-bargaining units are the most excluded group. Management, however, is not solely responsible for this; it is also true that many unions have simply ignored ESOPs in their companies. In addition, there is no evidence that the trade-union movement ever tried to influence this aspect of the design of employee-ownership law. Some observers have suggested that trade unions want to rely on contracts to control all forms of compensation benefitting their members and hence are suspicious of employee-ownership plans that tie a worker's capital accumulation to decisions by management and/or the performance of the firm. Unions, then, must bear as much responsibility as management for truncated forms of employee ownership in the United States: ESOPs can mainly be plans for salaried workers when either unions or management exclude unionized workers.

The surprise in Table 2–3, however, is that 32.8 percent of the workers in all these companies are excluded because they do not meet minimum age or service requirements or because they are ineligible (this first category may include part-time workers). There may be substantial room to include more employees in ESOPs by altering these requirements. The fundamental question here is not at all technical: For an employee-owned firm to benefit from increased employee identification and motivation, should it not be necessary to include as many employees as possible in the ownership?

Some Changes in the Law. This substantial exclusion led to proposals for reform in the 1986 tax act. The House of Representatives proposed that no more than one-third of a corporation's contributions to a worker-equity plan in any year could go to a group of employees consisting of officers, 10-percent shareholders, or highly compensated individuals. This would have forced enterprises either to include more employees or to cut back on the amount of equity. The proposal was rejected.

The new law does tighten the participation requirements for all employee-benefit plans a bit (see Table 2–1, *Tax Reform Act of 1986*, item 4). One Senate staff member has noted, "What we have done is increase the number of participating workers from 56 percent to 70 percent."[19] At first glance, this appears to be true. Close study, however, reveals that the claim is unjustified. There may be improvements, but the opportunities for exclusion remain generous.

An indisputably important achievement of the new law was a definition of "highly compensated."[20] Previously, the lack of such a definition, the limited information a company was required to provide on its application for an ESOP, and the rarity of government investigations of challenges by employees permitted serious abuses by companies ostensibly adhering to the principles behind the legislation.

The old law provided ample opportunity for some firms to include far fewer than 56 percent of their employees in their ESOPs. The new law makes employee ownership somewhat more inclusive. A minimum of 50 employees or 40 percent of all employees must be included. Again, many unionized or other employees can be disallowed before this standard is applied, but this does prevent a more extreme kind of abuse. For example, under the old law, a company with 1,000 workers could, in theory, exclude 500 unionized workers, establish three salary categories for the remaining 500, and include in its plan only a "fair cross-section," say, 10 people in each of these categories. This is no longer possible.

Although the new law still allows a corporation to exclude unionized and other employees before applying its percentage test, it does make it more difficult to exclude workers based on length of service. The number of years an employee must work before being allowed to participate has been reduced from three to two; if a worker has completed more than one year of service, he or she can only be excluded if the plan has 100-percent immediate vesting.

However, the law still allows the exclusion of at least 30 percent of the remaining employees through various ways to test for nondiscrimination. Now either 70 percent of all remaining non-highly compensated employees must be included or the percentage of non-highly compensated employees included must be at least 70 percent of the percentage of highly compensated employees included. In other words, companies must now maintain a certain proportion of non-highly compensated to highly compensated employees in the plan. These numbers can be manipulated, however, and some companies may actually include fewer employees in their ESOPs under the new law.

The upshot is that the new tax law prohibits some of the most extreme forms of limited worker ownership but still permits significant exclusion. And these new rulings will not be implemented until January 1, 1989—perhaps later in collectively bargained plans. One caveat: The rules on inclusion for ESOPs are the same as those for other employee-benefit plans. The bulk of the abuse of the old rules was by employee-benefit plans other than ESOPs. But the point still remains: Is this how U.S. law should deal with employee ownership?

The Division of Ownership

How ownership is divided among participating employees is another important moving part of each ESOP.[21] In every such plan, the company annually contributes stock or cash to buy stock to the ESOT. The company's tax benefits are keyed to these contributions, and the government presumably wants a say in how this worker equity is apportioned. There are three aspects of the law that determine this division: a general principle, guides for a formula, and a set of upper limits.

The Principle: No Discrimination in Favor of Highly Compensated Employees. In general, the allocation format may not discriminate in favor of corporate officers, significant shareholders in the firm, or highly compensated employees. This is the same rule that applies to other employee-benefit plans, as is the case with many regulations affecting ESOPs.

It sounds fair to say that ESOPs should not discriminate in favor of highly compensated employees, but the law defines "highly compensated" so narrowly that the principle affords little protection. Indeed, up to 1987 the law did not even define the term but merely mentioned it; what determined who was highly compensated depended on the circumstances in each case.

As of December 31, 1986, this was tightened by the new tax law. An employee is considered highly compensated if he or she has a salary in excess of $75,000, owns 5 percent or more of the employer company, receives more than $50,000 in annual compensation and belongs to the most highly paid group in the company (i.e., in the top 20-percent salary range), or is an officer in the employer company. Highly compensated employees must be identified in terms of the entire company not just a line of business or an operating unit.[22] Until this last stricture went into effect, it was possible to "discriminate" without breaking any restrictions in many ESOPs as well as in other pension plans.

All of the tax expenditures on ESOPs prior to 1986, then, have subsidized worker ownership that has not carefully measured whether highly paid groups of employees were profiting unduly from the program. A principle of nondiscrimination has actually served to justify discrimination. This reveals something about the ideology of those responsible for extending the rules governing pension plans to employee ownership, an ideology that says it is all the more important to benefit the highly paid and top management when a company is worker owned. Although as yet no one has proven that this is in fact necessary for firms to maintain healthy, motivating forms of employee ownership, corporations generally accept without question the notion that status should be the main determinant of pay.[23]

The tax-credit ESOP illustrates this point of view, particularly since in its case the principle of nondiscrimination and the actual mandated allocation formula were severely at odds. Although the government rigorously applied the general principle of nondiscrimination, it also stipulated that worker equity had to be allocated strictly according to differences in salary. Thus, since tax-credit ESOPs used 89 percent of all federal tax expenditures on ESOPs during their eleven-year history and generally excluded many salaried and unionized workers—particularly in the large publicly held corporations where they were most likely to be installed—nine out of ten dollars in tax incentives for ESOPs did in fact get allocated precisely according to salary differences during this period. Companies were prohibited from considering compensation in excess of $100,000 when figuring an employee's allocation (Internal Revenue Code 409 [b][2]), but this only prevented the worst abuse.

Guides for a Formula. In nonleveraged and leveraged ESOPs, the government says that every company must develop its own specific formula that puts the principle of nondiscrimination into practice. Legal manuals say that the formula will normally be proportionate to an employee's compensation although other factors such as years of service may be considered.[24] Yet many persons—even those familiar with ESOPs—believe that the formula must be based solely on relative compensation or that differences in pay must be the central mechanism of such a formula.

What is behind this misapprehension? Many lawyers have correctly noted that allocating worker equity according to salary differences is a good, quick, legal approach since one can certainly be sure that an ESOP with such a formula will not be disqualified. Unfortunately, this formula has become an ESOP canon that has precluded attempts to design imaginative approaches to the allocation of worker equity. Few firms consult managers and employees about what they think would be a fair and equitable way of distributing worker ownership—the issue is either prepackaged or considered irrelevant or threatening. Indeed, one reputable Connecticut law firm recently told a highly participatory 100-

percent worker-owned firm that it would be illegal to allocate worker equity according to the number of hours worked. The opinion was subsequently seconded by another attorney. Unfortunately, this was a case of lawyers presenting their opinions as the law.

In fact, there are a number of allocation methods from which to choose, as long as the resulting formula is at least as favorable to nonhighly compensated employees as would be allocation according to compensation. For example, all employees and managers could get equal portions of employee ownership each year without regard to salary. Or the allocation could be based on the number of hours worked. (This would eliminate problems such as that at a firm where a middle manager making an annual salary of $60,000 who spent several months in the hospital got six times more worker ownership allocated to his account in one year than an employee who worked full time and overtime throughout that same year.) PACE of Philadelphia designed ESOPs for the O & O Supermarkets using this approach, which qualified for IRS approval.[25] Years of service could be factored in as well, although some lawyers have noted that a formula based solely on years of service might be quite discriminatory in favor of managers, who often remain at firms much longer than the average worker. As we will detail later in this book, reseachers have found that compensation systems that are perceived as fair and equitable have the greatest chance of motivating employees. This must be carefully considered in the case of ESOPs, especially when allocation according to salary differences combines with the ability to exclude large numbers of employees to make some ESOPs appear as stock plans for the better off. In this area, it is certainly not clear that ESOP regulations should so closely follow those for all pension plans.

Limits on Annual Worker Equity. A ceiling on the amount of worker equity that can be added annually to any one account controls some of the inequity. Allocation cannot exceed the lesser of 25 percent of an individual's yearly compensation or $30,000, this last to be adjusted annually for cost-of-living increases beginning in 1988. If, however, officers, shareholders with more than 10 percent of the shares, or highly compensated employees do not receive more than one-third of the allocations in any year, the ceiling is doubled to $60,000. These ceilings have also applied to the tax-credit ESOPs.

The law also tries to guard against extremely discriminatory retirement plans of all types, including ESOPs, that primarily benefit officers, the employees who own the ten largest interests in the firm, and owners of 5 percent or more of the company with over $150,000 in annual compensation. If these key employees hold more than 60 percent of the trust's assets in any year, the plan is considered top heavy and must abide by special rules to reduce the inequity: Only the first $200,000 of any employee's annual compensation can be counted in computing allocation of worker ownership; vesting for all employees must be speeded up; and the company must make a contribution on behalf of each non-key employee equal to at least 3 percent of annual compensation. The new tax law somewhat tightens these adjustments.[26]

Who Gets the Resources? The weak protections provided under the law apply only to employees participating in the worker-ownership plan. In addition, as noted, most legal manuals recommend the use of salary differences to determine allocation. Thus, whether the original framers intended it or not, the interaction of the eligibility and the allocation formulas of the law has produced worker-ownership plans that favor the inclusion of more highly paid workers, to whom more equity is allotted. According to a 1981 survey by the ESOP Association, more than two-thirds of ESOPs allocated at least half of their stock—an average of 69 percent, in fact—to their salaried employees' accounts.[27] Another survey of 229 leveraged and nonleveraged ESOPs confirmed these findings (see Table 5–4c).

The creation in 1982 of the laws against top-heavy retirement plans of all types suggests that potential inequality had been even more severe, and they did not eliminate the problem. For example, they protect against plans in which key employees get more than 60 percent of the benefits—but the definition "key employees" does not extend to all highly paid managers or salaried employees. While the 1986 definition of a highly compensated employee corrects this to a point, there may still be ample room to get around the intent of the new law by way of various loopholes and the regulatory discretion allowed the secretary of labor.

An alternative allocation formula used by some lawyers tends to discriminate even more in favor of highly paid and long-term employees. This unit formula figures allocation according to a complex credit system based on salary and years of service. Depending on how far the formula is carried, allocations can be made even more stratified.

All of this points to one major pattern: The definition of highly paid employees was so vague under the previous law and and is so focused on exceedingly highly paid employees under the new law that in practice ESOPs can drastically favor moderately paid workers over low paid workers or highly paid workers over moderately paid workers.

Vesting: When Does One Get the Rights of Ownership?[28] The main function of vesting is to give workers an incentive to stay with the company. Assets may be allocated to a worker's account, but the vesting schedule determines when they belong to the worker. Defined-benefit plans and defined-contribution plans share many of the same regulations, but the latter have historically vested benefits faster.

Prior to 1986, vesting could not be less generous than one of the following schedules: (1) 100 percent of the benefit after ten years of service; (2) 25 percent of the benefit after five years of service, then 5 percent yearly for five years followed by 10 percent yearly for five years; (3) 50 percent after five years of service if the sum of the worker's age and service years is 45 or more, then 10 percent a year for five years (in this scenario, any worker with ten years of service must be vested 50 percent and then 10 percent a year for the next five years); (4) 40 percent after four years, 5 percent for the fifth and sixth years, then 10 percent for the next five years. Also, a worker may be vested according to the year in which the employer contributions were made, in which case he or she must be 100-percent vested within five years after the end of the plan year in which the contribution was made.

Since vesting is based on years of service, a company can disregard years that were not completed by the worker or that were completed before the worker was 18, as well as certain periods of employment, even if there was no break in service, when the worker declined to make a mandatory contribution or the plan was not maintained by the employer. The law prohibits arbitrary dismissal of workers before their benefits are vested and any unintentional pattern of vesting that discriminates in favor of officers, important shareholders, or highly compensated workers.

When a worker leaves the company, his or her unvested assets are forfeited and divided among other employees or used to reduce corporate contributions to the ESOP. The vesting schedule determines when a worker's ownership is nonforfeitable. In tax-credit ESOPs, vesting is 100 percent, immediately. There are no forfeitures, but worker stock must stay in the trust for seven years.

Vesting governs both how long a corporation can use the worker's equity in its business operations and when an employee actually controls his or her ownership. One study indicates that 97 percent of ESOP companies begin vesting after five years of actual company service or less—the average is 2.9 years—and complete it after ten years. Public companies tend to finish vesting earlier (7.7 years) than private companies (10.4 years). Company size does not affect these patterns. When an employee separates from company service, dies, or is disabled, he or she (or the heirs) can take the vested benefit. Employees leaving for any reason before they are completely vested forfeit all their benefits.

The current ESOP vesting mechanism was designed to reward length of service, yet the average worker now stays in a job only three-and-a-half to five years. In other words, many workers lose their equity. Recently, further research has indicated how many employees leave ESOP firms before retirement. A 1986 survey of 237 ESOP companies found that only 11 percent of the companies had no employees who left prior to retirement; 58 percent had 1 to 50 such employees; and 28 percent had 51 to 1,000. This is especially common in closely held firms.[29]

These vesting provisions have guided the organization of employee ownership and have likely dampened incentive and motivation. The most radical changes in vesting in the 1986 tax reform law responded to the widely held view that many retirement benefits were imaginary because of the drawn-out scheduling of property rights. Now vesting must be either 20 percent a year after three years or 100 percent after five years. Thus, workers get nonforfeitable rights after five to seven years instead of after ten to fifteen years. The new vesting does not become effective until 1989—1991 for some collectively bargained plans—and, while it cuts the vesting period in half, it will still leave many ESOP employees out in the cold.[30] Still, the new tax law mandates companies to begin paying worker-ownership benefits even if the employee leaves the firm for reasons other than death, retirement, or disability.[31]

Giving Workers Their Money.[32] The whole point of employee ownership is for the worker to have an ongoing stake in the company—quite reasonably, employees cannot remove their assets at will. A worker will generally receive benefits upon retirement or if he or she is disabled; in case of death, the worker's beneficiary has a right to the benefits. These will be distributed in cash or stock. The worker can demand stock unless the company's charter or bylaws provide that current workers or the ESOP must own 80 percent or more of the stock. In this case, the distribution is made in cash, and the ESOP has the right of first refusal in the sale of any stock. This provision protects companies that wish to remain substantially employee owned.

In a publicly traded company, workers can sell stock on the open market. Workers in closely held firms do not have this option and will typically want cash in any case, in order to pay the tax due on distribution. ESOPs in such firms are required to give the worker a "put option," according to which the corporation must redeem the stock for cash at fair market value within sixty days after it is distributed. Workers have two years to exercise their option. Some state laws require that corporations redeem stock only from retained earnings; in these cases put options will be deferred until the company has the funds to repurchase the shares. The ESOP cannot be forced to repurchase the stock, but it may be permitted to do so if the corporation cannot.

Distributions may be made in lump sums or in installments. When a company repurchases a worker's stock, it can pay the worker in a lump sum or on an installment basis. A corporation will usually project what it will need to cash out retiring, disabled, or deceased workers and make tax-deductible contributions to the ESOP, establish a sinking fund (of annuities, life insurance, certificates of deposit, and so on), or a combination of both to accumulate the necessary cash. Lump-sum distribution is more popular (70 percent) than installments (7 percent) because it is easier for plan administrators and has more tax advantages for employees. Eighteen percent of companies let the workers choose how they would like to receive benefits. Every company using the installment method was closely held, probably because these firms prefer to put off repurchasing stock as long as possible.[33]

The General Accounting Office has pointed out that the final measure of an ESOP's benefit to employees is their ability to convert their equity to cash or its equivalent at fair market value. Corporations were not required to convert to cash worker stock acquired up to September 30, 1976; workers in closely held firms were completely at the company's mercy. In 1976 the Department of Labor proposed a regulation to require such conversion in all ESOPs, but it was established only for leveraged ESOPs. The staff of the Joint Committee on Taxation made the surprising move of sharply criticizing that proposal in its statutory report on the 1976 tax act, saying that a put option requiring the employer to pay for the stock over a short period of time "would effectively deny the employer the benefits of capital formation the Congress sought to provide under an ESOP."[34]

But all evidence indicates that ESOPs are generally not used for new capital formation. By adhering to this pleasant fiction, a policy that benefitted corporate financial management rather than the worker-owners could be justified. In 1979 the GAO researched this issue and found that only two of the thirteen companies it investigated provided the put option. In the same year a more thorough survey found that 41 percent of leveraged and nonleveraged ESOPs did not offer a put option, regardless of the size of the companies in which they were installed. Some of the companies indicated that they intended to repurchase shares from workers voluntarily, and indeed this evidence does not disprove their claim. The GAO strongly recommended that Congress pass legislation requiring all nonpublicly traded companies to redeem worker stock at fair market value whether it was acquired from a leveraged ESOP or not. This recommendation was finally adopted in 1981.

From 1973 to 1981, over 90 percent of all nonleveraged and leverageable ESOPs had not been required to buy back worker stock, and over 85 percent of all nontax-credit ESOPs in closely held companies had not been required to put a commitment to buy back worker stock in their plans. The ESOP Association found that all leveraged ESOPs were complying with the law in 1983 and again in 1985. Although the put option was extended to all ESOPs after 1981, 12 to 13 percent of nonleveraged ESOPs in closely held companies still had made no provisions to comply at the time of the 1985 survey. The new tax reform act requires a put option for all stock-bonus plans.[35]

A basic problem remains: Will closely held companies match their promises to redeem stock with plans to have the money on hand? Figures indicate that only about half of ESOP companies have done actuarial studies to see how much cash they will need to meet their obligations, and about a third have specific plans to come up with this money. However, a 1986 survey of 237 ESOPs indicated that 84 percent showed an increase in stock value in the last three years; of the remaining 16 percent that had a decrease in stock value, overhalf had decreased less than 10 percent. Thus, although further study is needed, ESOPs seem to be appearing in many healthy companies, which will be more likely to meet their responsibilities to workers.[36]

To guarantee benefits further, the new tax law states that 55-year-old employees who have been in an ESOP for ten years can demand that the company distribute to them 25 percent of their assets or offer them three diversified investment options within the worker-ownership plan for a like amount. At age 60 the percentage increases to 50 percent. This ensures that workers will reap some of the benefits of their years in the plan even if the company has not sufficiently planned for stock redemption.[37]

The reforms of 1986 undoubtedly make it easier and surer for employees to get their ESOP benefits. That such adjustments had to be made at all suggests that there were indeed problems during the ESOP's first fifteen years.

Representation

The right to vote stock comes with allocation. In a leveraged ESOP, a worker-ownership trust can hold 100 percent of a company's stock, but only the trustees will be able to vote it until the stock is allocated.[38] Who instructs the trustees on how to vote?

In publicly held firms, workers have the legal right to direct the trustees how to vote their shares on all matters. The law requires this of any company with a class of securities that must be registered under the Securities and Exchange Act of 1934 (that is, any corporation with assets of at least $1 million and 500 or more stockholders). A law that became effective on December 31, 1979, required that ESOPs in privately held firms pass through voting rights to workers on major corporate issues, usually those that state law or the corporate charter stated must be decided by more than a majority (i.e., more than 51 percent) of the outstanding common shares, such as merger, acquisition, consolidation, or sale of all or most of the company's assets.[39] Up to 1979, 90 percent of all the nontax-credit ESOPs were established in closely held companies, accounting for 77 percent of all such ESOPs established from 1973 to 1983. None of these was required to pass through voting rights on stock acquired before the effective date of the law.[40] The events at Galaxy Manufacturing indicate what such a denial can mean.

All this applies only to allocated shares—the trustees still vote unallocated shares as they choose. These trustees also have exclusive authority to manage and control the assets of the plan, although a provision can be made that the trustee will be subject to the direction of a fiduciary who may appoint an investment manager. A recent study by the ESOP Association shows that a bank, trust company, or officers of the firm itself serve as the ESOP trustees in 95 percent of the cases.[41]

Stock is usually voted on a one-share/one-vote basis. Some observers believe that this approach is inherently undemocratic and argue for a one-person/one-vote system, which would stress the common interest of all employee-shareholders. A one-person/one-vote company can still reward special skills or performance through greater ownership, but that ownership would not be tied to greater power. Very few firms—one of which is Seymour Specialty Steel—have actually experimented with this approach, which is viewed as a compromise between unequal ownership and unequal control.[42]

Dividends

Louis Kelso's original design for the ESOP included substantial dividends to workers. The abstract ownership expected to inspire greater commitment and motivation was to be buttressed by a tangible "second income." Of all the original intentions behind the ESOP, this has been the least respected in actual legislation.

In fifteen years of federal law, no ESOP was required to pay dividends. The law does, however, require ESOP stock to combine voting power and dividend rights in a way comparable to or better than the class of stock having the greatest voting and dividend rights. Because ESOP law favors management domination of the trust and does not require employee representation on the board, employees usually have no say about dividends, unless they initially negotiated for such a voice or control of management through some other means.

During their existence, tax-credit ESOPs could allocate dividends to individual worker accounts for distribution at retirement or pass them through the trust directly to the workers. The dividend law is much more relevant in leveraged and nonleveraged ESOPs, where workers may hold a greater percentage of the company and where their stock and dividends may constitute a meaningful addition to their total compensation. In these ESOPs, dividends may be used to buy stock, which is allocated to individual accounts—the employees receive nothing until retirement or separation from service. Dividends can be passed through the trust and paid currently to the employee, but this happens infrequently. In the leveraged ESOP, dividends may be used to repay the loan incurred by the trust. If an ESOP chooses to pay dividends, it can require that they be paid automatically or periodically according to the will of the trustees, the board of directors, or the employees themselves.

Prior to 1984, only about a third of ESOP companies overall paid dividends; of all nontax-credit ESOPs that paid dividends, less than 10 percent distributed them immediately to workers. Tax-credit ESOPs were twice as likely to pay dividends as nontax-credit ESOPs.[43] In 1982, 80 percent of the publicly traded firms surveyed by the ESOP Association paid dividends, compared to only 35 percent of the closely held companies surveyed. The association commented that market pressures force the publicly traded firms to pay dividends; in fact, most of these publicly traded firms probably had tax-credit ESOPs.[44] Thus, when dividends were paid prior to 1984, they were likely paid in the tax-credit ESOPs, where the amount of worker equity was irrelevant, or generally retained in the trust, which muffled their effect as an incentive.

Tax Law and Dividends. For years American corporations and stockholders have opposed the current system that taxes corporations' gross profits, thereby reducing dividends, and then taxes dividends as individual income, further reducing stockholders' returns on investment. Congress's 1984 Deficit Reduction Act changed all of this by exempting companies with ESOPs from double taxation, thus distinguishing them from all other corporations. Employee-owned companies can now take a dollar-for-dollar tax deduction for dividends paid in cash to participating employees. A 1982 ESOP Association survey reported that half of the firms not paying dividends indicated they would start paying them and that half of the firms paying them but not passing them through the trust to employees said they would begin doing so. A quarter of the companies who paid dividends directly to employees said they would also increase their dividends.[45] The 1986 ESOP Association survey reported that, after the passage of the 1984 law allowing companies to deduct dividends paid to workers on ESOP stock, slightly more companies paid dividends, but 80 percent began to pass them through to the workers.[46] This one law significantly transformed the behavior of dividend-paying ESOP companies. However, 66 percent of all companies still do not pay dividends, including 70 percent of majority employee-owned firms. Clearly, companies did not change their behavior as much as they said they would.

The 1986 tax reform law may actually decrease the number of companies paying dividends to employees directly by allowing firms to deduct dividend payments that go to individual ESOP accounts as long as the trust uses the payments to pay back an ESOP loan. The deduction is in addition to all other deductions. This allows a corporation to repay larger loans faster to purchase worker equity, but it will reduce short-term income for the employees. So far, employee ownership has not gone far toward generating a motivating second income for worker-owners, and many of the factors discussed here injure the incentive value of ESOPs.

Other Crucial Issues

A number of other factors shape employee ownership in an ESOP. Just as the definition of a worker is amorphous, so can be that of the company. A parent company that owns 50 percent or more of another corporation's stock can use those securities in its own ESOP. The original minimum was 80 percent, but this was changed in the Revenue Act of 1978 when Congress decided that "this 80 percent . . . requirement was unduly restrictive and that the interests of the public in broader employee stock ownership would be better served by a 50-percent stock ownership requirement." There is little evidence about how many of these arrangements exist—certainly the change was intended mainly to accommodate the large Fortune 1000 firms that used the tax-credit ESOP—but it is yet another distortion of the original notion behind the ESOP.[47]

Next, for an employer security to be acceptable for an ESOP, it must be common stock that is readily tradeable on an established market or that has a combination of dividend rights and voting power equal to or in excess of those classes of common stock with the greatest voting power or dividend rights, or it must be noncallable preferred stock that is convertible into common stock at any time at a reasonable price. But, as noted above, employer securities issued by any member of a controlled group of corporations are treated as if they are stock of any other member of the group.

Additional twists resulting from the interaction of a majority or wholly worker-owned ESOP with unexpected future situations in a company can limit and divide the meaning of worker ownership. In effect, ESOP law's habit of reshaping the meaning of ownership can also work to the employees' disadvantage even in what seem like completely worker-owned firms. Congress has dealt with one aspect of this problem by allowing companies to subject stock to a right of first refusal or by allowing companies that largely restrict stock ownership to employees or a trust to distribute benefits in cash without granting departing employees the right to demand stock. In this case, workers to whom stock is distributed can be compelled to offer it to the ESOP or the company when they leave. This can prevent the disappearance of employee ownership as the company matures.

Another problem is that if the company is sold at some future point, under certain circumstances employees with a sizable stake in the firm may find that they may lose ownership with little alternative. To avoid this possibility, one labor advisor, Randy Barber, has stressed worker negotiation of rights of first refusal to purchase a company, along with special rights in case of merger, takeover, or consolidation.

If a firm is publicly held, the absence of employee involvement on the board of directors might mean that a new stock issue could be launched to dilute the percentage of worker ownership significantly. This could not happen if preemptive rights guaranteed employees the option to purchase enough shares from a new offering to preserve their ownership.

Management can create subsidiaries or holding companies that seriously affect the business. In one company, management created a foreign subsidiary that manufactured the same product at such a low cost that many of the U.S. worker-owners lost their jobs. Required worker approval of such decisions could be an important addition to some ESOPs.

If a substantial portion of compensation were being diverted into the trust or wage cuts became the price of the ESOP, protection of the employee ownership through liquidation preferences for worker stock or other options in case of bankruptcy or liquidation would be a useful provision to which to turn.

This presentation of potential wrenches in the works of the ESOP machine suggests the importance of a broad outlook when designing a plan. The company's future, the myriad possible problems that may arise, and the rights and responsibilities of all people involved must be considered. Some scholars have confined their studies to the role of organized labor, but all employees, salaried and nonsalaried, among them many members of middle management, must be taken into account.[48] The ESOP should provide for as many variables as its designers can envision.

Conclusion

No evidence has yet been accumulated on how efficiently employee ownership—in any of its many forms, as evidenced by the examples at the beginning of this chapter—achieves its official goals of broadening the wealth, increasing capital formation, promoting labor-management cooperation, improving economic performance, and renovating the general structure of the economy. The model emphasizes the creation of as much employee ownership as possible; the instrument itself provides countless ways to limit, diminish, and defer this ownership, eliminate its immediate rewards, and restrict its meaning. Nor is the ESOP used primarily for its official purpose; individuals and firms considering the concept will be motivated by its wide variety of possible corporate uses and tax incentives (see Appendices A and B).

Employee ownership can be insignificant or extremely minimal (up to 15 percent), sizable (16 percent to 50 percent), majority (51 percent to 99 percent), or complete (100 percent). It can involve inconsequential or total employee involvement and endow employees with many or few of the rights and responsibilities associated with ownership.

The moving parts of the ESOP machine can be arranged in four basic configurations:

1. Minimal employee ownership and very little employee involvement in the ownership or management of the firm. The justification for this arrangement is that when employees own only a small part of the company, it makes no sense to involve them in the rights and responsibilities of ownership. Ownership is intended merely to supplement wages.

2. Minimal employee ownership and some or extensive employee involvement in the ownership and management of the firm. The reasoning here is that when employees own a small part of the company, it makes sense to provide them with the rights and responsibilities of ownership because this will help a little equity go a long way.

3. Sizable, majority, or total employee ownership and very little employee involvement in the ownership and management of the firm. In this case, the theory is that when employees own a large part of the company, it makes no sense for them to have many of the rights and responsibilities of ownership because workers simply cannot manage such rights and responsibilities efficiently, both in terms of the firm's interests and their own.

4. Sizable, majority, or total employee ownership and some or extensive employee involvement in the ownership or management of the firm. Here the idea is that when employees own a large part of the company, it makes sense for them to have many of the rights and responsibilities of ownership because that is the way a private-property system works.

Each type of worker ownership will not always be limited to a specific set of proponents. Management will not consistently fight for minimal worker-owner participation. Existing owners who are selling an entire firm to employees may actually prefer them to have responsibilities. Of course, this may be most likely when the owners are leaving or when they no longer control a majority interest. They may then be happy to experiment with sharing ownership and its responsibilities as long as the process can be managed efficiently. Or perhaps they feel that the company is theirs regardless of their actual share of ownership. When managers and nonsalaried employees share majority ownership of a firm, managers may come to identify more with the worker-owners than with the traditional power elite. On the other hand, managers may always identify with the existing power structure of a firm and refuse ever to involve workers in the rights and responsibilities of ownership. Workers themselves may reject responsibility if their ownership stake is small or fear it if the stake is large.

In its current state, the ESOP machine can be operated in a way that respects a richer concept of employee ownership, but only if all parties involved are prepared to share the woes and rewards of ownership. Unfortunately, based as it is on the personal ideologies of the would-be participants, the odds are against such an equitable arrangement.

CHAPTER 3

Capital Formation and Corporate Finance

The Old Stone Bank of Providence, Rhode Island, is a publicly traded firm with assets of over $3 billion. It recently used an ESOP to leverage new capital into the bank, create a block of stock to defend against possible takeover, and motivate employees to identify more closely with the company. The bank is now 33-percent employee owned. Initially, management had worried that the new shares would dilute shareholder equity, but instead the restructuring increased earnings for all shareholders.[1]

In the summer of 1981, Pan Am realized it had to reduce direct labor costs to remain competitive. The five unions representing the airline's employees ratified concessions including a 10-percent wage cut and a 15-month freeze on wage increases in exchange for 13-percent equity in the company and a seat on the board of directors. In July 1987, a coalition of four unions hired Drexel Burnham Lambert to restructure the plan after management and labor were unable to agree on how much the worker stake would increase in exchange for new concessions.[2]

On December 31, 1986, the Kroch family sold half of the stock in Kroch's and Brentano's, the largest bookstore chain in Chicago, to its 700 employees. The remaining half of the privately held firm is to be sold to the ESOP over the next five years. Kroch had refused a tempting offer from another chain for fear that layoffs would be imposed on the firm's loyal workforce. The reorganization helps protect the company from takeover and provides financial and tax benefits to the Kroch family and the employees.[3]

In 1986, Robertshaw Controls of Richmond, Virginia, was put up for sale by Reynolds Metal Co. The United Auto Workers and the United Steel Workers engaged American Capital Strategies, Inc., of Bethesda, Maryland, to structure and arrange financing for a bid of $418 million on behalf of the 7,000 employees—the first hostile tender offer by employees to purchase a major American corporation. Britain's Siebe PLC topped the bid with an offer of $467 million, but an important precedent had been set: Wall Street would loan workers big money to buy large firms.[4]

What are the options for corporate finance available with the ESOP? What are their advantages and disadvantages? How do these advantages and disadvantages explain the actual diffusion of ESOPs? Does the ESOP represent an innovative and efficient use of resources? Does it broaden wealth, boost the economic performance of firms, and bolster the economy as a whole? Concerns about the efficacy of the ESOP's working parts and the contradictions in the law become less dire if these questions can be answered affirmatively. If the answer is no, then the framers' central justification for the program must be reexamined.

We now turn to an analysis of the financial features of the three types of ESOPs.[5] To talk about "*the* ESOP" is seriously misleading. The tax-credit ESOP, leveraged ESOP, and nonleveraged ESOP each have unique features, knowledge of which is essential to understand their socioeconomic implications. The tax-credit ESOP (i.e., the TRASOP and the PAYSOP), although now discontinued, is particularly noteworthy in its distortion of the original intent of the program and, as such, will be considered at length. The others, all still functioning, will be analyzed more briefly and with a specific focus on their financial attributes.

Table 3–1 presents the background against which these details about the financial features of the three types of ESOPs should be considered. It shows the various approaches to corporate finance used by nonfinancial corporations in 1985. (For a historical view, see Appendix C, Table C–1.) Corporations create new capital mainly through internal sources, while debt serves as the main external source. The tax-credit ESOP was essentially designed to encourage corporations to make worker equity available when they benefitted from government tax credits for capital spending. The leveraged ESOP was mainly designed to encourage corporations to sell workers equity when they used debt. The nonleveraged ESOP was primarily designed to give corporations a way to sell workers equity without necessarily borrowing new funds or dispensing cash. As noted, it is almost identical to the standard stock-bonus plan.

Table 3–1.   Capital Formation by Nonfarm Nonfinancial Corporations in 1985
(percent)[a]

Retained earnings	5.5	
Depreciation	53.1	
Inventory, capital-consumption adjustments, and foreign earnings	20.4	
Total internal capital formation		79.0
New equity issues	-18.9[b]	
Debt	31.8	
Other	8.2	
Total external capital formation		21.0

a. Debt securities will not be considered in the text.
b. Corporations bought more stock than they sold, mainly because of mergers and acquisitions.

Source: U.S. General Accounting Office, *Employee Stock Ownership Plans: Interim Report on a Survey and Related Economic Trends* (Washington, D.C.: U.S. General Accounting Office, February 1986), p. 49.

The Nonleveraged ESOP

Companies do not use the nonleveraged ESOP for corporate finance or credit. Its main advantage is that the employer can take a cash deduction for contributions of stock or cash to buy stock to a worker trust. In all cases cash flow will improve. With the top current marginal corporate tax rate of 34 percent, for every dollar a company contributes to an ESOP to purchase worker stock, thirty-four cents of the initial value of that stock is paid for by the U.S. Treasury. That thirty-four cents increases the company's working capital.

If new shares are issued to contribute to the ESOT, previously existing shareholders control a smaller percentage of stock and can thus anticipate diminished future earnings. Net income and equity per share are diluted, and some commentators note that the market value of shares may suffer as well. Total assets and net income will generally increase because of the tax subsidy.

If a company contributes existing stock to the ESOP, or cash with which to buy stock from existing shareholders, these dilution effects are tempered. Presumably, owners who sell want to cash out their holdings; those remaining suffer no dilution in net earnings per share nor do they lose rights to future earnings. Since taxes are saved, working capital and net income still increase.

The financial impact of this ESOP will vary depending on which scenario is followed, but either way there will be a substantial repurchase liability for the privately held company since no established market will exist for the stocks when the time comes to convert them to cash. Indeed, it is probable that some companies discover that they have benefitted from the ESOP tax advantages without adequately planning for the repurchase of shares. In a 1985 survey of managers in companies maintaining nonleveraged ESOPs, 23 percent cited the diluted value of the stock and 22 percent cited the repurchase liability as a disadvantage. Although it must be noted that 54 percent saw no drawbacks whatsoever in the nonleveraged ESOP, it seems that there is some incentive for firms to abandon existing plans. This may explain the extremely high rate—almost 40 percent—of companies terminating nonleveraged ESOPs.[6]

A profitable company may choose to install a nonleveraged ESOP to gain certain short-term capital advantages. The plan can help remedy—in the short term—lack of access to capital, a major reason that businesses fail. However, such a company must weigh the dilution of net income and equity per share against the increases in net income and assets from tax savings and investment of those savings.

The owner or some shareholder(s) may need to cash out shares for which a public market does not exist. The owner may want to sell the company to the workers slowly in order to prepare for retirement or because sale to another buyer is not likely.[7] When new stock is issued, the nonleveraged ESOP is clearly disadvantageous to existing owners, but when the aim is to transform ownership, the owner does not care about dilution. He or she has decided that the tax gains and the creation of a market for stock justify the dilution effects during a specified period or that company growth and improved performance will offset the loss in potential earnings. The ability to create a benefit without a cash outlay—an impossibility with profit-sharing or defined-benefit plans—may be viewed as a labor-relations or incentive stratagem by management. A profitable company in a highly competitive market might require wage and benefit concessions; the nonleveraged ESOP could serve as a deferred-compensation program to shore up the company in the short term. A start-up firm without a track record, unable to get a secured or unsecured loan for a leveraged ESOP or to afford a pension plan, may turn to the nonleveraged ESOP instead.

This financial analysis helps explain why almost 90 percent of nonleveraged ESOPs are in privately held companies. The nonleveraged ESOP provides a means to cash out existing shareholders in companies with restricted markets. Most of the corporate uses are available to these companies. When ownership is being transformed, the disincentives of the nonleveraged ESOP are considerably reduced, particularly since the repurchase liability can be passed on to the new employee-owners. It should also be noted that a nonleveraged ESOP might compare quite favorably to the possibility of a successful unfriendly takeover.

This analysis also clarifies why there are so few nonleveraged ESOPs in publicly traded companies, even though these firms do not suffer from the repurchase liability.[8] Profitable publicly held companies in the era of the investment tax credit, accelerated depreciation, and other tax incentives have ample opportunities to reduce taxes, although this may change with the new tax law. Dominant owner/manager shareholders can use the market to transform their ownership. Thus, in such firms, the main reason to choose a nonleveraged ESOP over other means to save taxes would be to satisfy a philosophical commitment to employee ownership.

Would a profitable publicly held firm ever choose a nonleveraged ESOP over conventional equity financing? As an example, let us look at a profitable firm with 10,000 shares of common stock. Instead of an immediate equity offering of, say, 5,000 shares of stock, for five years the company would contribute annually 1,000 shares of stock to its nonleveraged ESOP and get a tax write-off. If the company is in the 50-percent income-tax bracket, the government would in effect provide 50 percent of the new equity. If the firm is publicly traded, non-ESOP equity financing would be advantageous: equity per share would be greater, the ESOP would do no more to increase working capital, and net income would be equal or better. If, however, the equity-financed firm raised all of its equity in the first year, the ESOP would have one clear advantage: Its net income per share for the first five years would be greater than or equal to that of the equity-financed firm, because the latter would be dividing income among 15,000 shares in one year, while the ESOP would gradually add the 5,000 new shares over a five-year period. In addition, it is possible that the ability of ESOPs to deduct their dividends from federal income taxes since 1984 might influence some publicly traded companies in its favor.

Generally, the nonleveraged ESOP does not lead to new private-sector capital formation in the classic ESOP sense. It does not use credit to produce new worker ownership that is paid for later out of productivity. Thus, it does not conform to the legislation's main promise to further increased ownership through self-liquidating credit. If it does issue new shares and create new capital, some redistribution of wealth takes place from the dilution of the stock value of current shareholders, although certain ESOP enthusiasts claim that increased worker motivation and the availability of more working capital lead to a higher rate of return, which compensates for this dilution. Evidence indicates, however, that most ESOPs—both leveraged and nonleveraged—acquired existing stock rather than new issue and that they are used largely to transfer ownership rather than to produce new capital ownership.[9]

The Leveraged ESOP

Loan to the Trust

A hybrid of debt and equity financing, this is the classic Kelso ESOP. It always involves corporate finance and the use of self-liquidating credit for worker ownership, and it is worth remembering as well that Kelso intended ESOPs to buy newly issued shares of corporate stock.[10] Its main financial advantage is that it permits the corporation to raise additional capital and repay principal and interest with pretax dollars.

Considered here is the trust-financed leveraged ESOP, where credit is extended to the ESOT itself rather than directly to the company. The ESOT borrows funds from a lender and then creates equity through the purchase of new shares of stock in the worker company. The company guarantees the loan and makes a commitment to contribute annually to the trust so it can amortize the loan.

The leveraged ESOP increases working capital and total assets in both the short and long term through tax savings greater than those a debt-financed company would enjoy. It improves the ratio of working capital to debt service and moderately increases the overall debt capacity of the company. After 1984, a company choosing to pay dividends could deduct them from its income for tax purposes; before 1984 such dividends would have reduced cash flow.[11]

There are a number of disadvantages to leveraged-ESOP financing. Equity per share is diluted since the same amount of assets is divided among more shares. Although the after-tax rate of return is greater, the earning base is divided among more shareholders, thus net income per share is also diluted. Net income is significantly reduced until the company completes its contribution to the ESOP trust. Also, the ownership percentage of non-ESOP stockholders—often the principal stockholders—is diluted.

Table 3–2. Comparison of Leveraged-ESOP Financing with Debt Financing over Ten Years.

A. Direct Borrowing by Corporation—No ESOP (in thousands of dollars).

Year	Payments to Corporation	Payments by Corporation		Cash Value of Deductions	After-Tax Cash Cost
		Cash	Stock		
1	$1,000	$ 180	—	$ 40	$ 140
2	—	172	—	36	136
3	—	164	—	32	132
4	—	156	—	28	128
5	—	148	—	24	124
6	—	140	—	20	120
7	—	132	—	16	116
8	—	124	—	12	112
9	—	116	—	8	108
10	—	108	—	4	104
	$1,000	$1,440	—	$220	$1,220

B. Borrowing by Leveraged ESOP (in thousands of dollars).

Year	Payments to Corporation	Payments by Corporation		Cash Value of Deductions	After-Tax Cash Cost
		Cash	Stock		
1	$1,000	$ 180	$1,000	$ 90	$ 90
2	—	172	—	86	86
3	—	164	—	82	82
4	—	156	—	78	78
5	—	148	—	74	74
6	—	140	—	70	70
7	—	132	—	66	66
8	—	124	—	62	62
9	—	116	—	58	58
10	—	108	—	54	54
	$1,000	$1,440	$1,000	$720	$720

Parameters: (1) The corporation is raising $1 million, repayable over ten years in equal annual installments of principal plus interest at the annual rate of 8 percent; (2) fair market value of stock is $10 per share and the corporation is in the 50-percent income-tax bracket.

Source: Jared Kaplan, Gregory Brown, and Ronald Ludwig, *Tax Management: ESOPs* (Washington, D.C.: Bureau of National Affairs, 1985), p. A20.

In a leveraged transaction the block of stock acquired by the ESOP is put in a suspense account and shares of stock are later allocated to the accounts of individual participants as the loan is repaid. This allocation process is based on the original price paid by the ESOP, not the current fair market value. Thus, when share values are increasing rapidly [particularly in the case of a fast-growth company], a leveraged ESOP will distribute a greater number of shares to participants than would a nonleveraged ESOP contributing the same percentage of payroll each year.[12]

From another point of view, the disadvantages are even greater. Table 3–2 compares debt financing to leveraged-ESOP financing. The leveraged ESOP results in an after-tax cash savings of $500,000 on a $1-million loan, but employees have received $1 million in stock, which creates a repurchase liability for the company. As in the nonleveraged ESOP, this presents a substantial long-term disadvantage for the privately held firm that mitigates to a large extent the short-term benefits. Indeed, the repurchase problem is even more serious for the leveraged ESOP. Robert R. Bumgarner has analyzed the problem:

The company can pay off the loan and still owe its employees. The after-tax cost to the leveraged ESOP corporation is thus greater than the cost of direct borrowing.

Leveraged-ESOP financing will be most advantageous for a publicly held company that can easily handle repurchasing the shares. It will also be useful in a privately held firm where the repurchase liability can be passed on to a new set of owners. If the present users of the leveraged ESOP plan to be nonowners of the company (as in the case of a retiring owner) or new owners of the company (as in the case of a leveraged buyout by management, perhaps in combination with a takeover defense), the company usually will not issue new shares—leveraging will be used simply to replace one set of owners with another. When it does not result in new equity, the leveraged ESOP has more advantages.

It is also conceivable that management may decide to use a leveraged ESOP instead of debt financing for the short-term advantages of cheaper credit or lower interest rates or because a specific lender may decide that the ESOP ameliorates an otherwise unacceptable credit scenario.

The leveraged ESOP has few advantages compared to conventional equity financing. It will be able to deduct its dividends (not shown in Table 3–2) from federal taxes. It may be structured to retain dividends in the trust; in this way cash flow will not be reduced, but the worker incentive may be lost. It will not have the administrative costs of an equity offering. Both the leveraged ESOP and conventional equity financing will dilute the proportionate interest of existing shareholders in the corporation's net income.

Conventional equity financing, however, will not reduce income or working capital to pay debt retirement and interest costs. Net income, net income per share, working capital, and equity per share will be higher than in the leveraged ESOP, which must deduct its debt install-ment from net income annually, thus reducing cash flow. The issuance of new equity shares will result in the full proceeds of the offering being added to the permanent capital of the company, whereas sale to a lever-aged ESOP merely retains cash that would have been paid in taxes. The ESOP generates new equity capital based on debt that creates fixed obligations for the company—it is thus considerably more expensive than conventional equity financing.[13]

The U.S. General Accounting Office has reported that some banks may have been reluctant to loan to corporations planning to use such funds for employee ownership, "fearing for the stability of the com-pany and its ability to repay the loan." This may have been the case in the early years of ESOPs,but the lack of any substantial evidence that employee ownership leads to more business failure and the wider acceptance of employee ownership have reduced this problem. Never-theless, the GAO notes that the provisions in the Deficit Reduction Act of 1984 making half of a bank's interest earnings on loans to leveraged ESOPs tax free addressed the concerns of commercial lenders by pro-viding a premium for ESOP-financed loans. Banks may be sharing this benefit with ESOPs by charging lower interest rates on loans to ESOPs than on loans to other borrowers. A recent study by the National Center for Employee Ownership has found evidence of considerable support for employee ownership on the part of many large banks.[14]

A further disincentive of the leveraged ESOP is its accounting treat-ment. Assets held by the ESOP are not included in the financial state-ments of the employer, and the obligation of a leveraged ESOP must be recorded as a liability when it is covered by the employer's guarantee or commitment to make future contributions to the leveraged ESOP suffi-cient to meet debt-service requirements.[15]

Loan to the Company

Confronted with these drawbacks, some ESOP financial planners designed an alternate method of leveraging funds into ESOPs. The company, not the ESOP, takes out the loan directly from the lender. Interest on the loan is deductible as usual. The company then makes annual stock contributions to the ESOP to offset the loan-principal payments and receives the tax advantages. Technically, the ESOP is not leveraged and so can abide by looser legal restrictions, which require fewer protections for workers.[16]

In the alternate financing approach, the company annually contributes to the ESOP only the number of shares that equals the value of the principal payment to the bank. The dilution of net income per share, the ownership percentage, and the access to ongoing rate of return of previous owners is eliminated from the company-financed ESOP until the ESOP has bought all the shares. Equity per share is higher under ESOP financing by the company versus ESOP financing by the trust, although it is still greater under debt financing. A company may use this method to reduce the disadvantages of the leveraged ESOP for a few years and then transform the ownership structure the year when the tax and other benefits run out. But all in all debt financing remains preferable.

Equity financing continues to provide more working capital, greater equity per share, and more equity and assets. The advantage of the company-financed ESOP over equity financing exists only if the firm—usually privately held—does not have easy access to an equity market.

It becomes obvious why a large number of these alternative arrangements occur in privately held firms. The company-financed ESOP in any form provides publicly held companies with little improvement over equity financing. Even in privately held companies, the repurchase liability, the dilution of equity per share, and net income per share will probably be weighed against the possible advantages. Compared to debt financing, the major disadvantage "is the requirement that employees receive stock in the company as a part of the transaction," as the GAO puts it.[17]

If owners or management decides it is a philosophical goal to share ownership with employees, philanthropic concerns will override the negative aspects. This does not happen often.

A Means to Transform Ownership

Transformation of ownership, then, rather than new capital formation emerges as the major catalyst of new ESOP growth. An owner wishing to sell his or her business or retire leverages credit for the employees to carry off the deal. Or an existing owner uses a nonleveraged ESOP to transfer ownership gradually to employees. Workers and management wanting to acquire a subsidiary of a publicly or privately held company buy the stock through an ESOP.[18] Employees of a firm threatened with shutdown buy all or part of the company. A company uses an ESOP to acquire another company. (These examples show how employee ownership is becoming an important part of corporate financial planning.) A corporation actively threatened with a takeover installs an ESOP as a preferred alternative or sets one up as a built-in takeover defense.[19] A corporation in a competitive market simultaneously seeking wage and benefit concessions and new capital turns to a leveraged ESOP, which receives the capital and allocates shares according to the concessions each worker makes. Management and workers decide on a leveraged buyout of a whole firm that is for sale. The management or some owners of a publicly held firm want to take it private and include employees as partners in the deal. An ESOP is used as part of a stock-buyback program in order to restructure a firm, support its stock price, defend against a takeover, and so forth.

In each of these examples a transformation of ownership or a serious reevaluation of its current structure is taking place. The disadvantages of the leveraged ESOP to existing shareholders are minimized because the shareholders themselves are in favor of the transformation.

Managers surveyed for a 1986 GAO study report that ownership transformation is the main motivation behind their ESOPs, and, as shown above, the financial incentives and disincentives of the ESOP encourage this outcome. These situations are the most likely to lead to sizable or majority employee ownership—indeed, the transfer of ownership of successful privately held firms to their employees accounts for more than half of the new ESOPs with sizable and majority worker ownership.[20] It is not surprising that leveraged ESOPs are found in a large percentage of both sizably and majority worker-owned firms. The study revealed that almost 60 percent of surveyed managers in ESOP companies reported that they used the ESOP to buy the stock of a major owner, and almost 40 percent reported that they used it to transfer majority ownership to employees.[21] Worker buyouts of failing firms have received extensive media coverage, but this special use accounts for under 4 percent of the sizably and majority worker-owned firms.

Substantial evidence suggests that the most common way that leveraged ESOPs acquire company stock is to purchase it directly from a principal shareholder or on the open market (if publicly held). According to the 1985 ESOP Association survey, only 11 percent of leveraged

ESOPs purchased newly issued stock. (That figure is probably a good estimate of how many companies find reasons to consider instituting the leveraged ESOP in spite of the financial disincentives discussed above.) As the association states, "The power of leveraging is used far more frequently for purposes of buyout than for purposes of financing corporate growth."[22] More recent evidence from the GAO survey of thousands of ESOPs confirms this. Only 12 percent of the leveraged ESOPs responding purchased new treasury shares of stock from the sponsoring corporation. Seventy-six percent used at least part of the proceeds from the loan to buy outstanding shares from other stockholders. For the small percentage of ESOPs that have leveraged using newly issued stock, it still cannot be presumed that these funds were used solely for new capital formation. Forty-nine percent of the respondents to the GAO survey reported that they used at least some of the funds for the purchase of new plant or equipment, while the balance used the funds to repair plant or equipment, pay off corporate debt, or cover operating costs.

The GAO examined the special case of leveraged buyouts of plants threatened with shutdown because they are especially relevant to understanding the leveraged ESOP. As noted, these account for only 4 percent of all ESOPs, yet one-third of the cases are leveraged ESOPs. Ninety-one percent purchased stock from existing shareholders and no treasury stock. The funds were not used to invest in new plant or equipment, and only 17 percent was used to modernize existing equipment. The GAO concludes, "Essentially these firms borrowed through ESOPs to buy out the previous owners (individuals or parent corporations) in order to keep the businesses in operation. They may have retained existing capital in operation, but they usually did not add to the capital stock through these leveraged transactions."[23]

Thus, the leveraged ESOP, structured to promote new capital formation, actually leads to very little formation of new capital. It does result in worker ownership through self-liquidating credit, a major goal of the legislation, but it generally replaces one set of owners with existing capital with employee-owners. Essentially, in a leveraged-ESOP transaction, a corporation in the top current marginal corporate tax bracket of 34 percent finds that, for every borrowed dollar it uses to purchase worker stock, the government gives it thirty-four cents.[24] If a share costs $1 the company receives $1 worth of stock but also receives a tax deduction for the full market value of the stock. The thirty-four cents per share the government gives the company increases working capital and is the government's incentive to use this type of financing. This thirty-four cents represents a redistribution of tax revenue. Further redistribution occurs when the company deducts dividends paid out to the worker-owners and interest on the credit used to buy their shares. And, as noted, the fine print of ESOP leveraging means that firms will still use this cheaper capital only in a special set of circumstances that cancel out the disadvantages of the leveraged ESOP.

Over a third of majority employee-owned firms stem from ownership being transferred from a family to the employees to avoid a succession problem. While this occurs mainly in privately held companies, family owners of large publicly held firms do sometimes sell their shares to the employees. Another quarter of ownership transfers are the result of worker buyouts of both failing firms and successful companies that are being divested. Start-ups of new firms, similar to the Jefferson Masonry case discussed at the beginning of Chapter 4, do not occur very often.[25]

A review of national reportage suggests that many ESOP companies with minority employee ownership represent the beginning of a gradual transfer of ownership to employees or an existing owner's incomplete attempt to remove his or her capital from the company. Yet, while these companies are usually privately held small businesses, it cannot be presumed that privately held automatically means small. Table 3–3 lists twelve such companies that are among the top 400 firms in the country.

Table 3–3. Largely or Completely Employee-Owned Firms among the 400 Largest Private Companies in the United States.

Publix Supermarkets (#10)
Avondale Industries (#45)
Weirton Steel (#65)
Raymond International (#74)
Parsons (#75)
Dan River Textiles (#122)
Science Applications (#214)
The Journal Company (#261)
Thomson-McKinnon (#267)
APICO (#281)
Otasco (#302)
W. L. Gore (#350)

Source: National Center for Employee Ownership, Majority Employee Owned Firms (Oakland, Calif.: National Center for Employee Ownership, August 1986).

Although employee ownership has not been a major factor with large publicly held corporations, many such corporations have cooperated with worker buyouts of a failing firm or a divestiture of a successful subsidiary. In fact, one in ten major employee-owned firms with more than 20-percent ownership and 1,000 employees resulted from such divestitures. Unions are disproportionately involved in such cases because of their greater involvement with larger publicly held companies. The resultant corporation is usually private, but initiative to form it often comes from a public company. ESOPs are seldom used to start up new companies, but, interestingly, transformations of ownership occasionally create large employee-owned firms. Table 3–4 reviews the major cases of the use of worker ownership as a takeover defense and leveraged buyouts of large publicly held companies, providing examples of worker buyouts of failing firms or successful divestitures. The parent corporation is listed first, followed by the name of the new worker-owned enterprise.

Table 3–4.   Employee Ownership Affecting Publicly Traded Companies: Buyouts, Divestitures, Takeover Defenses, Leveraged Buyouts.

A. Buyout of a Failing Firm or Successful Divestiture: Some Examples Primarily Touching Large Publicly Traded Companies.

A&P—O&O Supermarkets
Allegheny International—Clarion Sintered Metals
Allied Corporation—Scully-Jones
Allis-Chambers (via Wesray Corporation)—Simplicity Manufacturing
Amcast Industrial Corporation—Ironton Iron
American Standard—Mosler Safe
Amsted—South Bend Lathe
Cluett Peabody—Saratoga Knitting Mills
Colt Industries—Crucible Materials
Control Data—Kerotest Valve Company
GAF Corp.—Vermont Asbestos
General Motors—Hyatt-Clark
Gerber—Infants Specialty Company
W. R. Grace—Rich Sea-Pak Corp.
A Japanese conglomerate—Denka Chemical
Kaiser Aluminum—National Refractories Division
LTV—Republic Storage
Louisiana Pacific—Ketchikan pulp mill
Marnid—Webb's City
Merrill Lynch—Lionel D. Edie & Co.

National Distillers and Chemical Corp.—Seymour Specialty Steel
National Steel—Weirton Steel
Occidental Petroleum—W & A
Ogden—Avondale
Omega Alpha—Okonite Corporation
Pfitzer—Morflex
Phillips Petroleum—Duraco
Rapid American—Otasco Division
Rath Packing Co.—Rath
Renold Power Transmission—Atlas Chain Company
Sperry Rand—Mohawk Valley Community Development Corporation
Wickes Company (in Chapter 11)—Engineering Materials Division

B. Purchases Currently under Discussion

Copperweld Steel
General Dynamic Corp.'s Quincy, Massachusetts, shipyard
Nantahala Power and Light Co. of Alcoa
Volkswagen Corporation and one of its American plants

C. Tried Successfully or Unsuccessfully to Use Employee Ownership as a Takeover Defense

American Sterilizer
Anderson-Clayton
Ashland Oil
Michael Baker Corp.
Bendix[a]
Calumet[a]
Carter-Hawley
Chicago Pneumatic Tool[a]
Continental Airlines[a]
Dan River
El Paso Gas
FMC
Grumman[a]
Hi-Shear
Landmark Savings
National Can
National Convenience Stores
Norlin
Phillips Petroleum
Raymond International
Texas American[a]

D. Large Leveraged Buyouts

American Sterilizer Company
Amsted Industries
Blue Bell (maker of Wranglers)

Cone Mills Textiles
Dan River Textiles
Denstply International
Duff and Phelps
Gravely Furniture
Indiana Limestone
Leslie Company
National Color Labs
Parsons Engineering
Raymond International
Ripley Industries

E. Partial Leveraged Buyouts for Possible Takeover Defenses

Clark Industries
Toro, Inc.

F. LBOs that Failed for One Reason or Another

Dunlop Tire
Formost-McKesson
G. C. Murphy
Scott and Fetzer
U.S. Industries

---

a. Led to a court case.

Source: Joseph Raphael Blasi, *Employee Ownership through ESOPs: Implications for the Public Corporation* (Scarsdale, N.Y.: Work in America Institute, 1987), pp. 16–32.

The Tax-Credit ESOP

The tax-credit ESOP was introduced in 1974. Through 1982, as the TRASOP, it allowed firms an additional 1 percent of investment tax credit if part of a corporation's funds for capital expenditures were put into an ESOP and an additional 1/2 percent if employees matched company contributions. In 1983 the plan, renamed the PAYSOP, was based instead on 1/2 percent of total payroll of covered employees. The tax-credit ESOP was discontinued in 1986.

The tax credit was contingent on a company's investment in capital equipment (for the TRASOP) or its payroll (for the PAYSOP)—both variations were designed to benefit capital-intensive and payroll-intensive companies respectively. This ESOP could exist alone or with other ESOPs; its tax credit was in addition to the deductions allowed the other plans.

The TRASOP/PAYSOP involved the most extreme redistribution of tax dollars—it was not even allowed to borrow money to purchase the worker stock. It provided a total subsidy, not a modest incentive such as the tax benefits for leveraged and nonleveraged ESOPs. Since most companies that used this format were either very large or generated a small amount of employee ownership, it is difficult to believe that improved economic performance to offset these tax expenditures was a realistic expectation. This was worker ownership by direct state fiat, a Homestead Act turned on its head: government distribution of shares of private capital, instead of public land.

The History of the Tax-Credit ESOP

The tax-credit ESOP was signed into law by President Ford on March 29, 1975, six months after the basic deductions for nonleveraged and leveraged ESOPs were passed as part of ERISA on September 2, 1974. What happened in those six months to change completely the direction of employee-ownership legislation? Why did Senator Long change course by designing the tax-credit ESOP?

The use of business tax incentives as instruments of public policy rather than mere revenue-collection devices began in 1954 with the introduction of accelerated depreciation, which reduced the actual rate of taxation on new investments from 60 to around 54 percent. The Kennedy Tax Cut of 1962 introduced the investment tax credit and the shortening of the useful lives of assets for the purposes of depreciation deductions. By 1965 the effective tax rate for corporations had fallen to about 28 percent, although it rose through the economic boom to greater than 56 percent in 1969. The investment tax credit was periodically suspended in these years. After the recession of 1970–71, the investment tax credit was made permanent and the useful lives of assets for the purposes of depreciation were shortened even more. Effective tax rates fell again, averaging about 40 percent from 1971 to 1980. The Reagan tax cut of 1981 lowered the effective tax rates on new investment to an estimated 16 to 22 percent through the Accelerated Cost Recovery System (ACRS). As tax scholar Peter Fisher notes, "The net effect of these changes, which were in addition to reductions in the maximum statutory tax rate from 52 percent in 1952–63 to 46 percent since 1979, has been to reduce corporate income tax revenues from 28 percent of total federal receipts in the 1950s to about 8 percent in 1983."[26]

In 1974 Congress was debating a massive change in the tax laws to continue to accelerate depreciation allowances and the investment tax credit, which was raised from 7 to 10 percent. These new laws would allow business to reduce its tax bill significantly, retain more capital for internal financing, and, it was hoped, increase capital investment. From 1975 to 1986 corporate tax savings on the depreciation deduction would total about $856 billion and about $170 billion on the investment tax credit.[27] With such a massive return of capital to business, the question of whether wealth redistribution had a place in a capitalist democracy must have lost some of its urgency.[28]

Russell Long correctly observed that "the standard investment tax credit . . . in the interests of stimulating investment makes the rich already richer still. . . . It operates to further concentrate ownership of that newly formed capital in existing shareholders."[29] He wanted to avert this concentration of wealth and "link a larger portion of this tax incentive to expanded ownership."[30]

Enthusiasm about the new ESOP was not universal. Senators Humphrey, Javits, Muskie (D-Maine), Proxmire (D-Wis.), Percy (R-Ill.), and Kennedy (D-Mass.) strongly opposed Long's 1976 attempt to make it permanent and increase the employee-ownership tax credit to 2 percent over and above the 10-percent investment tax credit. They believed that it favored highly paid employees and did nothing to achieve equitable broadened ownership. They also suspected that Long would eventually try to make the entire investment tax credit contingent on the use of the TRASOP. Humphrey quoted statistical projections—which proved to be very close to the true measure of the TRASOP—suggesting that 72 percent of the labor force would receive no benefit from the TRASOP. He wanted more careful investigation of the best means to achieve broadened ownership in American society.[31]

Long's response to an intensive debate with these senators was that "these people are talking about . . . continuing a system under which the majority of Americans get nothing. . . . But you have to get it started somewhere. The question is, do you want to move ahead with employee stock ownership or . . . just leave it where it is . . . ?" After a last-ditch effort by Senator Muskie to derail the idea, Long won the vote by more than a two-to-one margin. Later, in the House-Senate Conference Committee, it was cut back to 1 percent and limited to four years.[32]

A more comprehensive program to broaden the wealth would never receive full consideration—although a wide variety of options were discussed in a Joint Economic Committee report.[33] The ESOP device would never be supplemented; the tax-credit ESOP, which quickly outstripped the nonleveraged and leveraged ESOPs' use of tax expenditures, made the Treasury Department unwilling to entertain further increases in the ESOP tax bill. In his January 19, 1976, State of the Union Speech, President Ford proposed a Broadened Stock Ownership Plan, which would give progressive tax deductions to individuals with lower incomes who bought stock. However, the proposal offered no suggestions on how to change the system of credit or make credit available for the plan. It never got the serious attention of Congress.

Legislation never required that ESOPs issue new stock partially or fully, despite the centrality of capital formation to ESOP ideology. On June 23, 1978, Senator Long introduced the Expanded Stock Ownership Act of 1978 (S.3241), which would require that at least one-half of the tax credit for TRASOP contributions (whether based on the additional investment tax credit or the payroll credit) could be claimed only if newly issued securities had been transferred to the TRASOP. Corporations immediately opposed this proposal on the grounds it would lead to the dilution of equity and earnings per share. It never became law.[34]

From 1979 to 1987, neither the House nor the Senate held further hearings. Instead, even after he lost the chairmanship of the Senate Finance Committee to a Republican Senate, Long slowly garnered support from his colleagues and horsetraded with the administration, making adjustments to his ESOPs in the tax bill at the end of each legislative season. Until it was eliminated in President Reagan's 1986 tax reform, the tax-credit ESOP was extended every time the investment tax credit came up for discussion. In 1984 amendments to the tax reform bill made dividends paid by corporations on ESOP stock tax deductible, essentially eliminating double taxation for ESOP companies. Capital-gains taxes and estate taxes for owners or their estates transferring businesses to their employees were excluded or heavily reduced. Banks were allowed to deduct 50 percent of their interest income on loans to ESOPs, which led to lower interest rates for bank loans to establish worker equity. In the 1986 tax bill, ESOPs were given many more tax incentives (see Appendix A), but these were relatively minor compared to the huge support for the tax-credit ESOP that had effectively squelched any further serious review of the more significant leveraged and nonleveraged ESOPs. For an overview of all these laws and amendments, see Table 2–1.

Comparison with Other Forms of Financing

At first glance, TRASOP equity financing appears to have no advantages over conventional debt financing—the dilution of net income per share and share ownership was huge. However, if the TRASOP purchased existing shares, either on a public market if the firm was publicly held or from cash-hungry shareholders if privately traded, the corporation could enjoy the tax credit without any dilution at all.

As we have noted, new capital formation would be largely undercut by this approach. An ESOP Association survey suggests that over 90 percent of tax-credit ESOP companies did not purchase newly issued stock.[35]

The tax-credit ESOP depended on the presence of corporate taxes or the possibility of tax carryforwards to be useful to companies. Most of the possible corporate uses enumerated in Appendix B could serve as the motivation behind the ESOP—getting the tax credit, defending against a takeover defense, buying out an existing shareholder, supplementing a leveraged buyout by management, or a combination of the above.

It is easy to understand why there was such a high incidence of the tax-credit ESOP in publicly held companies. Investment or payroll in these firms was large enough to create a substantial credit based on such a small percentage of investment/payroll that little ownership resulted, thus eliminating worries about a potential voting block of worker-shareholders. Their established markets allowed them to avoid the repurchase liability and the dilution effects of creating new shares for the worker ownership.

The tax-credit ESOP involved direct redistribution of tax revenue to buy stock for workers: every dollar a company contributed to a tax-credit ESOP for worker stock cost the U.S. Treasury a dollar. (If employee matching was used, every $1.50 of employee benefit cost the U.S. Treasury $1.00.) In effect, the company contributed nothing—it was the treasury's dollar that increased the company's working capital. The company could use the credit for new capital formation, but it was unlikely to do so. If the company decided to issue new shares, only better economic performance could compensate for the dilution.

Curiously, up to 1983 only about 700 of all publicly traded companies decided to use the tax-credit ESOP. To some extent this is explained by the early dependence of the tax credit on the amount of capital investment. Once the government converted the tax credit to 1/2 percent of payroll, more companies could take advantage of the benefits. Eighty-four percent of the companies with TRASOPs switched to PAYSOPs. By 1984, almost 65 percent of the Fortune Directory Companies had PAYSOPs, and 11 percent were considering them.[36]

The Tax-Credit ESOP—In Principle and In Practice

It is easy to see why Senator Long pursued the TRASOP/PAYSOP even though it was not an innovative method of corporate finance. The federal government gave business $1.1 trillion in special deductions from 1975 to 1982. To Long, making a few billion of this available to broaden worker ownership of stock during the same period surely seemed a worthy goal. It is inescapable, however, that the tax-credit ESOP turned the Treasury Department against a further expansion of incentives to use debt to produce worker equity.

The public-relations campaign for the ESOP had emphasized that no redistribution of wealth was involved, but the huge tax expenditure of the TRASOP effectively refuted that claim. In 1975, the revenue loss to the treasury from leveraged and nonleveraged ESOPs was only $10 million; TRASOPs accounted for $741 million in the same year. Upwards of 89 percent of the total federal tax subsidy for ESOPs from 1973 to 1986 was used for this ESOP, which did absolutely nothing to open up credit markets for workers. In 1986, the General Accounting Office estimated that tax incentives for ESOPs cost $12.1 to $13.3 billion from 1977 to 1983, saying that these costs "are high relative to the $19 billion in assets participants [i.e. employees] have accumulated to date."[37] Most of this inefficiency is accounted for by the tax-credit ESOP. Official legislative reports on ESOP law, as well as Long himself, continued to describe the ESOP as a revolutionary form of corporate finance from 1976 to 1986. The reality was that almost 90 percent of the tax expenditures on employee-ownership programs eliminated the possibility of corporate-finance innovations. Companies with tax-credit ESOPs bought existing stock instead of issuing new shares; they generally excluded—quite legally—more than 50 percent of their employees from participating, usually the less highly paid workers most in need of the program; they allocated shares exclusively according to salary, so more highly paid professionals always got two to five times more stock than the average blue-collar employee.

Responsibility for this, however, cannot be ascribed solely to the managers who designed the tax-credit ESOPs for their corporations. Organized labor never fought in Congress to have workers in collective-bargaining units automatically included in tax-credit ESOPs. There is also little evidence that unions concerned themselves with the actual details of the formulas of tax-credit ESOPs in many corporations. And the main culprit remains the government: Those who legislated the tax-credit ESOP designed the law to resemble that covering pension plans, which allowed the exclusion of large numbers of workers for a variety of reasons.

The law also mandated that the stock in a tax-credit ESOP could not be distributed to workers remaining with the company, who were not disabled or deceased, for seven years after the securities were allocated to workers' accounts. In effect, the government gave companies a grant to buy stock for their employees and then gave them the actual dollars for their own corporate use for seven years. This was another way in which the corporate-finance aspect of the tax-credit ESOP overshadowed its employee-ownership aspect.[38]

It is ironic that Russell Long's most successful legislative coup—the creation of the TRASOP over the objections of many powerful senators—seen by him as a way to force employee ownership on the big corporations, became instead a massive benefit for these corporations and their highly paid employees. The diversion of some of the capital dispensed by the government in the investment tax credit to worker stock as a just approach to economics came to dominate the whole ESOP legislative program, despite the fact that this use of employee ownership failed utterly to create new wealth. The tax-credit ESOP diminished the integrity of the ESOP as a whole. The weight of its dead hand will be felt for some time.

The Diffusion of the ESOP

The tax incentives for employee ownership and its corporate uses make up an impressive list (see Appendix A). Apparently, however, they have been quite resistible in practice. What accounts for the discrepancy between the popular perception of their wide appeal and their actual rate of diffusion? Why have all these advantages produced far fewer than 10,000 ESOPs and 10 million worker-participants in the fifteen-year history of the legislation?

Certainly, the main reason is that the tax-credit ESOP's version of employee ownership practically eliminated the possibility of a significant increase in the federal government's support for the other types of ESOPs that promote employee ownership at a reasonable cost to the treasury, which would probably be more widely acceptable to the American public at large. This can be illustrated by examining how the variable efficiency of the government's encouragement of different types of ESOPs made the tab for tax-credit ESOPs so high that a more aggressive ESOP legislative program was blocked.

A recent 1986 report by the U.S. General Accounting Office attempted to estimate the costs of ESOPs. These costs included the tax credits given to tax-credit ESOPs and the revenue loss from corporate deductions from taxable income allowed to nonleveraged and leveraged ESOPs. Also, individual income taxes are deferred on the equity contributed to employees' accounts until they receive those funds—say, at retirement. At that time, employees may pay less in taxes than had they gotten this compensation as salary and wages, since they may have lower incomes.

The GAO developed upper- and lower-bound estimates of the government's tax expenditure on employee ownership from 1977 to 1983. The upper-bound estimates simply added together the tax expenditures for credit, deductions, and deferrals. For tax-credit ESOPs, the total was $11.8 billion; for nonleveraged and leveraged ESOPs, the total was $1.5 billion. The lower-bound estimates are based on the assumption that if all the tax benefits for ESOPs were not available, firms would probably make contributions to other tax-favored employee-benefit plans, such as pension or profit-sharing plans. This probably would not have affected the results for tax-credit ESOPs, since those credits could not be recaptured through contributions to other plans. But with nonleveraged and leveraged ESOPs it does appear that contributions could have been switched to other types of plans or replaced by wages and salaries. Also, without the ESOP, worker buyouts of failing firms would probably have resulted more frequently in liquidation, hence no tax revenues from those companies. The GAO assumed that worker buyouts using ESOPs did not add to revenue losses; in fact they probably generated tax revenue. The result is a lower-bound estimate of only about $227 million in tax expenditures for the leveraged and nonleveraged ESOPs.

While radically illustrating the historical mistake of the tax-credit ESOP, the GAO goes on to make a further assessment of the efficiency of the state's encouragement of employee ownership. Its conclusions are enlightening.

First, when either the total upper-bound or lower-bound estimates for all types of ESOP tax expenditures are compared with the actual amounts of worker ownership, the whole ESOP program's costs seem to be very high compared to the assets: Based on the upper-bound estimate, $1 of federal money produced $1.40 of employee ownership; based on the lower-bound estimate, $1 of federal money produced

$1.55 of employee ownership. When the *Wall Street Journal* spotlighted the GAO report on its front page in 1987, it strongly emphasized this point. However, when the efficiency of the tax-credit ESOP is compared to that of the leveraged and nonleveraged ESOPs, a completely different picture emerges. Based on upper- and lower-bound estimates of tax expenditures, $1 of federal money spent on the tax-credit ESOP produced $1.25 of actual employee ownership. Based on upper-bound estimates, $1 of federal money spent on leveraged and nonleveraged ESOPs produced $2.56 of actual employee ownership; based on lower-bound estimates, $1 produced $16.99 of actual employee ownership.[39]

This is the clearest evidence that the tax-credit ESOP has been the crucial impediment to a stronger employee-ownership policy—it completely eclipsed the simpler and fairer approaches to employee ownership, yet was grossly inefficient in comparison. It is in this context that other barriers to ESOP diffusion are discussed.

Barriers to ESOP Diffusion

Enterprises Must Be Profit Making and Corporate. An ESOP generally requires a profitable taxpaying corporation or a firm that can use carryforwards. Worker buyouts of failing companies are the exception, but they constitute less than 300 of all ESOPs. If a profitable firm has a history of poor earnings, low expectation of growth, and bad prospects for credit, it may not be able to cover the repurchase liability of a leveraged or nonleveraged ESOP or to use a leveraged ESOP at all. The amount of leverage a profitable company requires for optimum operation may be limited by the nature of its business. Many businesses are not corporations, and many are not profitable.

Other Tax Incentives May Exist. Firms that can install ESOPs may have many other opportunities to save taxes. Remember that the actual corporate tax rate and the statutory tax rate are very different: Since 1981 the actual rate has been estimated at 16 to 22 percent, compared to the statutory rate of 46 percent.[40] The tax-credit ESOP may have seemed to offer a useful tax break to large publicly traded companies, but few of them needed to take advantage of it. From 1981 to 1983, for example, 118 of 250 profitable nonfinancial corporations paid zero or less in taxes in at least one of the three years. The average tax rate of the fifty-eight companies in the group paying the least in taxes was -8.4 percent.[41] Also, between 1975 and 1982 corporations saved $105 billion in taxes with the investment tax credit and $515.6 billion from the depreciation deduction against taxable income. Indeed, throughout this period the depreciation deduction provided more than half of all corporate funds used for capital formation.[42]

Privately held firms can gain tax advantages by reducing taxable income through increasing a whole range of business expenses: management/owner salaries, employment, minor renovations, and so on. Larger firms that might consider ESOPs are likely to have defined-benefit pension plans that offer tax deductions. Many also have other defined-contribution plans providing additional deductions. If defined-benefit plans are not present, their establishment may take precedence over an ESOP for labor-relations reasons.

Profit-sharing plans are generally the only employee-benefit plans in smaller companies, although many ESOP consultants have said that these firms might find it worth their while to convert to ESOPs. But those small companies that invest largely in their own stock already enjoy the cash-flow advantage promised by the ESOP; those that don't, even though they would surely experience improved cash flow in a conversion, must still find their own reasons to overlook the ESOP's inescapable disadvantages. Indeed, employees or the company may prefer some diversified investment to protect their assets, especially since most of these companies do not supplement their profit-sharing plans with defined-benefit plans. Finally, most small firms would not establish an ESOP for the same reasons they do not have another pension plan: Administrative costs may be too high, and in any case they may not be profitable enough to fund a plan—even with the subsidies—much less benefit from tax deductions.[43]

It is possible that the new tax reform law's lower corporate tax rates may make tax deductions less attractive for some companies, although the full effect of the new law on the incentive structure for ESOPs cannot be estimated at this time.

Financial Disadvantages of Employee Ownership. As we have seen, even if a business is corporate and taxpaying, debt financing and equity financing will generally be preferable to an ESOP, although one may well be chosen if a transfer of ownership is contemplated or management or the current owners have a strong commitment to share ownership—in which last case, other means to do so also exist.[44]

Corporations finance capital formation mainly through internal sources, and tax incentives to increase cash flow provide the major impetus. But the nonleveraged ESOP is decidedly less attractive than other tax alternatives. Even the leveraging possible with ESOPs is not enough to offset their financial disadvantages for existing owners and shareholders when they are used for new capital formation. When corporations do turn to external sources, they prefer debt financing, compared to which the ESOP is even less attractive. Corporate use of new equity issues to form capital averaged -4 percent from 1980 to 1985—companies bought more stock than they issued. (See Appendix C, Table C–1, for a complete review of capital-formation trends.)

For the ESOP to appear, its uses must outweigh the financial disadvantages. Finding a ready market for shares, securing survival of the firm (worker buyout, takeover, or acquisition), sharing equity and profit, or short-term improvements in working capital and tax savings—all these can make the ESOP a first choice. Sizable and majority worker ownership frequently spring from these cases, except when the company is merely seeking short-term improvements. Indeed, some firms in this last category may find that they have misjudged what they are getting into, which may explain the large number of ESOP terminations.

Technical Limitations. The administrative and set-up costs of an ESOP may be too high. A company may have too few employees or too small a payroll for the percentage of payroll allowed as a tax deduction to be worthwhile. If a leveraged ESOP is being considered, the deduction limits may make it impossible for the trust to service the loan.

Removing Some of the Barriers

The diffusion rate for ESOPs has not been constant for the last decade and a half. While Congress has been unable or unwilling to eliminate the incentives in the economic system that favor debt or equity financing, it has tried to alter the balance a bit in favor of employee ownership. In 1981, 1984, and 1986, several refinements were added that may tip the corporate scale in favor of ESOPs (see Table 2–1). Since much of the GAO's data is based on pre–1983 ESOPs, it isn't possible to gauge the effects of the bulk of these changes, which were made in 1984 and 1986. However, their combined impact, composed of seemingly small technicalities, has greatly contributed to the existing incentives for ownership transformation and even led companies uninterested in such transfers to take a new look at the uses of employee ownership.[45]

Tax Incentives. The leveraged ESOP is now allowed a deduction of 25 percent of payroll—no other employee-benefit plan can deduct more than

15 percent. Companies can deduct dividends paid on employee-owned stock. In 1986, a major tax loophole was removed for all but ESOP companies: In the past, it was not uncommon for a profitable company to purchase an unprofitable one with many years of losses so that it could claim those losses on its tax return. Under the new tax law, a company cannot use this net operating-loss carryforward after a significant ownership change (i.e., more than 50 percent of equity); this applies to certain tax credits as well. ESOPs are exempted from this new ruling.

Financing Incentives. Interest on loans to buy worker equity is now deductible without limits or ceilings under certain conditions. Because banks, commercial lenders, and mutual funds can now deduct their interest income on ESOPs, they pass on their savings through loans at lower-than-prime rates. The Federal Reserve Board has lifted rules enjoining banks from lending ESOPs more than 50 percent of the value of securities held in the ESOP as collateral on a loan. Because of this and other relaxations in the law, ESOPs can now borrow up to 100 percent of what they need to buy securities.[46] From 1986 publicly traded corporations doing stock buybacks are allowed a tax benefit on corporate borrowing for the buyback when it is coordinated with contribution of stock to a nonleveraged ESOP. In practice, this means that a public company can now use an ESOP to buy a large amount of its stock off the market and complete the transaction and allocate the stock to employees all in one year, so that it can get control quickly despite the fact that it will not pay the loan off for seven years. The new deductibility of dividends paid to an ESOT will make it easier to pay back worker-equity loans using dividends. Employee ownership now becomes a tax-favored way of performing stock buybacks.

Individual Incentives. As long as no more than one third of all the annual allocations goes to a small group of highly paid employees, an ESOP can allocate up to $60,000 of worker equity to an employee; other employee-benefit plans must stop at $30,000. Existing owners are allowed various exclusions from capital-gains and estate taxes when they sell their businesses to their employees.

Employee-Benefit Incentives. A company can now use excess assets from an overfunded defined-benefit pension plan to establish worker equity without terminating the pension plan. While part of the 1986 tax law says that when a company recovers excess assets from a terminated pension plan it must pay a 10-percent excise tax, the rollover of such assets into an ESOP is exempted up to 1989. In addition, although this is not the product of regulatory changes, many corporations have found that they can convert a profit-sharing plan not heavily invested in employer securities into an ESOP or a profit-sharing plan that does so and thus retain use of those assets.

Growth in Publicly Held Firms? Employee ownership has largely occurred in privately held companies, either as a result of transfers of ownership in such firms or transformations from public to private corporations. But this situation is changing. The assertion that ESOPs won't work in publicly held companies just is not true in an era of leveraged buyouts, takeover wars, human-resource management, stock buybacks, and capital transactions involving employee-benefit plans. Just when the passing of the tax-credit ESOP seemed to ensure that employee ownership in the publicly held corporation would disappear or severely decline, the use of leveraged and nonleveraged ESOPs has become increasingly important.[47]

In 1974, only thirteen public companies reported that employee-benefit plans were their largest stockholders, and only one plan (Sears, Roebuck, and Company's profit-sharing plan) attained 20-percent ownership, while five others—Ford, U.S. Steel, Textron, McDonnell-Douglas, and Burlington Industries—averaged 12 percent. By 1981, employee-investment funds were among the top stockholders in sixty-nine of the Fortune 500 companies and attained close to 20-percent ownership in eleven cases.[48] In a second 1981 study, forty-three ESOPs in publicly held firms were randomly surveyed. The ESOPs held an average 9 percent of stock. Sixty-four percent of the companies had no union, and all generally excluded unionized employees. Forty percent were companies with more than 1000 employees. Only 17 percent of the firms included all employees.[49]

A complete survey for all types of employee-benefit plans is not available, but one survey indicates that many Fortune Directory Companies have multiple stock ownership plans, usually including an ESOP. These firms are listed in Tables 3–5 and 3–6. The chapters on The Lowe's Companies and Up-right, Inc., in *Taking Stock: Employee Ownership at Work*, by Quarrey, Blasi, and Rosen, discuss how two of these firms actively integrate employee ownership into their corporate cultures.[50]

Table 3–5.   A Selection of Publicly Traded Corporations Averaging Employee
Ownership of 10 to 49 Percent.

ARCO
Action Packets
Alamo Savings (11.5%)
American First Corp.
American Western
Atlantic Financial Federal Inc. (10%)
Badger Meter
Bank of N.Y. (12%)
Butler Manufacturing (14%)
Clark Equipment Co. (18%)
Coastal Tank Lines (18%)
Comfed Savings
Communications Systems, Inc.
Crown Zellerbach (9%)
Dennison Manufacturing (17%)
First Albany (10%)
Harcourt Brace Jovanovich (16%)
Jackson National Life
Kerr Glass (16%)
Key Corp. (12.5%)
Landmark Savings (10%)
Mehoce Electronics (12%)
Met Coil (10%)
Herman Miller
National Convenience Stores (14%)
Pacific Southwest Airlines (15%)
Pan Am (13%)
Pay 'n Pak
Petro-Lewis (7%)
Ply-Gem Manufacturing (13%)
Presidential Airlines
Roadway Express (15%)
Rohma Haas
Roper Corp.
Savannah Foods (10+%)
Scope
Shop 'n Go (6%)
Stanley Works
L. S. Starett (10%)
Synergex Corp. (16%)
SysCon, Inc. (8%)
System Integrators

Table 3–5.   (continued)

Texas American Energy Corp. (15%)
Times Mirror Co.
Ultra Systems (12%)
Viking Motor Freight (10%)
Western Union (10%)

Source: National Center for Employee Ownership, *Non-majority Employee Owned Firms* (Oakland, Calif.: National Center for Employee Ownership, August 1986).

Table 3–6.   Publicly Held Firms with Total Workforces of Generally 1,000 or More and Employee Ownership of 20 Percent or More.

Alco Standard (industrial products manufacturing)
2,000 employees; 20%; NYSE

American Medical Services (nursing homes)
2,000 employees; 20%; NASDAQ

American Recreation Centers (bowling centers and real estate)
800 employees; 25%; NASDAQ,

America West Airlines (airline)
1,000 employees; 20%; NASDAQ

Ashland Oil Company (oil refinery)
32,000 employees; 27%; NYSE

Continental Steel (steel manufacturing)
1,700 employees; 37%; NYSE

E-Systems (electronics)
9,500 employees; 25%; NYSE

FMC Corporation (industrial manufacturing)
31,000 employees; 32%; NYSE

Kaiser Aluminum (aluminum products)
15,000 employees; 20%; NYSE

Tony Lama Company (boot maker)
1,250 employees; 20%; NASDAQ

Landmark Savings Bank (bank)
365 employees; 41%; ASE

The Lowe's Companies (retail lumber/hardware)
14,000 employees; 30%; NYSE

Marsh Supermarkets (supermarkets)

Table 3–6.   (continued)

7,000 employees; 20%; OTC

STV Engineers, Inc. (engineering)
1,200 employees; 46%; NASDAQ

Taco Viva (fast-food chain)
625 employees; 40%; NASDAQ

Tandem Computers (manufacturing)
7,000 employees; 25–30%; NASDAQ

Transcon (trucking)
3,650 employees; 49%; NYSE

U.S. Sugar (sugar processor)
2,100 employees; 47%; NASDAQ

Recently Sold Companies Previously in This Group

Eastern Airlines (25%)
People Express Airlines (30–45%)
Republic Airlines (15%)
Western Airlines (32%)

Others

LTV Corporation (bankruptcy reorganization with an earlier program of trading stock for wages that has led to an undetermined amount of equity)

Wheeling Pittsburgh Steel (bankruptcy reorganization with 33-percent employee ownership in a stock trust)

Source: National Center for Employee Ownership, "Major Employee Ownership Companies," *Employee Ownership* 6 (May/June 1986): 12.

It is possible that the coming years will see a growth in employee ownership in publicly traded companies. First, there are more and more working ESOP companies with minimal or sizable employee ownership to serve as models for those just starting out. The radical redirection in ESOP incentives will change the attitudes of publicly held corporations. Employee ownership has not yet altered industrial relations, but the concept is now considered legitimate. Many companies now feel that employee ownership is central to their corporate culture.

Second, stock buybacks are becoming increasingly common in such companies. Solomon Brothers announced in 1984 that 190 companies announced or completed buybacks of 5 to 10 percent of their outstanding shares, with almost $20 billion expected to change hands. Employee ownership is now one of the most tax-advantageous ways of perform-ing a stock buyback and the stock crash will expand this.[51]

Third, there is a new corporate-finance philosophy that considers the conversion of existing benefit plans, the creation and deployment of worker-equity funds in corporate control battles, and the phasing-out of expensive defined-benefit plans to be an important way to cut the cost of capital and increase its efficient use by the company. A 1986 survey by the ESOP Association indicated that 33 percent of ESOPs resulted from conversion of profit-sharing plans and 10 percent from conver-sions of defined-benefit plans.[52]

Fourth, mergers and acquisitions now seem to be a major activity of public corporations. Because of the new financial attractions of ESOPs, employee ownership in a target company will increasingly figure in an acquirer's strategy to reduce the cost of an acquisition or leverage cheaper capital into an acquisition.

Fifth, employee ownership is completely transforming certain sec-tors of the economy. When an industry with labor agreements runs into problems with its cost structure, it cannot simply decide to reduce labor costs. A pattern of negotiation has emerged where capital and labor make concessions and gains: Stock is traded for wages; wage cuts are traded for board seats, equity, and worker participation in manage-ment. In industries such as airlines, steel, and trucking, deregulation and increased competition from more efficient smaller and newer pro-ducers have caused existing cost structures to totter. Large numbers of firms have turned to employee ownership, either to gain wage conces-sions or as a different, perhaps more efficient form of compensation. Table 3–7 illustrates these five catalysts of employee ownership in the public sector.

Table 3–7.   Five Engines of Employee Ownership among Publicly Held Cor-porations.

A. Working Models

American Recreation Centers; E-Systems; The Lowe's Companies; People Express Airlines (until recently); Southwest Airlines; Up-right Corporation.

B. Stock Buybacks

The Bache Group, Inc.; IBM; Marsh Supermarkets; National Chemsearch Corp.; Roper Corp.; Tokheim Corp.

Table 3–7. Five Engines of Employee Ownership among Publicly Held Corporations.

C. Employee-Investment Plans as a Source of Capital

1. Harper & Row—termination of profit-sharing plans and use of assets to buy 33 percent of stock from a major stockholder to avoid disruption of business operations from a possible sale to other parties. (Subsequently, Harper & Row was taken over.)

2. Harcourt Brace Jovanovich—conversion of two retirement plans to an ESOP.

3. Dan River; Raymond International and Bluebell—use of excess assets in employee-benefit plans to perform leveraged buyouts to go private.

4. Am International—use of employee-investment plan as part of a financial reorganization.

5. City Federal Savings Bank—reorganization of entire benefits program to stress incentive by basing some benefits on employee ownership and to recapture excess pension assets into company earnings.

6. Ashland Oil; Bank of New York; Clark Equipment Company; Hartmarx Corporation; Old Stone Bank; Up-right Corp.—combination of a defined-benefit pension plan and an ESOP for use as a floor-offset plan.

D. Acquisitions

E. Reorganizing Whole Sectors

1. Airlines—Air Florida; Air Virginia; America West; Capital Air; Eastern Airlines; PSA; Pan Am; Presidential Air; Pride Air; Republic Air; Southwest; TWA; Wein Air Alaska; Western Airlines.

2. Trucking—Associated Van Lines; Branch; CL Industries; Clairmont Trucking; Clark Group; Coastal Tank Lines; Commercial Lovelace; GMW; Halls; ICX; Interstate; MRF4; McLean; PIE; Pre-Fab Transit; Roadway Express; Smiths; System 99; Transcom; Viking Motor Freight.

3. Steel—Armco; Bethlehem; Continental; Eastmet; Gilmore; Johnstown; LTV; Lone Star; McLouth; Nucor; Sharon; Weirton; Wheeling Pitt (i.e., 24 percent of steel-industry employees).

Note: Not all these firms are publicly traded, but the complete list is included hereto illustrate the extent of the phenomenon. Also, many of the companies include only salaried employees in their employee-ownership plans. Concession bargaining in unionized industries tends to create more inclusive forms of employee ownership, and where it is present this has led to a new, strong union presence on the national employee-ownership scene.

Source: Joseph Raphael Blasi, *Employee Ownership through ESOPs: Implications for the Public Corporation* (Scarsdale, N.Y.: Work in America Institute, 1987), pp. 28–32; 56–57.

Conclusion

Employee ownership and worker-investment funds are part of a larger movement to connect labor and capital in a more mutually beneficial way. Employee-ownership law has indeed led to national employee ownership of surprising proportions in just fifteen years.

A number of considerations may encourage a firm to install an ESOP: future company performance, which may offset dilution; the effect of employee ownership on labor relations; the expected market for the company's product or service; the use of assets from employee-benefit plans to finance employee ownership; the need to keep equity safe during an actual or potential takeover (usually in a publicly traded corporation); and a major stockholder's desire to cash out shares (usually in a closely held corporation).

Nevertheless, the financial features of the three ESOPs have not been enough to tempt many privately held and publicly traded corporations, who still rely on debt financing, equity financing, and retained earnings. The tax-credit ESOP may have sprung from praiseworthy motives, but its serious defects tainted its performance and the employee ownership program as a whole. Leveraged and nonleveraged ESOPs are used largely to transform ownership situations and they do supply employee ownership more efficiently. But, all in all, employee ownership has not arisen from new capital formation; it has been purchased with subsidized capital from the government.

While ESOP financing does not always compare favorably with other avenues of corporate financing, Corey Rosen of the National Center for Employee Ownership has emphasized that "if a company has two goals—creating an employee-benefit plan and worker equity and commitment AND financing—that ESOP financing looks better. The problem is that not many companies have come to the decision that they really want ownership as a benefit." This line of reasoning implies that the appearance of employee ownership is really a function of several factors—the financial and tax incentives, the benefit and philosophical incentives, and the special uses and opportunities that arise for corporations and workers.

As shown in this chapter, the government can influence the first factor through changes in the tax law. But, generally speaking, observers of ESOP growth have pointed out that major changes in the tax laws (as reviewed in Table 2-1) have not appreciably affected the growth rates of nonleveraged and leveraged ESOPs and stock-bonus plans. This suggests that the other factors are quite important. If the American labor economy moves toward a system of flexible compensation, profit sharing, and tying economic rewards to performance in the workplace, it is likely that the benefit and philosophical incentives for employee ownership will be substantially expanded. This is already evident in the marked shift away from defined-benefit plans to defined-contribution or capital-accumulation plans for compensation. Also, to the extent that labor and management see innovative uses for employee ownership— such as in defensive stock buybacks or even union or labor bidding for firms in leveraged buyouts, as in the United Airlines example (discussed at the begining of the following chapter)—we are likely to see more employee ownership.[53]

From 1973 to 1983 the federal program of employee ownership altered the ownership of about 1 percent of the corporate stock. A tax expenditure of $12 to $14 billion helped produce about $18.6 billion in worker equity. Based on a total national wealth of $12 trillion, about .0016 percent of total wealth was affected. Still, when the tax-credit ESOP is removed from the picture, it becomes clear that government encouragement of leveraged credit to purchase employer stocks (the leveraged ESOP) or company creation of worker equity through retained earnings (the nonleveraged ESOP) could have tremendous significance. Certainly, the state increased worker equity far more efficiently with these kinds of ESOPs. Yet this classic employee-ownership program, so stressed in the legislative record, has not really been given a chance to prove itself. If, from 1977 to 1983, $10 billion in tax expenditures had been used for leveraged and nonleveraged ESOPs alone, instead of the roughly $2 billion they actually absorbed, the total worker equity would have been closer to $25 billion than $3.8 billion. If the General Accounting Office's assumptions about lower-bound revenue losses for leveraged and nonleveraged ESOPs are accepted, $10 billion in tax expenditures could have resulted in almost $170 billion in worker equity in the same period.[54]

1987 has marked an increase in ESOP tax incentives, but a decrease in the federal government's tax-expenditure commitment to ESOPs. The elimination of the tax-credit ESOP program alone cuts down this support by 90 percent. It is still uncertain whether the new state-sponsored attractions of 1984 and 1986 will persuade many publicly traded corporations to adopt leveraged and nonleveraged ESOPs. Eighty to ninety percent of the government's annual tax expenditure on ESOPs disappeared between 1986 and

1987, dropping from $2.5 billion to roughly $200 million. Of course, the tax expenditure could theoretically grow to any amount, depending on the number of firms that choose to adopt leveraged and nonleveraged ESOPs, but the remaining barriers to ESOP diffusion will probably still prevent a substantial increase in employee ownership. For example, if publicly traded companies begin to use employee ownership widely for stock buybacks, partial leveraged buyouts, acquisitions, and employee benefits and concession bargaining, it is possible that they, not the privately held firms, will continue to use the bulk of the tax expenditures for ESOPs. Several investment banks have already noted some signs of a move in this direction. If it really happens, it will only serve to sharpen the arguments about the kind of employee ownership the government is supporting.

CHAPTER 4

Sharing Wealth Through the
ESOP

*Arnold and Company is a Boston advertising agency with 142 employees. Arnold Z.
Rosoff, who had founded the privately held firm thirty-nine years before and wanted to
ease out of the agency both financially and professionally, decided to sell a majority of his
stock to the employees' profit-sharing plan. One hundred and thirty-five workers will
participate in the plan.*[1]

---

*The first worker-owned construction company, Jefferson Masonry, Inc., of Birmingham,
Alabama, was organized as part of an attempt by the International Union of Bricklayers
and Allied Craftsmen to pursue employee ownership through new business start-ups
rather than wage concessions or buyouts of failing firms. The union's consultant, the
Industrial Cooperative Association of Somerville, Massachusetts, has said that the struggle for better wages and benefits must lead unions to a new strategy of worker entrepreneurship.*[2]

---

*In 1987, United Airlines' 7,000 pilots initiated a bid to purchase full control of the
company. At first, United's parent company's board of directors unanimously rejected
the bid, but a fund-raising strategy by a group of investment bankers, in addition to the
ESOP tax benefits that would allow the pilots to leverage funds at a lower interest rate
and the possibility of using excess pension assets, gave the union sufficient strength to
take a credible stand. The transaction marked one of the first instances of a coalition of
labor and investors using employee ownership as a negotiating weapon.*[3]

---

*Bank Building & Equipment Corporation, a publicly traded company, designs buildings
for financial institutions. To ward off a possible takeover by Amcat Corporation of Hart-
ford, Connecticut, the company initiated a joint tender offer with its employee stock
ownership plan to buy back as much as 47 percent of its common shares. Stock buybacks
can also serve to support a company's stock price. The Tax Reform Act of 1986 gives
special tax advantages to firms using ESOPs in such buybacks. Eugene Keilin of the
Lazard Freres investment bank reports that the incidence of such cases is increasing.*[4]

T hus far, we have seen how a corporation adopting an ESOP can put it to use and how the components of the ESOP can be legally manipulated to reap the largest possible benefit for existing power-holders and for the corporation as a whole. These corporate-finance uses, though less effective in their promotion of capital formation than many legislators had hoped, can be justified in part. Certainly, it can be argued that without the purely financial advantages of ESOPs, corporations might not consider employee ownership at all.

But the ESOP was not developed to help out business. This aspect is incidental to its primary purpose: broadening worker ownership of their own companies as a first step toward a revitalization of the American economy. Has the ESOP lived up to the expectations of its framers? To ascertain this, we must determine how much ownership has actually been established through the ESOP during its fifteen-year history, and what effect it has had on the distribution of wealth in the country as a whole.

None of this would be relevant if employee-ownership legislation had merely diffused a minimal amount of worker equity throughout the economy—something along the lines of a bonus in addition to other employee benefits. This is indeed what has happened in many corporations, but the story doesn't end there. The ESOP has in fact begun to create an employee-owned sector in this country. Table 4–1 is based on a General Accounting Office survey of about half of all ESOPs in existence in 1985. Overall, half of all ESOPs own at least 10 percent of their companies' stock, while half of all leveraged ESOPs own at least 20 percent of their companies' stock. But the table indicates that almost a fifth of the companies described as minority owned may in fact have been sizably owned (25 to 50 percent) by their employees. On average, 20 percent, 13 percent, and 3 percent respectively of leveraged, leverageable, and nonleveraged ESOPs are majority owned.[5] The survey also discovered that, while less than 2 percent of all ESOPs are completely owned by their employees, 6 percent of leveraged ESOPs are completely employee owned. And, of course, we must remember that most leveraged and nonleveraged ESOPs will have accumulated additional equity since this survey and that each year more and more minimally owned firms become sizably owned, more and more sizably owned firms become majority owned, and so forth.[6] The author estimates that about 1,500 firms were majority or fully owned by their employees in 1987. An evolution toward greater employee ownership is taking place.

Table 4–1. ESOPs: Quality and Quantity (percent).[a]

	Tax-Credit	Leveraged	Leverage-able	Non-Leveraged	Total
Minority owned	97	80	87	97	91
Majority owned	3	20	13	3	9
Median percent of stock owned	2	20	15	13	10
Own up to 25%	95	56	68	77	75
Own more than 25%	5	44	32	23	25
Reasons for Formation					
Employee benefit	95	88	90	92	91
Tax advantages	77	64	77	74	74
Improve productivity	65	73	74	70	70
Purchase stock from major owner	21	59	45	35	38
Reduce turnover	29	36	40	36	36
Transfer majority ownership to employees	23	37	37	32	32
Raise capital for investment	21	26	30	18	24
Decrease absenteeism	13	11	16	14	14
Avoid unionization	7	7	7	9	8
Avoid hostile takeovers	6	6	4	5	5
Save failing company	3	8	2	4	4

Table 4–1.   (continued)

	Tax-Credit	Leveraged	Leverage-able	Non-Leveraged	Total
Exchange for wage concessions	3	1	2	4	3
Take company private	2	4	b	b	1
Other	10	10	7	8	b
Total number	1,015	579	1,250	853	3,698

a. Some totals do not balance because of rounding. Data is based on two surveys of 3,052 and 3,287 ESOPs respectively.

b. 0.5 percent or less.

Source: U.S. General Accounting Office, Employee Stock Ownership Plans: Benefits and Costs of ESOP Tax Incentives for Broadening Stock Ownership (Washington, D.C.: U.S. General Accounting Office, December 1986), pp. 20, 39. Figures on majority- and minority-owned ESOPs appeared in an earlier unpaginated, unpublished draft of the report.

Analysis shows that, while providing an employee benefit and gaining tax advantages were uppermost in the minds of the managers of the surveyed firms, employee ownership was being used in many cases to transform the nature of the firm by transferring majority ownership to employees, buying the stock of a major owner, making firms less vulnerable to hostile takeovers, taking companies private, saving failing firms, and exchanging stock for wage concessions. This pattern is emerging in both publicly and closely held corporations, contrary to the popular notion that employee ownership is mainly a phenomenon of small privately held business. The emergence of companies that are largely employee owned, combined with far-reaching tax incentives and multiple corporate uses (see Appendices A and B), makes it all the more important to establish the true nature of employee ownership.

Major ESOP Trends

The widely quoted 1987 estimate that there are 7.5 million workers in about 7,500 employee-owned companies comprising about 7 percent of the private-sector labor force in the United States is grossly misleading when taken out of context. In 1985, the General Accounting Office compiled data on 2,004 ESOPs from Internal Revenue Service files and used this survey to trace national employee-ownership trends. Based on this information, Table 4–2 presents further facts on the types of ESOPs, their distribution between publicly and closely held firms, their participants, and their assets. What are the major ESOP trends?[7]

Table 4–2. Types of ESOPs, Total Employees Participating, Trading Status of Stock, Assets, and Median Worker Stake in 1983.

A. Estimates of Participants and Assets of ESOPs.[a]

Type	Participants		Assets[b]		
	Number (in thousands)	Percent	Total (in millions)	Percent	Median/ Participant
Tax-credit	6,391	90	$14,800	79	$2,952
Leveraged	158	2	1,450	8	8,660
Leverageable	293	4	1,445	8	7,149
Nonleveraged	238	3	961	5	5,098
Other	2	[c]	1	[c]	0
Total	7,083	99	$18,660	100	$5,226

a. Based on plans active in 1983, the last year for which complete data are available. Totals do not add up because of rounding.
b. In constant 1983 dollars.
c. Less than 0.05

B. Trading Status of Stock.[a]

Type	Privately Held		Publicly Traded		Total Number
	Percent	Number[b]	Percent	Number[b]	
Tax-credit	35.4	377	64.6	687	1,064
Leveraged	84.7	573	15.3	103	676
Leverageable	94.4	1,380	5.6	82	1,462
Nonleveraged	86.3	786	13.7	125	911
Other	—	—	100.0	12	12
Total	75.5	3,116	24.5	1,009	4,125

a. Data missing on forty-nine ESOPs.
b. Numbers are approximate, figured by author.

C. Participants, Assets, and Median Value of Assets by Trading Status of Employer Firm.[a]

	Privately Held	Publicly Traded	Total[b]
Total participants	495,757	6,574,833	7,070,590
Median number of participants	39	631	54
Total assets[c]	$3,109,983	$15,488,434	$18,598,417
Median value of assets[c]	$277	$1,464	$337

a. Based on plans active in 1983, the last year for which complete data are available.
b. Excludes eighty-one ESOPs for which trading status data were not ascertained.
c. In thousands of 1983 dollars.

Sources: a. U.S. General Accounting Office, *Employee Stock Ownership Plans: Benefits and Costs of ESOP Tax Incentives for Broadening Stock Ownership* (Washington, D.C.: U.S. General Accounting Office, December 1986), p. 19; b. *Ibid.*, *Employee Stock Ownership Plans: Interim Report on a Survey and Related Economic Trends* (Washington, D.C.: U.S. General Accounting Office, February 1986), p. 19; c. *Ibid.*, p. 25.

1. Tax-credit ESOPs accounted for 90 percent of the participants and about 80 percent of the assets. The mean tax-credit ESOP was installed in a company with approximately 11,000 employees, of which 6,000 were eligible to participate.[8] The average participant had fewer assets than a worker in a leveraged or nonleveraged ESOP, although the median tax-credit ESOP had more assets than other ESOPs. Surprisingly, in some cases these ESOPs produced notable amounts of worker equity (see Appendix C, Table C–2). Tax-credit ESOPs have now been revoked and so no longer need be considered except in terms of their repercussions; the following conclusions focus mainly on the other ESOPs. As noted in Table 4–1, the median percentage of stock owned in a tax-credit ESOP is 2 percent; however, as Table 6–1C establishes, the insignificance of these ESOPs is even greater—their median voting strength is only 1 percent.

2. Leveraged and nonleveraged ESOPs have thus far accounted for only about 10 percent of the participants and 20 percent of the assets. The average leveraged or nonleveraged ESOP has approximately 1,000 to 1,200 employees, of which 300 to 500 participate in the ESOP. The fact that 50 percent of the leveraged and nonleveraged ESOPs have less than 43 participants indicates either that there is a sizable number of ESOPs in smaller companies with less than 500 workers or that many companies are excluding substantial numbers of their employees.[9] However, because of powerful incentives in the 1984 and 1986 tax laws (see Table 2–1 and Appendix A) and the repeal of the tax-credit ESOP, these ESOPs are now growing more rapidly. Nevertheless, although the leveraged ESOP represents the core principle behind these plans— the use of credit to purchase worker equity—it covers only 2.2 percent of all ESOP participants and represents only 7.8 percent of all the assets in all ESOPs. Only 676 leveraged ESOPs appeared by 1983.[10]

3. Over 90 percent of these leveraged and nonleveraged ESOPs are in privately held companies with a current average worker equity of just over $5,000 and a median equity of about $7,000. This stake will grow in many of these plans because new stock is still being purchased,

and there is also the possibility of continued appreciation and dividend payments. Recent information, however, shows sizable and growing employee ownership in publicly held corporations (see Table 3–4), many of which already had notable worker stakes through various benefit plans (see Appendix C, Table C–2).

4. There are signs of significant employee ownership in the publicly traded corporate sector. The prevalence of tax-credit ESOPs in publicly held firms has led many observers to assume that significant employee ownership is not to be found in such businesses. This is not the case. The predominance of ESOPs in closely held corporations is indisputable, but even when the tax-credit ESOP is set aside, the publicly traded sector should not be overlooked. First, there are indications that employee ownership has definitely expanded among publicly traded companies since the Senate Committee on Government Operation's survey of the subject in 1974. Second, before 1981, internal employee-investment funds were among the top five stockholders in one-third or 151 of the Fortune 500 companies and they were the largest stockholder in 69 firms. ESOPs played a modest part in this development, as the figures show (see Appendix C, Table C–2). Third, in researching files of the National Center for Employee Ownership and public stock exchanges, the author has identified almost twenty-five publicly traded corporations with more than 20-percent employee ownership and 1,000 employees, and about fifty publicly traded corporations with about 10-percent or more employee ownership. Many of these plans use ESOPs (see Tables 3–5 and 3–6). Fourth, unlike smaller and privately held companies, the publicly traded corporation, especially a Fortune Directory company, tends to further employee ownership through diverse company stock plans at the present time (see Appendix C, Table C–3). Fifth, five major engines of growth for employee ownership other than the tax-credit ESOP have emerged in the publicly traded corporation: the use of employee ownership in stock buybacks, takeover defenses, corporate restructurings, acquisitions, and reorganizations of entire business sectors (see Table 3–7). Recently, the author predicted in *Business Week* that coalitions of employees and institutional shareholders will eventually form to challenge managers.[11]

5. ESOPs exist in all industries and regions of the country and have spread widely in their fifteen-year existence, although they are still a minor phenomenon compared to other employee-benefit plans (see Chapter 1). Overall, ESOPs are highly concentrated in manufacturing and moderately represented in somewhat equal proportions in whole-

sale trade, services, finance, insurance, and real estate. ESOPs are also present in smaller numbers in transportation, utilities, and construction and minimally in agriculture, forestry, fishing, and mining.[12]

6. Substantial employee ownership is growing, as indicated in Table 4–1. ESOP members grew almost by a factor of nine between 1975 and 1983 with fairly consistent growth rates for the different types of ESOPs.[13] The employees participating in ESOPs, however, constitute just a fraction of the total workforce. Also, best estimates indicate that the average ESOP legally excludes about half of the employees of a firm. Obviously, this colors all subsequent data concerning the employee ownership produced through the ESOP.

7. Employee ownership is not found mainly in failing firms. The 1986 GAO report confirms that this widely held assumption is utterly mistaken. Evidently, the large amount of media attention to cases such as Weirton Steel has led to this misconception. In fact, as shown in Table 4–1, 4 percent or fewer cases represent this use of employee ownership, and these companies often cannot benefit from ESOP tax deductions because they are unprofitable.[14] The truth is that profitable enterprises pursue employee ownership as a means to benefit employees, gain tax advantages, and increase productivity—indeed, over half the time, the main purpose of the ESOP is a major transformation of ownership in favor of the employees. As noted in Chapter 3, over a third of majority employee-owned firms have resulted from retiring owners selling ongoing small businesses to the employees. Also, many of the subsidiaries of large Fortune 1000 firms that have been sold to workers are not failing units, even though they are identified in the press as "worker buyouts"—a popular term often implying the rescue of a failing firm.

The Distribution of Wealth

The growth rate of the ESOP may seem remarkable, and the amounts of stock involved may appear considerable. However, the true impact of the ESOP on broadening the ownership of wealth in this country can be fully assessed only in the context of the distribution of wealth as a whole and how this distribution has evolved in recent U.S. history.

Wealth is not equivalent to income. One can have a large income and accumulate little wealth or be very wealthy with little net income. In 1983, the total private wealth—that is, ownership of real estate, corporate stock, bonds, debt instruments, life insurance, trusts, and holdings in cash—of U.S. families was estimated at about $11.5 trillion dollars. Debts were $1.5 trillion and total net worth was $10 trillion. Researchers have concluded that hard work and savings account for about a third of this. The Joint Economic Committee has said that the rest stems partly from inheritance and partly from money making money, as it inevitably does.[15]

The Components of Wealth

Table 4–3 shows how the components and shares of this wealth for individuals have changed between 1958 and 1976. Most important to remember here is that wealth is extremely concentrated in the United States. Who owns wealth does not change much over time, but where they hold it does.

Table 4–3. Total U.S. Wealth Distribution over the Top 1 Percent and 1/2 Percent of the Population in 1958 and 1976.

Kinds of Wealth	1958			1976		
	% of Total Wealth	% Owned by Top 1/2%	% Owned by Top 1%	% of Total Wealth	% Owned by Top 1/2%	% Owned by Top 1%
Real estate	38	10	15	43	9	13
Corporate stock	18	61	69	11	38	46
Bonds	5	37	43	4	26	30
Debt instruments	3	27	35	2	27	37
Cash	13	10	15	18	7	11
Trusts	2	83	89	2	—	—
Miscellaneous	19	6	8	17	—	—
Total Assets	100[a]	20	25	100[a]	14	18
Liabilities	14	13	17	19	11	14
Net Worth	86	21	27	81	14	19

a. Totals may not balance due to rounding.

Source: U.S. General Accounting Office, *Employee Stock Ownership Plans: Interim Report on a Survey and Related Economic Trends* (Washington, D.C.: U.S. General Accounting Office, February 1986), p. 36. Computed from the actual dollar amounts in James D. Smith, "The Concentration of Personal Wealth in the United States, 1958–1976," *Review of Income and Wealth*, series 30, no. 4 (December 1984): 422–23.

Real estate has constituted an average 39 percent of total wealth while corporate stock has constituted an average 18 percent from 1958 to 1976. The components of wealth remained fairly constant during this period. Throughout this period, the wealthiest 1 percent of the population averaged about 1.5 million individuals, who owned an average 10 percent of all real estate and 53 percent of corporate stock, or 21 percent of all wealth (i.e., net worth).[16] In order to understand better whether wealth broadens beyond the richest 1 percent, let's look at 1972, for which more figures are available, showing that the wealthiest 6 percent of the population owned 43 percent of the real estate and 72 percent of all corporate stock.[17] Research confirms that not only is wealth highly concentrated, but it does not significantly broaden outside the top 10 percent of the population. The old saw that the poor get what they deserve while everyone else enjoys the just fruits of their own hard work is wrong. Either the top 10 percent of the population works very hard and everyone else is lazy, or hard work alone does not explain why people accumulate wealth.

Since 1958 there has been a decline of about a third in the amount of corporate stock owned by the wealthiest 1 percent of the population. It looks as though this may have been prompted by poor market performance and increasing interest rates over the latter part of the period under discussion. This group also continued to reduce their holdings in bonds in response to the high inflation rates of the 1970s and increased their interest in noncorporate assets such as partnerships. This shift has closely paralleled corporations' reduced use of equity to fund operations.[18]

Nevertheless, who holds corporate stock is remarkable testimony to the narrowness of wealth holding. Its ownership is more concentrated than that of other assets and remains indicative of the concentration of ownership of total assets, despite a decline in both. Indeed, the concentration of ownership of all wealth has not declined as drastically: From 1958 to 1976 the top 1 percent's holdings of all assets only declined from 25 percent to 18 percent.

In 1983, the Federal Reserve Board and the Department of Health and Human Services joined together to sponsor a survey of consumer finances that focused on families rather than individuals. This study gives a far more detailed picture of the distribution of wealth.[19] The Joint Economic Committee of the U.S. Congress based a recent report on this study. As Table 4-4 shows, wealth is highly concentrated at the top of our society, where the wealthiest have a strong grip on all types of business assets. Beyond the richest 1/2 percent, wealth does not significantly broaden—indeed a marked decline is already evident in the next 1/2 percent. The fact is that the concentration of wealth is not an issue only for the very poor or the working classes; wealth is not distributed equitably even among the middle and upper-middle classes.

Table 4–4.   1983 Assets of All Households and of the Wealthiest Households.

| | | Percent of Total for Wealthiest Households | | |
Type of Asset	All Households $ Amount[a]	Top 0.5%	Top 1%	Top 10%
Trusts	495.7	77.0	81.6	95.1
Corporate stock[b]	1,005.0	45.6	58.4	89.8
Bonds	328.1	41.3	49.6	88.0
Business assets[c]	2,274.6	39.0	51.6	90.9
Money-market accounts	265.0	15.9	22.5	58.8
Real estate	5,355.0	14.9	19.3	49.2
Land contracts	111.0	13.9	15.2	50.4
IRAs and Keoghs	142.2	13.0	21.1	67.3
Checking accounts	115.9	9.7	17.2	46.3
Insurance cash-surrender value	259.8	6.7	10.5	34.9
Certificates of deposit	383.1	4.8	10.7	49.9
Savings accounts	189.5	2.1	5.2	31.1
Automobiles	359.5	1.6	3.0	20.1
Miscellaneous[d]	201.1	15.2	22.1	70.2
Gross assets	11,485.4	24.6	31.6	63.5
Net worth	10,038.9	26.7	34.3	67.92

a. In billions of dollars.
b. Including stock owned directly or through mutual funds, but excluding holdings of pension-plan trusts.
c. Business assets are all interests in unincorporated businesses, farms, and professional practices.
d. Miscellaneous assets are boats, aircraft, works of art, classic automobiles, campers, trailers, motorcycles, precious metals, loans owed to family members, and gas leases.

Source: U.S. Congress, Joint Economic Committee, Democratic Staff, and James D. Smith, *The Concentration of Wealth in the United States: Trends in the Distribution of Wealth Among American Families*(Washington, D.C.: Joint Economic Committee, July 1986), p. 24. The figures in the table are based on revised estimates provided by the Federal Reserve Board following publication of the Joint Economic Committee report.

The Concentration of Wealth at Present

Evidence indicates the 1929 stock market crash started a decline in the concentration of wealth that continued into the mid-seventies. However, this has stabilized in recent years, and there has even been a slight increase in the concentration, as Table 4–5 shows. More wealth is owned by fewer families, and more poorer families find themselves less well off. The richest 20 percent of families increased their share of total national income from 45 percent in 1969 to 48 percent in 1982, while the shares of the middle-class , upper-middle–class, and moderately rich families actually shrank during the same period. Home ownership, the biggest asset most of the population will ever possess, declined from 65 to 60 percent of all nonfarm families between 1977 and 1983. The family car is often the most valuble property of low-income families, and the National Bureau of Economic Research has reported that most American families count their entitlements under the Social Security system as their greatest wealth.[20] The percentage of families owning stock increased steadily between 1964 and 1971 and then declined to less than 20 percent of all families, where it had been nineteen years earlier.[21] All of this leads to one conclusion: A great many people—and not just the poor—are remaining in much the same financial positions that they've always occupied.

Table 4–5. Concentration of All Wealth in 1963 and 1983 (percent).

	1963	1983
Top 1/2%	25.0	26.7
Next 1/2%	6.6	7.4
Next 9%	32.4	33.6
Bottom 90%	36.0	32.1

Source: U.S. Congress, Joint Economic Committee, Democratic Staff, and James D. Smith, *The Concentration of Wealth in the United States: Trends in the Distribution of Wealth Among American Families* (Washington, D.C.: Joint Economic Committee, July 1986). Revised figures based on a November 1986 telephone interview with a committee spokesperson.

Indeed, the 1983 Federal Reserve Board study showed that 52 percent of the families surveyed had a total income of less than $20,000, and on average these families had assets of less than $10,000 each.[22] The importance of credit in expanding ownership becomes obvious—most people do not have a lot of money to spare, and one can easily understand why they might not want to take risks with what they do have. In essence, purchasing stock requires jeopardizing what is for many their major social and economic objective: home ownership. A substantial amount of worker equity through an ESOP would have a profound effect on income groups below $50,000—even a relatively modest stake in worker equity could be quite meaningful for this group.

The proportion of owners of stock and the dollar amounts of holdings rise dramatically with income. Income, far more than age, determines all forms of asset holding—corporate-stock ownership is quite rare in families with lower incomes. Only 5 percent of the families with incomes under $10,000 and 13 percent of families with incomes under $20,000 hold corporate stock. Families in all income groups under $30,000 average less than $10,000 in total financial assets. Fifty percent of these have total financial assets of under $2,000. Interestingly, more than half of stock-holding families with incomes between $30,000 and $50,000 have quite insignificant holdings. And most striking of all, less than 50 percent of families with incomes between $50,000 and $99,000 own any publicly traded stock, and pension assets often represent a significant chunk of wealth to managers employed by others. Broadened stock ownership appears to be an issue for the middle and upper-middle classes as well.

Status and Stock Ownership

The disparities in wealth distribution prompted the government to focus more carefully on the issue by studying the super-rich. Its study showed that professionals or managers in the service or manufacturing sectors made up a large percentage of the heads of families with substantial incomes, as shown in Table 4–6. There were also respectable numbers of lawyers, accountants, health-service professionals, and banking, insurance, and real-estate professionals who on average made up another 35 percent of each category. These nonself-employed professionals and managers in service and manufacturing industries held 17 percent and 27 percent respectively of their total assets in bonds, trust accounts, and stocks. They also had 8 percent of their total assets in retirement instruments, among them defined-benefit plans, defined-contribution plans, IRAs, Keoghs, and the cash value of whole-life insurance policies. Clerical and sales employees had 22 percent of their assets in bonds, stocks, and trusts and 13 percent in retirement instruments. By contrast, operatives', laborers', and service workers' families had a negligible amount of their total assets in bonds, trust accounts, and stocks and 10 percent in retirement instruments, an investment matched by craftspeople and supervisors, who had 7 percent in bonds, stocks, or trusts.

Table 4–6.   Managers/Professionals, Income Group, and Stock Ownership.

Income Group	Percent Managers/Professionals	Percent Owning Publicly Held Stock
$ 50,000 – $99,000	39	47
$100,000 – $149,000	26	61
$150,000 – $279,000	29	75
$280,000 +	17	90

Source: Based on Robert B. Avery, Gregory B. Elliehausen, Glenn B. Canner, Thomas A. Gustafson, and Julia Springer, "Financial Characteristics of High-Income Families," *Federal Reserve Bulletin*, March 1986: 169–71.

Several other studies, focusing on individuals, confirm that managers, professionals, and office workers hold a relatively high proportion of corporate stock. A 1984 New York Stock Exchange study found that one of three American shareowners was participating in a direct-ownership employee stock-purchase plan at his or her company. But 46.4 percent of them were professionals/managers, 25.7 percent were in clerical/sales, and only 19.3 percent were craftspeople/supervisors.[23] These studies note that stock-option programs stack the decks even more heavily in favor of highly paid managerial and professional employees and include very few lower-ranking employees. As we have shown, rank-and-file employees simply do not have the wherewithal to take advantage of these kinds of opportunities—their liquid assets average about $6,000 compared to about $20,000 for professionals and managers.

According to the Federal Reserve Board study, illustrated in Table 4–7, the key to these investment patterns is that the richer families are, the less concerned they are about taking risks. High-income families are much more likely to take average or above-average financial risks and they are also willing to invest their savings for a long period of time in illiquid assets in the hope of higher returns. The study further showed that the families with higher incomes hold proportionately more business assets and smaller shares in their housing, other property, and liquid assets. For all families, their houses represent 68 percent of their assets; even vehicles represent a significant portion of many families' wealth. Wealthier families become capital owners by using leverage; they have larger debt-to-equity ratios and use more financial services.[24]

Table 4–7.   Proportion of High-Income Families, and of All Families, Holding
Various Attitudes toward Financial Risk and Liquidity, 1983.[a]

Attitude	Family Income (in dollars)				All Families
	50,000–99,000	100,000–149,999	150,000–279,999	280,000–or more	
Financial Risk					
Take substantial financial risk to earn substantial return	6	8	5	10	6
Take above-average financial risk to earn above-average return	22	25	36	34	11
Take average financial risk to earn average return	55	57	52	46	38
Take no financial risk	17	9	3	5	43
Liquidity					
Tie up money for long term to earn substantial return	20	30	22	26	12
Tie up money for intermediate term to earn above-average return	42	48	56	47	26
Tie up money for short term to earn average return	30	17	18	18	30
Do not tie up money at all	5	3	2	2	29

a. Does not report cases in which attitude was not ascertained.

Source: Robert B. Avery, Gregory B. Elliehausen, Glenn B. Canner, Thomas A. Gustafson, and Julia Springer, "Financial Characteristics of High-Income Families," *Federal Reserve Bulletin*, March 1986: 171.

The ESOP's Effect on the Ownership of Wealth

The way the ESOP alters wealth distribution is not immediately clear. One cannot assume that broadened stock ownership or deconcentration of wealth automatically accompanies each extension of stock ownership. ESOPs generally allocate stock according to salary. They also tend not to include employees with lower incomes or fewer years of service, and those who are young or unionized. As Chapter 2 makes plain, these two forms of exclusion are allowed in the statutes of the law—

although the nondiscrimination rules tend to draw attention away from them—and both are widely practiced. Moreover, the most expensive and hitherto most popular ESOP—the TRASOP/PAYSOP—has practiced more discrimination than the others.

The General Accounting Office engages in apologetics on the issues of stock allocation and the exclusion of employees from ESOPs. Their final report claims that since the distribution of stock ownership is even more concentrated than that of total wealth and since the median rate of employee participation in ESOPs is 71 percent compared to 19 percent of all American families owning stock in 1983, then "ESOPs appear to provide a broader distribution of stock than generally prevails."[25] On the contrary, as this book has demonstrated, this assumption is false: (1) excluded employees tend to be nonprofessional, nonmanagers, younger, and/or unionized, with lower incomes; (2) the vague definition of highly compensated employees has encouraged even more discrimination; and (3) the wide practice of allocating worker ownership strictly according to salary—which some lawyers come close to citing as law—ends up skewing stock ownership even in ESOPs that include all employees.

Even if distribution of corporate stock is not the only or even the best way to broaden wealth, with the vague definition of highly compensated workers that prevails in ESOPs until 1989 and other ways of excluding employees, many ESOPs are essentially government-subsidized stock plans for workers with salaries up to $100,000. However, as we established earlier, even these relatively highly paid employees are substantially less well off than the top 10 percent of the population, so arguments can be made that they, too, deserve greater stock ownership and financial assets.

The key point remains that employee-ownership law has reproduced the system of economic stratification in American society rather than attempting to reverse it. In so doing, the law has given the power over the employee ownership and the control over property rights to the more highly paid groups, even in those employee-owned companies where all employees are allowed to participate.

The assets of all ESOPs were $18.7 billion in 1983—0.16 percent of the total wealth and 0.81 percent of the total corporate stock. How is this broadening of ownership to be interpreted?[26]

Table 4–8 shows who owns all the stock, both publicly and privately held, in the country. Compared to the total of publicly held stock owned by all individuals and the total amount of all equities, the ESOP has barely broadened stock ownership. Despite its massive use of billions of dollars through tax-credit ESOPs, mainly in publicly held companies, employee ownership has scarcely touched the stock concentrated in that top 2 percent of individuals that controlled 50 percent of all stock in 1983.

Table 4–8. Stock Ownership Patterns (percent).[a]

	1960	1965	1970	1975
Total Stock Outstanding[b]	$451.0	$749.0	$906.2	$892.5
Held by				
Households	87.7	84.9	80.4	72.5
Private pension funds (self-administered)	3.7	5.4	7.4	11.4
State and local government retirement funds	0.1	0.3	1.1	2.7
Mutual funds	3.3	4.1	4.4	3.8
Brokers and dealers	0.1	0.2	0.2	0.4
Life insurance companies	1.1	1.2	1.7	3.1
Other insurance	1.7	1.6	1.5	1.6
Commercial banking[c]				
Mutual savings banks	0.3	0.3	0.3	0.5
Foreign owners	2.1	1.9	3.0	4.0

	1980	1981	1982	1983
Total Stock Outstanding[b]	$1,635.6	$1,568.5	$1,810.5	$2,151.5
Held by				
Households	72.6	72.3	70.4	68.1
Private pension funds (self-administered)	12.8	12.5	13.7	14.2
State and local government retirement funds	2.7	3.0	3.3	4.2
Mutual funds	2.6	2.4	2.7	3.4
Brokers and dealers	0.2	0.4	0.2	0.1
Life insurance companies	2.9	3.0	3.1	3.0
Other insurance	2.0	2.1	2.1	2.2
Commercial banking[c]				
Mutual savings banks	0.3	0.2	0.2	0.2
Foreign owners	3.9	4.1	4.2	4.5

a. Totals may not balance due to rounding.
b. Current dollars in billions.
c. Less than 0.05 percent.

Source: U.S. General Accounting Office, *Employee Stock Ownership Plans: Interim Report on a Survey and Related Economic Trends* (Washington, D.C.: U.S. General Accounting Office, February 1986), p. 39.

The Tax-Credit ESOP

The now-defunct tax-credit ESOPs were required by law to allocate stock strictly according to compensation. They generally excluded over 40 to 50 percent of their employees from participation. As a result, these ESOPs promoted stock ownership among a segment of the population that already had modest access to the stock market.

Even when rank-and-file employees were included, they generally received much less stock than managerial and professional employees, since a highly paid employee making $50,000 would have received two-and-a-half times more stock than an employee with a salary of $20,000 if stock was allocated according to compensation. They had little say in the determination of dividends or anything else in the corporation. Also, as we have seen, managerial, professional, and office employees had access to stock-option plans, generally closed to the mass of workers, and stock-purchase plans, which either exclude such workers or are not financially feasible for them. The provision of several stock ownership programs is characteristic of many Fortune Directory firms (see Appendix C, Table C–3)—the New York Stock Exchange study reveals that 45.2 percent of the firms that were likely to have tax-credit ESOPs also had direct ownership plans. In fact, many of the managerial and professional employees most likely to be included in tax-credit ESOPs were often also covered by both employee stock-purchase plans and stock-option plans.[27]

The tax-credit ESOP not only absorbed 80 percent of the assets of ESOPs and 90 percent of the participants—but as a dollar-for-dollar credit, it also represented 90 percent of the lost tax revenue. It came close to being a direct grant from the federal government, mainly to the large publicly held corporations. In effect, a large number of tax-credit ESOPs simply provided a supplemental compensation program for favored categories of workers.

The tax-credit ESOP was eliminated by the Reagan Tax Reform of 1986. Not a single congressional or public supporter of ESOPs fought against its demise—a remarkable reversal of the aid and comfort they gave the tax-credit ESOP during the ten wasteful years of its existence. All told, $11.8 billion in government tax expenditures served as an incentive to produce $14.8 billion in assets; $1.00 of government money bought $1.25 in "broadened" ownership.[28]

The Leveraged and Nonleveraged ESOP. The statistical portrait of wealth in America supports the investment logic behind the classic ESOP. Most working people—rank-and-file and managerial/professional alike—just do not have the financial base, the liquid assets, or the gambler's instinct to leverage their way to meaningful capital ownership. Inheritance makes little difference to most families—70 percent accumulate more than half of their assets solely from earnings, while 93 percent can trace more than half of their assets to both earnings and savings. Even those that have inherited most of their wealth do not veer far from the familiar patterns of investment.

Families with heads who work in commercial and investment banking, insurance, and real estate (61 percent), who are lawyers or accountants (38 percent), health-service professionals (23 percent), self-employed entrepreneurs in the manufacturing sector (21 percent), self-employed entrepreneurs in the service sector (46 percent), or professionals or managers in manufacturing (50 percent) or the service sector (22 percent) are most likely to hoist themselves into the top 2 percent.[29]

As we have shown, the main determinants of wealth in the United States are occupation, position, and the ability to leverage current assets into future accumulation—not hard work. This means that the core of the leveraged and nonleveraged ESOP is sound: It provides a way for the government to put ownership in the hands of people who could not otherwise afford it or achieve it through most efforts of their own, by encouraging companies to establish worker equity out of retained earnings in return for either tax-advantaged credit (the leveraged ESOP) or tax advantages (the nonleveraged ESOP.)

The leveraged and nonleveraged ESOPs have not yet had a chance to show what they can do. From 1973 to 1983, leveraged ESOPs resulted in about $1.45 billion in assets for 158,238 employees; nonleveraged ESOPs hold $961 million in assets for another 238,406 employees; and leverageable ESOPs produced $1.445 billion in assets for 293,274 employees. Together, these three programs have been responsible for $3.856 billion in ownership, representing O.03 percent of all assets and O.18 percent of the value of all corporate stock in 1983. Nationally, the ESOP has been insignificant. However, from another perspective, the picture is rosier—these assets of $3.856 billion cost the federal government about $1.5 billion; $1.00 of government tax expenditures served as an incentive to produce $2.56 of employee ownership.[30] To produce the same amount of ownership through the tax-credit ESOP would have cost about $5 billion.

Even if these dollar amounts are negligible, leveraged and nonleveraged ESOPs have unarguably realized substantial changes in ownership in some firms. An examination of this area indicates the potential of the ESOP. The National Center for Employee Ownership studied 108 representative ESOP firms to see how much money they put into their employees' pockets. The center computed how much an employee making a given salary could expect to receive if the company contribution and the stock price continued to change at the same rate and employees remained long enough to be vested.

From 1980 to 1984, the average company contributed 10.1 percent of payroll to its ESOP annually. The average stock price changed by about 11.5 percent every year during this period. Workers at the 1983 median wage level of $18,058 would receive about $30,000 worth of stock after ten years and more than $120,000 after twenty years. Workers at a salary level of $11,792 could expect about $20,000 after ten years and $80,000 after twenty years. Workers at a salary level of $27,277 could expect about $47,000 after ten years and about $190,000 after twenty years. A $30,000 stock estate for a median-wage worker making $18,058 would still comprise about 50 percent of that family's net worth in constant 1983 dollars ten years hence. When one considers that 50 percent of all families had a net worth of less than $25,000 in 1983 and the median financial assets of families at retirement were only $11,000, this becomes quite meaningful.

The actual median employee-equity estates of the leveraged ($7,904) and nonleveraged ($5,098) ESOPs in 1983 were two to three times larger than the ownership estates of the tax-credit ESOP ($2,952).[31] In the individual firm, widespread adoption of one of these two plans would have a notable impact on the net worth of a worker with an annual income under $30,000, as well as providing an otherwise unlikely opportunity to become a stock owner. It would also be a significant supplement to retirement assets if the ESOP had not been installed at the price of reduced compensation or the elimination of a pension plan. In a smaller firm unlikely to have a defined-benefit pension plan, the ESOP would constitute the primary retirement asset after Social Security.[32]

Conclusion

In the end, the ESOP has done very little to broaden the wealth in the country. Relatively speaking, an insignificant amount of employee ownership has been established through ESOPs in the last fifteen years. Where it has taken hold, widespread exclusion of lower- and middle-paid workers from the plans and stock allocations weighted in favor of more highly paid employees have meant that workers who are already stockowners are receiving the most ownership. The wealth structure in this country is well established and rigid—different and more energetic interventions would be required to change it.

Yet even though the ESOP's current contribution to the broadening of wealth is negligible, it cannot be called a failure. The original framers had untested views of what the legislative program would accomplish. They ignored or minimized the sizable barriers to ESOP diffusion that partially neutralized the successive tax incentives. Excitement about the novelty and swift growth of ESOPs led to a mistaken impression of actual progress. The final legislated program was meant to constitute one small component of an extensive plan to dilute the concentration of wealth, yet the major levers of this plan were never applied, and, quite unrealistically, the ESOP alone has been expected to work the transformation.

CHAPTER 5

The Law and Employee Rights

One of the largest sellers of prepared cocktails, Federal Distillers of Cambridge, Massachusetts, employs about 140 people. In 1985 salaried employees agreed to convert their profit-sharing plan into an ESOP so that the company president could buy the firm. The ESOP's share came to 17 percent. The plan does not include the company's fifty-five unionized workers, represented by the Teamsters. Voting rights are not passed through the trust, and worker-owners generally have little say in management decisions, although they elect one ESOP trustee.[1]

Hall-Mark Electronics executives arranged for the workers' retirement plan to sell its shares back to the company for $4 each shortly before they planned to sell the company for $100 a share. The Department of Labor felt that an earlier out-of-court settlement was unfair to the employees, and the case is under review by the U.S. Court of Appeals in Atlanta. Hall-Mark illustrates the problems that arise when employee-owners' holdings are managed by corporate executives.[2]

In late 1985, a group of senior management officials at Amsted Industries, a construction and building-products company in Chicago, attempted to take the firm private. The management group and a newly formed ESOP would buy the company. The Labor Department questioned the proposal, and four shareholders filed suits charging officers, directors, and their advisors with breaching their fiduciary duties to employees through self-dealing and overreaching. The offer was abandoned. In 1986 the purchase, presumably intended to block a takeover, was concluded under new terms.[3]

In March 1986, the Belzberg family of Canada proposed a $1.8-billion takeover of Ashland Oil Co. Ashland countered with a buyback of stock that netted the Belzbergs a profit of $16 million. An ESOP bought 20 percent of the stock with loans at 78 percent of prime. Only Ashland's 8,000 salaried employees were included in the plan. $200 to $300 million in excess assets from their pension plan were recovered for general corporate uses as the company used the worker ownership as part of a new retirement program.[4]

E SOP law is not merely a neutral object that people use or abuse to achieve their private purposes. It constitutes a specific outline of employee ownership to which owners adhere. The form can be fleshed out in ways that distort or enhance its basic composition, but it possesses certain constant attributes that will inevitably influence any structure it supports. What the law intends and what it actually promotes can be surprisingly different. Thus, it is vital to understand the kind of ownership favored by this law. Owners in this country are endowed with certain rights and responsibilities. They expect certain benefits from their property and from their ownership of that property. The question with ESOPs is whether they establish workers as actual owners or whether they result in a new variety of ownership, tailored almost as much to the uses of the corporations as to the needs and expectations of the worker-owners.

In order to establish the ideology inherent in the law and its effect on the quality of employee ownership in this country, Chapters 5 and 6 will examine its basic elements in terms of six broad areas in which its ideology can be clearly seen at work: (1) the principle of exclusive benefit to workers and how it is carried out in practice; (2) workers' roles as investors in their companies and whether they enjoy their traditional rights as capitalists; (3) the doctrine of discrimination and how it is used to shape employee ownership according to management's taste; (4) where employee ownership has been placed in the law, and whether this placement suggests that it is perceived as true ownership; (5) the question of worker versus management involvement—who holds the power?; and (6) the vision of the corporation and the impact of labor law on ESOPs. This chapter will focus on issues of employees' rights under the law, while Chapter 6 will concentrate on the responsibilities ESOP law allots to labor and management.

The Exclusive Benefit of Employees

An investor group has sued managers of Western Kentucky Gas Company and its holding company and announced plans to seek control of the parent firm . . . . Western Kentucky Gas, the second largest natural gas supplier in the state is the major asset of Texas American Energy Corp. (TAE) of Midland, Texas. Texas American bought the Ownesboro-based firm in 1980 for about $23 million. . . . The suit claims Texas American managers in December formed an ESOP that was financed by Texas American to buy 1,263,157 shares, or about 15 percent of the common stock. "The ESOP was created and structured with the sole purpose of placing a large block of TAE voting stock in the hands of persons who would be adversely affected if [the shares] were to vote . . . in opposition to management."[5]

It was obvious to the framers of ESOP law that the corporate-finance uses attendant on ESOPs made it all too likely that companies would choose these plans purely for their business advantages, attempting to minimize the actual benefits to the workers. As a result, a principle was written into ESOP regulations by which all these plans must abide: The Internal Revenue Code defines the ESOP as a stock-bonus plan whose trust must be for the exclusive benefit of the participants; any loan to an ESOP must be primarily for the benefit of the participants and their beneficiaries. The IRS does accept that members of management may participate and that employee-ownership plans may serve a variety of corporate-finance purposes (see Appendix B).

What constitutes the exclusive benefit of the employees is vague. In ESOPs it differs from the principle as it is applied in other employee-benefit plans. A trustee of an ESOP does not have to diversify the ESOT's investments to benefit the workers, even if such diversification seems prudent and in the workers' best interests, nor does the trustee have to be sure the investments yield a fair return. The increasing number of cases such as the Texas American Corporation suit target this particular issue.

Such issues, though not unimportant, are secondary to the fundamental flaw in the law itself. The primary problem is not alleged acts against the law, but innate in the law itself. The law says that ESOPs are for the exclusive benefit of the employees participating in the trust. Yet, as we have seen, companies are allowed to exclude large numbers of workers from their plans; the exclusive-benefit rule does not go into effect until after these exclusions have been made. Without question, the framers of the original model for employee ownership had intended ESOPs to benefit a wide range of employees; the accepted definition, however, guarantees protection only for the select employees who are permitted to participate. This contradiction at the center of ESOP law must be acknowledged at the outset. It must be emphasized that, with the exception of some special provisions, the general rules for all employee-benefit plans apply to ESOPs. But, as a relatively new phenomenon, employee ownership can often be hurt rather than helped by this treatment under the law.

Many professional law, tax, and finance articles on ESOPs are essentially manuals for managers, owners, and existing nonworker shareholders on how to use the ESOP for personal or corporate advantage. One boasts messages such as "How Mr. Big Can Remove His Capital, Retain Control, and Perpetuate the Company" and "How to Sell Your Company and Still Keep It."[6] Even the ESOP Association of America speaks of "installing" ESOPs in companies. Respected summaries of ESOP law, such as the guide published by the Bureau of National Affairs, Inc., limit themselves to the legal workings of the ESOP and make no mention of possible conflicts between corporate and employee interests. There are some exceptions, notably the materials of the National Center for Employee Ownership; the Industrial Cooperative Association, of Somerville, Massachusetts; PACE of Philadelphia; American Capital Strategies, Inc., of Bethesda, Maryland; and the Michigan Employee Ownership Center in Detroit, Michigan.

The Ideology of ESOP Practitioners

A 1983 survey of 200 employee-ownership consultants confirms that ESOP lawyers and consultants are predominantly management-oriented:[7]

Employee ownership is so important that our company would set up a plan even if there were no tax benefits.	7%
Making employees owners makes sense, but we would not do it if there were no tax benefits.	50%
If we could get the tax or financial benefits of employee ownership without making employees owners, we would prefer that arrangement.	43%

Most of those surveyed were attorneys who are deeply involved in the initiative stages of these plans. Although these statements reflect only what the consultants considered to be company motivations, they show quite clearly whose benefit was being sought.

In 1980, the Comptroller General issued a study entitled *Employee Stock Ownership Plans: Who Benefits Most in Closely-Held Companies?*.[8] ESOPs in sixteen companies in eight states were reviewed. The plan documents, trust agreements, minutes of ESOP meetings, trust transactions, and allocations to workers' accounts were examined. Key company officials and company employees were interviewed about the reasons for establishing the ESOP and its operational problems. The report determined that most plan transactions were not being operated in the best interests of participants—the price at which the company sold or contributed stock to the ESOP was often questionable. The study also found that the ESOPs held mainly employer stock and that there were few provisions for funds to be made available to repurchase the stock distributed by the ESOP. Managers often failed to understand the ESOP or to meet even the minimal requirements of formal communication about it to employees, several of whom were unfamiliar with its basic elements and some of whom were unaware that their company had such a plan. The study concluded that most employers were concerned only with the corporate-finance aspects of the ESOP.

The price charged for stock sold to the ESOP can be a particularly telling indicator of corporate interests taking precedence over employee benefits. This price, important for obvious reasons, also determines the size of the tax deduction. Fiduciaries in ESOPs have always been required to pay a fair market value for stock, but until recently they were permitted to set this value themselves. For fifteen years, Congress and regulatory agencies ignored repeated evidence suggesting that this should be corrected. The new tax reform law finally addressed the problem. As of January 1, 1987, a regular independent valuation of company shares is required. Some observers believe employer-dominated ESOP trustees will now be less likely to overvalue stock. Others say that companies generally hire consultants who will give them the stock valuation they want, rendering this law irrelevant.

Avondale Industries, recently spun off from the Ogden Corp. in a leveraged-ESOP buyout, illustrates just how confused interests can become. The ESOP bought the company for $282 million in cash and $105 million in preferred stock. Avondale is now 100-percent employee owned by 8,000 of its 10,000 employees. William F. Connell, Avondale's current CEO, a former executive of Ogden, is leading a battle in Boston's federal court, contending that Ogden overcharged the workers over $100 million. Former executives and salaried workers have joined together to fight their former employer. Yet Avondale, which company executives claim has real employee ownership, excludes all of its unionized employees from participation and severely limits the involvement of other workers and lower-level managers.[9]

The U.S. Comptroller General's report proffers significant evidence of the conflict between corporate-finance uses and exclusive employee benefit in ESOPs. In essence, it rejected Congress's identification of workers' exclusive benefit with corporate-finance uses, given the lack of measures to keep these two goals in balance (see Appendix B and consider how the corporate uses listed might not correspond with the exclusive benefit of participant employees).

Initiation and Termination

What can be more fundamental in employee ownership than the decision to initiate the ESOP and the decision to terminate it? There are many facets of this problem. The law essentially defines the nonemployee owner or management of a company as the initiator and terminator of an ESOP. Reinforcing this, most of the tax incentives are designed specifically to attract those two parties (see Appendix A). The main tax break to employees is that they do not have to pay income tax on the deferred compensation that goes into the trust until it is distributed to them.[10] The only exception to this implicit delegation of initiative is when management and/or the nonemployee owner agrees to sell the company to a group of workers and/or managers in a buyout, spinoff, or related arrangement. In that case, workers and/or managers will often set up a shell corporation with an ESOP, which then usually purchases all of the original company's stock. This ESOP is designed by them. The Robertshaw Controls and United Airlines cases discussed in Chapters 3 and 4 illustrate how employees in public companies are using the public market for corporate control and shell companies with ESOPs to become initiators of hostile employee takeovers in this area.

Senators Javits and Humphrey proposed an Employee Stock Ownership Fund Act of 1976 (S. 3300), which would have changed labor's right to initiate an ESOP.[11] In a 1976 review, the Joint Economic Committee noted that

most ownership programs have been established for the sole benefit of managers and supervisors . . . [S.3300] is designed to address concerns expressed by organized labor and management that actual stock benefits not be illusory. . . . The bill expands the Taft-Hartley Act provisions which allow the formation of jointly trusteed pension funds, health and welfare funds, and legal service funds to permit the establishment of a jointly trusteed fund for investment in stock for the benefit of bargaining unit employees.[12]

The act was never considered.

The corporate and individual uses encouraged by the law and practitioners largely foster the conversion of existing firms to employee ownership—they are based on tax deductions, and start-up companies tend not to have profits for four or five years. Because of this, it is unlikely that many groups of employees will initiate ESOPs through start-ups, although this may change significantly if employees begin to use ESOPs for hostile or friendly takeovers of firms. The law takes no special action to encourage the creation of new worker-owned companies. This in itself is strong evidence that employee-ownership law is structured mainly for corporate uses by existing corporations.

As one writer says, an ESOP can be terminated "in the event it does not work out as well as the employer has hoped."[13] When this happens, assets are fully vested and distributed to the employees. Alternatively, the ESOP can be frozen, and contributions to a nonleveraged or company-financed ESOP stopped. Assets can also be put into a profit-sharing plan or even rolled over into IRAs within sixty days of the distribution. Conversion into a profit-sharing plan is an important option. An initiator of an ESOP can simply decide he or she does not want worker ownership any more, but profit-sharing plans provide worker ownership without being required to pass through any voting rights. With this option, an initiator can keep worker ownership but rescind worker involvement at any time as long as the profit-sharing plan document does not specify otherwise.

Such easy termination invalidates the long-term effect of voting rights in any ESOP. Of particular concern are ESOPs in closely held companies where the employees own 51 to 100 percent of the stock without voting rights. If such a company is contemplating a merger, consolidation, or sale of substantially all of its assets, trustees of the ESOP could conceivably terminate the worker-ownership trust to avoid an employee vote on the action. Little empirical data is available on whether this actually occurs, but the frequency of terminations, as shown in Table 5–1, suggests a need for further study. It is important to note that the government does not require an employer to establish or keep indefinitely any kind of retirement plan. After a reasonable period, perhaps five years, almost any plan can be terminated without raising questions. The issue of termination rights has not received any attention in the studies conducted by Congress.

Table 5–1. Estimated Terminations of Types of ESOPs Compared to the Total Number of ESOPs.[a]

Type	Terminated ESOPs		Total ESOPs	
	Number	Percent	Number	Percent
TRASOP/PAYSOP	166	23.1	1,244	25.4
Leveraged ESOP	58	8.1	733	15.0
Leverageable	192	26.7	1,659	33.9
Nonleveraged	287	39.9	1,221	24.9
Other	16	2.2	36	.7
Total	719	100.0	4,893	99.9

a. Weighted totals do not balance because of rounding.

Source: U.S. General Accounting Office, *Employee Stock Ownership Plans: Interim Report on a Survey and Related Economic Trends* (Washington, D.C.: U.S. General Accounting Office, February 1986), p. 9.

The General Accounting Office followed up the U.S. Comptroller General's report with a survey of 745 cases of termination, the results of which are summarized in Table 5–2. While most respondents' reasons for termination were not related to employee ownership—adverse business conditions (32 percent), a change in ownership (12 percent), or a merger (13 percent)—18 percent blamed the burdens of ERISA and 14 percent cited the disadvantages of ESOPs.

Table 5–2. Reasons for Terminating, Converting, or Discontinuing Contributions to an ESOP (percent).

Reason	Tax-Credit	Leveraged	Leverageable	Non-leveraged	Overall
Adverse business conditions	11	39	30	54	32
Burdens of ERISA	10	32	22	20	18
End of TRASOP credit	46	0	3	1	15
Disadvantages of ESOPs	4	28	19	13	14
Merger	22	14	4	11	13
Change in ownership	13	0	9	16	12
Liquidation of company	6	0	10	0	5
Collective-bargaining agreement	0	0	3	0	1
Other	14	10	40	26	24
Total weighted cases	243	66	238	247	765[a]

a. Weighted subtotals do not add up to overall total because of rounding.

Source: U.S. General Accounting Office, *Employee Stock Ownership Plans: Benefits and Costs of ESOP Tax Incentives for Broadening Stock Ownership* (Washington, D.C.: U.S. General Accounting Office, December 1986), p. 24.

In order to have a say in the termination of their ESOP, employees would have to be represented on the board of directors of their company and have some authority over the trustees of the plan. The Copper Range ESOP, featured at the beginning of Chapter 6, provides that the plan can be terminated only after a majority vote of the board of directors, which is partly controlled by labor; approval by the board member representing employees who do not belong to a bargaining unit; and, finally, approval by at least a majority of all employee-participants, voting on a one-person/one-vote basis. This provision was negotiated by the United Steelworkers of America, nonunionized salaried workers, and management at that plant.[14]

In a strange twist, the Securities and Exchange Commission has created a situation where the company and workers are actually penalized if employees are given a say. It ruled that when an ESOP is converted into another type of retirement plan rather than terminated, if the employees are offered a choice between a new plan and receipt of funds or other benefits from the old plan, this constitutes a sale subject to the Securities Act. If none of the funds transferred had been invested in employer stock, the conversion might be exempt from registration under the Securities Act. Kaplan, Brown, and Ludwig conclude that "to avoid this problem, plan conversions may be made without giving employees such an option."[15]

Who Protects the Workers' Interests?

The problem of who benefits in ESOPs is aggravated because they are not under the shield that protects workers in all federally regulated pension plans. Certainly, the protections the federal government affords defined-benefit pension plans, which are intended to avoid both putting all of workers' eggs in one basket and risking the future benefit, are not always appropriate when workers own a small or large portion of their company and must accept "playing the stock market" with their property. But the elimination of most of the protections must be carefully analyzed.

A major innovation of the giant Employee Retirement Income Security Act of 1974 (Public Law 93–406) was the creation of clear-cut protections for employees in all benefit plans for "the well-being and security of millions of employees" and "the successful development of industrial relations." Prohibitions against tinkering with the benefit plans were established as barriers to both company and union connivance. As noted, ESOPs are exempt from the rulings requiring holdings of no

more than 10 percent in company stock, diversification of plan investments to reduce risk, and prudent investment, and forbidding sale and
credit transactions between the worker-ownership trust and parties in
interest who may be plan participants or somehow tied to the
employer, the union, or their relatives or agents. Subsequent regulations have extended these exemptions. For example, a direct loan to an
ESOP from a bank is not subject to the margin rules governing the use
of credit to buy stock. Also, a company need not recognize gain or loss
for tax purposes when it sells or contributes stock to an ESOP.[16]

Why did the law allow these exemptions to employee ownership but
give management control over them through permission to self-deal
and self-police without limit? The law gives absolute discretionary
authority over the trust, not to workers and company officials jointly,
not to the workers alone, not to independent third parties, but to fiduciaries. Further, the fiduciary standards of ESOPs, although guided by
principles of trust law, depart from the common-law rule prohibiting
fiduciaries from maintaining dual loyalties. Thus, they are often disqualified persons or parties in interest—company officials or people
appointed or hired by them who could otherwise not police and deal
with such a trust under ERISA's normal prohibitions. Technically, the
fiduciary can be anyone; in practice, since nonemployee-owned companies commonly initiate ESOPs, since the initiative is often with the company and not labor, and since the law allows self-dealing, the fiduciary
is often someone handpicked by management, if not management
itself.[17]

The list of exemptions for fiduciaries is particularly interesting reading. Not only is the fiduciary in an ESOP exempted from self-dealing
shields—for example, he or she can set the price at which the stock is
sold to the trust—he or she is also exempted from performance-based
shields. In a profit-sharing plan, if the return on investments is 2 percent rather than the 9 percent typical of many other plans, some lawyers believe they can use the prudence principle as a basis for legal
action. In an ESOP, however, it is presumed that the standard definition of prudence cannot feasibly be applied since ESOPs invest primarily in the workers' own companies; as long as the trustees invest primarily in company stock at a fair market value, that is considered to be
fundamentally prudent. By both excluding workers from governance
and eliminating the prudence requirement, the importance of performance is de-emphasized in an ESOP. Rational alternatives—encouraging some form of profit sharing as a reward for superior performance or

developing practical forms of shared governance of the company (in sizably or wholly employee-owned companies)—have never been considered.

The upshot of this is a complete return to a prelabor-law manager/ worker relationship in some worker-ownership plans, where the fiduciary—a manager or a management appointee—exercises absolute discretionary authority. It is true that the usual severe penalties of pension law apply to ESOP fiduciaries—they are open to personal liability and civil suit if they do not act in the exclusive interests of the workers—but the problem lies in the design itself, not in the judicial response to abuses of it. One recent development circumvents even this obstacle, thus removing the final shield. Some companies are insuring law firms and investment-management companies involved in designing and managing trusts against any liabilities resulting from breaking federal law. It is now the opinion of the Labor Department that indemnifying fiduciaries out of corporate assets for liability resulting from their participation in a leveraged-ESOP buyout is "unenforceable and improper."[18]

A number of commentators suggest that ESOPs run counter to the main thrust of ERISA. As Carlson notes:

Their central purpose is to accomplish exactly what ERISA bans: to turn the funds of an employee benefit plan over to a sponsoring employer for uncontrolled use in the employer's business in exchange for the issuance of stock acquired through financing guaranteed by the employer. Every aspect of such a transaction is contrary to the policy of ERISA.[19]

ERISA sought to eliminate the risks of retirement plans by regulating them closely, yet ESOPs have been set outside most of these regulations—workers thus bear the risks of investment as capitalists without having capitalists' rights.

Congress recognized that allowing ESOPs these exemptions and delegating policing authority to fiduciaries might present problems. The 1980 report of the U.S. Comptroller General found these concerns to be justified and concluded that neither the Labor Department nor the IRS had the resources to monitor ESOPs effectively. (Indeed, Labor admitted that it was focusing on significant cases involving legal precedent, large dollar values, or large numbers of participants.) But, again, the main defect is structural: A trustee, perhaps appointed by people who might act against the exclusive benefit of the employees, is made the guard of that exclusive benefit. The argument could be raised that as long as the law requires adherence to the exclusive-benefit rule, that is sufficient. But the fact is that the rest of ERISA specifically builds many other rules into worker-investment trusts precisely because the mere statement of an exclusive-benefit requirement is not viewed as sufficient. In ESOPs the trustees are freer to define the employees' interests as they see fit.[20]

Workers' Roles as Investors

We've seen how ESOPs were placed outside the sanctuary of ERISA and how the worker-owners, denied the status of participants in pension plans, were expected to bear the burdens attendant on their ownership. Yet, incongruously, the law also denies the worker-owner the role of investor. It seems patently obvious that a worker-equity fund would involve worker investment, but the ESOP trust potentially separates the rights of control from the rights of ownership. This is hardly defensible in light of the supposed objectives of employee-ownership law, particularly when a company is sizably, majority, or totally employee owned. As David Ellerman remarks, trusts are usually set up for people who are not competent to manage their affairs; even assuming trusts are appropriate, why should the law favor their domination by management?[21]

One might countenance this abrogation of workers' rights as investors if workers were at least afforded the protections due to them as investors. Yet, while a worker's holdings and the company securities purchased by the ESOP could well be considered subject to the fraud and registration sections of the Securities Act of 1933, they have been exempted. This and other securities laws require issuers and sellers of stock to make broad disclosures so that investors can make informed choices. But the ownership right of informed choice about one's assets has been detached from the definition of employee ownership. The information freeze can be taken to outlandish extremes. At Hyatt-Clark Industries and South Bend Lathe, Inc., workers' representatives on the board of directors learned the amount of management's salaries and salary increases only after substantial conflict—and these firms are 100-percent worker owned![22]

What can be the reasoning behind these exemptions? First of all, it represents an extension of a general exemption in the securities laws of worker-owned equities in pension, profit-sharing, and stock-bonus plans as long as they do not involve worker contributions. Such an extension would be justified if ESOPs found alternative organizational ways to give employees access to the information and decisionmaking of investors. Yet not only is this not the case, but, as we have shown, the investment test used both before and after ERISA removed many responsibilities from the trustees. As long as the investment in employer securities is prudent and fair market value is paid for the stock, the diversity of the investment and the rate of return need not be protected.

Second, the idea that worker-owners are not true investors seems based on the notion that their ownership is a gift and so their substantial investments in their own companies do not require the same protection afforded distant investors. It is true that workers do not pay for their stock out of their savings and that part of the stock is purchased through government tax subsidies. Is it, however, logical to deny workers investor status in sizably, majority, or completely employee-owned companies where the production of most of the workers is paying for the contribution to the ESOP? In a leveraged ESOP, the funds that the worker trust borrowed to purchase its ownership are used for company operations, and those improved operations are used to pay off the loan over time. In this instance, the ownership can in no way be considered a gift from management, any more than funds borrowed from a bank for a management buyout of a corporation can be considered a gift.

Let us clarify this with a straightforward example. Worker Capitalism, Inc., sets up an ESOP to do a partial leveraged buyout of the company (it does not matter if the company is public or private). Management has already acquired 5 percent of the firm through stock options. The ESOP borrows $100 million and buys 50 percent of the firm. Employees now own half of the firm and are using profits from company operations financed with this borrowed money to pay back the loan. If the employees do not create value with this borrowed money, they will have a smaller worker-equity account in their ESOP. Their risk is total. True, they have not used their savings to purchase their equity, but in 1985 all nonfinancial corporations funded 21 percent of their business operations with debt and 79 percent internally (see Appendix C, Table C–1). Certainly managers in an ongoing business do not typically put up their savings. The simple truth is that a great deal of purchasing in this country, whether corporate, personal, or otherwise, is done on credit; stock ownership by means of a loan should be as valid as home ownership by means of a mortgage.

After ten years, suppose that the firm is now worth $300 million, making the value of the stock in workers' accounts $150 million. Where did that $150 million come from? It has five sources: (1) the $100 million in credit that was leveraged in to buy the stock; (2) the increase or decrease in the value of the stock; (3) dividends retained in the trust used to pay back the loan; (4) money that the company did not have to pay the government on its profits because of ESOP-related tax breaks; and (5) the firm's savings on interest on the borrowed capital stemming from the lender's ability to deduct its interest income on the loan to the ESOP.

The worker equity is obviously not a gift or bestowal or grant from the management or the previous owner. It is derived mainly from the use of credit to make money and partially from a subsidy of this credit by the federal tax system through ESOP incentives. In fact, the previous owner may have received a tax break for his or her sale to the ESOP.

This discussion is not academic. In late 1986 the Department of Labor promised to issue guidelines on how the exclusive benefit of the employee participants should be interpreted in large leveraged buyouts. In the final analysis, Labor will have to base its ideas on a particular view of the property rights of employee-owners. Lawyers representing key ESOP investment banks and attorneys pressed Assistant Secretary Kass (who has since left the government), himself an investment banker, to ensure that these guidelines would leave as much flexibility as possible for using employee ownership as a technique of corporate finance. Their position paper attempts to resolve the key dispute: Are the ERISA principles protecting worker rights incompatible with leveraged buyouts involving ESOPs and other types of investors?[23] Kelso and Company's lawyers argue that since employees in ESOP-leveraged buyouts do not put up their own cash, they should not participate in the new employee-owned company on terms equal to or better than other investors, such as management, who may invest cash. This argument ignores the fact that management often does not put up its own cash from personal savings, but may use stock options or loans from the company itself or from other sources. In addition, the brief appears to treat the credit used for employee ownership as a courtesy of "the company," as though the company in a largely employee-owned corporation is distinct from the employees. It verges on terming ESOP worker equity a gift and stresses the importance of reward premiums for management as if they were the only or main group responsible for production in an employee-owned company.[24] However, conservative legal scholars of ERISA point out that when a company transfers funds to a qualified employee-benefit trust that money is viewed as assets of the trust and as a payment to employees for services. Tax deductions are allowed because these payments are seen as a necessary expense of doing business. In a leveraged ESOP, workers are essentially borrowing part of their own expanded compensation and investing it in the firm. In nonleveraged ESOPs, although workers are not using credit to create value, the federal government is providing tax subsidies to corporations so that they can increase their working capital in order to establish employee equity.

In essence, proponents of minimal property rights for worker-owners want to take advantage of the tax incentives that come with employee ownership without conferring ownership rights to a degree that they feel might interfere with the operations of the business. Recently, Deputy Under-Secretary of Labor Stephen Schlossberg issued a study showing how the way federal law regulates the roles of labor and management effectively prevents new forms of cooperation between labor and management.[25]

Emasculated Capitalism

The discussion of the source of worker rights in ESOPs pinpoints one of the major faults in the structure of ESOP law: ESOPs are generally treated as if they are distant benefit plans, involving minimal ownership. It might be reasonable for employees who own only a small part of a company not to have intensive ownership rights, but why should this hold for all amounts and types of worker ownership? Those who claim that workers are not investors seem to consider worker equity to be part of compensation, an addition to the wage, a supplement given by management, rather than worker stockholding. Indeed, one legal case in support of this view cites a Supreme Court ruling that an employee sells his or her labor primarily to obtain a livelihood and not to make an investment. Laws written for an era when "workers worked and owners owned" are being applied to circumstances to which they are no longer suited.

Another aspect of the Securities and Exchange Commission's own reasoning about the exemption of ESOPs from traditional stockholder protections supports this way of thinking—the protections disappear because workers are not defined as traditional stockholders. The SEC claims that a sale or offer to sell stock has not occurred between the worker stock ownership trust and the company since the worker "does not have any discretion with respect to participation in the plan or the investment of the employee's funds."[26] This is tantamount to a catch-22. Because workers have no discretionary authority in an ESOP, they are given no discretionary authority as investors. The SEC does not take into account the fact that when a corporation borrows money or uses retained earnings instead of new equity issues to expand its business, existing stockholders benefit as the value of their stock increases (if the company succeeds). No discretion regarding investment occurred in this case either, but those stockholders have property rights over their stock—which now includes the increased value from that credit or those reinvested earnings. The SEC, perhaps unwittingly, reinforces employees' weak position in ESOPs conferring the minimal ownership rights prescribed by ESOP law. The SEC reasoning is explicitly based on the notion that workers are not contributing anything to the equity fund and so have earned no rights.

Again, a serious contradiction becomes obvious. Enthusiasts of the ESOP cannot have it both ways. The state cannot both encourage an ESOP structure that secures absolute management rights and at the same time suggest that this will create a common interest between labor and management and a joint partnership in the firm. It treats employee ownership as an extension of the wage with which management purchases worker compliance, rather than as a source of new property rights and responsibilities. This stance contradicts both the legislative claims and the facts about ESOPs—which are that the new ownership is a result of government tax subsidies, leveraged credit, worker involvement in production, and the rate of return on worker investments. Perhaps when a lone entrepreneur uses savings to give gifts of ownership, he or she should be able to control the extent of the rights conferred by that ownership, but when the ownership results from a general state tax subsidy and credit, should management have that authority?

Another aspect of the SEC reasoning further clarifies the ideology at work here. In a private company or a company going private or in an intrastate offering of stock, it is presumed that the purchasers are insiders or in close proximity and hence have access to sufficient data about the company, so that the time-consuming process of being regulated is unnecessary. This might be a persuasive argument for exempting ESOPs from the laws requiring disclosure of information if worker-owners actually had the same rights and access that typical investors have in a closely held company. But, again, the law removes protections without providing an alternative means for workers and managers/owners to participate together in safeguarding their own interests by giving employees the same access to information that shareholders in closely held firms are presumed to have. This is in spite of the fact that the GAO reported that the threats to these interests were pervasive, related to the lack of voting rights in ESOPs and compounded by the lack of formal communication and informal employee involvement in management. One legal scholar says that, if these plans are indeed to benefit the employees, full disclosure would more probably promote employee acceptance of ESOPs and encourage their growth.[27]

The Publicly Held Corporation

The U.S. Comptroller General's 1980 report stated that the key problems associated with fair stock valuation, marketability of shares, and voting were not found in ESOPs in publicly traded companies. This is because the shares are traded on an established market determined by willing buyers and sellers, registered with the SEC and subject to its reporting and disclosure requirements, and in possession of full voting rights as prescribed by federal law. This observation has since proven to be too optimistic since the sheer value of combining some of the ESOP tax incentives makes it easier to use an ESOP to convert a large public company to one that is private. In *Employee Ownership through ESOPs: Implications for the Public Corporation,* the author has demonstrated how a radical shift has taken place in the incentives for employee ownership in such corporations and their actual use of it between 1983 and 1987.[28]

Recently, a number of large leveraged buyouts of publicly held companies were attempted by management groups using ESOPs. Several of these cases raised serious questions with lawyers from the Pension and Welfare Benefits Section of the Department of Labor. While many of the approaches developed by Labor have not yet been fully tested in the courts, they do indicate that there is substantial concern about who is benefitting from ESOPs.

In 1984, the U.S. Court of Appeals upheld an order preventing Norlin Corporation from voting its ESOP stock. Norlin had sought to avert a takeover by transferring large blocks of its common and voting preferred stock to a subsidiary and a newly formed Norlin ESOP. By adding this stock to shares already under its control, the board controlled 49 percent of the corporation's outstanding stock. The transactions, however, were performed without shareholder approval, and so Norlin was suspended from trading on the New York Stock Exchange. Piezo Electric Products, Inc., the would-be acquirer, wanted to bar Norlin from voting the shares it had transferred to the subsidiary and the ESOP, claiming that the transfer of stock to the ESOP lacked a valid business purpose and was intended merely to entrench management. The court agreed, reasoning that "the wide latitude normally afforded management in the exercise of their business judgment is not applicable where management is acting in their self interest; under such circumstances, the burden shifts to the directors to demonstrate that their actions are fair and reasonable." The court concluded that the ESOP was being used mainly to solidify management's control of the corporation. Had the Norlin board been able to show that the ESOP was created primarily to benefit the employees, it could have rebutted these charges.[29]

The Department of Labor alleged that the fiduciaries of an ESOP that owned 100 percent of the company's shares violated their duties by selling the stock without "prudently determining whether a sale transaction was in the plan's interests and under what terms." With the consent of the parties, the court ordered an independent fiduciary to make the decisions.[30]

Labor also evaluated the leveraged buyout of Blue Bell, Inc., proposed in 1984 by its profit-sharing and retirement plan and management, and judged that it raised significant questions regarding the prudence standard of ERISA and reflected the regulatory problems of employee ownership in leveraged buyouts. This case also illustrates how different formats for employee ownership share the same problems. The total cost of the buyout was approximately $650 million. The credit would be leveraged in by a syndicate of savings-and-loan associations ($75 million), a group of institutional investors represented by Drexel Burnham Lambert, Inc. ($138 million), a group of banks ($357 million), a group of managers exercising stock options and using a loan made at below-market interest rates by the company ($12 million), Kelso and Company ($1.5 million), and the profit-sharing plan ($67 million).

The department felt that the committee of the profit-sharing plan had not sufficiently established the soundness of the investment or whether the terms of the buyout were fair and prudent. It rejected as overly optimistic an analysis by the firm Houlihan, Lokey, Howard and Zukin, claiming that the internal rate of return of the plan's investment was greater than the institutional investor's projected internal rate of return. Labor objected to the stipulation that no cash dividends would be paid on the plan's stock for six years. It questioned whether the workers would be adequately compensated for the investment of their accumulated profit-sharing and retirement assets.

Labor was also concerned about the management-appointed fiduciaries making this decision without qualified investment-banking advice. It felt that the equity rights, or percentage of ownership, each of the parties would get for its investment were not figured sufficiently to the advantage of the workers who had traded in their profit-sharing plan, while the institutional investors were granted higher dividends and interest incomes, and concluded that the relative potential for appreciation was wrongly distributed. The institutional investors would get 36 percent of the common stock for a certain investment of $62.5 million, while the workers would receive 32.8 percent of the ownership for an investment of $67 million. The Labor Department said it could understand this difference if the workers' plan was subject to lower risks, but in fact the institutional investors' notes enjoyed a liquidation preference. It computed that management was ultimately getting a 24.6-percent share of the common stock with a post-buyout value of $22 to $30 million for a nominal investment of $9 million, $3.5 million of which was supplied through the low-interest company loan they had arranged for themselves. It figured the internal rate of return for management to be 54 percent, as compared to 31 percent for the worker-ownership plan.

The management team asserted that they deserved this bigger reward to make up for the possible loss of their personal assets and that this higher rate of return, by attracting outside investors, would have a favorable impact on the whole company. A study by lawyers and investment-banking consultants hired by management supplied the justification for this structuring of the deal. The Department of Labor's response was that "even accepting the need to provide incentives to management, the management group's potential share in the company relative to the plan appears out of proportion to any reasonable incentive scheme."

While this was not an ESOP, it was a profit-sharing plan that shared some ESOP characteristics, such as being able to invest more than 10 percent of its assets in employer stock. In the end, management amended the Blue Bell arrangement. But the company's employee ownership was short-lived. In 1986, Blue Bell Industries, the maker of Wrangler, agreed to be acquired by VF Corporation, the maker of Lee clothing.[31]

The Department of Labor found similar problems with several ESOP arrangements, including Scott and Fetzer, Inc., the owner of World Book Encyclopedia and Kirby Vacuum Cleaners (in 1985—a $574-million buyout), and Raymond International, Inc., an engineering firm (in 1983—a $219. million buyout). The Labor Department review of the Raymond case was requested by the Securities and Exchange Commission.

Labor's conclusions from these cases confirm the conflicts mentioned above:

1. The transactions are prearranged, and the fiduciaries do not meaningfully evaluate and represent the worker-ownership plan's interests, and this violates the Internal Revenue Code's principle of prudence and the principle that the exemption from prohibitive transactions in using credit in an ESOP arrangement requires that the loan primarily benefit the plan participants.
2. The potential for conflicts is extreme where corporate officers who are engineering the transaction also serve as fiduciaries or appoint those who do. Independent fiduciaries with independent counsel and advisors are preferable, while advisors previously connected to the company are not likely to be viewed as independent.
3. The type of fairness opinion traditionally issued to a corporate board of directors saying the transaction is fair from a financial point of view may not constitute an adequate basis for a plan fiduciary since it may satisfy the bottom-line conclusion of the board acting in the broad latitude of the "business judgement" rule, but it may not be sufficient to satisfy the standards of prudence and "solely in the interests." A conclusion that the plan is paying no more than fair market value is the minimum on which the fiduciary should rely.
4. A plan fiduciary cannot prudently rely on an investment advisor if the advisor's compensation may be increased by virtue of the substance and nature of the advice it provides.
5. The interests of the workers may differ depending on the type of worker-ownership plan involved. For example, an existing plan with substantial assets that is being converted or used in the transaction will have different considerations than a newly created plan. (This is based on the fact that such buyouts often involve using the assets of several existing types of defined-contribution plans and new plans.) If there are several plans, the existing plan with substantial assets should have a bargaining position exercised independently of the other plans.
6. Lenders to the new corporation or to the worker-ownership plan should not serve as fiduciaries for the plan. A bank's position as a

lender poses unacceptable conflicts. The contention that a bank's trust department can act independently on behalf of workers while the commercial department acts as the lender would not likely be viewed as a defense.[32]

These principles were drafted by Norman Goldberg who served as the counsel for fiduciary litigation in the Department of Labor's Plan Benefits Security Division. As mentioned earlier, investment banker Louis Kelso and his firm, Kelso and Company, subsequently launched a well-publicized lobbying campaign against the restrictive effect of these principles on employee ownership. *Business Week* reported on the significant pressure being exerted on the Department of Labor, as well as on the secretary himself, by investment-banking groups who argued that such constraints prevented employee ownership from occurring, since architects of leveraged buyouts just would not use ESOPs if they could not have a freer hand. They claimed that the primary purpose of ESOPs is to serve as a tool of corporate finance, which broadens the ownership of capital, choosing to ignore the other equally important legal and policy goals clearly intended by Congress.[33] Recently, however, the firm of Houlihan, Lokey, Howard and Zukin prepared detailed proposals on how a firm being recapitalized with an ESOP can avoid providing an economic disincentive to other equity investors while being fair to the ESOP. American Capital Strategies, the investment-banking firm, has also designed suitable approaches to leveraged buyouts that protect labor's interests.[34]

Obviously, these arguments miss the central point: ESOPs are not simply corporate-finance techniques that incidentally benefit workers, but rather employee-ownership plans for the exclusive benefit of workers that also happen to be useful in corporate finance. While the Department of Labor has applied the guidelines noted above to alter several leveraged buyouts by consent of the parties involved, all of the details of these various guidelines have not been tested in court. Nevertheless, leading members of the legal profession are beginning to take these cases into account in their approaches to employee ownership.

In these cases and guidelines, the Labor Department is interpreting the concepts of "prudence" and "exclusive benefit of the participants" as they apply to ESOPs in a way more consistent with the general tenor of ERISA and case law on conflicts between the rights of participants and the role of fiduciaries in worker-benefit trusts. The main problem here, as Corey Rosen has put it, is "whether employee ownership devolves into a game to see how much management can get away with or whether it leads to a different concept, a partnership concept of the work relationship."[35]

Despite all this, the Department of the Treasury still has not issued the definitive regulations on ESOPs that it and the GAO agreed in 1980 might address some of these issues—in practice, ESOP trustees are almost always chosen exclusively by boards of directors. Large leveraged buyouts in publicly held companies have drawn the most attention; the abusive ESOP in the closely held firm is apparently too small for available resources both to identify and to examine. As noted above, the 1980 U.S. Comptroller General's report was quite critical of the Department of Labor's willingness and ability to carry out appropriate investigations. The primary issue, however, is that these problems arise from structural and doctrinal contradictions within ESOP law itself that stopgap programs of review cannot begin to address.[36] All eyes are now on the Pension Benefits Welfare Administration to see who Labor's guidelines on these issues will favor.

It cannot be assumed that the opinions of Kelso and Company reflect the attitudes of large world-class corporations or large banks. For example, when T. Boone Pickens threatened Phillips Petroleum with a takeover, Phillips proposed one of the largest leveraged ESOPs in history. Phillips, feeling that its employees were loyal and potential partners, wanted them to be as involved as possible. According to federal law, the employees were entitled to vote their shares, but, because Phillips was going to use leveraged credit to buy the ESOP's shares off the market, the company realized that in reality the trustees would be voting workers' shares for many years until the loan was repaid. The firm decided that its ESOP would be different: Trustees would be required to vote unallocated shares according to workers' instructions for allocated shares. In a strange twist, the Labor Department subsequently said that labor law made this unacceptable and ended up supporting a position that limited employee involvement.[37]

Discrimination

A trust . . . shall constitute a qualified trust under this section . . . (4) if the contributions or the benefits provided under the plan do not discriminate in favor of employees who are (a) officers, (b) shareholders, or (c) highly compensated. . . . A classification shall not be considered discriminatory within the meaning of paragraph (4) . . . merely because it excludes employees the whole of whose remuneration constitutes "wages" . . . or merely because it is limited to salaried or clerical employees. Neither shall a plan be considered discriminatory within the meaning of such provisions merely because the contributions or benefits of or on the behalf of the employees under the plan bear a uniform relationship to the total compensation, or the basic or regular rate of such compensation of such employees or merely because the contributions or benefits based on that part of an employee's remuneration which is excluded from wages by section 3121 (a)(1) differ from the contributions or benefits based on employee's remuneration not so excluded.[38]

The doctrine of nondiscrimination in employee-benefit plans as it is applied to ESOPs essentially permits discrimination: It is double-talk. The law governing ESOPs contains a number of discriminatory elements in addition to eligibility requirements and allocation schedules. Chapter 2 described the mechanics of discrimination as they related to worker ownership and suggested that it was fairly widespread. This section looks at the data in terms of the ideology of legal practice. Given that those who should exclusively benefit from ESOPs have little say in defining the use of these mechanisms, they are potentially all the more harmful.

Because a company and its managers can decide who a worker is, they can discriminate against groups of workers they do not want in the plan. Indeed, a major legal text on ESOPs discusses just this kind of social engineering. Such support of management entrenchment fills popular and legal literature on employee ownership.[39]

The moving parts of ESOPs have a complex interaction effect. Using this effect is one of the main ways of discriminating in an ESOP. Its nature can be completely transformed by varying the definition of a worker, the presence of voting rights, the structure of voting rights, the provisions for voting unallocated stock, the formula for the allocation of ownership, the vesting schedule, the commitment to contribute annually to the ESOP, the cost and classes of stock, the percentage of ownership of the company, the provisions for future company ownership, the plans for distributing ownership to employees, the composition and selection of the board of directors, the identity and selection of the ESOP trustees, and the amount and attendant voting rights of non-ESOP stock held by employees.

The possibilities are myriad within the law's definitions of fairness and nondiscrimination. A largely democratic ESOP can be constructed, yet as long as it is nonleveraged and does not have a money-purchase pension plan feature, its annual contributions are completely discretionary. The employer can terminate or limit the extent of the plan at any time as long as he or she controls the board of directors. These two small changes alone can totally transform the scenario. The vesting schedule, allocation formulas, and worker definitions, too, can be altered to exclude workers of a certain age, sex, and so on, as long as they are conveniently concentrated in sectors affected by these schedules. If enough nonsalaried employees are excluded, enough highly compensated and salaried employees are included, the allocation of stock is according to relative income, and stock is voted on a one-vote/one-share basis, management and/or salaried employees will always be able to outvote other employee groups. Yet the ESOP will appear to be as liberal as the law allows, providing worker influence—even employee selection of trustees—and full pass-through of voting rights.

Discrimination as a concept in the law is taken to refer narrowly to the definition of who the participants are, and the principle is evaluated in this context. But, obviously, the design of an ESOP allows for strategies to vary distribution of power, prestige, and resources according to class of employee. Please note, the problem here is not that everyone cannot participate in ESOPs and everybody should be able to do so, nor is it that all ESOPs grievously misuse this part of the law. The difficulty is with the actual definition of discrimination and who has the authority to apply it. It is probable that this problem restrains the ability of all employees to work together for better economic performance and labor-management relations—the image of the employee-owned firm projected at hearings and in the popular literature.

The allocation schedule also offers substantial opportunity for discrimination. The law says explicitly that the allocation formula may not discriminate in favor of officers, shareholders, or highly paid employees who make more than $50,000 a year (Internal Revenue Code 401[a]). But, as noted, under present law this definition has been so vague that it applies only to a small number of people in any company. In addition, the law both allows and encourages allocation formulas based on compensation, in effect favoring unlimited discrimination among different pay levels. This law will continue in force until January 1, 1989, when the tighter definitions of highly compensated employees in the Tax Reform Act of 1986 become effective.

Discrimination in the Tax-Credit ESOP

With the repeal of the tax-credit ESOP, analysts have tried to forget it. Yet it demands close attention since it reveals so much about how the interaction between eligibility and allocation can create discrimination. If only in its massive distortion of the aim of the classic ESOP—to encourage the use of credit for worker equity—it is central to an understanding of the worldview inherent in much of ESOP law. As noted, TRASOP/PAYSOP law required allocation according to compensation, and TRASOPs/PAYSOPs accounted for 89 percent, or $11.8 billion, of the $13.3 billion in federal tax expenditures (upper-bound estimate) for ESOPs from 1977 to 1983. The government thus mandated that almost 90 percent of the ESOP tax expenditure be allocated in a way that most favors highly compensated members of generally large publicly held firms. True, there was a ceiling of $100,000 on the amount of a worker's income that could be taken into account in allocation, but this limit was more than cancelled out by the fact that a large number of TRASOPs/ PAYSOPs were found in publicly traded Fortune 1000 companies, which have many highly compensated management employees.

Still, our claim is justified only if most TRASOP/PAYSOP plans did actually exclude groups of employees. The research of Harvard economist Steven Bloom indicates that this was in fact quite common, as Table 5–3 shows. In 1985 he matched the overall company data from COMPUSTAT with ESOP data from the IRS Form 5500 Series return. All but one of the firms were publicly held, and most had TRASOPs/ PAYSOPs. Discrimination through nondiscrimination was rampant.

Table 5–3.   Percentage of Employees Participating in Tax-Credit ESOPs.

Percentage of Employees in Tax-Credit ESOPs	*Percentage of Tax-Credit ESOPs*
0– 35	43.9
35– 70	28.4
70–100	26.5

Source: Steven Bloom, *Employee Ownership and Firm Performance* (Cambridge: Harvard University Department of Economics, 1986), p.104.

Two other surveys provide conclusive evidence about just who has been excluded. Hewitt Associates studied the TRASOP in 1978 and the PAYSOP in 1985. In 1978, 40.7 percent of the plans covered all or most employees, but 34.4 percent only covered all or most salaried or nonunion employees and 25 percent only covered all or most salaried employees. The trend toward exclusion had actually increased since their 1977 study, although Hewitt and other observers had noted that the change from the tax-credit ESOP to the payroll-based ESOP would reward firms for being more inclusive. In Chapter 2, however, this author suggests that large companies with huge payrolls could exclude workers and still get sizable tax credits because one salaried professional receiving $100,000 could deliver five times the tax credit of a unionized or nonunionized laborer making $20,000. Hewitt's 1984 study of PAYSOPs supports this conclusion: 48.3 percent included all employees; 27.8 percent covered salaried and nonunion hourly employees; 19.2 percent covered salaried employees only; and 4.7 percent used other options, primarily including all employees except those belonging to a union. Only 9.1 percent of the PAYSOPs excluded officers, directors, 10-percent shareholders, or other employees subject to SEC "insider" rules.[40]

The reader should appreciate the catch here. In the technical legal sense, because the government has defined "highly compensated employees" so narrowly—and will continue to do so until 1989—it could give the better part of almost $12 billion to highly paid employees while remaining true to the letter of its laws. It is sheer sophistry, much the same as saying that there will be no discrimination in favor of light-haired people, but only Albinos shall be considered to have light hair, and, furthermore, all those with hair darker than light brown will be excluded before anyone determines whether discrimination has occurred.

Discrimination in Leveraged and Nonleveraged ESOPs

In 1981 the *Journal of Corporation Law* released a study that examined this problem in leveraged and nonleveraged ESOPs. Through the use of median statistics, the 1986 General Accounting Office data and conclusions cited in Table 2–2 understate the amount of discriminatory non-discrimination, indicating that half of all leveraged and nonleveraged ESOPs excluded 26.7 percent of their employees.[41] Kruse's analysis, summarized in Table 2–3, partially exposed this understatement. In fact, of the ESOPs covered in that study, almost a third excluded at least 50 to 75 percent of their employees, and over half excluded at least a quarter. Table 5–4 examines exclusion in more detail. The bigger the firm, the more employees it excludes, which may be because such firms employ more salaried or nonunionized workers whom they can favor. Indeed, a close look at Table 5–4B shows this to be true. Seventy percent of the companies with union representation have ESOPs that do not cover union employees, and, as the percentage of a company's employees covered by a union increases, the mean employee coverage by the ESOP generally decreases. A 1985 survey of all types of ESOPs confirms that 61 percent of ESOP firms with union members exclude the union members from participation. Finally, Table 5–4C provides evidence of the strong interaction of nondiscrimination with a rule of allocation that also "does not discriminate in favor of highly compensated employees"—69 percent of all these ESOPs have more than 51 percent of their holdings in company stock in the accounts of salaried workers. Unfortunately, the General Accounting Office neglected to include this type of analysis in its most recent study.

Who is responsible for the state of affairs revealed by these numbers? First of all, we must remember that these aggregate figures obscure many ESOPs that take pains to involve as many employees as possible, and, in any case, businesspeople surely cannot be blamed for abiding by the law. Members of Congress systematically designed and supported this version of employee ownership while promising to broaden and improve American capitalism. Primary responsibility must lie with them and a small group of misguided ESOP supporters—many of them lawyers and consultants—who have had an inordinate and unacceptable influence over the shape of national employee-ownership legislation. Finally, organized labor must be faulted for passively, and in many cases actively, keeping their collective-bargaining units out of such plans and for making no attempt whatsoever to direct the evolution of the legislation.

The Placement of the Law

Most observers agree that the placement of the major part of employee-ownership law within tax and pension law is due both to Senator Russell Long, who chaired the powerful Senate Finance Committee for many years, and to the fact that ERISA was being written at the time and employee ownership looked like a close cousin of tax-qualified employee-benefit plans. This very placement emphasizes the passive role of the worker.

Yet another factor in the contradictions in ESOP law may be the historical baggage and the complex evolution of laws on pension funds in the United States. These are a very recent phenomenon. The first pension plan dates from 1875, created by American Express for disabled elderly employees. By 1929 about 400 industrial plans existed. The plans, used to discourage workers from striking, were seen as voluntary gifts from the company, which constituted no contract and conferred no legal rights on any

Table 5–4. Employee Coverage by Size, Unionization, and Control of Stock.

A. Mean Employee Coverage by Company Size.

		Mean Coverage[a]	
Total sample		(N = 219)	68%
Size[b]:	10 – 50	(N = 36)	84
	51 – 100	(N = 45)	73
	101 – 500	(N = 84)	65
	501 –1,000	(N = 27)	61
	1,001 +	(N = 27)	51

B. Coverage of Union Employees.

	Union Employees Covered by the ESOP			
	All	Some	None	Total
Percentage of those companies with union representation (N = 77)	20	10	70	100

	Percent of Company Employees Represented by a Union			
	0	1–20	21–50	51–100
Mean Coverage[a]	76 (N = 142)	61 (N = 27)	61 (N = 17)	40 (N = 32)

C. Percent of ESOP Holdings of Company Stock Allocated to Accounts of Salaried and Non-salaried Personnel.

			Percentage of Sample
0 – 25	in salaried accounts, balance in nonsalaried accounts	(N = 15)	8
26 – 50	in salaried accounts, balance in nonsalaried accounts	(N = 41)	23
51 – 75	in salaried accounts, balance in nonsalaried accounts	(N = 42)	23
76 – 99	in salaried accounts, balance in nonsalaried accounts	(N = 27)	15
100	in salaried accounts	(N = 56)	31
Total sample		(N = 181)	100

a. In terms of the percent of company employees covered by the ESOP.
b. In terms of the number of company employees.

Source: Thomas R. Marsh and Dale E. McAllister, "ESOP Tables: A Survey of Companies with Employee Stock Ownership Plans," Journal of Corporation Law 6, no. 3 (1981): 591–92, 600–601.

employee.[42] Workers were frequently excluded from the plans for various reasons, such as joining a union. Often fewer than 10 percent of the members would actually qualify for benefits.

Generally, an employee earns credits based on length of service and gets a pension determined by the number of credits he or she has accumulated. Some plans are paid for partly by the employer and partly by the employee. A company may buy the benefit plan from an insurance company or set up the fund alone or in concert with other employers. In 1940 only 3.8 million employees were covered by private pension plans—about 13.6 percent of private nonagricultural employment. The state played a key role in the growth of these plans. At the end of World War II, the United Mine Workers and the federal government, which then controlled the mines, negotiated a pension plan. In 1948 the National Labor Relations Board ruled that the Inland Steel Company was required to bargain with the steelworkers' union about pensions, and the next year pension plans were adopted by the automobile and steel industries in general. They appeared in the mid- to late fifties in trucking and construction. In July 1986 the most recent statistics released by the Bureau of Labor Statistics showed that 80 percent of American workers in certain medium and large companies were covered by defined-benefit pension plans, a figure that had held constant since 1980.

When excess-profits taxes went into effect during World War II, the government started to give tax breaks for company contributions to pension plans. Because they were considered fringe benefits rather than wages, these were not covered by federal wage freezes. Subsequently, the Taft-Hartley Act said unions could not control funds made up of employer contributions, yet the funds themselves were part of collective bargaining. As Andrew Strom notes in one study, this lessened the voluntary and paternalistic nature of the plans but perpetuated the image of the passive worker.

The government then developed a system of regulating the fairness of such funds and established Social Security as a supplementary system. In the fifties, in an arrangement called a Social Security offset, most pension agreements were actually tied to Social Security benefits, with the company paying the difference between Social Security and a specified benefit. This provision was eliminated from many plans in the sixties, although a number of employers are trying to resuscitate the offset concept.

ERISA came along in the early seventies to clean up abuses in the structural features of pension plans related to eligibility, vesting, allocation, funding, disclosure, fiduciary standards, discrimination, and employee rights. It, too, did not substantially change the passive role of the worker, but it did give workers some protections. Yet, as noted, ESOPs, which owe most of their core features and principles to ERISA, were exempted from many of these protections, even though they retained the general structure of pensions. Their major distinction was that they could result in substantial worker ownership, because, as noted in Section 407(3)(d)(6) they were "designed to invest primarily in qualifying employer securities."

From the very beginning, then, the placement of ESOPs in pension law created contradictions. The ESOP was intended to invest primarily employer securities and to encourage as much employee ownership as possible, yet nothing in ESOP law said that worker ownership should contain the rights and responsibilities that normally accompany ownership. Despite the tremendous exemptions from both taxes and government controls that benefit ESOPs, thorough review of the legislative record indicates that these plans were hardly mentioned in the extensive hearings, debate, or official research conducted for ERISA. They constitute a minor part of the act itself—a few paragraphs out of 246 pages. In its official report on ERISA, Congress expressed concern about the lack of protections for ESOP employees.

The congressional motivations for ESOPs and for pension plans differed drastically. Yet, although ESOPs were never identified as retirement plans in the ERISA debate, they automatically took on many of their features. The result was that the law developed a very clear ideology on what employee ownership should look like. Returning to the four possible types of firms described in Chapter 2, we see that ESOP law essentially postulates that, whether a firm is minimally, sizably, majority, or totally owned by its employees, there should be little employee involvement in the company, and indeed, with the exception of certain guidelines for economic fairness, employees have few rights of influence in these plans.

The Battle over the Meaning of Ownership

A fundamental contradiction in the official definition of the ESOP is visible in the initial interpretations issued by the Senate Finance Committee in 1975 and 1976.

[A] key element of the employee stock ownership plan is that it provides a new technique of corporate finance. . . . [I]t may be used: (i) to meet general financing requirements of the corporation including capital growth and transfers in the ownership of corporate stock; (ii) to *build into employees* [emphasis added] beneficial ownership of stock of their employers . . . *without requiring any cash outlay, any reduction in pay or other employee benefits, or the surrender of any other rights on the part of the employees* [emphasis added]; and (iii) to receive loans or other forms of credit to acquire stock. . . ."[43]

The worldview expressed above unabashedly focuses on the corporate uses of employee ownership in discreet opposition to the notion of the "exclusive benefit of employees" and the legislative goals expressed in Chapter 1. Note that this language almost implies that employee ownership is a gift requiring nothing from the employee. This contradiction has been gradually intensified in succeeding official representations of employee ownership.[44]

Two aspects of the statement above reveal the root of all the problems that later emerged. First, as noted earlier, the psychology of ownership expressed here is based on the belief that the mere presence of ownership is sufficient. The law is "building ownership into employees" rather than sharing its rights and responsibilities. It is, indeed, free ownership: It requires nothing from the employees—no cash outlay or reduction in benefits, and no participation in management or involvement in decisionmaking. This is the source of the notion that employee ownership is a gift of management. In fact, as we have seen, the financial stake of employees in leveraged ESOPs and large transfers of ownership definitely does involve them in taking responsibility for creating the absolute value that will pay for their ownership. Furthermore, there is no objective evidence that corporations making contributions to both leveraged and nonleveraged ESOPs do not moderate wages or other benefits.

Second, let us examine the observation that this arrangement must not involve "the surrender of any other rights on the part of the employees." Given the evidence provided above, this statement is patently duplicitous. Almost every conceivable shield and right provided to employees in other benefit plans under ERISA is removed. In this instance, the problem lies with neither the actual concept of employee ownership nor its use in corporate finance, but with an ideology that pretends to support substantial employee participation in ownership and corporate finance yet removes the rights and responsibilities of ownership and provides no alternative avenues of involvement and influence to protect these interests. This would remain an ongoing confusion and a bitter under-the-surface conflict for the next decade and a half.

The first major hearings on the ESOP in 1975 constituted an extensive debate on ESOPs as a plan to further worker ownership in the economy. This is how the senators, administration witnesses, and economists understood the idea. No evidence exists that the framers had in mind a minor supplementary benefit plan, and, certainly, the ESOP has not evolved that way. Economists were asked to compare the ESOP to a number of other worker-equity ideas, and during those hearings members of Congress and company witnesses gave repeated examples of increased worker interest and motivation in employee-ownership companies. This earliest record makes it apparent that the framers and supporters of employee ownership truly intended to change industrial relations, not just to institute another passive pension plan. But the issue of worker rights and concrete mechanisms to involve workers in their ESOPs or their companies was never really addressed.[45]

On the contrary, members of the Senate Finance Committee would slowly defend and strengthen the passive role of workers in ESOPs. The official House and Senate Reports interpreting ESOP legislation after 1974 repeatedly insist that ESOPs are not retirement plans, but a subtle shift has been noticeable. The concept of "beneficial ownership," underscoring the passive role of workers, has received ever-increasing emphasis in the texts, as has the corporate-finance side of the dual ESOP definition. A rationale claiming that ESOPs were not retirement plans when their broadened-ownership and corporate-finance facets were stressed allowed supporters in and out of Congress to argue that the ESOP should be exempt from ERISA's normal protections for employees. Yet ESOPs are treated as retirement plans or beneficial funds when it is in the interest of the speaker or writer to underline the passive role of workers within them. In direct contradiction to the original objective of ESOPs, this response reflects some ESOP enthusiasts' increasing resistance to intensified labor-management cooperation or worker participation in employee ownership.

In 1975 the TRASOP was enacted as an afterthought to the investment tax credit. As we have shown, it was not a real ESOP because it did not produce new ownership by means of credit. The fact that it would quickly become a major corporate-financing tactic for large corporations again powerfully points up how Congress allowed this aspect of the ESOP to dominate. The TRASOP/PAYSOP stands as the most irrefutable evidence of an employee-ownership worldview in opposition to much of the original populist philosophy that Senator Long ascribed to the idea.

The absence of the protective ERISA shield for ESOPs and the promise of their quick growth with the TRASOP apparently caused some eyebrows to be raised at the Department of the Treasury and the Department of Labor. In 1976 they issued proposed regulations that would put more rigorous limits on ESOPs under ERISA or at least restrict their exemptions from various ERISA rules. It was an attempt to change course quickly on a few issues. The regulations called for independent third-party trustees, mandatory put options and voting rights in leveraged ESOPs, stricter provisions on issuing nonvoting stock to employees, and nondiscrimination. While some of these regulations would have made ESOPs more difficult to establish—and in the author's opinion they would have seriously retarded the evolution of employee ownership—several directly addressed the questions of whom ESOPs were intended to benefit, what the participation rights of workers should be, and how much self-dealing by companies and management would be tolerated.[46]

Congress and ESOP practitioners reacted strongly. On December 29, 1976, Congress made the bold move of specifically attacking and debating each of the proposed regulations in its official report on the Tax Reform Act of 1976:

The Act reaffirms Congressional intent with respect to employee stock ownership plans and *expresses concern that administrative rules and regulations may frustrate Congressional intent* [emphasis added]. In this connection it has come to the attention of the Congress that proposed regulations issued by both the Department of Treasury and the Department of Labor on July 30, 1976, may make it virtually impossible for ESOPs [this reference included TRASOPs] and especially leveraged ESOPs, to be established and to function effectively.

The report contained strident arguments against voting rights and the need for independent trustees. Congress also noted that "it is deeply concerned that the objectives sought by this series of laws [encouraging ESOPs] will be made unattainable *by regulations and rulings treating ESOPs as conventional retirement plans* [emphasis added]." Again, since here proponents wanted to emphasize the special exemptions of ESOPs, they argued that they were not akin to retirement plans.[47]

The regulations were withdrawn, but it is interesting to note that several of the Treasury and Labor Departments' proposals dealing with the financial structure and fairness of ESOPs were subsequently made law. Ultimately, however, none of them altered the balance of power in ESOPs. All proposals that dealt with increased worker influence, such as those regarding voting rights and independent fiduciaries, were left substantially unchanged. It must be underlined, however, that the entire tradition of employee-benefit law reflects prevailing norms about equity and control in the corporation; the problem is not unique to employee ownership. Nor is management alone to blame: Trade unions themselves never objected vigorously to the unequal allocation, discrimination, and exclusion that ERISA itself upheld.

The Most Recent Skirmish

In 1985 concern about the role of workers in worker ownership surfaced in an unexpected quarter. In proposals that stunned traditional supporters of ESOPs, the Reagan administration, acting through the Treasury Department, called for fundamental changes in the ESOP as part of the giant tax reform package. The administration said that employees must have all the rights of direct ownership, including voting rights and in some circumstances dividend rights, if employee ownership were to merit the tax expenditures it demanded. It questioned whether ESOPs that restrict the "traditional incidents of ownership" could really improve profitability or employee motivation. The administration proposed to remove ESOPs from retirement law and continue to encourage them with tax incentives as a socially desirable goal. It called the bluff of ESOP apologists by saying plainly that, if ESOPs were not retirement plans, they should be vehicles of real ownership.

The theory behind the Reagan proposal may have seemed sound, but the proposal itself was not based on a careful analysis of all the intricate issues involved. It went to such extremes that the worker ownership it intended to promote would have become impossible. Certainly, the recommendation that workers have the right to vote, the right to dividends, and the right to prohibit self-dealing and conflict of interest by existing owners and managers appeared reasonable.[48] But if workers could demand immediate distribution of their stock, require the company to repurchase it within three years, and transfer it in an unlimited manner, the fundamental purpose of the ESOP—to establish substantial worker ownership and involvement in companies—would be undercut. These new structures would instead encourage workers to bolt with their stock whenever it was convenient, which would be incompatible with ongoing amounts of substantial worker ownership in American companies that might serve as a basis for greater labor-management cooperation and a new way of organizing corporations. If the goal is to encourage a meaningful quantity of employee ownership, some limits on property rights are probably necessary—perhaps a vesting period to invite longer service and some limits on the distribution of equity to eliminate a wholesale drain on a firm's capital. In short, the administration's proposal took to its extreme a radical free-market Chicago School approach to all points of the problem.

On September 20, 1985, the staff of the Joint Committee on Taxation issued a detailed conceptual analysis of the positions of both sides for use in the tax reform debate. This represented the first official documentation of the contradictory motives behind ESOPs. A full reading is invaluable to understanding all the nuances of this debate:

Opponents of the Administration proposal argue that: (1) ESOPs were never intended to provide employees immediately with traditional incidents of actual stock ownership . . . but to create a capital-accumulation device designed to . . . facilitate corporate financing on favorable terms, . . . provide a market for employer securities, especially in the case of a closely held corporation, . . . and to enable employees to accumulate a capital estate sufficient to generate an additional income stream unrelated to compensation; . . . (2) if direct ownership is required and the corporate-finance incentives are weakened, the ESOP goals would be undermined because few employers would maintain ESOTs; . . . (3) full pass-through of voting rights is not a necessary element of the primary goals of expanding capital ownership, individual capital accumulation, and capital-income generation; (4) Congress has addressed this issue and has concluded that full traditional ownership rights are inappropriate and, in fact, may operate to deny employees an opportunity to begin to accumulate a capital estate; . . . (5) the ownership rights available through ESOP financing can justifiably differ from more traditional stock ownership rights . . . because traditionally stock owners pay cash for their ownership whereas ESOP participants generally receive employer stock without personal investment of capital; . . . and (6) . . . ESOPs historically have been designed to ensure that employees share in the appreciation in value of employer securities, not to facilitate direct transfers of the stock and all indicia of ownership.[49]

In response to this attack—originating, interestingly enough, from the property-rights right rather than the worker-sympathetic left—Russell Long drafted an extensive statement on ESOP policy, which he proposed for permanent inclusion in the U.S. Code. His final term in the Senate had just a few more months to run—this was intended as his parting shot, the summing-up of his ideology, and he fought hard for its inclusion in the 1986 tax reform package:

The Congress has made clear its interest in encouraging employee stock ownership plans as a bold and innovative technique of corporate finance for strengthening the free enterprise system. The Congress intends that such plans be used in a wide variety of corporate financing transactions as a means of encouraging employers to include their employees as beneficiaries of such transactions. The Congress is deeply concerned that the objectives sought by this series of laws will be made unattainable by regulations and rulings which treat employee stock ownership plans as conventional retirement plans, which reduce the freedom of employee stock ownership trusts and employers to take the necessary steps to utilize ESOPs in a wide variety of corporate transactions, and which otherwise impede the establishment and success of these plans.[50]

At a time when critics were suggesting that perhaps some of ERISA's protections should be extended to ESOPs, this amendment argued that ESOPs are not retirement plans and even proposed that state actions to increase the rights and responsibilities of employees should be outside of the law and the intent of Congress.

The policy was not adopted—Long's point of view eventually received a stinging rejection. Long had originally introduced what was known as the "Long amendment" as part of a bill that contained a host of tax incentives for ESOPs. The bill passed the Senate, with many members voting for it as a sign of respect to the senator. Later, In the House-Senate conference, the amendment was deleted. The House of Representatives had made a number of reform proposals, all of which were defeated. The administration's modifications were not fully conceived; they, too, all lost. In the end, the new tax reform law improved employee rights only slightly.

The administration's ESOP reform proposals were drafted in the Treasury Department, and Treasury's point of view was largely shared by the Labor Department. Informed sources in both departments and in the Congress say that Senator Long personally asked the White House to make no major changes to ESOPs during his last session in Congress. Presumably, Long accompanied his request with a promise of problems with elements of tax reform if it was not granted. Congressional sources close to the House-Senate Conference Committee that hammered out the final tax reform law report that senior White House officials relayed to Treasury and Labor the president's directive that it was "hands off of ESOPs for this session."

Observers of the House-Senate conference point out that, even after Long was assured passage of virtually all of his more practical ESOP proposals, he kept pushing for the adoption of his "ideological law." His insistence becomes more understandable when one remembers that this was his last chance to get a specific interpretation of ESOPs made law, one that attempted to resolve the main debate about employee ownership: Which was fundamental and which was incidental—corporate-finance uses or a transformation of capitalism that would allow employees to own and participate more fully in their companies?[51]

Conclusion

The quality of worker ownership enshrined in the legal implications of ESOPs raises two sets of issues. One is political: Is this what it was meant to be; is this what populist capitalism is all about? The other is quite practical: Regardless of the ideology underlying ESOP law, do ESOPs deliver the results they promised? And if they don't, then we must anticipate problems arising from future public policy in this area.

CHAPTER 6

The Responsibilities of Capitalism

In 1983 managers of Raymond International, a Houston-based engineering firm, used $41 million in accrued employee benefits, including funds from the company's terminated pension plan, to finance a $219-million buyout. The board of directors appointed the ESOP trustees, who were advised by Drexel Burnham Lambert, whom Raymond indemnified from liability under federal securities laws. Worker stock was nonvoting. The lack of attention to worker interests drew criticism from the Wall Street Journal. Three years later, bankers forced the company into a major restructuring.[1]

The Boston Bank of Commerce employs twenty-seven workers. Its ESOP owns around 40 percent of the stock, and managers and outside investors own about a thrid each. The president and four directors, who already own a third of the stock, also control the ESOP. The ESOP holds voting stock, but since stock is distributed according to salary, the more highly paid managers have more voting power. In addition, the ESOP is leveraged, so management-appointed trustees will vote all unallocated shares until the loan is repaid.[2]

Eberhard Foods has a chain of six stores in Michigan. Its ESOP, set up in 1975 to provide a market for the owner's stock, excluded unionized employees until 1981. As the ESOP's share of the firm approached a majority, the company limited the issues on which employees could vote. In 1986 the United Food and Commercial Workers Union filed a suit in federal court challenging the voting-rights restrictions, which blocked a sale pending to outsiders and led to negotiations with the owner for full worker ownership and voting rights.[3]

The Copper Range Company is 70-percent worker-owned mine, a spinoff organized by the Steelworkers Union. Management owns 30 percent but must sell back its stock below appraised value if the board is dissatisfied with its performance. Stock is allocated according to compensation, which is capped. An initial board represents all parties, but in five years workers will elect the full board. Workers will vote on a one-person/one-vote basis regarding termination of the plan, discontinuation of ESOP contributions, or any proposed sale, transfer, or tendering of stock by the ESOP trustee.[4]

W ithout question, the framers of the ESOP hoped to influence industrial relations through their innovation. How does the worldview inherent in employee-ownership law affect the realization of this hope? To what extent does it encourage workers to take responsibility in their own companies? This chapter explores these questions through an examination of voting rights in ESOPs, an analysis of the common American views of the corporation and their effect on employee ownership, and the relationship of labor law to the rights of worker-owners.

Voting Rights

The question of voting has been preeminent in the controversy over the rights and responsibilities of employee ownership. As noted in Chapter 2, ESOPs must pass through full voting rights on all issues in publicly traded companies, but only on certain major issues in closely held firms. A recent study by the National Center for Employee Ownership of sixteen majority-owned closely held firms found that stockholders vote on very few issues. Half of the firms provided voting on only one issue: the board of directors. Several had voting for the board members, the number of people on the board, and the selection of ESOP administrators. Except for two firms where shareholders voted on more specific management issues, voting was limited to broad policy rather than specific future actions. Only one of these two firms extended the scope to include decisions on issues such as wage structures and work rules.[5]

Voting rights are relevant in most firms' governance systems in only four rather modest respects: They provide a minimum guaranteed voice on big policy issues, which can even be defined in advance in the company's charter; they interact with other features of the ESOP to affect the balance of power; they symbolize a worldview that places importance on property rights for the employees; and they frequently allow employees to choose or recall the board of directors, which, as a representative group for shareholder interests, makes decisions affecting the interests of owners in the firm.

But even the presence of full voting rights does not solve the governance problem of an ESOP. As the analyses in Chapters 2 and 5 demonstrate, full voting rights on worker stock for all issues can be rendered meaningless by other structural features in an ESOP. There is also a distinction between full and partial voting rights. With full voting rights, employees can vote on all issues that are brought to the stockholders; partial voting rights permit employees to vote only on specific issues. In both cases, unless otherwise specified, employees vote only allocated stock, so they are at a disadvantage during the early years of a leveraged ESOP when large amounts of stock remain to be allocated. And if, as is usually the case, highly paid employees are allocated many times more stock than rank-and-file workers, no degree of voting rights will ever amount to real power for the plurality of workers.

History of Voting Rights

Table 2–1 traces how voting-rights legislation evolved, but a tabular format does not show just how uneven that evolution was. It was not immediately clear where Congress was going on this issue. When the Joint Economic Committee recommended voting rights in 1976, it noted that two of the four extant ESOP laws favored them: The Trade Act of 1974 mandated voting rights, and the Tax Reduction Act of 1975 required voting rights for all TRASOPs. TRASOPs however were predominantly (64.6 percent) in publicly traded companies, so this last was not as radical as it may seem. In addition, as we have seen, tax-credit ESOPs were able to limit their participants in many ways that attenuated the impact of this requirement. It is ironic that the most liberal provisions for voting rights existed in companies that were likely to average the least amount of employee ownership.

In keeping with the reasoning that ESOPs should be treated as retirement plans when the goal is to ensure worker passivity, the official report on the Tax Reform Act of 1976 said that ESOPs—meaning those other than TRASOPs—should not have voting rights since "Congress believes that the regulations should not distinguish between leveraged ESOPs and other employee plans in this regard."[6] In its official report on the Revenue Act of 1978, Congress said that it considered voting rights in closely held firms to be "unduly burdensome."[7] Put bluntly, the staff members who made these observations and the congresspeople who voted for the legislation that prompted them were saying that it would be burdensome for managers and existing minority nonemployee owners if employees owning the majority of their own companies were permitted to vote their own stock.

In 1981 a major lobbying effort by the ESOP Association resulted in a bill to eliminate voting rights on all issues in closely held companies. This passed the Senate ninety-seven to three, but died in the House-Senate conference. The following year the House of Representatives passed a bill proposed by New York's Stanley Lundine giving the Economic Development Administration of the Department of Commerce statutory authority to make loans for worker buyouts. It required that full voting rights be provided on all ESOP stock. In 1982 Senator Dixon (D-Ill.) and Congressman William Frenzel reintroduced the bill that had failed in 1981, and Senator Dixon sponsored it again in early 1983. In both instances, it did not pass.

The battle was joined again in the conflict over the 1986 tax reform bill. Opponents tried to dissuade the Reagan administration from supporting voting rights, claiming that lenders would be reluctant to provide financing to ESOPs unless the entity (i.e., the management team) was certain to remain intact. Others have contended that lenders also want management to take a substantial and personal equity interest in any employee-owned company. But research by the National Center for Employee Ownership of 100 bankers, including most of the large money-center banks has indicated that these contentions are false. Most of the banks were comfortable with full voting rights; only one of the nine banks with over $1 billion in assets was not. Many banks are developing ESOP loan products, and Ken Winslow, who heads that department for Chemical Bank, has said that employee involvement is preferable and should be part of employee ownership.[8]

In the 1986 tax bill proposals, the House of Representatives tried to strengthen voting rights somewhat, the Department of the Treasury made far-reaching proposals, and the Senate recommended eliminating even limited voting rights for closely held newspapers. This last amendment was a political favor to one senator and must be viewed as an outrageous precedent. The Treasury lost out completely, the Senate got its way, and the House got those important corporate issues for limited voting rights more carefully defined.

In any piece of tax legislation, changing a word or a sentence without any public discussion can affect the rights in question, and this can cause unforeseen problems in the future. Subtleties can be introduced that people do not fully understand, may not favor, and have not been able to influence because there has been no discussion. But the history of the legislation also reflects the indifference to employee ownership shown by the AFL-CIO and the union movement in general. Evidently, because the legislative discussions have not focused on the traditional adversarial topics of labor relations, labor's interest in defending worker rights or even monitoring the developments in employee ownership has not been awakened.

Growing public knowledge about the increasing presence of ESOPs made it impossible for the ESOP Association and traditional congressional supporters always to restrict voting rights. Congress's mixed record reflects this conflict. In 1976 a Joint Economic Committee staff study recommended that ESOPs in publicly held companies pass through full voting rights to the employees and that at minimum an advisory committee to the trustees be established by vote of the employees in all ESOP companies. Their motivations were clear: "to increase employees' interests in such plans and to better insure that they definitely benefit employees," "to help prevent management's domination of the ESOP," and "to insure that ESOPs are facilitating genuine worker ownership." The committee did not recommend full voting rights in closely held firms, feeling that owners of such companies would be "unwilling to transfer substantial portions of equity for fear of losing voting control."[9] In essence, they argued for the minimal worker involvement described at the end of Chapter 2, no matter how much ownership existed.

The recommendation in the U.S. Comptroller General's 1980 report to the Congress was broader, claiming that employees' voting rights should be as extensive as their holdings. In 1979 the Treasury Department also recommended full voting rights. The 1985/6 Reagan administration proposals went even farther, recommending voting rights for all ESOP stock no matter how the corporation itself structured voting and whether or not the stock was allocated to the employees' accounts. The president's advisors stated that the lack of voting rights "is inconsistent with the goal of employee stock ownership" and that there is "no clear policy justification for permitting different treatment based on whether the employer is publicly traded or closely held." They even questioned whether tax benefits should be given to such diluted ESOPs, which mimic stock-appreciation or stock-purchase plans.[10] All three government initiatives questioned whether ESOPs could improve employee motivation and economic performance without voting rights and strongly enjoined Congress's point of view. Indeed, the U.S. Comptroller General and the Joint Economic Committee staff study judged evidence of the achievement of these goals to be lacking.[11] Quite clearly, then, early studies questioned the validity of extensive worker ownership without more intensive worker involvement.

The Complexity of Voting

The impact of voting rights in ESOPs is complex; the actual law is simple (Internal Revenue Code 401[a][22] and 409[e]). Voting rights are passed through to workers on allocated stock in all publicly traded companies. Since 1979, voting rights must be passed through to workers in privately held companies for major corporate issues that bylaws or state law require to be decided by a more-than-majority vote; otherwise they are optional.

This supermajority provision is unquestionably an important protection. But, as noted earlier, there are many ways to structure an ESOP to circumvent such authority. And, in any case, short of these vital questions, the people who set up the ESOP in privately held firms—usually initial owners, managers, and their consultants—can decide how stock will be voted no matter how much the employees own. In the 1986 tax reform act, Congress specified the major corporate issues to which limited voting rights should be applied as corporate merger or consolidation, recapitalization, reclassification, liquidation, dissolution, or sale of substantially all of the assets.

Voting rights are not a mandatory topic of collective bargaining, so the presence of a union does not change the situation. Other options are available but not often used. Thus, a leveraged ESOP in a privately held firm can be largely controlled by the trustees until a substantial portion of the loan is repaid. Allocation schedules and eligibility definitions can be manipulated so that the only worker-owners with a real voice are those closest to management. In any event, management can retain ultimate control if it chooses to do so.

Voting control, even if granted, can be weakened or revoked in all manner of ways. The plan can be terminated, converted to a plan that does not require voting, or, if the ESOP is in a publicly held firm, taken private and transformed through recapitalization of the corporation and dilution of previous stock blocks. Arrangements can be made to sell workers' shares to outside sources or nonworker inside sources when workers leave the company or to keep the company worker owned only for the period during which management-appointed trustees hold voting control. Indeed, the establishment of an ESOP firm with secure voting rights requires careful and extensive planning around the loopholes of the law.

Yet another difficulty is that Congress strengthened voting rights only for stock allocated after 1979. And the new definition of mandatory issues for limited voting rights will not become effective until 1989. The law does not even consider the possibility that worker-owners will have representatives on the board of directors or a hand in electing the trustees. Since the boards initiate and determine the evolution of ESOPs and in many cases direct the trustees, and since trustees vote unallocated stock in almost all cases and allocated stock in a large number of cases, even this indirect means of asserting influence is curbed. One recent study finds that ESOP trustees are generally not chosen by the employees: Officers choose themselves in 47 percent of the cases in ESOP companies, in 38 percent of the cases they choose banks, and in 10 percent of the cases they choose trust companies.[12]

The Evidence on Voting Rights

If voting rights are irrelevant in closely held companies, as some observers claim, it is hard to explain why ESOP conservatives fight so hard to limit them. ESOP enthusiasts and the ESOP Association of America repeatedly lobbied against the extension of voting rights. As late as 1986 the association featured in its publications the fight to reduce voting rights in ESOPs as its major lobbying initiative. Luis Granados, the former legal counsel of the association, provides the most cogent discussion of their view.[13] He says that a voice cannot be achieved through voting rights in closely held firms where the preexisting nonworker owners retain a controlling interest, nor is there any evidence that voting rights will improve productivity or motivation.

Both observations are only partly correct. First of all, why should every structural feature of ESOPs rise or fall on its connection to productivity and motivation? More to the point, when workers have made significant wage or benefit concessions or arranged to purchase most of a firm, they may demand in return a heavy hand in the design of the ESOP and/or ongoing policymaking of the firm. Finally, the NCEO found that a strong philosophical commitment to employee ownership by management did predict positive employee attitudes and that votings rights were a main determinant of such a commitment.[14]

According to Granados, the most telling argument against voting rights is that existing owners of closely held firms do not want them: "Many owners of closely held companies have devoted their careers to building up their firms and are willing to share the fruits of their success with their employees, but they are not willing to give up control of their assets."[15] Certainly, this argument is appropriate where small businesspeople are using an ESOP to transfer majority or full ownership gradually to the employees—flexibility and an awareness of the difficulty of a culture change are essential during such a transition.

In the same article, Granados calls the ESOP trustees the legal owners of the stock. His point is not without weight. A 1983 ESOP Association survey found that 75 percent of the members opposed voting rights, and many indicated that they planned to terminate their ESOP or drastically curtail the company's contribution if Congress passed voting rights. Only 7 percent opposed the repeal. In its 1982 survey on the same issue, the association had found that 67 percent of the companies with ESOPs holding large or controlling interests (greater than 50 percent) wanted voting rights repealed. There was evidence that these firms intended to slow the growth of their ESOPs in response to the law.[16] These findings were soon borne out: A decline in the growth of nonleveraged ESOPs began the year the supermajority minimum voting rights were discussed and accelerated after the law went into effect.[17] Existing owners and managers in many closely held firms simply do not want to deal with workers as owners.

The basis for this attitude appears to lie more in management's ideology than in the actual behavior of employee-owners. The 1986 NCEO study indicates that (1) employees generally have little desire to control company decisions; (2) most companies with voting rights report that irreconcilable splits never occur; (3) employees almost never use their voting rights to change management and seem, rather, to be extremely loyal to the firm's leadership; (4) concerns that giving employees sensitive information might hurt the company have been generally unfounded; and (5) boards consist primarily of managers even when workers have a say in the selection. The fact of the matter is that, while voting rights do not appear to have a big day-to-day impact on company decisions, they do seem to support labor-management cooperation by making managers and employees more aware of each other's concerns, to facilitate implementation of decisions by building consensus, and generally to play an important role in demonstrating the company's commitment to labor-management cooperation through more pragmatic forms of informal employee involvement.

Several companies have been experimenting with combining full voting rights in a one-person/one-vote format and some informal worker participation in management, among them Seymour Specialty Steel, described at the beginning of Chapter 2, the Solar Center, which is discussed in *Taking Stock: Employee Ownership at Work*, and Republic Container, described at the beginning of Chapter 7.[18] Until 1986 the law made this difficult if not technically illegal. A special provision of the 1986 tax reform act permits the option of a fully democratic ESOP for the first time.[19]

Let's review the evidence. The most comprehensive study of voting rights was done by the General Accounting Office in 1986, based on a sample of 3,000 firms.[20] Nearly 70 percent of those ESOPs surveyed held stock with some voting rights. As Table 6–1B shows, about a third of nontax-credit ESOPs passed through full voting rights. This suggests that the ESOP Association membership is skewed toward companies with particular views on this issue and thus is not representative.

Table 6–1.   Voting Rights in ESOPs.

A. Voting Rights in Companies by Size and Unionization.

	Total	Under 250 Partic.	Over 250 Partic.	Union Included
Full voting pass-through on all issues	19 9%	14 9	4 10	3 14
Pass-through on some issues	19 9%	16 10	2 3	2 9
No pass-through, trustee votes stock	177 81%	131 81	45 87	17 77

B. Pass-Through of Full Voting Rights by Type of ESOP (percent).

Tax-Credit ESOPs	66%
Leveraged	33
Leverageable	30
Nonleveraged	25

C. The Overall Voting Strength of ESOPs (percent).

	Tax Credit	Leveraged	Leverage-able	Non leveraged	Overall
Own up to 25 percent	96	68	72	85	81
Own more than 25 percent	4	32	28	15	19
Median percent of voting strength	1	14	10	5	5
Total weighted cases	847	491	1,034	633	3,005

Sources: a. ESOP Association, *ESOP Survey: 1986* (Washington, D.C.: ESOP Association of America,1986), pp. 54–55; b. U.S. General Accounting Office, *Employee Stock Ownership Plans: Benefits and Costs of ESOP Tax Incentives for Broadening Stock Ownership* (Washington, D.C.: U.S. General Accounting Office, December 1986), p. 39; c. Ibid., p. 40.

But the GAO dug deeper to understand the implications of voting rights in these firms. Table 6–1C indicates the voting strengths of ESOPs, that is, the percentage of all voting shares in a corporation that is controlled by the ESOP (note that this table does not indicate whether shares are voted by trustees or workers). Only 7 percent of all ESOPs control a majority of voting strength in their firms, including a high of 10 percent of leveraged ESOPs, although 19 percent of all ESOPs control more than 25 percent of voting strength. These findings reveal another way that government policy has limited property rights in ESOPs: Before 1978, ESOPs were not required to own classes of stock with the best voting rights, so some employee-owned firms that bought such pre–1978 stock have nonvoting shares today. Further, because the IRS does not distinguish between a stock-bonus plan and a nonleveraged ESOP, it does not require voting shares in nonleveraged ESOPs.

The inevitable conclusion here is that the government, while not utterly opposing voting rights or employee involvement, has favored a worldview that endows employee ownership with few property rights. Admittedly, the issue of property rights is not straightforward in every case. Extensive (51 percent or more worker-owned) and nonextensive (1-to 50-percent worker-owned) ESOPs are difficult to address within the context of the same law. Certainly, the views of existing owners of closely held firms are understandable as well. Perhaps, when a retiring businessperson is selling his or her firm to the employees gradually, it would be reasonable not to allow voting on employee stock until the 51-percent mark is passed. Maybe ESOPs involving minimal employee ownership (less than 15 percent) should be viewed as retirement or benefit plans in which the ownership constitutes a trust investment. But the state makes no such distinctions. Nor does the ESOP Association, which favors eliminating the pass-through of voting rights on all issues in all closely held companies, even those that are or will soon be majority or totally worker owned. ESOP proponents in Congress simply adopted this position, in an instance of undue influence by an obviously self-interested organization.

The Responsibilities of Owners and Employees

When the U.S. Comptroller General's office studied ESOPs in 1980, it noted that "companies generally had not established formal means for allowing participants to communicate their desires, as stockholders, to management."[21] This raises the issue of who is responsible in a capitalist corporation.

Capitalism and the Corporation

Perhaps the main problem here is that an adequate theory of capitalism under democracy does not exist. Indeed, despite Milton Friedman's belief that the shareholders control the corporation and management are *their* employees—"in a free-enterprise private-property system, a corporate executive is an employee of the owners of the business"[22]— the corporation does not fit into democratic theory, as Carl Icahn describes:

When America built its economic leadership, managers were accountable to owners. . . . But as ownership got dispersed management became accountable to no one. . . . All this makes a modern chief executive much like a feudal baron. The top man, what's more, usually finds expanding his power more important than rewarding owners . . . . Bureaucracy has produced a corporate welfare state . . . . Senior management must be accountable to true owners. Corporate staffers must deal directly with workers on the line. My experience and other, similar experiments illustrate the dramatic improvement that occurs when management is accountable to ownership.[23]

What is the state's right to limit or define property rights in the service of democracy? Somehow, the law has been allowed to develop into an entity that supports limited property rights, yet its framers have never been forced to gather together and justify publicly all of the various arguments and ideological assumptions behind this law.

Nicholas Wolfson, author of *The Modern Corporation: Free Markets vs. Regulation,* has written that corporate law in the United States is based on the assumption that the publicly held corporation is a powerful ministate run by control groups requiring legal checks and balances and that the principal object of corporate law is to articulate a constitution to define and limit the power of senior management and the board of directors. In the thirties A. A. Berle and Gardiner Means had provided evidence in *The Corporation and Private Property* that 65 percent of companies and 85 percent of their combined wealth were controlled by management or by a legal device—for example, voting trusts or nonvoting stock—involving a small proportion of ownership. They had argued that this separation of ownership and control eliminated an important efficiency aspect of the enterprise, in accordance with Adam Smith's view that businesses should be managed by their owners. They had further claimed that shareholders' tenuous connections with their property meant that they had surrendered their right to have the corporation operated for their exclusive benefit. Berle and Means concluded that, as an "economic state," the modern corporation needed a constitution; this resulted in a series of corporate reform movements: SEC disclosure, independent directors, legal devices to increase shareholder democracy, and federal efforts to strengthen duty of care and loyalty concepts.[24]

Wolfson argues that these reform attempts have not succeeded and claims that shareholders want ownership separated from control so that management can use its control to maximize profits. He fears the result of these reforms will be some type of state control of corporations. But he does not offer an opinion about what should happen if the *employees* own part or all of a company and they are the shareholders, not outsiders. Should all property rights still be denied? Such a denial would appear to twist even Wolfson's view of capitalism.[25]

Capitalism and Takeover Battles

In fact, while employee ownership has been used in a number of takeover battles (see Table 3–4), it should not be seen as just another tool but more broadly as part of the struggle over corporate control.[26] Corporate raiders are reviving the issue of entrenched, irresponsible management. But frequently their assaults do not result in more efficient, entrepreneurial companies or prompt threatened firms to become more efficient and entrepreneurial in self-defense. Instead, they often lead to greenmail, protracted public drama, and a narrow fixation on the stock price of the target firm rather than the integrity of its operations or the relationship between the performance and rewards of management and workers. There are cases, however, where management is streamlined and made more accountable and even employees have an ownership stake, as Carl Icahn tried to do with TWA.

Frequently, management responds to a potential takeover by loading on mechanisms to make it impossible. These "shark repellants," which are plans to dilute voting rights or force certain harsh financial terms on raiders, or "golden parachutes," which are payoffs to management in case of a successful takeover, are the antithesis of shareholder democracy and efficient operations. Sometimes management saddles the firm with huge debt by designing recapitalization plans that offer bigger payoffs to existing shareholders than the raider can promise. Management will even use ESOPs to entrench itself.

None of these measures unites ownership and control in the corporation, making it a more responsible entity. Employee ownership and the design of a comprehensive program of labor-management problem solving, profit sharing, and flexible performance-based wages for both workers and managers, however, are one way to confront this problem. Various parties can initiate the process: (1) managers themselves seeking to restructure the company, who combine employee, management, and public ownership; (2) employees seeking to do the same but to replace existing management or completely or partially take over the company; (3) coalitions of large institutional or individual public shareholders working in concert with employees against or with current management; and (4) a raider offering a better plan for running the company. In any of these four scenarios, a well-planned employee-ownership program practically immunizes the firm from takeover while energetically reorganizing its operations. Institutional and even some farsighted individual shareholders prefer it to outrageous recapitalization schemes, even when these are accompanied by larger dividends. The Robertshaw and United Airlines cases (Chapters 3 and 4) are proof that such scenarios are no longer fantasy, although the mere appearance of employee ownership does not guarantee that the initiating parties will act responsibly.

Control in the Private Company

The situation is different with the closely held corporation, where a very subtle manipulation was necessary to defend a view of employee ownership encompassing limited property rights. No specific federal definition of this entity exists; its origins were outside the law. The law in this instance is more of a social charter, describing the norms and practices businesspeople and their lawyers have adopted over time. Various laws have been passed over the years to accommodate the perceived needs of the closely held corporation, but they do not follow a standard definition and can vary from state to state.[27] The following is one practitioner's description of the closely held firm:

[T]he term "close corporation" means a corporation whose shares are not generally traded in the securities markets. This definition seems to be most nearly in accord with the linguistic usages of the legal profession . . . . A close corporation typically has the following attributes: (1) the shareholders are few in number, often only two or three; (2) they usually live the same geographical area, know each other, and are well acquainted with each other's business skills; (3) all or most of the shareholders are active in the business, usually serving as directors or officers or as key men in some managerial capacity; and (4) there is no established market for the corporate stock, the shares not being listed on a stock exchange or actively dealt in by brokers; little or no trading takes place in the shares.[28]

The absence of a federal definition of the closely held firm and the bias in favor of management and existing owners in ESOP law work together to reverse these generally accepted social characteristics. When workers become the owners of a closely held corporation, the corporate-finance problem of the lack of an established market is solved, but the legal tradition is ignored. The law suddenly allows, encourages, and even protects the suspension of most the firm's unwritten tenets. Few ESOPs in closely held companies pursue even informal attempts at labor-management cooperation.

Legal scholars generally agree that a major advantage of the closely held corporation is the degree of mutual loyalty and flexibility among its members. Yet some have argued that more protection of minority shareholders is necessary. Some believe that the absence of an effective market for corporate control eliminates a check on inefficient management and that shareholders should be held to an even higher standard of fiduciary duty to each other to compensate for this. Rather than burdening the firm with bureaucracy and making it into a mine field of potential litigation, the solution might well be to emphasize this closely knit character. This would involve a change in the roles of labor and management that ESOP law would need to support more actively. In fact, the opposite is the case in ESOPs. Not only is self-dealing blatantly allowed, but the definition of the duty of the fiduciary and trustee is itself limiting because the fiduciary by law can consider the interests of the workers only as shareholders and beneficiaries, not as workers in the company.

The law's response to this problem is generally to regulate extreme financial misdealing while ignoring highly inequitable distribution of power or rewards. It does make a real effort to prevent such abuse, focusing primarily on cheating, stealing, self-profit, and the use of almost all of the tax incentives and allocations for highly compensated workers. But struggles for corporate control are also possible in these firms; employees and others may well discover how to buy blocks of such companies.

The Deregulation of the American Labor Law Tradition

One study of the ESOP lists eight necessary components of true ownership according to legal philosophers Lawrence Becker and A. M. Honore: (1) the right to possess something, to have exclusive physical control of it; (2) the right to use something, to derive pleasure from it; (3) the right to manage one's property, that is, to decide how it is used;

(4) the right to claim income; (5) the right to consume or destroy; (6) the right to modify, to effect changes less extensive than annihilation; (7) the right to alienate, to exchange or abandon ownership, and (8) the right to transmit, to give or bequeath property. Only the last right is absolute for a worker in an ESOP.[29]

Does it have to be this way? Are worker ownership and the goals ascribed to it by its framers best achieved by means of this particular structure of rights and definition of fairness? Obviously, if each of these rights were absolute for worker-owners—or indeed for any owners—most firms as we know them could not exist. The breadth of property rights in all companies is affected by the modern capitalist state. For example, the government has the authority to intervene in citizens' lives to modify these rights through the tax system.

It would, however, be equally irresponsible to limit the rights of property purely to further management's interests. Neither the strict protection of management's interests nor absolute worker control is the solution. At this point, one can only conclude that the ESOP now promotes a skewed definition of property rights in worker ownership.

Traditionally, U.S. labor law is conservative. Not exclusively pro-labor, it enforces a strict compromise of powersharing between the parties within the context of institutionalized conflict. Labor law scholar Karl Klare has analyzed the vision of the firm contained in U.S. labor law—a vision that attempts to preserve a social relationship between labor and management that alienates and separates them from each other and takes an approach to capitalism that stresses lack of worker participation in the broader capitalist enterprise.[30] In essence, labor law doles out property rights in the firm. Labor is allotted the power to curtail management's absolute control through the institution of collective bargaining. It is required to elect and run its organizations according to the principles of democracy and must represent the community of interests of its members fairly without being arbitrary, capricious, or discriminatory. Labor must abide by certain rules and agreements in its struggles with management. For its part, management is required to bargain in good faith with organized workers about a variety of issues. It cannot interfere in labor's right to organize itself and cannot dominate the union.

These limits on management's absolute right to manage were developed before the presence of sizable or even minimal employee ownership in the economy. Many contracts include management-rights clauses; management wants to be explicit about which of its rights are not to be infringed upon. As a counterbalance, the National Labor Relations Act protects workers' rights to self-organization, collective bargaining, and democratic procedures in constituting a labor organization. The state takes a central role in this compromise; these rights are government enforced, not self-enforced. In recent years, however, there has also been substantial growth of nonunion protections of workers based on their rights as individuals in business organizations.[31] Although created in tax-writing committees and purporting to deal primarily with tax issues, ESOP law, too, is labor law, with profound implications for the relationship between labor and management.

ESOPs do not take away workers' existing rights or prevent workers from organizing unions. However, the law neither mandates nor encourages minimal worker involvement when workers gain significant ownership of a firm by denying them a corresponding extension of property rights. ESOP law, in theory based on a belief in the value of ownership, in reality favors a structure that does not involve shared power and shared involvement in managing risk, but, rather, benevolent domination. This introduces a strange anomaly into the U.S. legal system—the ESOP falls between the cracks in federal law. When workers do not own part or all of their company, they are protected by federally enforced rights of self-organization to limit through unions management's absolute right to manage. When they do own part or even all of their company, they are guaranteed "financial fairness" but are almost completely at management's mercy regarding everything else. If workers in ESOPs do not choose to unionize, they lose the ability both as workers and as owners to limit management's absolute right to manage.[32] However, if workers do unionize, the union is prevented from representing them as owners on the grounds that it is an "outside organization." The law mainly recognizes the workers' adversarial role in this case.

When American labor law came into being, worker ownership of their own firms was not an option. The law was constructed to deal with the relationship between owners/managers who owned/managed and workers who worked for their wages. Recognizing that the laws relating to labor unions cannot necessarily be extended to employee ownership, the law has removed ESOPs from those protections. But instead of developing new approaches to address new circumstances, it has reverted to a pre-labor law ideology. Before ESOPs became well known and widespread, it was possible for the law to go unanalyzed.

But now that more and more workers own part, most, or even all of their companies and management and owners work with and sometimes "for" worker-shareholders, the contradictions within U.S. labor law and between U.S. labor law and ESOP law are becoming apparent.

The very occurrence of ESOPs strengthens the myth of the separation of management and labor. Only a small number of ESOPs involve unions, which often have limited rights when they are present. Scattered data suggest that about 20 percent of nontax-credit ESOP firms are unionized.[33] Unions are more prevalent in midsized (100 to 500 employees) ESOP firms. These unionized firms are twice as likely to have defined-benefit pension plans as nonunionized ESOP firms and tend to be majority owned. Most ESOPs, though, begin in nonunionized companies; where unions are present, they are usually excluded. However, the extent of employee ownership and the intensity of worker involvement in their ownership tend to be greater when management and unions are forced to adopt an ESOP because of worker buyouts, the need for wage concessions, or the restructuring of certain industries. Indeed, 16 percent of ESOPs with wage concessions had unions, as opposed to 3 percent without unions. One other exception is still strong. A sizable number of retiring small businesspeople are selling their businesses to all their employees, even when unions are present, and the departing owners do not seem to care how the firm is governed. The barriers to organizing unions even when workers want them and their continuing decline in nonagricultural private-sector firms are likely to aggravate further the general trend toward the unions' alienation from employee ownership.

In any case, the presence of a union in an ESOP provides workers with little opportunity for bargaining. An employer need not inform a union that he or she is going to establish an ESOP; as long as the employer has negotiated with the union in good faith about employee benefits, the issue need never be raised. Various decisions on cases before the National Labor Relations Board have established that the only mandatory subjects for collective bargaining in an ESOP are issues relating to compensation or the accumulation of credits that affect compensation: wages; vesting schedules; whether layoffs, strikes, and lockouts count as breaks in service; and whether the company alone may define this status. These issues are viewed by the board as deferred compensation and conditions of employment.[34]

The major case establishing this policy was an NLRB ruling on a non-ESOP employee stock-purchase plan by the Richfield Oil Corporation. The company complained that any union bargaining would allow the union "to interfere with matters solely within the province of management." The NLRB decided that the union's bargaining capability was strictly limited to compensation and the accumulation of various credits. While the union made no demands over other ownership-related issues, the board ruled this out explicitly:

On the occasion of stockholder meetings, corporate elections, or any other matter in which only stockholders have the right to be heard, *the union has no voice whatever as a statutory representative* [emphasis added]. It by no means follows that the effect of our decision here is to require the Respondent [the Company] to bargain with respect to its dividend, debt, and financial policies, simply because, as the dissenting opinion would have it, such matters are "relevant" to the establishment of a stock-purchase plan. Indeed, these factors are no less relevant where a union seeks to bargain about higher wages, pension plans, or profit-sharing plans, all of which have been held by this Board and by the courts to be mandatory subjects of collective bargaining. Yet, no one can seriously contend that these decisions have forced employers to bargain as to their dividend, debt, or financial policies.[35]

This decision was upheld by the District of Columbia Court of Appeals. Voting rights were not explored in that case, but there is no evidence that they have ever been considered a mandatory subject of collective bargaining. Because the law requires labor and management only to bargain in good faith about these limited issues, because these issues do not include defining who is eligible for participation and many other structural features of ESOPs, and because ESOPs have not been a priority in bargaining for union officials, it seems that it would be fairly easy to exclude unionized workers from ESOPs after relatively perfunctory bargaining.

The contradiction within ESOP law—as supported by relevant rulings of the NLRB—is summarized by Deborah Groban Olson, who has written the authoritative law article on the matter:

The concept of management rights, protected by labor law, protects the interests of the equityholders or stockholders from undue interference from labor. However, the balance of legal equities shifts when the majority of stockholders are employees represented by the union. Employees, as majority stockholders, should be able to enjoy the rights and privileges of majority stockholders . . . . Furthermore, in such a situation, the concept of management rights is not truly a protection of ownership or property rights. It is, in fact, a counterfeit argument aimed at giving managers rights in their capacity as managers that do not derive from property rights and thus are not legitimate for consideration in the balance struck by labor law between the rights of property and the rights to organize and bargain.[36]

The separation of management and labor is artificial—worker ownership throws together these two supposedly opposing interests in a new way, which the law and many National Labor Relations Board rulings do not recognize. In the current system, if a group of workers privately purchases with cash 51 percent of the stock of the closely held company where they work directly from a minority shareholder, they can control the company. If they buy 100 percent through a leveraged ESOP, they may find themselves controlled. Unionized and nonunionized workers must separately negotiate any issue related to the rights and responsibilities of their ownership. The unionized workers can get a modicum of representation only by organizing under an adversarial system and bargaining with management as if they do not own the company. Their bargaining rights specifically exclude the majority of ownership-related issues. The nonunionized workers are not protected as owners or as workers. They must become experts at juggling the moving parts to achieve even the most basic rights of private property.

Ignoring most forms of labor-management cooperation, the law does little to counterbalance this unmistakable bias. The federal labor law that predated ESOPs intensifies this split with its own contradictions. Labor law contains elements meant to create an adversarial relationship, such as barriers to union memberships on corporate boards and the ability of union officers to hold stock.[37] But most significant is a question that arose before the National Labor Relations Board concerning whether worker-stockholders who are also unionized are legally "employees" protected by the National Labor Relations Act. The basic principle is that a worker-stockholder is protected as a worker by labor law unless he or she has an "effective voice in management." In other words, if an employee-owner adds some characteristics of ownership to his or her role as a worker, the law removes employee protections.

For example, in the Mutual Rough Hat Company, worker-stockholders who were directors were held to be employees because corporate officers held all control and none of the other worker-stockholders could "participate in management conferences or determine management policy."[38] In the Everett Plywood and Door Corporation, all employees were stockholders and received equal pay. Supervisors assigned work, and the board of directors had discharge powers. Worker-stockholders could appeal such charges to the membership of the whole corporation, which could advise but not overrule the board.

The board decided that supervisors and employees who served on the board of directors could not be in the bargaining unit.

But the rulings on this controversy are mixed, reflecting the difficulty with which the law handles alterations of the social roles of labor and management. The board has counted worker-stockholders as non-employees; it has required worker-stockholders and workers who do not hold stock to belong to separate bargaining units; it has included both groups in the same bargaining unit. In one case, a group of worker-owners tried to decertify their union, and the union argued before the board that because "they control a substantial proportion of the outstanding stock and can effect management decisions," worker-owners who were union members should not be allowed to participate in the decertification vote.[39]

Certainly, part of this system stems from the need to prevent the same kind of self-dealing and Rube Goldberg manipulations of power on the part of unions in worker-owned firms that management has long enjoyed. Thus, when some workers are stockholders and others are not, if the worker-stockholders have created special employment preferences for themselves, the board has held that they must be completely excluded from any bargaining unit or form another bargaining unit. This rule of "effective voice in management" disqualifying union representation does not apply in 100-percent employee-owned firms, where the board says that workers can have the privileges and rights of both a stockholder and a worker. The implication is that workers can have protections when management and worker roles are polarized, but when workers have common interests with management, they must be separated from those who do not.

Essentially, the system of labor law, based on adversarial rights but limited responsibilities for workers in unionized firms, is inadequate to deal with the new roles that are emerging, which frustrates the potential for labor-management cooperation. This is now the focus of a Labor Department study.[40]

Yet these problems have not completely thwarted union involvement. Frequently, ESOPs are considered in the context of wage concessions or other bargaining issues, where the union's role is key, or attempted takeovers of the company by the union's members, as in the United Airlines case (see beginning of Chapter 4). Thus, unions have some means to negotiate about ESOP structure and take responsibility for their companies' futures, even though labor and ESOP law give them little assistance.

More significantly, large numbers of nonunionized firms have ESOPs, and workers in these companies are beginning to examine ESOP structure more closely. Some observers predict that, as employee ownership spreads throughout the American economy, unions may begin an organizing campaign focused on these firms, the goal of which will be to promote more worker understanding and involvement. This worries some ESOP enthusiasts who had hoped that employee ownership would help to eliminate unions—which it certainly will not do as long as it is combined with an ideology of management entrenchment.

An Ideology of Bureaucracy in American Law

One of the problems in examining the social phenomenon of the ESOP is that lawyers either claim that the workings of their craft are incomprehensible to nonprofessionals or assert that the law is an objective tool and hence outside the arena of interpretation and adjustment that such a review would promote. Consider the following syllogism: (1) Employee ownership is a good thing; (2) employee-ownership law is a special tool established by Congress to build employee ownership; (3) there are excellent, functioning examples of employee ownership in the country; (4) if we apply employee-ownership law carefully, the idea will work.

Only blind faith can accept these claims unquestioningly; a detailed structural analysis is necessary to prove or disprove them. Written into the law is a particular worldview. Only with reference to this ideology can the actual formation of employee ownership in this country be justified and understood. Without an understanding of the principles behind the law, the structure of ownership that it encourages appears utterly arbitrary. Harvard law professor Gerald Frug's *The Ideology of Bureaucracy in American Law*, which traces the ideology from which the conservative ESOP worldview flows, helps explain where the law has drawn support for its approach to employee ownership.[41] Frug suggests that corporate law should be viewed as an attempt to reconcile the individual with the bureaucratic group that affects his or her life. His analysis clarifies why the coresponsibility of labor and management in American corporations has received so little emphasis.

Max Weber's notion of bureaucracy required the hierarchical organization of the workforce, the separation of workers from shareholders, the separation of bureaucratic officials from ownership of the organizations they administer, and a permanent domination of the organization by the bureaucratic managers. Frug focuses on the relationship between the bureaucracy and the shareholders but suggests that his analysis can also be applied to the relationship between the bureaucracy and the workforce.

The argument begins with the notion that the bureaucratic way is the only way, that it furthers progress and is necessary for an advanced modern society. The goal of the bureaucracy is not only to make corporations run efficiently and deliver the goods; in addition, it must devise a way to protect the individual from domination in a liberal democratic society. The idea that bureaucracies involve tremendous power and that their constituents must be protected has a long history in American law. Frug enumerates four legal and social schools of thought for protecting the individual in the bureaucracy while securing the collective goals of the organization. Each seeks to limit a concentration of political and economic power that would permit unlimited management discretion against the interests of the shareholders they purport to serve. Elements of the controversies in the structure of ESOP law are apparent in each model.

The Formalist Model

The formalist model draws on the theories of Max Weber, Frederick Taylor, Ernst Freund, and A. A. Berle. It tries to limit the bureaucratic discretion of managers in order to ensure shareholder control of the bureaucracy. This model is very close to Milton Friedman's idea of the corporation: managers are servants of shareholders. It sees the bureaucracy as a disciplined machine intended to execute the wishes of the shareholders. Bureaucratic power is unthreatening because the wielders of this power—management—are controlled by the shareholders, who delegate it to management by way of the board of directors. The shareholders are freed by this system to have their own personal lives, to pursue their own goals with the comfortable assurance that the managerial bureaucracy is working for their best interests. There is also an equal opportunity to rise in the hierarchy of the bureaucracy. This approach reflects the agency theory, popularized by V. Morawetz and Robert Hessen.

The law, however, vests corporate power in the board of the directors, which undercuts the notion that the delegation is voluntary or that somehow the shareholders can exercise it themselves. Some scholars have claimed that the election of the directors would truly enforce shareholder control, but this has not been the case. These claims have been largely abandoned by corporate theorists because they do not reflect the realities of the corporation.

Another version of this model, trustee theory, portrayed the directors as fiduciaries who, although not amenable to shareholder control, serve shareholder interests. The fiduciary must (within limits) abide by the subjective desires of a beneficiary, not his or her own. This approach eliminates the illusion that shareholders actually control management or delegate power or that shareholder elections are a meaningful exercise of authority. Trustee theory was argued in the early 1930s by A. A. Berle. Within a few years, it went into a long decline, although it was somewhat revived in the sixties in a theory that identified shareholder interest with profit maximization.

Current ESOP law contains many elements of the formalist model, although it rejects outright the agency theory. Russell Long's assertion of a "common interest and incentive" between management and workers carefully skirts the issue of shared control. The ESOP relies heavily on traditional trustee theory to justify its version of management control. The law allows management to choose and dominate the trustees. By not binding management to any specific profit maximization in the ESOP, the law frees management and the trustees from the need to meet defined performance goals.

Employee ownership presents a unique problem for trustee theory, which is based on the assumption that shareholders are diffuse, inaccessible, and unknowledgeable about, or at least uninterested in, the business. It also considers that the shareholders' interests will be best served by the most efficient organization of employees possible. When the employees are the shareholders, these assumptions are no longer justified. In employee ownership, trustee theory promotes a twisted application of capitalism that deliberately limits the property rights of a specific group. The truth is that these shareholders may be quite knowledgeable and capable of contributing to efficient organization. However, what they have seen of production operations may have made them leery—their definition of efficiency may not resemble management's on all counts.

Frug correctly notes that the prospect of shareholder influence causes managers to worry about the introduction of arbitrary and uncontrollable desires that have no place in the bureaucracy. Certainly, the author has heard manager after manager echo this fear, as they transmute potential employee influence into the most threatening and inefficient kind of interference—at worst, total control by incompetent workers. Evidence suggests, however, that such apprehensions are mere fantasies, projected by people who must possess absolute control. It is simply untrue that employees with a say in their firms impede day-to-day operations. They do sometimes prevent corporate dictatorships.

The Expertise Model

The expertise model became the dominant corporate theory in America after the decline of formalism. It actually encourages the bureaucratic discretion of management by limiting the intervention of outsiders. It stresses the professional expertise of the manager as leader and sees the firm as a social system rather than a machine, "a natural community" that is built on loyalty rather than discipline and rules. Some proponents of this view are Philip Selznick, Chester Barnard, Elton Mayo, Peter Drucker, Douglas McGregor, Woodrow Wilson, and James Landis. They focus on the sociological issue of how organizations can foster the common pursuit of a common goal.

According to the expertise model, organizational success depends on creating a successful organizational personality. The manager's good judgment and professional competence are the basis of his or her leadership and serve to control any tendencies to abuse power. This manager is the "indispensable fulminator" who defines the goals of the organization and develops a strategy to achieve them. He or she does not exercise personal power over employees; instead, this manager leads, inspires, energizes, and catalyzes.

The model further states that decisions should be made by corporate insiders, who are the experts with the most competence and knowledge. This view is supported by the "business judgment rule" in corporate law, which protects management from the consequences of their decisions, as long as these are informed and free of arbitrariness or conflict of interest. A related "duty of care" principle commits the manager to act prudently and in the best interests of the corporation, while a "duty of loyalty" principle requires the manager to acknowledge that the interests of the corporation and the shareholders must take precedence over self-interest.

The problem with the expertise model is that it allows virtually complete discretion. It becomes difficult for managers to distinguish expertise from bias. Some scholars have recommended the use of outside experts or independent corporate directors to help corporate managers maintain impartiality, but often the familiarity of these same "outsiders" with corporate officials and their reliance on corporate staff undercut their objectivity. Some critics also claim that corporate managers encourage a mystique of expertise that may involve substantial pretense.

ESOP law relies heavily on this model, especially on its definition of management's role. The statement by one of Senator Long's former legislative assistants that workers in employee-owned companies are employees in the daytime and stockholders at night exemplifies this point of view.[42] Congressional hearings are replete with stories of the creative owner or manager who is using employee ownership to bind employee loyalty solely by means of cash, without any changes in corporate culture. Indeed, the book *Taking Stock* shows clearly that managerial leaders play a major role in employee-owned firms.[43] But the law makes no place for worker involvement in the management of business and strictly insulates the worker from participating in key decisions about starting, maintaining, or terminating the ESOP itself or providing input through an advisory committee, seats on the board, and so forth. Management can control the trustees—or even be trustees—and is self-policing in this process.

The use of closely tied trustees or experts came under fire repeatedly in the Labor and Treasury Departments' initial proposed regulations in 1975, the Joint Economic Committee's study in 1979, the U.S. Comptroller General's Report in 1980, and the Labor Department's harsh criticism of ESOPs in leveraged buyouts in 1986. The proxy statement of one proposed ESOP buyout, Raymond International, Inc., contained many outrageous examples of close relationships between management, the board, ESOP trustees, and financial experts and was singled out in an unusually critical article in the *Wall Street Journal*.[44]

Again, employee ownership poses special problems for this model of the corporation, because employee-owners may in fact be knowledgeable insiders who are amply qualified to work with management to improve the company.

The Judicial-Review Model

This model has emerged in reaction to the excesses of the expertise approach. It questions whether constituent control or managerial expertise can limit the exercise of bureaucratic power and recommends the threat of review, actual review, or even the interference of the courts as the solution. Scholars promoting this approach include Felix Frankfurter, Lon Fuller, Louis Jaffe, and Kenneth Culp Davis. The model avers that no form of social organization can be self-policing but suggests that serious abuse can be prevented by the rule of law and the dispassionate involvement of judges.

Obviously, the problem here is where to draw the line between the role of the bureaucracy and the role of the courts. Frug observes that this model has not worked because the courts have been concerned that interference might diminish the efficiency with which corporate bureaucracies function. Courts also do not have the experience, information, and intimacy with a company's workings that are vital to making valid business decisions. They lack the resources to become involved in every case; at most, they issue abstract warnings. Frug claims that the practice of letting the facts of each case speak for themselves has led to contradictory decisions. Courts will actually defend various versions of the formalist or expertise models and have sometimes created even greater roles for experts in the organization, who then take over the courts' role as arbiter. The courts will also often retreat into procedure when they have trouble deciding whether or not to intervene. Indeed, the lengthy process of distinguishing between legal and illegal activity contributes to unfettered corporate bureaucratic power.

In ESOPs the judicial model can be perceived in the appointment of independent trustees as a result of court cases and the Labor Department's opinions on the use of experts and trustees. Sometimes the courts have mandated widespread worker participation in the bureaucratic process and urged performance-based rewards for both workers and managers to resolve the problem. As mentioned, Labor has looked carefully at some large highly publicized ESOP-leveraged buyouts and plays a quasijudicial role in reviewing ESOPs, as do the IRS and, to a lesser extent, the NLRB.

Judicial-review theorists do not suggest that intervention in every case is realistic or even possible. Some recommend stronger bureaucratic procedures as a solution, and this seems to be the direction in which the Department of Labor wishes to move in its courtlike regulatory role with ESOPs. Congress, however, continues to oppose restrictions on ESOPs.

The judicial-review method is least useful in the many cases that are inconsequential. Workers are often unaware of their rights, and unions, if present, are uninterested or uninformed. Often the law is so promanagement that it does not acknowledge grounds for a case.

A variety of suits are likely to occur until worker rights in ESOPs are clarified in detail by the courts or Congress. Because of the structure of

ESOP ownership, it is not clear whether workers can bring derivative suits against the company. There is, however, increasing evidence that some law firms and ESOP experts are recommending more influence for workers in ESOPs mainly to prevent possible court problems. In any regard, ESOP lawsuits are definitely on the rise, and the Hall-Mark Electronics example (see the beginning of Chapter 5) is cited more and more frequently in the press.

Management may begin to turn increasingly to experts and "independent directors" to forestall charges of self-interest that might lead to the courts. This would, in Frug's terms, affirm the free-enterprise system as we know it while restraining it, "reinvigorate capitalism and correct its excesses" by replacing one elite with another. Frug emphasizes that this alternative overlooks a sensible and natural check on bureaucratic power: the people affected by it. Surely, in companies where workers are stockholders, this option suggests itself even more strongly. More worker responsibility for problem solving and more labor-management collaboration in sizably, majority, or fully employee-owned firms would be preferable to regulations and court cases alone. But Frug says that, although judicial-review theorists accept the democratic process as desirable, they do not see it as a way to operate social organizations; rather, it is a means of choosing among competing elites for leadership. He suggests that each compromise between democracy and elitism worked out by judicial-review theorists has contained the same contradictions. This raises the possibility of increased worker participation as an alternative response to the structural problems of ESOPs.

The Market/Pluralist Model

This model was popularized by liberal democrats and members of the Chicago school. It claims that corporate structures are legitimate because of a political or market mechanism within them that allows individuals to express themselves about how the bureaucracy should operate. It questions whether bureaucracy alone can balance subjective individual interests and objective collective interests harmoniously. This doubt is key, given that the policing function in this model depends on modifications to the bureaucratic form of social organization, rather than the judiciary. The market and the pluralist versions shall each be reviewed separately here.

The market version claims that individuals can express their preferences through the market. Corporate abuse of power is not a concern since shareholders can simply sell their stock if they dislike what management is doing, and this exit provides adequate protection. One problem with this theory is whether shareholder attitudes toward the corporation can be reduced to buying and selling. Another problem is that many shareholders do not directly control their shares and hence have no legal authority to control their preferences. In closely held firms there may not even be a market where those preferences can be expressed. Finally, it is unclear if exit can prevent managerial domination; it may in fact encourage it. These objections are relevant in light of the Reagan administration's suggestion that easy exit might be the solution to the ESOP quandary.

One sophisticated version of this model contends that the "market in corporate control" allows shareholders to discipline management. It was first developed by Henry Manne and is now popular among conservative law-and-economics scholars. This view holds that shareholders want to maximize profit, but managers, who frequently do not directly benefit if they work hard, often frustrate this desire by slacking off. The conflict between managers' lack of incentive and shareholders' desire for more money is overcome by the threat of a takeover or an actual takeover that can improve management's productivity or replace it. This approach to outside takeover is often unrealistic in closely held companies and offers no way for minority shareholders to express their desires, but the Robertshaw and United Airlines cases (see Chapters 3 and 4) suggest that it is a direction that employee ownership is taking in publicly held corporations. Many scholars believe that this model actually promotes takeovers and favors acquiring companies. What has emerged is an argument about whether corporate law should protect the defending or the acquiring managers.

The disadvantages of takeovers as a solution to excessive management control are exacerbated in a firm partially or fully owned by its employees. Not only may there be no market for the stock, but management may actively desire both worker ownership and worker passivity while it maximizes profits that it allots to itself through salaries, special stock options, and so on. Individual exit in this situation diminishes the collective worker stake—and thus the collective worker voice—while the individual reverts to being a mere employee, with no stake or voice at all. Also, worker ownership has been put to an unforeseen use by existing managers, who can entrench their positions vis-à-vis acquiring managers by using the ESOP to remove stock quickly from a public market or a group of closely held shareholders to the control of its trustees. So, ironically, the ESOP without worker influence can actually serve as a superior tool for protecting management. Management can propose to use worker's assets, control the firm, and arrange substantial personal profits without having to reach specific performance goals. Indeed, when a departing owner sells the firm to the workers, existing management may be both the acquiring and the acquired group by virtue of the way both initiative and power are structured in the ESOP.

This intellectual tradition was clearly behind the Reagan administration's abortive ESOP recommendations in 1986. The proposals would have justly provided traditional characteristics of ownership, such as voting and rights to dividends, but would have mistakenly allowed the worker to sell shares back to the company within three years. Turning a worker-owned firm into a totally free market would destroy the chances of stable ongoing investment of employee equity and renewed commitment and interest that would facilitate labor-management cooperation.

The market theorists are telling the workers, "You get to vote your stock and receive dividends and, if you don't like that, you must exit." Their model does not seek to alter the essential role of management or labor but tries only to assure attainment of the formal goal of profit maximization. It goes beyond the traditional ideology behind the structure of ESOP law by admitting that workers are active owners and investors, not passive beneficiaries of free gifts. But, as noted, depending on the circumstances in a particular ESOP company, voting rights may or may not present an opportunity for real participation. In fact, this view does not go far enough and still denies workers the practical influence commensurate with their ownership.

The pluralist version says that all people affected by a corporation—employees, customers, neighbors, shareholders—comprise a variety of interest groups that form the constituency to which management owes allegiance. Proponents of this theory wish to inject interest-group politics into corporate decisionmaking. For example, the board of directors might include representatives of the various groups.

This model is based on a radical rejection of expertise. The firm is transformed into a kind of parliament. Pluralist theorists have not succeeded in having their ideas adopted by the legal system; they have simply suggested that interest-group representatives be corporate directors. One controversy about the model's workability has been over conflicts these directors might experience between allegiance to the interest group and to the corporation as a whole. Also, it would be impossible for everyone affected to serve on the board so some criteria to determine eligibility would have to be established. Another issue is whether the outcome of interest-group conflict would be a fair means to arrive at decisions—perhaps the results of such conflicts would be distorted by the varying power of different groups.

The pluralist version's impact on the ESOP phenomenon can be seen in the frequency with which including a worker on the board is viewed as the solution to management entrenchment in worker-owned firms. While the pluralist model seeks to capitalize on its appeal to a democratic process in companies, its lofty promises frequently get reduced to appointing one representative to the board, instead of developing a system of practical labor-management cooperation to solve problems of strategic importance to the firm's performance. Even in this limited application, the model has provided effective ammunition for legislators and businesspeople who oppose any major changes in power in ESOPs as leading inevitably to worker assemblies running and ruining companies.

Frug concludes that none of these models envisions an alternative to the Weberian bureaucracy. Each rejects the classical idea of active popular participation in social decisionmaking. Each tries to assure us that it removes the threat of misused power, but the instruments of their defenses are artificial legal arguments, contradictions, and spurious tests and principles that essentially retain the problem they are trying to solve.

Conclusion

Employee ownership not only provides flimsy and minimal protection of workers' rights, it does not encourage managers and workers to embrace the responsibilties of worker-owners. This state of affairs must be attributed to a twisted view of the corporation and a market for corporate control that benefit entrenched management and irresponsible speculators. As America is threatened by its lack of competitiveness, the sad fact is that labor, management, and government often seem equally committed to ascribed, rather than earned, status and rewards, and ESOP law is only one reflection of this conflict. Finding ways to involve workers more in their companies is not just a matter of philosophy—as *Fortune* magazine has noted, "today's workplace is filled with sophisticated machinery and it is increasingly organized to make workers responsible for what they do."[45]

Chapter 7

Labor-Management Cooperation

O & O Supermarkets are a group of unionized worker-owned stores in Philadelphia. Organized by the Philadelphia Association for Cooperative Enterprise (PACE), the stores conduct extensive training and education programs stressing cooperation. Workers participate in ad hoc committees, attend employee meetings, are encouraged to suggest ways to improve service and performance, and share in profits.[1]

Max O. DePree, CEO of Herman Miller, Inc., a nonunion office-furniture manufacturer in Zeeland, Minnesota, espouses "inclusive capitalism in the firm by giving more than a few people meaningful involvement in running the company and sharing in the results." The company has sizable employee ownership through a profit-sharing plan, an employee stock-purchase program, and a Scanlon Plan where employees meet monthly to discuss how to improve their performance and then share in the results if measurable goals are attained. Problem-solving teams have worked to cut costs, slash delivery times, and penetrate new markets.[2]

Republic Container in Nitro, West Virginia, was an LTV spinoff of a successful division to its sixty-six employees. The Steelworkers' local union worked with Deborah Groban Olson of the Michigan Employee Ownership Center to create a participatory company. The entire workforce helped plan the buyout, which included some minor concessions. The worker-elected board includes representatives from management, the local union, and the lenders, plus two outside directors and one nonvoting member from the United Steelworkers.[3]

Quad/Graphics, Inc., of Pewaukee, Wisconsin, is a 20-percent employee-owned nonunion printing firm that produces 100 different national magazines. Each new employee gets on-the-job training and formal courses in a trust-oriented, problem-solving approach to the profession. Communication is stressed, while bureaucracy and the usual work rules of union shops get short shrift. All employees receive annual bonuses tied to profits, typically 10 to 12 percent of salary, with an additional 8 or 9 percent contributed to the ESOP.[4]

Labor-management cooperation may be a strategy to deal with increased competition, a changing workforce, and insufficient involvement of employees in their companies. Competition is on the rise globally and extends to the inner workings of business. Post-industrial societies are now vying for superior labor-management cooperation, and in this country both sides of that equation are being faulted for their failure to improve relations. The tremendous anxiety in the United States about Japanese management, the abundance of new "quick-fix" approaches to business success, and news of trade deficits and waning productivity are all signs of this increased competition.

Obviously, drastically lower wages, protectionist legislation, substantial decreases in corporate taxes, heavily reduced energy costs, wage and price controls, or radically increased automation could improve the performance of American business without disturbing the status quo of labor-management relations. Because these alternatives are either politically or economically unfeasible, however, each of these solutions seems unlikely. In any case, most individuals prefer cooperation over competition as long as it does not dramatically alter other aspects of their lives.

More and more, demographers are talking about a new class of workers, better educated and more actively resentful of a lack of involvement and fairness. The research firm of Yankelovich, Skelley and White says that these workers, who made up 40 percent of the workforce in 1980, are divided into two groups:

One new class group dislikes formal job structures and rejects money as a substitute for fulfillment; the primary objective of the second group is to earn money not for the sake of money but to buy a certain lifestyle. Once that is achieved this group tends to hold back on the job.[5]

As mentioned in Chapter 1, Senator Long felt employee ownership could respond to the crisis of labor and management in the United States. He cited a 1980 Gallup poll finding that 84 percent of those surveyed said they would worker harder and better if they were involved in decisionmaking. However only 9 percent felt that they, the workers, would benefit from any improvements; most assumed that the beneficiaries would be others—consumers, stockholders, managers. In the seventies, Lou Harris conducted a poll for the National Commission on Productivity and found that over 70 percent of hourly wage earners felt that management and stockholders benefitted a great deal from increased productivity while less than 20 percent felt that the workers themselves benefitted. In 1982 the Public Agenda Foundation researched what individuals think about their possible contributions to their jobs. Seventy-eight percent said they have an inner need to do the very best job regardless of pay, but only 16 percent said they were doing the best job possible. Eighty-eight percent responded that they had control over the quality of work they performed. A mere 7 percent thought of work as a business transaction in which one regulates effort according to the size of the paycheck.[6]

As we have seen, the actions of the federal government have a powerful effect on how labor and management interact in the workplace. Many experimental approaches to work were explored in this country in the early seventies. The ESOP, however, merits particular attention because in its case the tax system was essentially paying labor and management to take part in the experiment.

Cooperation Between Labor and Capital

Keith Bradley of the London School of Economics notes that under a nonworker-owned system the interests of various parties are diverse: Owners and shareholders want profitability; managers want job security, good pay, and high status, which they may not consider to be related to profits; employees want job security and, within that context, a variety of private objectives.[7] Worker ownership seeks to eliminate the basic capital-labor conflict by making the employee a representative of both and to reduce conflicts between labor and management at every level of the company through the promotion of common interest and joint effort. The words "at every level" are revealing—in addition to the strict divisions between management and labor, which are maintained in employee ownership by the structural features of the ESOP and related law, there are many other layers of hierarchy within any organization: Middle management is managed by upper management; supervisors are managed by middle management; some workers have higher status than others. Workers may feel "managed" by a union bureaucracy or a tradition-ridden informal hierarchy unrelated to unions. Upper management may or may not feel itself to be under the supervisory authority of the board, various stockholders or major owners, and bankers/investors. Corporate organization expert Rosabeth Moss Kanter has proven that the structure of corporations affects all individuals in subordinate positions and that middle management's power over lower employees does not eliminate their own requirements for involvement and commitment.[8]

The theory of labor-management cooperation is based on the notion that that, given an opportunity, the workforce could understand the market, collect product or service information, analyze relationships between the use of a product or service and consumers' needs, improve quality, evaluate production processes or the delivery of a service, help solve the problems that emerge, and even monitor coworkers and managers. John Dunlop, Harvard economist and former secretary of labor, although critical of naive conceptions of employee ownership and participation, has suggested that tapping this source could conceivably improve productivity by 50 percent in many worksites.[9] Wages alone are not sufficient to release this potential.

Table 7–1 suggests a variety of activities that might be involved in cooperation. Each activity can also be classified according to the levels of the organization where it takes place, the range of issues it addresses, the degree of control it puts in the hands of the participants, and the reasons for its institution. Labor and management may cooperate in production but not in the office, or on the board of directors but not on the shop floor. Certain departments, such as marketing or shipping, may be specifically targeted for cooperation. The issues addressed might range from immediate, individual concerns—physical working conditions and the like—to more distant and complex problems, such as the raising of capital. Authority may be limited to making suggestions or extend to include the right to get information and influence decisions, to work in tandem with management, or even to have full control.

Table 7–1.   Types of Labor-Management Cooperation.

These categories, illustrating the spectrum of labor-management cooperation in a company, range from more informal, less substantial forms of labor-management cooperation to intense collaboration by both labor and management in all aspects of company policy and practices. In many cases, although not always, more advanced forms of cooperation will incorporate the more basic approaches.

Table 7–1.   (continued)

Mutual Awareness

   Access to information
   Relating company objectives to individual departments
   Increasing common social activities and community involvement
   Surveys of employee attitudes
   Open-door policies and frequent meetings with management
   Setting employee goals
   Suggestion systems
   Employee appraisal and feedback
   Formal or informal training and instruction

Flexibility

   Structuring physical space of plant and office
   Personalized work hours
   Scheduling workflow
   Training managers and workers in participatory approaches
   Job rotation
   Job enlargement and enrichment
   Putting blue-collar workers on salary

Problem Solving

   Quality circles at departmental level
   Task forces
   Labor advisory groups
   Individual training in specific work areas in problem-solving skills
      and use of sophisticated information

Close Cooperation

   Companywide quality circles (QC) or labor-management committees (LMC)
   Steering committee for QCs and LMCs
   Formation of internal consulting group to train workers and managers in
      problem solving and cooperation
   Companywide training in cooperative and problem-solving skills
   Companywide task forces on strategic issues
   Employee representatives on board of directors
   Forms of gainsharing

Joint Control

   Majority employee ownership of firm
   Employee election of board of directors
   Worker-selected managers or supervisors
   General employee meetings and problem-oriented subcommittees

   A mandate for increasing cooperation may be imposed from above
by labor or management, or all relevant internal subgroups may jointly

decide to design and plan the program and process of cooperation. The reason for seeking to increase cooperation may be instrumental, philosophical, or both. If instrumental, cooperation is chosen to improve the performance of the firm directly or to influence factors that will improve performance. If philosophical, cooperation is chosen to uphold the dignity of the individual employee, improve relations, and foster a more humane working environment.

Firm performance and even cooperation do not necessarily improve in step with the institution of each type of labor-management cooperation listed in Table 7–1, and, regardless of the reasons for pursuing cooperation, the frequently opposing interests of efficiency and rights must be balanced. The instrumental motive will initiate and terminate any cooperative program based on the bottom line. Yet the bottom line can be variously defined—in terms of measurable improvements in productivity or profitability, changes in labor relations that do not directly affect production but help profitability in the long run (reductions in turnover, tardiness, absenteeism, health-care costs, or grievances), or modifications in production that have no immediate effect on productivity and profitability (improved quality and design). What is good for the bottom line may be quite different for different people—management might favor innovations in automation, while labor looks for improved employment and job security.

Nevertheless, quality-circle expert Edward Cohen-Rosenthal has argued that idealism alone cannot be the motive; expenses and income must also be taken into account. Employee-involvement programs are often complex and roundabout cost-containment efforts with little emphasis on larger organizational issues, such as improving market position, product development, customer service, and investment opportunities and plans. Cohen-Rosenthal claims that the world's best quality circle is no substitute for demand, an intact distribution network, or proper advertising. A strategy of labor-management cooperation that focuses on costs alone may carefully and cooperatively speed a firm's decline.[10] The bottom-line motive alone, the most conservative reason to promote labor-management cooperation, may in fact be inefficient and shortsighted in its failure to recognize the wider philosophical possibilities. A sincere, ongoing commitment to cooperation will continually search out human-resource solutions to bottom-line problems.

An observer, manager, or worker can quickly assess the character of labor-management cooperation at a worksite by asking what kinds of cooperation exist dealing with which issues at what levels with what degrees of control based on what motives. Unfortunately, despite what messiahs of the New Corporation proclaim in popular books, successful labor-management cooperation is not a simple matter of identifying what is missing and quickly developing it.

A recent New York Stock Exchange study examined the diffusion of many of the varieties of labor-management cooperation in U.S. industry. In brief, the study found that the types of cooperation involving mutual awareness and flexibility are most prevalent, and those that stress problem solving, cooperation, and joint control are the least common. Generally, the larger the corporation, the more experimentation takes place.[11] Let's look at two extreme perspectives on cooperation, each characterized by a preoccupation with who dominates rather than how to get the best results.

An extreme worker-control perspective might argue that employee rights and control are the exclusive criteria for judging a system of labor-management cooperation. In this system efficiency is viewed as a by-product of control and often unworthy of independent assessment. This point of view is really a reaction-formation (in Freud's terminology) against the oligarchical views of many managers; there is no evidence that workers actually desire the complete elimination of management or the management function. This extreme view also conveniently dismisses the complexities of designing a realistic system of cooperation. It does not recognize the impracticability of cooperation at all levels, on all issues, with maximum day-to-day power for all employees and rejects the need for careful partitioning of rights and control both between labor and management and among the various levels of labor and management. It ignores the fact that even in a liberal system some "workers" will have more management functions than others, just as some "managers" will have more routine functions than others.

This view's main effect is to upset and threaten management. As such, it is not a practical program. Managers and politicians and workers—some trade unionists among them—who oppose cooperation between labor and capital cite this extreme scenario as evidence that worker control would transform an imperfect but working system into total chaos.

The opposite point of view espouses absolute control by management or dominant owners. In this system, labor and management would cooperate only enough to ensure an efficient business where management's control would be unquestionable and unshakable. Yet, in practical terms, it is not certain that a business could continue to meet the challenges of a rapidly changing world and marketplace if it denied itself access to the useful knowledge of many of its members. Can an overauthoritarian management avoid blocking the creativity of other managers and all employees?

This view, too, has a psychological basis. It is a projection of management's fear of the uncooperative, uncaring, dishonest, and incompetent employee. Proponents of this extreme perspective use it to explain why even small experiments in cooperation must be tightly controlled. Opponents of this view—workers, labor leaders, and even some other managers—find it a handy scapegoat and point to it in arguments that cooperation will merely lead to more power for management by reducing labor's right to fight.

These extreme attitudes are responsible for much of the opposition to labor-management cooperation in America. The truth is, however, that as much as management and labor blame each other for the problems, in the end both fear change and loss of familiar status, position, and structure. A look at two working systems of labor-management cooperation—the Mondragon industrial cooperatives in the Basque Autonomous Region of Spain and the kibbutzim in Israel—suggests that a breakdown of the business system itself is not a likely outcome of cooperation. Obviously, neither of these systems could be transplanted as is to the United States, but each is an illuminating example of how differently relations between labor and management can be approached and incentives and assets can be organized. Both may provide insight into how firm cooperation could be restructured in this country.

Mondragon: A Labor-Management Partnership

In 1956 a Catholic priest, Jose Maria Arizmendi, rejected the extremes of Smith and Marx and founded the Mondragon system, which now comprises eighty industrial cooperatives that are completely employee owned by their 18,000 members. The cooperatives produce machine tools, refrigerators, kitchen appliances, electronic and electrical devices, plastics, and some agricultural produce. The cooperative conglomerate has an Entrepreneurial Division that helps members and prospective members prepare detailed business proposals and plans and choose competent management for new cooperatives. Each firm provides a steady flow of financial data by computer to this division, which monitors the bottom line, exercises accounting authority, oversees the performance of management, and supplies a range of professional services to the businesses. The Caja Laboral Popular savings bank, with modern branches and automatic tellers throughout Basque cities and towns, collects deposits from over 300,000 customer accounts. The bank provides a health-care and social-security system for the employee-members, who are considered self-employed by Spanish law, and their families. It also runs an engineering college and a combination cooperative factory/vocational school.

Internally, the cooperative is structured similarly to a corporation. All workers in a general assembly elect the board of directors on a one-person/one-vote basis, and the board then selects trained managers from among the workers or hires outside management. The general manager attends board meetings but has no vote. A management council of workers provides advice in monthly consultation meetings. A social council, made up of one representative for every ten workers, advises management on social and personnel matters. Wages, considered to be an advance on profits, are figured at a rate slightly greater than that of surrounding industry. The most highly paid manager does not get more than four-and-a-half times the salary of the least paid worker in a company. Individual salaries are further calculated according to an evaluation, based on a point scale, of skills, responsibilities, attitudes, and the nature of the work itself. In addition to wages, each worker receives an annual profit distribution. The conglomerate strives to maintain solidarity by standardizing average earnings in its member companies.

To join, employees must make a contribution, which can be borrowed from the cooperative and/or deducted from weekly income. This investment is usually a year's salary and does not escalate with the value of the company, as is usual in many other cooperatives. Up to 70 percent of net profits are distributed annually to individual worker accounts. A social fund is given 10 percent to support the surrounding community. The balance goes into a collective reserve. Unlike many failed cooperatives throughout history—and like the ESOP—the firm retains individual employees' account capital for use in investment. Workers are paid a fixed rate of interest yearly for essentially "loaning" this money to the business, and their accounts are revaluated annually to correct for changing economic conditions. This capital account cannot be sold, and departing employees can be fined up to 30 percent of their accumulated profits. Rather than using unemployment insurance when an individual cooperative fails, even though the system has its own unemployment fund that provides 80 percent of salary, the conglomerate attempts to expand business and increase capital investments by retraining employees and establishing new businesses. Mondragon is export oriented, and its productivity and profitability equal or exceed those of comparable companies.

The firm is committed to providing employment to the surrounding towns. Local worker ownership protects this commitment from capital flight. Management retains its executive function; only the source of its power and the degree of performance evaluation are altered drastically. Evidence indicates that managers who do not perform are frequently replaced. Sometimes the Entrepreneurial Division steps in if the numbers on their computer screens suggest something is awry. This system of labor relations relies primarily on close cooperation, control, and mutual awareness. Mondragon has not widely used problem-solving groups, quality circles, or redesign of the workplace. Indeed, compared to employees in similar firms, Mondragon workers feel quite inhibited about expressing opinions and do not consider that they participate greatly in important decisions. They report they have just as much supervision as comparable workers but also expend substantial energy in informal monitoring of their coworkers. Workers and managers have a high degree of trust in each other; each group is confident that the other respects its interests. Much of this is due to the emphasis on equality—all members, workers and managers, are copartners, although Mondragon has been faulted for substantial sexual inequality. Mondragon's cooperation predominantly concentrates on creating a work environment that involves the careful selection of workers and member participation in setting overall company policy on incomes and discipline.[12]

The Kibbutz: A Labor-Management Community

Unlike Mondragon, the kibbutz integrates the workplace with the neighborhood. A kibbutz is essentially a small town that employs all its residents in owning and running social services or profit-making businesses located in the community. There are about 300 such communities in Israel, founded from 1910 to the present, with an average population of about 500 adults. Kibbutzim have developed a unique system of industrial relations. Each community may have from ten to twenty business branches, now split fairly evenly between capital-intensive industry and capital-intensive agriculture. Kibbutzim supply about 6 percent of the country's industrial output and 40 percent of its agricultural output and comprise 3.3 percent of the population. Decades of research indicate that the kibbutzim's industry and agriculture have adapted remarkably to Israel's high-powered economic development and hyperinflation, remaining competitive with and even surpassing comparable non-kibbutz firms in most periods.

All the members of a kibbutz "own" and control the businesses and assets through a weekly town meeting and through various subcommittees. However, the whole enterprise is considered a trust for existing members and future generations of participants. Assets cannot be sold and divided up by existing members, although departing members receive severance pay. There is no capital contribution upon entry.

Each individual business branch has a coordinator (manager), an assembly of workers, and often a management board. The management board handles technical problems. The worker assembly, or team in smaller branches, determines production plans, work schedules, the choice of candidates for training, and the selection of various plant officials. This assembly also chooses the managers of all the community businesses and sends out various individuals for professional training. Managers serve for three to four years to prevent the emergence of an elite and provide a continual source of new skills and insight for the business. One study of twenty-seven kibbutz factories found that 34 percent of the members were managers or supervisors, 48 percent had been in such positions and were not rank-and-file workers, and 18 percent had never held such a position. Kibbutz factories, service businesses, and agricultural branches tend toward small size, high investment in human capital, professionalization of the "worker," and sophisticated technology.[13]

All managers in a given firm are drawn from the workforce or from members of the community and trained internally. Notably, managers receive no special monetary rewards; indeed, throughout the kibbutz, rights to economic resources are never allotted according to occupation (i.e., doctors and garbage collectors receive different training and equipment, but their economic rewards, housing, etc., are the same).

Kibbutz federations provide planning, technical, and banking assistance, similar to Mondragon's Caja, although they are more consultative than authoritative in the naming of management. These federations play an important role in developing and improving general social and educational conditions in the member communities. They also run teacher-training colleges, schools of management, and regional high schools.

Instead of wages, kibbutzim have a flexible system of rights and accounts. Every adult member has an equal right to housing, health care, employment, education of his or her children in a cooperative school, community child care, food, meals, occupational training and higher education, social security through old age (members also pay into the national social-security system), access to a community car pool, unlimited public transportation throughout the country, a paid vacation, and expenses for cultural activities. Interestingly, all kibbutz members belong to the worker-owned division of the General Federation of Labor (the Israeli version of the AFL-CIO). They share in the union's mutual-aid projects, but individual kibbutz communities and firms do not maintain chapters. The union provides health care. Finally, each member gets a cash account for additional individual needs. Members are proscribed from starting businesses outside of the worker-owned context, but entrepreneurial initiative is encouraged throughout the federations and the businesses.

The kibbutz is clearly the purest example of labor-capital identification in any democratic country, and it would be too extreme for the United States, although it can teach us some lessons. Despite all attempts to eliminate the effects of hierarchy, management retains an unmistakable executive role, and evidence indicates that managers experience greater opportunities for self-realization, job satisfaction, and influence. The kibbutz emphasizes mutual awareness, flexibility, close cooperation, and control but has been surprisingly slow to develop quality circles and active problem-solving groups or to reorganize work in industry and the communities' social-service branches. Much of the participation takes place informally. However, strong conclusive evidence suggests that the kibbutz is increasingly accountable to the various participatory structures in both the community and the enterprises that monitor its affairs, since most individual members do not attend the weekly kibbutz town meeting in large numbers unless a particularly controversial issue is on the agenda. Much is worked out in small focused committees. The community character of the kibbutz leads to powerful mutual identification among members and with the economic-social community as a whole rather than with individual roles. Men and women both work, but there is clear evidence of unmistakable sexual hierarchy throughout most of the community's institutions.[14]

A Baseline for Our Expectations

These two examples reformulate labor-management relations dramatically, while avoiding the radical worker-control model and the extreme management-domination model. Indeed, they prove that management's fear of business disintegration or management mauling is unfounded. Once that fear is debunked, the justification for the management-domination model disappears. That model exists in business because some people want to protect their existing status and rewards, not because it is required for efficiency. Workers do not want to participate in every decision at every level of an organization.

Ironically, an examination of the most participatory industrial-relations systems in the world leads to an uncomfortable conclusion for proponents of extreme worker control: Cooperation and consensus, not control of one party by the other, seem to be key. In fact, kibbutz workers do not consider the workers' assembly to be the most salient aspect of their participation. The "pure" democracy involved in complete worker control is not what workers desire—even those in "pure" systems that might be able to achieve it. One of the abiding generalizations of worldwide research on the reorganization of the workplace is that participation in higher-level bodies such as general assemblies and corporate boards creates very little opportunity for participation by the average worker, who much prefers less elevated, but more practical, realistic, and immediate approaches to cooperation. In fact, keen inside observers of both Mondragon and the kibbutz fault both systems for stressing upper-level bodies of control over quality circles and problem-solving groups. This is also true of various European experiments—for example, the codetermination experiment in West Germany, where workers serve on management boards by law, and the self-management experiment in Yugoslavia, where the state has legislated that general assemblies of workers must elect councils that choose management and decide on a number of issues. One observer has even suggested that the strong identification of labor with management in Mondragon actually reduces demands for work reform.[15]

Patterns of Cooperation in ESOPs

One of the great claims for employee ownership is that worker-owners will tackle their jobs with new enthusiasm and energy, productivity and profitability will burgeon, and the United States will regain its position as a real contender in the global struggle for competitive superiority. Yet ownership alone does not spur workers to greater job commitment and motivation; a vigorous program to foster employee involvement is an essential corollary. Without that involvement, it is impossible to establish whether it leads to measurable increases in productivity and profitability. Our first task, then, must be to determine just how much labor-management cooperation is to be found in ESOPs. We will limit ourselves to an overview of majority employee-owned firms, where any changes will be most apparent; since tax-credit ESOPs so rarely involved majority or sizable employee ownership, they are irrelevant for our purposes. At the outset, let's establish a few basics.

There are about about 1,000 to 1,500 majority employee-owned firms in the country out of a total of about 8,000 ESOPs. About three in ten of the firms have full voting rights, and case-study data indicate that this number is higher for majority employee-owned companies. Although these rights are a crucial element in the property rights of employees, as we have seen, they are not a real factor in day-to-day labor-management cooperation; they come into play mainly when large questions about a corporation's future or present organization arise.[16]

Nearly 70 percent of ESOPs have boards of directors, but only about 4 percent include nonmanagerial employee representatives on their boards. In surveying over three thousand ESOPs in 1985, the U.S. General Accounting Office found no case of a board on which employee representatives constituted a majority. Employee representation on the board seems to be much higher—close to 10 to 15 percent of the companies—for majority employee-owned firms. In about half of these cases, employees choose management representatives. Table 7–2 reports on these firms in more detail.

Table 7–2.   Employee Involvement in ESOPs (percent).

A. Nonmanagerial Employee Involvement in Company Decisionmaking before and after ESOP Formation.

	Tax Credit	Leveraged	Leverage-able	Non-leveraged	Overall
More now	24	27	31	25	27
About the same	69	71	65	69	68
Less now	2	0	0	2	1
Not ascertained	5	2	4	4	4
Total weighted cases	936	552	1,174	786	3,447[a]

B. Nature of Increased Nonmanagerial Employee Involvement in Decisionmaking.

	Tax Credit	Leveraged	Leverage-able	Non-leveraged	Overall
Formal	3	27	16	17	15
Mixed formal and informal	14	15	5	3	8
Informal	83	58	77	80	76

Table 7–2 (continued)

Not ascertained	0	0	2	0	1
Total weighted cases	226	151	362	198	937

C. Issues on which Nonmanagerial Employees Have Input into Decisionmaking.

	Tax Credit	Leveraged	Leverage-able	Non-leveraged	Overall
Safety	51	34	40	38	42
Working conditions	36	38	33	28	34
Management-employee relations	38	30	36	25	33
Reducing costs	33	31	29	29	30
Product quality circles	25	18	15	17	19
New products	14	19	12	16	14
Planning	10	14	17	8	13
Budget or finance	13	10	10	8	11
Other	3	3	2	2	3
None	32	34	29	40	33
Total weighted cases	899	533	1,147	767	3,345[a]

D. Type of Decisionmaking Participation by Nonmanagerial Employees.

	Tax Credit	Leveraged	Leverage-able	Non-leveraged	Overall
Make suggestions	98	96	94	94	95
Share with management	20	36	42	35	33
Decide on their own	9	10	6	17	10
Other	1	4	0	0	1
Total weighted cases	563	298	648	375	1,834

a. Weighted subtotals do not add up to overall total because of rounding.

Source: U.S. General Accounting Office, *Employee Stock Ownership Plans: Benefits and Costs of ESOP Tax Incentives* for Broadening Stock Ownership (Washington, D.C.: U.S. General Accounting Office, December 1986), pp. 41–43.

Over two-thirds of the companies report no change in labor-management relations with employee ownership, although a quarter of the managers surveyed report a change. These findings must be examined more closely since most studies indicate that large numbers of both management and employees report improvements.

Labor-management cooperation is generally informal—the mutual awareness and flexibility described in Table 7–1—by means of casual meetings and discussions. Fewer than a quarter of the companies surveyed reported that the cooperation was formalized in committees or task forces. There is more institutionalization in the leveraged ESOPs, perhaps because the percentage of ownership is often higher and employees or their labor representatives want and demand more involvement.

Participation is largely restricted to issues regarding safety, working conditions, management-employee relations, and reducing costs—in other words, to issues relevant to the worker's immediate concerns rather than the organization's goals or the means to reach those goals. There is little attempt to develop quality circles or to encourage employee involvement in strategic or long-range planning, the development of new products and services, and financial control. In most cases, employees make suggestions rather than participate in decisions, although it is unclear from the sketchy data what sharing in decisions actually means.

Labor-management relations are quite traditional in ESOPs. Their emphasis on mutual awareness and flexibility rather than on close cooperation, problem-solving groups, or joint control resembles patterns prevalent in non-ESOP companies, according to the New York Stock Exchange study of about 1,100 companies conducted in 1982. A National Center for Employee Ownership finding reveals an exception to this pattern: those companies with labor representatives on their boards of directors—an experiment still widely viewed as radical in this country—are usually sizably or majority employee owned. In these companies, at least, management appears to be somewhat willing to share power.[17]

Do Unions Make a Difference?

Unfortunately, the General Accounting Office data did not report on unionization in the companies, but there are indications that unions may be one important form of employee involvement in ESOP firms. The ESOP Association reported in 1983 that 69 percent of its surveyed members did not have a union. Of the 31 percent that did, 42 percent of those companies included the union in the ESOP. Unions were present in 31 out of 229 ESOPs. About a third of the union ESOPs had full voting rights, constituting 20 percent of all companies with such rights. Further ESOP Association data indicate that unions are often present when substantial worker assets are being used to buy the firm or when wage and benefit concessions are traded for stock. Forty-two percent of all association ESOPs were financed at least in part by assets converted from other qualified retirement plans. Twenty-two percent of these included union members in the ESOP, but that amounts to only 9 percent of all the member companies. Only 3 percent of association members had wage or benefit reductions but 83 percent of those cases involved union members.[18]

The role of the trade union movement in the United States has often been to develop approaches to labor-management relations in specific companies, which are then extrapolated to nonunion ESOP companies in general. Unionized ESOPs are still the minority, although their concentration in larger companies in heavily unionized industries means that they influence comparatively great numbers of workers, especially as more and more firms in these sectors institute employee ownership. As mentioned, this involvement is concentrated in industries with bargaining over concessions, in return for which unions will often ask for greater involvement in management (for a list of such firms, see Table 3–7, item E).

Students of employee ownership commonly blame management for lack of cooperation and for the primacy of financial motives in initiating employee ownership. Certainly, the law's strong favoritism of management and management's dominance are inarguable. Yet the unions' responsibility must also be acknowledged. Substantial evidence, such as the analysis of several companies' experiences in *Taking Stock: Employee Ownership at Work*, shows that management has initiated cooperative experiments in nonunion ESOPs as often as unions have done when they are present.[19] The items at the beginning of each chapter in this book bear this out. Unions have largely limited their role in employee ownership to structuring fairly the distribution of economic resources and legal rights.

Studies evaluating such buyouts, conducted at Cornell University over a decade, have not found unions to be an especially progressive force in developing labor-management cooperation, with a few notable exceptions, such as the Rath Packing Company of Waterloo, Iowa, and the Atlas Chain Company of Pittsburgh, Pennsylvania. Both of these firms were floundering before their ESOPs were started and ended up in bankruptcy just the same. While the National Center for Employee Ownership estimates that about a quarter of worker buyouts involve unions, there is little evidence that unions attempt to transform labor-management relations in these companies.

Unions may speak of worker control, but very few invest energy in the development of real labor-management cooperation. There are some exceptions, such as Seymour Specialty Steel (discussed at beginning of Chapter 2), O & O Supermarkets and Republic Container (discussed at the beginning of this chapter), Weirton Steel (which will be discussed in more detail later in this chapter), Republic Cable, and North American Rayon, but these are the result of the energetic involvement of private consultants who worked with unions to develop cooperative forms of organization, while most ESOPs with heavy union involvement lack comprehensive approaches to labor-management cooperation.

Some Progress

Table 7–3 itemizes a number of companies that are working energetically to develop labor-management cooperation and participatory management. This partial list of fifty-six firms is not based on a systematic survey of employee-owned companies, and there may in fact be many more. Three central observations can be drawn from the list: (1) Most of the firms are closely held, which points to the lack of progress in combining employee ownership with labor-management cooperation in publicly held companies; (2) most are not unionized, which reinforces the finding that the presence or absence of a union does not predict labor-management cooperation; and (3) the firms range from majority/wholly to minority employee owned, which illustrates that the amount of ownership and the extent of labor-management cooperation are separate issues.

Table 7–3.   Companies Striving for More Labor-Management Cooperation.

Alaska Commercial Company
Allied Plywood[a,b]
America First Corporation
America West Airlines
American Building Corporation
American Recreation Center
American Western
Antioch Publishing[a]
Austin Engineering[a]
Burns & McDonnell Engineering Company[a]
Cardinal Cleaners[a]
M. W. Carr & Company[a,b]
Clay Equipment Company[a]
ComSonics[a]
Consumers United Group[a]
Cost-Cutter Stores[a]
Dakotah, Inc.[a]
Darwood Manufacturing[a]

Table 7–3.   (continued)

Dimco-Gray Company[a]
Fastener Industries[a b]
Frost, Inc.
Gore Associates[a]
Ironton Iron[a]
Kolbe and Kolbe[a]
Leslie Paper[a]
Lincoln Electric
Mansfield Ferrous Castings[a]
Herman Miller, Inc.
Nantahala Outdoor Center
New York Home Care Associates[a]
Norcal[a]
North American Rayon[a]
North American Telephone
North American Tool and Die
O & O Supermarkets[a]
Phillips Paper Company[b]
Preston Trucking
Quad/Graphics[b]
Reflexite Corporation
Republic Cable[a]
Republic Container Corp.[a]
St. Mary's Foundry[a]
Science Applications[a]
Scully-Jones Company[a]
Second Growth Forest Management[a]
Seymour Specialty Steel
Springfield Remanufacturing
Julien J. Studley, Inc.
TDI Industries[a]
Walnut Acres[a]
Weirton Steel[a]
White Pine Copper[a]
Workers Owned Sewing Company[ab]

a. Majority or wholly employee owned.
b. Studied in depth in Michael Quarrey, Joseph Raphael Blasi, and Corey Rosen, *Taking Stock: Employee Ownership at Work* (Cambridge, Mass.: Ballinger Publishing, 1986).

Source: Corey Rosen, National Center for Employee Ownership, Oakland, California, August 1987, based on public information in the center's files. Further information on each firm is available from the center.

These firms are by no means homogeneous, but all are characterized by the belief that the employees are the company and that as a group they have the ideas to make the company work. The distinction between employees and management is de-emphasized; instead, management is seen as coordinating and supervising an entrepreneurial opportunity for all the employees. Most of the companies make substantial contributions of stock and often supplement this ownership with profit sharing. A majority of the employees participate in the ownership. Most of these firms have a strong leader, whose commitment to ownership and cooperation is translated into voting rights and formal and informal structures for participation. Management tends to be strong and helps to build a culture of partnership, according to research by the National Center for Employee Ownership.[20] Recently, Karen Young of the center developed a handbook on how to increase participation and cooperation, based on the experiences of companies that have been successful in this sphere.[21]

Despite the real change that has occurred in a small number of companies, employee ownership in the United States is the loser in a struggle between labor and management in which both are striving to preserve their existing roles and retain their existing skills and worldviews. Because the state accepts and reinforces both the adversarial tradition and the rigid structure of roles, employee ownership has in fact produced very little innovation in cooperation that might be relevant to increasing productivity and competitiveness, with the result that the economy as a whole has barely been affected by the experiment.

Individual managers and entrepreneurs or retiring owners who believe in employee ownership, or union organizations and union officials with the same commitment, are the main catalysts of labor-management cooperation in ESOPs, and they must fight against the drag toward traditionalism inherent in the law. The mere presence of worker ownership leads to very little new cooperation and certainly not to control. No evidence exists that employees themselves, salaried or hourly, have taken much initiative in the many companies where they actually have majority ownership or voting rights. Ownership does not automatically create a common interest on which employees, their supervisors, and higher managers decide to act. As this book attempts to show, managerial bureaucracy and lack of interest or ability on the part of employees to explore new roles must be addressed as an issue separate from ownership.

Earlier in this chapter, two extreme experiments in employee ownership were described to put the ESOP in context. These examples demonstrated that, even when serious attempts are made to revolutionize the workplace, it is not easy to change the roles of labor and management. The vision of extreme worker control and a resultant loss of efficiency was revealed as a paranoid fantasy. More often than not, progressive employee ownership is typified by the following:

1. Management and labor identify with each other, and their social and cultural surroundings reinforce this common identification. Excessive differences in salary, status, and prestige are minimized.
2. A worldview of economic partnership in the enterprise motivates producers by means of aggressive problem solving and performance, rather than traditional authority.
3. Management is strong but is viewed as serving the larger interests of everyone in the enterprise rather than having special transcending authority. Managers are frequently removed or rotated, or new managers are continually retrained to maintain the best management team.
4. Labor-management cooperation is a continuing process, not a gimmick to be applied as a quick remedy and withdrawn the instant difficulties arise. Both the kibbutz and Mondragon are rather weak in developing concrete mechanisms for joint cooperation, such as practical problem-solving groups, but they have largely eliminated the perception that labor and management are in competition. In fact, they have done relatively little to reorganize work and educate workers for participation, yet both systems have managed to develop substantial cooperation.
5. Institutions and federations providing technical assistance help the enterprises maintain their financial stability and their participatory approaches.
6. Both the kibbutz and Mondragon emphasize the performance and profits of the enterprise, but also stress property rights, adequate representation of workers and disciplining of ineffective managers, equitable compensation arrangements, and inclusiveness.

Does Employees Ownership Lead to Cooperation?

The research on labor-management cooperation under employee ownership helps to explain why so little of it has emerged in this country. Appendix E summarizes the findings of eighteen major studies that, although limited in scope and purpose, reach similar conclusions about the labor-management dynamics involved.[22]

Labor-management cooperation is not an inevitable by-product of employee ownership. It requires effort, which is generally not forthcoming because of lack of support and follow-up by management, unions, and unorganized workers. Employee ownership does cause the worker-owner to identify more with the company and can engender greater commitment. But it is participation in management, usually at the shop floor and departmental levels, that increases an employee's motivation and provides opportunities for real change.

While employees generally have faith in management and rarely stage overthrows, all the studies discovered an alarming gap between how much participation workers have and how much they would like to have at all levels of the firm. Again, workers are most interested in participation at the job and departmental levels, but they are not completely indifferent to some formal status at higher levels of the company. It is simplistic to dismiss the problems as part of a class struggle between workers and bosses—many managers below the upper level are themselves frustrated by how little employee ownership affects their roles and jobs.

Management continually overestimates how much cooperation exists at their firms. Workers are more critical, but their unions—where they exist—also tend to do little to advance labor-management cooperation. Shareownership among individual employees created no desire for participation. In addition, it is so common for employee ownership to make no significant changes in the workplace that the adversarial function of the union is maintained, and even reinforced, as one of the few dependable forms of worker representation.

Employee-owners often feel that ownership has no real meaning for them. The organization of the firm empties employee ownership of its substance. As we have seen and the studies confirm, many companies exclude certain groups of workers or distribute the ownership according to status; even firms with voting rights and board representation have workers whose primary response to employee ownership is frustration or apathy. This suggests that formal legal property rights are not enough to give substance to employee ownership.

The studies decisively prove that the psychology of employee ownership at the root of ESOP legislation is misguided. Ownership does create an identity of interest, but without actual close involvement between labor and management, a true community of interest does not develop. Here is a case illustrating how labor and management can confront employee ownership and the role changes it can entail. Although buyouts of failing firms represent the rarest use of employee ownership, the Weirton Steel case illustrates how the pressure for a specific change can catalyze a complete transformation of a company.

Weirton Steel

In March 1982 National Steel Corporation announced that it intended to shut down its Weirton, West Virginia, plant, which was only marginally profitable and would require enormous capital investment to renovate.[23] National decided to cut its losses in a move that would throw a labor force of almost 9,000 out of work and eliminate the town's primary source of employment. National did suggest an alternative: Perhaps Weirton's workers would like to purchase the plant and run it themselves?

Employee buyouts of struggling companies were not unheard of in 1982, but this would be the largest ever, in an industry trammeled with economic hardship. Still, as William Doepken, general manager of Industrial Relations for Weirton Steel, put it, "It boils down to two choices. It's either jobs or no jobs, a new company or a shutdown."[24] A joint union-management committee hired a consultant to look into the feasibility of a leveraged-ESOP buyout. The findings, though encouraging, were not utterly rosy. For Weirton Steel to make an independent go of it, the workers would have to agree to substantial sacrifices: Employment costs would have to be cut by 32 percent and even then roughly 400 white-collar and 1,500 blue-collar workers would have to be laid off within ten years.

Represented by two unions, the Independent Steelworkers Union and the Independent Guard Union, Weirton Steel's 6,000 workers were receiving hourly wages $2 greater than the industry average. Clearly, the issue of wages had to be faced, but more important to the workers, who averaged twenty years of service, were the pension benefits accrued under National Steel's plan. Ironically, this source of anxiety proved to be a useful bargaining chip: The fate of the benefits would greatly influence the eventual sales price in favor of the workers. A joint study committee of Weirton's salaried and hourly employees, formed to address these and other issues involved in the purchase, proposed a compromise regarding National's future obligations on employee benefits. All former employees of the Weirton Division who retired before the ESOP was established would receive their defined-benefit pension benefits from National. All employees of the new Weirton Steel Corporation would retain their National benefits accrued up to the institution of the ESOP, after which Weirton would be responsible for additional defined-benefit coverage. This arrangement represented a substantial savings in shutdown and severance costs for National, and they returned the favor with flexibility in arriving at a sale price.

By September 23, 1983, the definitive purchase agreement was ready for a vote. Under the agreement, the new company would acquire most of the division's assets for $194 million in cash and notes plus debt. The ESOP would receive all of Weirton Steel Division's originally issued shares in exchange for an advance of $65,000, representing the par value of the common stock, and a $300-million promissory note, bearing interest at 12 percent and payable in ten equal installments by the ESOP. The take-home pay had been reduced from 32 to a total of 20 percent. The workers were asked to accept a no-strike clause and no cost-of-living pay increases. By an impressive majority of 84 percent, the 8,000 employees eligible to vote elected to proceed with the purchase and adopt the ESOP. The new 100-percent employee-owned Weirton Steel Corporation opened for business in January of 1984.

Weirton's ESOP. All stock purchased by the leveraged ESOP is held in a suspense account; as the loan is repaid, the shares are allocated pro rata according to salary. If Weirton's income exceeds $30 million in any year, it could save on its income taxes by contributing to the ESOP at a higher rate. Such extra contributions would then be paid back to the company to reduce the balance of the loan. The company must contribute to the ESOP every year whether it is making a profit or not. Weirton also has a nondeferred profit-sharing plan, which provides for cash distributions after the company attains $100 million in net worth, equal to one-third of adjusted net earnings before contributions to the ESOP. When net worth reaches $250 million, the profit-sharing distribution will increase to one-half of adjusted net earnings. Currently, Weirton has a bylaw stating that stock can be owned only by the ESOP trustee and active employees. Employees leaving the company who are entitled to the distribution of their stock must be paid entirely in cash, and active employees have a put option. This restriction may be removed eventually by the worker-stockholders, allowing ownership by former employees and/or others.

All Weirton employees (8,537 in all as of October 1986, including 7,251 unionized and 1,286 nonunionized workers), except probationary, summer, and co-op employees, participate in the ESOP. At present, Weirton's employees do not have full voting rights on this worker equity. The trustee of the ESOP votes all shares—allocated and unallocated—on all issues involving the election of directors, as specified by the ESOP Election Committee, which is formed of present board members. In October 1986, 2 million shares had been allocated and 4 1/2 million shares remained unallocated. By 1995, all shares will be distributed and individual workers will replace the ESOP trustees as the owners of record on Weirton's books. Shortly thereafter they will get full voting rights and be able to elect the board of directors. For now, the ESOP provides only the legal minimum, limiting full voting rights for all workers to issues that must be decided by a more-than-majority vote—matters such as amendments to the corporate charter, mergers, sales of corporate assets, and liquidation of the corporation. In these cases, the trustee must vote allocated shares according to the workers' instructions and must vote all unallocated shares proportionately.

The workers have control over other changes that are not mandated by law but constitute a special protection for worker-participants. They have the right to approve in advance any amendment and termination of the ESOP itself, any initial sale of stock by Weirton Steel to persons other than the ESOP trustee or the ESOP, and any sale of stock by the trustee in a tender or acquisition offer. On these issues, voting rights are exercised on a one-person/one-vote basis, and a majority of the workers must vote on an issue for the result to be approved. This provision prevents more highly compensated employees, who receive more stock because shares are allocated according to salary, from dominating such key decisions about the future of the company or employee ownership. These special provisions on votings rights, the participatory culture, and the mechanisms of labor-management cooperation discussed below allow for considerably more worker participation than is the norm in privately held firms without full voting rights.

Post-ESOP Follow-through. With the official instititution of the ESOP, Weirton's challenge was just beginning. National had originally decided to close the plant because of the huge capital expenditures necessary to make it commercially viable; those expenditures remained critical. The compensation cuts would liberate some capital and leveraging would supplement the company's coffers, but this left the newest and largest employee-owned firm in the country with enormous debt. The firm would have to meet a number of ambitious goals in order to survive.

The new CEO, Robert L. Loughhead, arrived at Weirton believing that "a large employee-owned company was the perfect environment to prove that employee participation could work."[25] Despite the majority support for the ESOP, labor relations at Weirton were strained. Loughhead's first step toward dismantling the old adversarial system was the institution of an intense program of communication. From his first day on the job, he began to visit a different section of the plant each week in order to meet with the workers. This alone did much to add credibility to the program of cooperation. In addition, the local union president and two other union representatives serve on the board of directors and on various committees, among them the profit-sharing committee and the retirement committee. An ESOP administrative committee composed of management and labor representatives acts as a kind of appeals court for gray areas in the ESOP, such as the time frame of stock distributions.

A Management for Productivity group (MFP) functions as an in-house management school in theories of motivation (x and y), Hertzberg's hierarchy of needs, teamwork, and more. Classes of about fifteen members of upper, middle, and first-line management go through this training. To date, 750 managers have completed the course, and many of the groups have stayed together as ongoing problem-solving teams.

Employee Participation Groups (EPGs), similar to quality circles, work in all areas of the company. Members of these groups receive training in problem-recognition techniques, receptivity to new ideas, becoming change agents in their areas, brainstorming, and problem-solving approaches. About 100 teams, involving about 1,500 people, have been trained and are in operation. These teams can include both managers and nonmanagers. A Facilitation Training Group provides support to the EPGs. Since May 1984, one to two teams a week have been trained.

The Operations Improvement Program (OIP) puts together teams of employees to solve specific problems relating to quality or productivity. Ideas generated by these teams go to a high-level steering committee comprising the CEO, the executive vice president, the head of operations, the CFO, and others. The OIP has its own staff, which assists groups in conducting their meetings and preparing and screening ideas so that only carefully researched proposals are sent on to the steering committee, which is intended to move quickly.

Workers are also trained in statistical process-control techniques, which provide another level of problem solving. This training sometimes overlaps with the EPGs, but is more technically oriented. Work teams undergo special instruction in the statistical analysis of industrial problems, focusing on very specific projects. Seventeen hundred employees have gone through the training.

Weirton has also held 500 cost sessions with hourly workers and a cost analyst for their area of the operation who has worked with them to identify opportunities for savings and provided information on how the area has actually operated in comparison with its budget. The company has various other ad hoc problem-solving teams as well.

Finally, Weirton has redesigned its internal communications system. There is now a hotline for immediate grievances. One hundred bulletin boards have been put up throughout the physical plant, on which pertinent information is regularly posted by individuals assigned to the task. A company newspaper has been started. An internal video system broadcasts news and views over one hundred television sets throughout the entire physical plant for twelve to fifteen minutes a week. The program provides news about quality, customer supply problems, the steel industry in general, the way customers use Weirton's steel, and so on. The company also encourages field research by labor-management teams, which visit customers to discuss and observe problems. Recently, a joint team of hourly workers and engineers visited several European operating hot mills to collect data for the renovation of Weirton's hot mill.

Rebirth of a Steel Mill. From its first year on, Weirton has operated profitably. The company's steelmaking and rolling operations are considered to be among the most technologically sophisticated in the industry. In 1985 the company had record sales and shipments. Demand was steady, although price erosion caused a loss of revenue of $48 million; significant cost reductions, higher volume, and an improved product mix offset the loss. Weirton officials report that important savings are resulting from nearly 700 cost-reduction projects developed by employee groups and other management initiatives. The company has also begun a study to reduce health-care costs without adversely affecting services. Profit sharing of $20.3 million was paid to employees in the first quarter of 1986—one-third of the company's $61 million in after-tax profits as provided under the profit-sharing agreement. (The company does not expect to pay taxes in its initial years because of various deductions, many related to the ESOP.)

Weirton's goal is to become a 100-percent continuous-cast producer, and engineering work has already begun to further this goal. In 1985 the company made capital expenditures of $47.5 million and committed a further $22.6 million for future installations. In 1986 expenditures in the range of $46 million were being undertaken. Facilities were being rehabilitated in almost every department. The company has a $100-million line of credit through 1989.

Growing Pains. But Weirton still isn't in the clear. It is estimated that the firm must make capital improvements of at least $350 to $400 million or more between 1987 and 1990 if it is to remain competitive. Weirton must find a way to close the gap between the $50 to $60 million that it can now afford for capital improvements annually and the $180 to $190 million it will require to upgrade its continuous caster and hot mill. In October 1986, management and labor discussed that goal and the mechanisms available to reach it. As one senior manager put it, "We are not negotiating with the union. We are sharing the problems and looking for a common solution."[26] Among the proposals under consideration are: the modification of profit sharing; a two-tier wage scale that would differentiate between steelworkers and non-steelworkers, and entry-level and existing workers; a practice called multi-crafting, which encourages cross-utilization of skilled craftspeople and reduces certain work rules; reducing crew sizes; and other means to improve Weirton's competitiveness.

In 1988–89, all of Weirton's shares will be distributed. Obviously, all employees are not likely to retire or leave service at that time, but if the firm is forced to redeem a massive number of shares at once, it would create an excessive burden, especially in light of any new capital-expenditure plans. A number of options have been proposed to deal with this situation—cost cutting and productivity improvements designed to maintain 100-percent employee ownership, or various combinations of partial employee ownership with public shareholders or other partners, such as the sale of 20-percent equity in the firm to an outside buyer, or capital infusion by a joint-venture partner.

Conclusion

Supporters of employee ownership expected it to transfigure the relations between labor and management. Judging from nationwide evidence, however, this has not happened. There have been some exceptions—often where other forms of employee ownership coexist—but by and large, as an experiment to test how labor and management might be able to cooperate in the American system, employee ownership has been unsuccessful. What are the shortcomings of the ESOP phenomenon that have undercut its ability to change labor relations? They can be narrowed down to four: lack of interest by both labor and management, lack of a well-structured incentive, lack of understanding productivity, and lack of state support for real innovation in this area.

Neither labor nor management seems to be sincerely interested in cooperation. ESOPs stand as an illustration of how deep and pervasive the adversarial ideology is in American society. Separate roles for labor and management are based on the idea that legitimate authority rests with property rights, which management either holds or represents. When labor owns, both management and the state tend to maintain the view that labor has no title to property rights. As we saw in the preceding chapter, the state has all too consistently structured the ESOP to protect management's authority. Unions have played into the hands of ESOP conservatives by generally ignoring employee ownership as a political and labor issue. The contradictions between the goals set out for employee ownership and the actual means for their realization could not fail to produce strains and suspicion that limit serious attempts at cooperation.

Employee ownership also reveals the weaknesses of labor in America. Some employees may want to be treated with respect and get involved, but they are unwilling to accept any significant responsibility; while employees complain about lack of participation, they seldom follow through, either as individuals or as a group, with useful suggestions for change. In short, the fault does not lie with management and the state alone—workers may not be taking advantage of the opportunities in employee ownership. Americans are unaccustomed to taking so much initiative in the workplace. This suggests that there may be a need for more education and training. Unions, too, may be part of the problem. Although they represent one of the few expressions of collective voice by workers in American companies, thus far they have treated employee ownership as more of a threat than a challenge to which they must respond. Yet the existing examples of how a union's democratic participatory ideology has changed employee ownership suggest that the unions hold great potential for constructive influence. An interest in labor-management cooperation will not emerge of its own accord in most cases.

Employee ownership was intended to reward the new common interests of labor and management, but this result has not materialized. ESOPs, and employee ownership in general, offer many opportunities to create incentives, but few are doing so effectively. What is the relative importance of long-term equity and short-term profit sharing? How significant are the size of the annual contribution, the distance of the worker from the retirement, the performance of the stock, the presence of property rights that allows an employee to feel like an owner?

Edward Lawler of the University of Southern California has researched the problems with reward systems. A list of his conclusions and their possible implications for employee ownership follows:

1. It is not true that reward systems are based on a simple and direct relationship between the amount of the reward and the employee's quality of working life. If this were true, designing incentives would be easy and highly effective. Implication: More and more worker equity may not be sufficient to create incentive.
2. Employees are influenced by how equitably they feel rewards are being distributed and compare their own circumstances to those of individuals within and outside of their organization. Implication: The flagrantly inequitable allocation schedules in ESOPs may provoke great skepticism in some employees.
3. Studies show that both extrinsic and intrinsic rewards are important, and that one does not replace the other. Implication: The notion that worker stock ownership alone can elicit commitment from the employee, no matter what else is happening in the work organization, is probably false.
4. People have widely different opinions about what constitutes a reward; no one reward can be generalized over a large group of people. Implication: Distributing equity over the workforce will not have the same effect on all workers.

Lawler recommends that reward systems be carefully examined because some practices contribute to organizational effectiveness while others do not. Such an analysis has not been applied to employee ownership. In fact, the law has mandated or encouraged an incentive design for ESOPs that conflicts with many of the observations above.[27]

The implicit theory of employee ownership's contribution to productivity is that employees will work harder and better. Let's assume that labor and management are interested in pragmatic cooperation and that an excellent incentive system is designed using various formulas of allocating worker equity, profit sharing, and so on. Will increased productivity result? Only if every firm focuses on problems that are particularly relevant to its own situation in order to improve productivity. This requires a careful assessment of the company's production, marketing, research, design, delivery, information handling, and more. A "piece of the action" will not magically release the skills, effort, communication, and trust necessary for groups of employees to engage such a process.

The only way employee ownership will improve a company's productivity is if it serves as a basis for practical labor-management problem solving of questions that have a strategic relationship to that company's productivity. If labor and management choose to cooperate on the wrong questions, the impact on productivity will be neutral or even negative. Here lies a serious flaw with employee ownership as it is now conceived. Kelso and Long picture the firm as having capital instruments on which the workers act—if workers have equity in these instruments, presumably they act with greater interest and effort. But economists are increasingly focusing on human capital, skills, and knowledge and immediate information important to efficiency that workers "produce," none of which is directly dependent on capital instruments.

Human capital refers to the investment people make in themselves and in their relationships with each other. It is nurtured through education and on-the-job training, which facilitate the transfer of knowledge between experienced and newer workers. Workers typically have knowledge about themselves and their jobs, but they have no incentive to pass it on to management. Employee ownership might provide such an incentive if labor-management cooperation made it possible. Productivity improvements are not simply limited to speeding up work, cutting sick leave, overtime, and staffing, or increasing business and reducing supervision. Every enterprise will be able to trim fat in these areas. But after these cuts, how does a business continue to improve its productivity?

Labor-management cooperation, through constant education, study, and problem solving, can transform an enterprise if investing in human capital becomes a permanent way of life for that company. This is the Weirton approach, whereby each worker begins to think actively and continually about the company. Unfortunately, the laws that govern employee ownership have discouraged labor-management cooperation and in fact have institutionalized rigid roles for both labor and management in employee-owned companies.

CHAPTER 8

Economic Performance

Katz Communications has nine branch offices that deal with broadcast advertising, sports syndication, TV stations, and radio stations. When its owner decided to divest himself of total interest in the company, its profit-sharing plan was used as the primary source of capital to buy the firm through an ESOP, which is open to all full-time employees and has about eleven hundred participants. The company is 58-percent owned by the ESOP and 42-percent owned independently by key managers. CEO Dick Mendelson says, "the ESOP is a tremendous motivating tool."[1]

Brooks Camera's profit-sharing plan was converted into an ESOP to purchase the company from its founder in 1971. After four years under employee ownership, the company had doubled its sales volume, expanded from one to six stores, and used more ESOP leverage to acquire a small chain. Concerned that the prospect of an enormous capital stake upon retirement provides little day-to-day motivation, Brooks began paying employees direct dividends to prompt them to think and act like owners. Management holds periodic meetings with small groups of workers to discuss the enterprise's progress.[2]

Forty-percent employee-owned ComSonics, Inc., rehabilitates and resells cable, satellite, and other electronic equipment. Inc. magazine featured the firm for its phenomenal growth of over 269 percent in five years. Employees establish three-year plans against which they check their progress throughout the year; upper management coalesces goals to maximize profitability; and managers, officers, and supervisors meet monthly to evaluate performance. In addition to the ESOP, employees share profits. The company also provides medical and life insurance, tuition reimbursement, and quarterly profit-sharing programs.[3]

Science Applications International Corporation, a fast-growing entrepreneurial company in San Diego, California, is a major contractor for the Strategic Defense Initiative with annual revenues of $600 million. The firm is mainly owned by its 7,000 primarily professional employees, but no single individual owns more than 3 percent of the company's stock. SAIC practices a form of consensus management that relies on an extensive network of committees and teams. In addition to its ESOP, profit-sharing, stock-option, and special bonus-compensation plans help tie pay to performance.[4]

Early observers and supporters of employee ownership were not unaware of the limitations of ESOP financing outlined in Chapter 3. But they often dismissed these problems by implying that reducing the concentration of wealth in the country was an overriding concern. They also presumed that the return on the investment of the additional cash available from increased working capital and better economic performance would compensate for the disadvantages of ESOP financing. Louis Kelso stated emphatically that greater ownership would give employees incentives to improve productivity and profitability (but an important aspect of Kelso's prediction was that workers would receive significant dividends, which rarely happens). Witness after witness at the congressional hearings pointed out that this increased efficiency was necessary to make the ESOP workable, but there was little evidence that it would actually take place.[5]

Professor Richard A. Musgrave, H. H. Burbank Professor of Political Economy at Harvard University, opened the 1975 hearings with an economic analysis of this problem, at the request of Senator Hubert Humphrey. The economics of ESOPs became central as observers tried to predict whether employee ownership would be used in existing firms or mainly to transform ownership. Investment bankers and accounting firms stressed that owners contemplating substantial employee ownership in their firms, where they intended to stay on, would need greater rates of return and efficiency to maintain the same income once equity per share, net income per share, and their percentage of ownership were diluted.[6]

Despite these criticisms, it would be grossly unfair to suggest that congressional and ideological advocates are solely responsible for the prediction of employee ownership's superior economic performance. According to economist Steven Bloom, substantial scientific literatures in the economic and social sciences, summarized in Table 8–1, have suggested such a positive effect on economic performance.[7]

Table 8–1.   Employee Ownership and Firm Performance: Relevant Scientific Literature.

1. Profit-Sharing Literature. Theretically, in companies run by managers and offering profit-sharing methods of compensation, employment will increase

until the supply constraints are binding, because the cost of hiring additional employees is always less than the extra revenue they help to generate. In actual practice, profit sharing, productivity sharing, and ESOPs represent different forms of gainsharing with possible incentive effects on productivity.

2. Labor-Managed Firm Literature. Some theorists in this area propose that wholly worker-owned or -managed companies will be more efficient because of greater incentives, worker identification with the firm, and worker involvement in improving production. Because workers would avoid hiring more workers, since this would decrease average income, firms will not grow beyond the most technically efficient scale or operation.

3. X-Efficiency Literature.[a] A latent potential for performance resides in labor in the capitalist enterprise. Productivity cannot be defined independently of workers' morale, attitudes, and wage rates. ESOPs may encourage workers to share knowledge and be more cooperative and cost conscious in the production process.

4. Trade-Union Literature. Unions, as the historic labor institution of collective voice, offer workers a formal mechanism for airing grievances on the shop floor, with potential positive impact on firm profits, productivity, labor turnover, and so on. Employee ownership may offer workers an alternative voice through shareholder influence, which may also have an impact on firm performance. Where employee ownership and unions coexist, this impact may be mutually reinforcing.

5. Pension Literature. Particular provisions in pension plans create substantial incentives for employees to adjust their labor-force participation, hours of work, turnover, human-capital investment, and effort on the job. Pension-plan contributions tend to be responsive to business conditions as well, introducing an added measure of wage flexibility from the firm's standpoint. ESOPs may be viewed as an alternative form of retirement security.

6. Public-Finance Literature. Some authors have shown that taxes have an impact on the ownership structure of productive assets. Also, the government can increase corporate net income through tax reductions. The ESOP may respond positively to such favorable tax treatment.

7. Other Literature. This literature has reappraised scientific management, which standardized work and de-emphasized involvement and innovative behavior. Under this form of management, short-term labor contracts, low trust, and lack of information became the norm. Firms and communities grew distant. Ownership and control were separated, and management managed assets, not people. This view suggests that employee ownership can potentially reunite the interests of labor and management.

---

a. "X-efficiency" is the efficiency with which a firm uses its various resources, that is, solves its organizational problems and undertakes all of its activities at a minimum cost. Generally, firms in competitive markets that maximize their profits should operate with maximum X-efficiency. See Harvey Leibenstein, *Beyond Economic Man: A New Foundation for Microeconomics* (Cambridge: Harvard University Press, 1976).

Source: Condensed from a list of sources and literature in Steven Bloom, *Employee Ownership and Firm Performance* (Cambridge: Department of Economics, Harvard University, 1986), pp. 65–66.

Even economists and government officials opposed to the ESOP legislative program tended to accept that employee ownership would improve firm performance. One of Kelso's harshest critics at the outset of the hearings, Professor Hans Brems, believed that short-term improvements in productivity would occur because of factors such as the elimination of waste. But he went on to point out that, historically, productivity has risen when new technology and capital investment make this possible, and this can be accomplished outside of worker ownership. Without the proper strategic decisions about capital investment, an increase in worker involvement could be bluntly described as "abundant effort and dedication in a paltry system." Paul Samuelson, Nobel laureate in economics, predicts that employee ownership would cause management to lose its incentive, which could in turn prompt some workers to shirk their own responsibilities.[8]

Until 1979, congressional proponents never debated the financial and motivational issues crucial to the achievement of the economic-performance goal, contenting themselves instead with reiterating two kinds of evidence to support their claim. The first was the simple notion that acquiring "a piece of the action" would increase the productivity of the worker. The second was a collection of success stories about employee-owned companies, supported by amateur "research" that mistakenly attributed everything positive in such firms to employee ownership (see Appendix D). Senator Long referred to one such study in the following remarks:

I am sure that you have seen some of the figures showing a close connection between employee ownership and productivity and profitability. A 1979 study of seventy-two companies which had employee stock ownership plans indicated that the sales per employee increased an average of 25 percent in the three years since they established an ESOP. Their total sales rose 72 percent; the total jobs in the company jumped by 37 percent; profits increased by 157 percent; and even Uncle Sam made something out of it because the taxes that they paid the government increased by an average of 150 percent. That just shows who all benefits when you have a greater interest among the workers in the companies in which they participate.[9]

But the key question remained: How do the investment of the government subsidy for working capital, the idea of worker ownership, the

incentive aspect of the ESOP dividend, and the employee stock ownership itself affect economic performance?

Defining Productivity and Profitability

Before responding to that question, let us pose a far simpler one: How
does one determine whether a company is operating more efficiently
under employee ownership? First we must define the elements used to
measure economic performance. *Profit* refers to the return on various
factors of investment, either before or after taxes. Researchers may measure profit differently, so their results may not be comparable. Further,
a company can be profitable—that is, have a net surplus after taxes—
but use its resources inefficiently.

Productivity refers to the relationship between output per unit of input
in a business. A profitable company can be less productive than an unprofitable or a less profitable competitor. *Labor productivity* refers to the fruitful-
ness of labor under various circumstances, such as the amount of equipment available, scale of output, method of production, and so on. It is
usually measured as the relationship of the number of employees, or the
total number of hours worked by all employees, to the dollar value of the
output. An increase in what is called labor productivity is not necessarily
due to workers. It may stem from an improvement in capital stock, management, or technical aspects of production, as well as the effort, expertise,
or quality of labor. Extremely careful testing is necessary to establish which
factor is responsible for an increase.[10]

Economists also gauge productivity in terms of *total-factor productivity*, which refers to the output produced by a fixed unit of labor and
capital combined. This approach to productivity takes into account all
the resources used in production—labor hours, intangible capital
invested in education, and tangible capital invested in equipment,
tools, and resources of all sorts. Economists use this measure to determine how to combine units of labor and units of capital most efficiently.
An increase in total-factor productivity in a company may result from
changes in technology, the size and character of economic organization,
management skills, and so forth. Output per unit of plant and equipment could fall, and a company could still be more efficient if there
were a saving of labor services per unit of product that exceeded the
increase in capital used per unit of product.

Managers and workers both tend to have very positive opinions of
how employee ownership has affected their firms. Yet, as this analysis

has shown, impressive increases in productivity may have nothing to do with labor-related factors such as motivation, working harder, working smarter, reducing labor conflict, and the like. Unfortunately, the so-called research on employee-owned firms that began to be available in the early eighties and congressional citation of that evidence failed to present conclusions based on the techniques just described.[11]

Research on Economic Performance

Taken as a whole, what is the bottom line of all the research on employee ownership? Let's examine the findings of some of these researchers. The tax-credit ESOPs and the leveraged and nonleveraged ESOPs will be discussed separately because of their distinct natures and effects on federal tax expenditures. Remember, too, that the tax-credit ESOP has been repealed, and the others will now receive even fuller support from the state. New legislative incentives are likely to give even greater tax subsidies to leveraged and nonleveraged ESOPs, thus making their economic performance look even better (see Chapter 3), but these had no impact on the studies mentioned here.

Tax-Credit ESOPs

Steven Bloom's research must be deemed seminal and pioneering because he controlled for alternative explanations of the economic performance of employee-owned companies. Bloom carefully matched 1981 Internal Revenue Service data on ESOPs with extensive economic and financial information on each company from Standard and Poor's COMPUSTAT II files. For most companies, income statements, balance sheets, and "Statements of Changes in Financial Position" are available for a period of ten to twenty years. Here we will concentrate on the 609 publicly traded companies Bloom surveyed, about 90 percent of which had tax-credit ESOPs (TRASOPs or PAYSOPs). The average number of participants in each ESOP was 7,178, out of a workforce of about 16,691. The study thus covers 4.4 million of the workers participating in ESOPs in 1981 in companies employing about 10.2 million workers in all. In 1981, these tax-credit ESOPs accounted for 80 percent of the national participants and $6.1 billion—over half of the total ESOP assets.

Bloom compared companies that had tax-credit ESOPs to those that did not, in order to determine what caused them to adopt their plans. He concluded that the average tax-credit ESOP firm had about three times more sales and twice the total assets. Differences in company size tended to diminish in industrywide comparisons. The tax-credit ESOP involved considerable legal and administrative costs and related to the size of the firm's capital investment or payroll—the larger the firm, the higher its return on the set-up cost of a tax-credit ESOP. TRASOP/ PAYSOP firms had an average investment tax credit that was five times that of non-ESOP firms in 1981.

Tax-credit ESOP firms appeared to be more leveraged with more long-term debt. Effective interest rates were lower by nearly 6 percent for these companies, many of which probably used the ESOP to retire debt with pretax dollars, which is more attractive for both the commercial lender and a highly leveraged borrower. The capital-labor ratios appeared to be more favorable in the tax-credit ESOP firms, but less so when comparisons were made throughout an industry.

Bloom found that the tax-credit ESOP participants constituted about 25 percent of the company's shareholders, with an average ownership of 3.4 percent of company stock. The average firm contributed about 15 percent of its pretax profits to the ESOP in 1981, or about 4 percent of labor costs. The plans averaged assets of $11.3 million or $3,977 per participant, but this figure was less than $2,000 in 43 percent and less than $1,000 in over 50 percent of the plans.

Bloom's first attempt to measure productivity—comparing expenses to sales—revealed that it seemed to be 50-percent higher in ESOP manufacturing firms than the non-ESOP sample. Nominal sales per employee grew by a factor of 3.7, and sales compared to net plant grew by a factor of 1.7. The computer analysis thus appeared to confirm predictions that employee ownership could affect company performance across the economy simply by shifting equity. However, when checked against "gross plant/employee" (the dollar value of gross plant divided by the number of employees), using the number of total employees (versus total participants in an ESOP), and controls for durable manufacturing, all significant differences completely disappeared. In nonmanufacturing, a 47.8-percent increase in productivity was similarly diminished.

Bloom then used the COMPUSTAT data on financial information of public companies to follow ESOP firms over time and compare each firm's pre-ESOP performance (from 1967 to 1974) with its ESOP performance (from 1974 to 1981). He discovered that firms with above-average productivity were more likely to adopt ESOPs. He also found that taxpaying firms were usually more productive and were four times more likely to adopt ESOPs. However, given the greater productivity of tax-paying firms in general, it was uncertain whether increases in productivity could be attributed to the ESOP.

Regarding profitability, Bloom studied firms in terms of their industry. In manufacturing, the gross rate of return for ESOP firms was 32.8 percent, or 11 percentage points lower than for non-ESOP firms. In nonmanufacturing, this return was noticeably higher in mining and agriculture but lower in communications, trade, and financial and other services. Measurements of profitablity after taxes indicated that ESOP firms enjoyed a greater return on equity and assets than did non-ESOP firms. This suggests that their profit advantage may be largely attributable to favorable tax treatment. In actual stock-market performance, ESOP firms outperformed non-ESOP firms.

Bloom concluded that the employee ownership in these largely tax-credit ESOP companies had no significant impact on the firm's economic performance. He noted that employees' holdings were too small to provide much incentive and suggested that the efforts of those employees who did work harder may have been cancelled out by others who did not. Performance did not appear to be affected if a larger percentage of employees participated in the plan or a larger percentage of employee ownership existed within a company. This conclusion must remain tentative, however, since tax-credit ESOPs by nature have smaller employee-ownership estates and an insignificant percentage of total employee ownership. Even with more employees participating, these plans may spread incentives too thinly to be meaningful. Bloom's study is noteworthy for its efforts to separate out and control for effects. However, its attempt to focus on design issues in ESOPs was irrelevant because of the nature of the ESOPs it analyzed; further, no attention was given to labor-management cooperation.[12]

Leveraged and Nonleveraged ESOPs

Much evidence suggests that the performance of leveraged and nonleveraged ESOP companies is comparable to that of firms without employee ownership. Twenty-six groups of studies on employee ownership and firm performance are summarized in detail in Appendix D. Generally, however, those studies that reported increased productivity and profitability did not use adequate checks and controls to verify the actual causes for the improvement. Many of the studies looked at either productivity or profitability, and most did not examine both. Few attempted to adjust their findings to reflect the paper improvement in economic performance that all ESOPs enjoy as a result of increases in working capital from reduced taxes.

In 1986 and 1987, the U.S. General Accounting Office complemented the Bloom research with another examination of ESOP financial data. It involved a very large sample of companies with nontax-credit ESOPs and included sizable numbers of leveraged and nonleveraged ESOPs in closely held companies—exactly the population Bloom did not study. As a branch of the U.S. government, the GAO went directly to the Internal Revenue Service files for accurate financial statistics. It compared matched samples of non-ESOP companies and ESOP firms established from 1976 to 1979. Like Bloom, the GAO collected data on firm performance before the adoption of the ESOP to test whether prosperous firms initially sponsor ESOPs. The study also examined a number of sizably or majority employee-owned companies where a large percentage of employees participated in the ESOP. The results of this research are that ESOPs do not improve productivity unless combined with employee involvement, as the Quarrey research below suggests.[13]

One drawback of both the Bloom and the GAO studies is their lack of detailed attention to the human side of the employee-owned firm. Those twenty-six studies summarized in Appendix D, suggest (but do not prove) that worker involvement in management combined with employee ownership in which a high proportion of workers participate may contribute to better economic performance: Employee ownership increases commitment to and identification with the company, while greater employee involvement increases motivation.

Michael Quarrey of the National Center for Employee Ownership addressed this issue in a study of 2,800 workers in thirty-seven companies, which were matched with non-ESOP firms in their industries to control for industrywide trends.[14] Excluding one large firm, these companies had an average of 380 employees. Pre- and post-ESOP data for each company were compared, and all firms registered a small improvement in productivity after the adoption of their ESOPs, measured by sales per employee and sales growth. Seventy percent of the ESOP companies performed better than the industry average. Sales in the ESOP companies grew 9.7 percent more than in the non-ESOP companies, although when Quarrey controlled for the firms' pre-ESOP performance, this edge in sales growth was cut to 3.7 percent. Quarrey observed increased employment growth as well. He also compared the ESOP firms to other companies within their industries, but his findings are open to some question. On the face of it, they eliminate the possibility that increased demand or inflation caused the sales growth in ESOP firms. This would seem to support the emerging hypothesis that better performers establish ESOPs. Nevertheless, the ESOP companies grew more slowly in both pre- and post-ESOP periods in sales per employee as opposed to sales growth. One major disadvantage of this study is that no data on capital/labor ratios in the companies were collected, so it is unclear whether worker output or capital input was responsible for certain changes. Thus, while Quarrey found that the mere presence of an ESOP did improve a firm's economic performance, one must question whether equating sales and employment growth with improved economic performance represents a proper measure of productivity and efficiency.

Quarrey tried to establish whether it was the percentage of ownership, the design aspects of the ESOP, the attitudes of workers, or participation in management that accounted for this increased performance of some ESOP companies. He found that neither the size of the company's annual contribution to the ESOP, the mode of vesting, the presence of formal communication about the ESOP, the percentage of employee ownership, company size, formal voting rights for the stock, board participation, the tax position of the company, nor a change in key management personnel was a factor in predicting the superior economic performance he measured. Instead, the amount of concrete worker participation in management, along with a management team that believed employees should be owners and actively sought to integrate them into the corporate culture, powerfully explained better performance—that is, increases in employment and sales growth. Participation was measured by the presence of company working groups involving both managers and workers in seven substantive areas of company operations, as well as by management's perception of workers' influence. Many participative companies have employees on the board of directors and pass through voting rights, but these measures alone do not improve sales performance; closer examination of the companies suggests that a wide variety of formal and informal types of labor-management cooperation are responsible. The participation programs of several of the most successful companies in the study were exhaustively explored in *Taking Stock: Employee Ownership at Work*, by Quarrey, Blasi, and Rosen.

How is the Quarrey study to be interpreted? All in all, this research does not contradict the mounting evidence on the nonexistence of an immediate connection between ESOPs and economic performance. It does suggest, however, that labor-management cooperation might explain some improvements in ESOP companies. When the participative companies were divided into high, medium, and low categories of participation, participation remained the key factor affecting sales and employment growth, although it did not significantly change the number of sales per employee. Now that the general accounting office has also discovered that employee participation can make a difference in ESOP's productivity, a cut may change.

What the Research Reveals

Do ESOPs truly improve economic performance? Proponents so emphasize the *superior* economic performance of ESOP companies, it might seem that the only acceptable outcome of employee ownership is *substantial* economic improvement over nonemployee-owned firms. Yet there is another crucial finding of the research: overwhelming evidence that companies with small or or large amounts of employee ownership *can* be profitable and productive. Appendix D summarizes findings on the performance of twenty-six firms, American and otherwise, under various forms of employee ownership. The research amply proves that employee-owned firms generally perform acceptably under varying designs of worker ownership, in different countries and cultural systems, at different times in history and economic growth cycles, no matter how productivity and profitability are measured. There is no evidence that employee ownership hurts companies. Any claim that modern economic organization requires centralized ownership by individual capitalists or clear domination by managers insulated from absentee owners is simply unfounded.[15]

The same evidence, however, also suggests that the mere fact of employee ownership does not automatically trigger increased productivity or profitability. Researchers who connected superior performance to employee ownership did not carefully test for alternative explanations. There are many causes of increased labor productivity, and greater profitability is not an indication of greater efficiency.

Unfortunately, the studies cannot really be compared. Different measures are used to examine performance in firms with varying amounts of ownership, participation, and tax subsidies during periods with different tax systems that affected net income variously. A profitability study comparing an ESOP firm with leveraged financing and a comparable non-ESOP firm, for example, will almost always find the ESOP firm to be more profitable than a conventional company using debt, equity, or internal financing simply because of the tax subsidy's effect.[16]

Two more serious problems weaken the ESOP research. First, the data on economic performance are not checked against the percentage of employees who are worker-owners. Studies of non-ESOP employee-owned firms that have looked into this have generally found that the potential impact on certain aspects of performance increased apace with the number of employees involved in the ownership. Second, no distinction is made between ownership involving long-term rewards, usually given upon retirement, and ownership that provides for short-term rewards, such as dividends or profit sharing. Both the presence and the size of these two distinctly different types of ownership contribute to the motivation effect in ESOPs. Isolating these factors is important because dividends in ESOPs have been tax deductible only since 1984 and so may now be playing a stronger role. In addition, the large number of profit-sharing plans in small to medium-size companies suggests that some firms with ESOPs may use profit-sharing plans to supply this short-term incentive.[17]

One key finding in the research is the discovery of an alarming gap between how managers perceive ESOPs' influence on motivation and productivity and the real impact that ESOPs have, coupled with the legislators' insistence on portraying the results of employee ownership as miraculous, again regardless of the facts. The 1985 ESOP Association survey of 239 firms found that 16 percent of the managers questioned believed that productivity in their companies was greatly improved, 56 percent found it somewhat improved, and 28 percent discerned an insignificant, negative, or uncertain change. Surprisingly, these views differed little according to whether the firm was large or small, minority or majority worker owned.[18] We now know that these perceptions are wrong, but why is the gap between such expectations and reality so large? It would seem that the legislative goal of superior economic performance was and is based on three fundamental fallacies.

A Fallacy of Politics

The fallacy of politics stems from a mistake in policy. Legislators and ESOP supporters believed that superior performance was a requirement of employee ownership. It was not sufficient for employee ownership to be another way of organizing businesses—it had to be a *better* way. The framers of ESOP legislation were clearly nervous about the public perception of their ideology, which they hoped to make more palatable by insisting that no redistribution of wealth was taking place. Perhaps the promise of superior economic performance reassured these men that they were on the right track. If the ESOP resulted in bigger and better business, then surely it must be right for America.

More cynically, the promise of superior performance was necessary to justify the tax expenditures. As Senator Long proclaimed, " . . . even Uncle Sam made something out of it because the taxes that [ESOP companies] paid the government increased by an average of 150 percent." Improved performance was to offset the financial disadvantages inherent in the ESOP outlined in Chapter 3. In fact, legislators and supporters should have emphasized that employee ownership can be a successful way of running a business that *might* improve productivity if both labor and management use increased identification with the firm as a basis for practical problem solving.

A Fallacy of Productivity

This fallacy is glaringly to blame for the discrepancy between managers' attitudes about improved economic performance in these companies and reality. It is based on the notion that workers can make a financial difference in a company simply by working harder and smarter, thus speeding up production. Yet it ignores the crucial point made by Professor Brems at the ESOP hearings: Labor productivity historically rises because of new technology and higher investment of physical and human capital per worker. At the root of the poor research and the exaggerated stories about ESOPs' performance is a refusal to recognize the complex interaction of forces in productivity. In reality, working harder and smarter will not necessarily make a difference if a company is not also utilizing new technology, physical capital, and human capital in the most efficient manner possible. The only way employee ownership can improve a firm's performance is to work directly on that crucial configuration of concerns that is strategically related to the company's efficiency and success. Anything else is window dressing.

A conviction that more worker participation of any kind in management will improve productivity is equally unmerited. If one could demonstrate that ESOPs lead to substantial, practical, ongoing labor-management cooperation in decisions about technology and the production process and the use of physical and human capital, it might be possible to claim that employee ownership improves productivity. Yet the goals and structure of ESOP law and the inner workings of the ESOP itself strongly militate against such cooperation.

A Fallacy of Psychology

As noted in Chapter 1, ownership was expected to unite labor and management in a common endeavor without changing the structure of power or prestige between them. Louis Kelso defends this worldview:

A basic tenet of two-factor economics is that the function of ownership and the function of management are two *entirely* distinct functions [emphasis added]. It is postulated that any human being can be an owner of productive capital and, that, ideally, every individual would actually own a viable holding of such shares. However it is not a postulate of two-factor economics that every individual is qualified to manage a corporation. The ideal corporation is one in which promotion from level to level in the corporate hierarchy is possible and easy. Nevertheless, management is a rare and difficult art; the health and success of the corporation as a whole depend upon its having the highest quality of management.[19]

The crucial word is "entirely." Neither Kelso nor Long, nor any other congressional supporters or ESOP enthusiasts and advocates foresaw any change in the corporate bureaucracy of American business, which generally does not relate rewards to performance for both managers and workers and tends to accord high status to managers no matter how they perform. As we have seen, ESOP law's allocation of worker equity, rights, and responsibilities magnifies these problems. The airtight defense of management's prerogatives and the emasculated rights of ownership can be explained only by a belief that there are just two possibilities in companies: efficient management control or chaotic worker control. Employees' main role in the affairs of the employee-owned company was to be better workers.

The pecuniary aspect of employee ownership was seriously flawed as well. As many observers have pointed out, real ownership is put off until the employee actually leaves the company. Motivation expert Saul Gellerman introduced the distinction between the ownership estate (the stock) and the ownership incentive (the dividend) and noted that the ownership estate will be dependent on the number of years the employee participates in the plan and on the allocation formula. Thus, older employees will accumulate smaller estates with an earlier reward, while younger employees will accumulate greater estates with a later reward. As demonstrated in Chapter 2, the allocation and eligibility requirements for many ESOPs can be combined to reduce the size of these estates drastically for some workers and even to eliminate other categories of workers completely.

Regarding dividends, Gellerman says that research on incentives suggests that the income paid a middle-income–bracket worker to encourage a desired change in behavior should be a minimum of 20 to 35 percent what he or she receives to reward current behavior. Payment of dividends below 20 percent of the worker's current earnings cannot reasonably be expected to affect productivity. Gellerman also posits that the quality of work, the worker's attitude, and his or her identification with the company may improve with the proper incentives. He further points out that research indicates that workers take a more active interest in their company if they have invested their own funds; where no financial risk is involved, workers may be apathetic.[20]

As noted in Chapter 2, the most extensive psychological study conducted on ESOPs concluded that the size of the company's annual contribution was the single greatest factor in creating positive worker attitudes toward employee ownership.[21] Yet even when workers feel better about the ESOP and their company, this does not always translate into better performance: An improvement in the estate provided by the ESOP may increase identification with the firm but may not increase motivation.

Many ESOP companies have programs of corporate communication on their ESOPs—posters, newsletters, meetings, and the like. These seem to be a direct outgrowth of a twisted employee-ownership psychology: If you tell people that they are owners, they will digest the information, become more motivated, and work harder. A culture of ownership does seem to be necessary for greater worker involvement in actually improving the company, but the limitations of this simplistic approach are expressed by two contradictory findings: National Center for Employee Ownership research on over thirty companies found that ESOP communication programs had little effect on employee attitudes, yet 71 percent of the managers polled by the ESOP Association of America felt (mistakenly) that employees have a good understanding of their ESOP.

As the National Center for Employee Ownership study proves, workers cannot have positive attitudes without a sincere philosophy of worker ownership on the part of managers. And various forms of labor-management cooperation may not be adequate unless workers can identify the productivity improvements springing from cooperation and a short-term incentive system allows them to share in the rewards. The strongest support for this theory comes from extensive research on the Mondragon system of worker cooperatives: The presence of short-term incentives and various forms of labor-management cooperation encourages mutual monitoring by workers, which researchers suggest directly affects productivity. This guards against the possibility that incentives may be diffused when individual employees slack off and continue to collect their share of a group incentive.[22]

Taxation and Social Behavior

The ESOP as an engine to change industrial organization is fueled by substantial tax credits and tax incentives. Any evaluation of the economic performance of ESOPs cannot escape one basic fact: The performance of American business is to some extent determined by the effect of the tax system on the balance sheet. Taxation, the direct commandeering of corporate assets, is the major tool of industrial state policy, even if Americans do not like to admit that such a policy exists.[23] The so-called private sector is tax driven in some profound ways.

Throughout the economy, the ESOP has not met the performance goals set for it regarding broadening ownership, labor-management cooperation, or improved productivity. This is because a comprehensive employee-ownership program was never really attempted, and the ESOP was improperly constructed. The ESOP was limited in kind and in degree. Yet, when it is viewed in terms of its real capacity for change rather than its hypothetical strengths, one cannot conclusively establish that the ESOP is a failure. Given that the government manages corporate profits through the tax system and continually decides how many resources to transfer from the public sector to the business sector, the ESOP can potentially serve as a corrective by ensuring that the ongoing redistribution of taxes helps to improve labor-management cooperation and to broaden ownership rather than to concentrate it further. In theory, if an ESOP really provided ownership to all of the employees in the various income strata, it would have this effect.

Admittedly, the tax-credit ESOP was a colossal mistake. Giving a dollar-for-dollar credit without substantially leveraging the government's money was excessive, even if one disregards the fact that many of the employees who most needed ownership were excluded and little new capital was formed. In the context of other corporate tax expenditures, however, even the tax-credit ESOP takes on a different light. From 1975 to 1982, corporations retained $142.3 billion as a result of the investment tax credit and $515.6 billion through the depreciation deduction. The total of $657.9 billion represents a massive tax return to business. During the same period, the tax-credit ESOP used $6.8 billion—less than 5 percent of the total investment tax credit and less than 1 percent of the corporate tax savings.[24]

The investment tax credit as a whole was a disaster, according to research collected by *Dun's Business Month*, the *Wall Street Journal*, and Citizens for Tax Justice.[25] One study of the tax returns of 238 profitable nonfinancial corporations between 1981 and 1983 found that the companies with the lowest tax rate (-8.4 percent) actually reduced investment by 21.6 percent, while the most heavily taxed companies (a rate of 33.1 percent) increased investments by 4.3 percent. The low-tax companies increased their dividends at a pace more than 30 percent greater than the high-tax companies. The companies that paid zero or less in taxes in any one of the three years reduced investment by 15.7 percent while increasing dividends by 21.2 percent.[26]

These data disprove the argument that corporate taxes artificially depress the return to investors and therefore discourage investment. In the real world, corporations invest when they need capital equipment to produce what consumers want. The investment tax credit added to corporate cash flow, which was used variously for investment or for increased dividends, mergers and acquisitions, executive pay, advertising budgets, stock buybacks, and expanded cash reserves. In this period from 1981 to 1983, many companies noted that they added substantially to their cash reserves.

The changes in tax laws that reduced the cost of capital for various firms were based on a claim that "the economy is a great spring held down by the weight of high marginal taxes and excessive spending. Take away the taxes that discourage risk taking and expansion, roll back the government spending that absorbs labor and resources that ought to be available to the private sector, and the inherent dynamism in the spring will manifest itself."[27] In retrospect, the extra claim made for the ESOP seems to have been a tactical mistake, since it held the ESOP to a higher set of expectations than firms in general. However, it must be squarely recognized that (1) the tax-credit ESOP represented the major waste, not employee ownership in general; (2) the excessive ESOP tax expenditure resulted from incompetent government use of the tax system to influence corporate behavior; and (3) the ESOP can be redesigned to maximize its benefit to the country.

Conclusion

A number of the ESOP's characteristics, all of which have been widely proven to be major patterns, are likely to reduce its incentive effect: the small percentage of compensation represented by the annual contribution to the plan; the indefiniteness of the contribution; the exclusion of large numbers of workers so that any incentive effect is attenuated; excessively long vesting periods that remove the reward from the immediate experience of the employee; the lack of dividend income; the lack of stock appreciation; the lack of information on the company and its operations that would be available to any other capitalist investor; the lack of adequate protections against self-dealing by management; the lack of property rights and voting rights to effect crucial company decisions. Several other factors may also powerfully diminish the ESOP's effectiveness—for example, the hierarchical way of allocating worker equity in most ESOPs, the lack of immediate short-term profit sharing, and minimal emphasis on labor-management cooperation to improve productivity. Finally, no one knows for certain how an ESOP affects employees who have acceptable versus unacceptable wages and assured retirement benefits versus no other retirement benefits.

Given the preponderance of all these factors, it should be no surprise that employee ownership is not an elixir. The relationship of employee ownership to positive economic performance is far more complicated than the proponents had anticipated. It requires the opposite of the psychology of ownership that underpins the ideology of the employee-ownership movement, the structure of ESOP law, and the moving parts of the ESOP itself.

Louis Kelso made great strides in designing alternative methods of finance and credit, but his view of economics, his concept of management, and his psychology of ownership woefully ignore the creativity of human capital, and this weakness is innate in the ESOP as it is now designed. An easy recipe for improving productivity in ESOP companies does not exist. Employee ownership does not automatically improve economic performance; it is not the sole answer to the nation's productivity problem. But employee involvement is crucial.

The ESOP's primary problem is that it started out burdened with an exaggerated economic claim, even though it was never more than a partial approach to reformulating the distribution of ownership and the industrial organization inside companies. A secondary problem is that the leveraged and nonleveraged ESOPs were never aggressively pushed by Congress. As such, the ESOP phenomenon has served as a demonstration of the complexities of changing industrial organization and ownership through a government-initiated program.

CHAPTER 9

Conclusion and
Recommendations

Employee ownership has evolved as a means to stabilize the current economic system, which has been thrown off balance by external and internal stresses. Externally, evidence indicates that industries facing competitive pressures because of foreign producers, trade policies, or deregulation turn to employee ownership and other cooperative labor-management approaches. Internally, companies are seeking new ways to benefit employees that involve lower costs and a departure from the postwar habit of constant wage increases; many are considering a shift from the fixed wage to flexible compensation. Privately held small businesses, especially when family owned, have serious continuity problems; employee ownership allows owners to remove their capital responsibly. Publicly held companies increasingly use employee ownership to become more entrepreneurial, avert takeovers, spin off less profitable units, or reform the union-management relationship. Recent new tax incentives for ESOPs, together with creative defenses against the dilution caused by the issue of new shares, have now cleared the way for publicly held firms to restructure themselves completely by means of employee ownership.[1] Unions and workers, beginning to take the initiative with employee ownership, are buying companies themselves. In general, uncertainty about how to organize work in modern American society has led to experiments with new approaches.

This book has demonstrated how employee ownership is largely predetermined by the social ideology behind the law and its ongoing interpretation, regulation, and application. The government has a tremendous ability to change the role of business in society through tax and other laws that determine business structure, and it has imposed its concept of employee ownership through the goals it laid out for the program and the tools it created to achieve them. But it is the details of the legislative program, the small moving parts of employee ownership, the often arcane aspects of the worldview behind the law and the regulations, along with the conflicts inherent in their interaction, that are responsible for the present incarnation of employee ownership, not the noble purpose that is supposedly at its base.

Evidence shows that the classic ESOP can broaden wealth: Modest tax incentives for credit to establish employee-ownership funds or tax-deductible corporate contributions out of profits to worker-equity funds are effective ways to change the structure of ownership in many corporations. Yet, for several reasons, the ESOP has not lived up to this economic promise. First, the tax-credit ESOP sabotaged the employee-ownership effort by producing such minimal results at so much expense that it became difficult for legislators to push for an intensive state role in broadening property ownership. Second, while many legislators supported the idea of broadened ownership and even declared it crucial to the survival of the political system, there appears to have been an abiding belief that ownership would naturally broaden as a result of a better economy. Third, there are evidently those who are uninterested in broadening ownership, contending that the rich and super-rich are being justly rewarded for their efforts while the rest have not worked as hard.

To understand the current incarnation of the ESOP, one must distinguish between its recognized and intended consequences and the unacknowledged and perhaps unforeseen aspects of the ESOP program. ESOPs are the direct result of rewards in the tax system, and this was certainly intended; it was not intended, however, that the tax advantages and corporate uses of employee ownership would come to dominate the entire phenomenon. Yet in its attempt to reform capitalism and broaden the base of democracy, the government strengthened a worldview that upheld many of the social characteristics that employee ownership was intended to change. Congress was unwilling to reorganize corporate finance and credit or restructure property rights in employee-benefit law for fear of being accused of violating private property and disturbing the status quo. In the end Congress managed to construct employee ownership in a way that diminished its ability to broaden wealth and still compromised property rights. The benefits to employees are seen as incidental. As William Foote Whyte of Cornell University has put it: "Worker ownership has been divorced from any notion of worker control."[2] If and when workers get ownership, they are denied the traditional property rights associated with capitalism because, according to the prevailing view, the most efficient way of running a corporation is to have rigid hierarchical authority centralized in very few managers.

Employee ownership has developed primarily as a nonunion work innovation, but there is very little evidence that it is reformulating industrial relations. Even in the unionized sector, it is a new tool in the old struggle between labor and management, but not as yet—in most cases—a transcendence of that struggle. In nonunion environments, employee ownership has served to ratify the differences between labor and management. In general, it has not changed firms or improved economic performance and motivation or changed incentives. It has not induced management to organize enterprises according to performance rather than authority and status.

On the contrary, the transformation occurring in American industrial relations by way of employee ownership usually involves the continuation—even the strengthening—of the rigid and adversarial roles of labor and management in the large majority of cases. Congress solidly supports management bureaucracy; both management and labor (organized and unorganized) resist modifications to their traditional roles. The face of labor-capital relationships is changing, but the underlying structure of these relationships remains the same. Under the current system, most industries could be completely employee owned without any noticeable change in labor-management relations, even when unions are present. In the end, employee ownership has involved workers more in risking capital, but has not given them greater property rights or increased involvement in their firms or improved cooperation with management.

Despite the rhetoric, government and business are committed to a feudal ideology of business, while unions have adopted systems of seniority, work rules, and pay that mimic the feudal approaches favored by management. Inherent in this feudal ideology is a belief in ascribed status and ascribed rewards. Status has no connection with performance—management has power by virtue of title, not deeds—and compensation, too, is based on position rather than performance. High wages for management, automatic cost-of-living increases for workers, and tying pension and ESOP benefits to relative compensation are all inspired by this feudal view.

A real entrepreneurial system of business directly links status and performance. Power and prestige are gained by increasing efficiency, and both management and workers vie for the same prizes. Rewards are linked to performance by providing management and workers with a long-term equity interest in the company and a short-term profit-sharing program to share the immediate benefits of increased productivity. American business is at an ideological crossroads, and it must solve two problems to negotiate that crossroads successfully: How to connect status and performance and how to connect reward with performance.

The government, business, and even labor have allowed employee ownership and participation to evolve along traditional feudal lines, yet only entrepreneurial employee ownership has been shown to change labor-management relations, broaden wealth equitably, and improve productivity. Some people have shared responsibility in a way that makes labor a partner in a company, opening the way for greater motivation, involvement, and even joint problem solving. Despite the general trend, there are some positive models of entrepreneurial employee ownership. What factors encourage individuals and organizations to buck the dominant social forces discovered in this study?

1. Leadership seems to be essential to any kind of innovation in labor-management relations. Strong managers and strong individuals are secure enough to invite participation in an employee-owned firm.
2. Companies that make a process out of labor-management cooperation work hard to create a new conformity based on cooperation, through encouraging intensive communication and interaction between individuals at different levels of the organization, teaching, skill development, and rewards for cooperative behavior.
3. Worker ownership promotes mutual identification among employees and with the enterprise. Sharing of short-term profits rewards productivity-oriented problem solving, while sensitivity to short-term performance goals creates a team spirit. More social contact among employees or even involvement in a community generates a new set of group norms based on joint interest rather than ascribed roles.
4. Various consultants can help individuals and enterprises sort out the complex issues involved in employee ownership and design a modest strategy for change. An entire firm may have to be redesigned through retooling, closing, acquisition, merger, reinvest-

ment, reskilling, research, and so forth. Only careful joint planning makes this possible.

5. There must be support for individual efforts at the top policy levels of business, government, and labor. The state can help through the tax and legal systems. Unions can help with the resources of the national union and labor federations. Business can help by assisting chambers of commerce and other business organizations.

6. Innovations in cooperation that persist over time tend to involve larger parts of the workforce, wider ranges of issues, different levels of the company, and more advanced states of involvement by workers and managers of all types. Team problem solving and close identification among all members of an enterprise are most useful both for individual workers and the achievement of practical goals.

Some Policy Recommendations

Employee ownership and participation are not the solution to the country's problem of competitiveness nor can they singlehandedly carry the burden of broadening the ownership of wealth in American society. Rather, employee ownership should be recommended as an important tool in a new labor-management system in the United States, the goal of which will be to encourage competitiveness and to create a better workplace. Properly structured, employee ownership can cause employees to identify more with the firm and perhaps with each other. It can provide a transition from the fixed-wage system by promoting wage flexibility through a share in long-term equity. Forms of short-term profit sharing through various combinations of cash profit sharing, dividends on stock, and immediate profits invested in more equity might increase worker incentive. This could buttress and stabilize pragmatic forms of labor-management cooperation involving joint problem solving and the kind of shared responsibility and partnership that research suggests might motivate workers and lead to innovation in productivity and service. Obviously, an important aspect of this problem solving would be the reorganization of some jobs and the effective integration of the worker with new technologies.

This study shows that without strong support from the state little in the labor-management system will actually change. The notion that the state should stay out of the private sector so that innovations can diffuse naturally is fallacious: State authority is deeply involved in structuring multiple elements of the labor-management relationship. Yet, although it can create favorable conditions for change, it clearly cannot make every decision for labor and management. The suggestions that follow are based on the presumption that employee ownership will continue to be a favored and complex part of the country's tax system. However, the incentives for employee ownership and labor-management cooperation must be restructured so that the main incentives will be built into the system itself rather than dependent on tax expenditures. The substance of the ideas must be the core attraction.

Promoting Employee Ownership

Philosophical Backing. Federal policy on ESOPs should be clarified once and for all to provide a sound structure on which to base administrative regulations over the coming years. The law should say that employee ownership is not a supplemental employee-benefit plan, that it is mainly for the benefit of the employees and to broaden capitalism, and that it is only incidentally a technique of corporate finance. The government should state that ESOP wealth is not a gift from management or a grant, but the result of the investment of worker-borrowed credit (the leveraged ESOP) or the investment of stock in place of compensation (the nonleveraged ESOP) in the company's ongoing operations.

A special commission comprising the Federal Reserve Board, the Department of the Treasury, the Department of Labor, academic experts, and Senate and House Finance and Labor committees should be set up to explore ways to redesign the mechanisms of corporate finance to favor broadened ownership of wealth. At minimum such a commission should focus on ways to foster more employee ownership through new capital formation and to develop new instruments of debt and equity financing based on employee ownership. A number of additional proposals to broaden the ownership of real estate, housing, and consumer services by extending credit to citizens should also be considered.

Restructuring the ESOP. There should be more focus on providing equity to those employees with the least stock ownership, savings, and access to credit. The limit on the amount of stock distributable to an employee should be substantially increased. As a corollary, allocations of worker equity among employees should not be based on salary but on a more equitable formula. I would retain vesting periods but shorten them in ESOP companies.

Fewer exclusions. Excluding workers because of their age should be eliminated. It should still be possible to exclude employees for not working a minimum number of hours in a year, but at least 80 percent of a firm's workers should eligible to participate. A limit should also be set on the number of part-time workers who can be excluded, since these represent a growing sector of the American workforce, yet currently constitute one of the most excluded groups. Labor law should be changed so that all aspects of ESOP structure are mandatory elements of collective bargaining, and it should not be possible to exclude employees in a collective-bargaining unit without actual bargaining sessions about the ESOP between labor and management.

Rights as owners. Employees' property rights and responsibilities should be related to the extent of employee ownership—the more employee ownership, the more mandated property rights should be present. Worker-owners should be able to protect their own rights through at least a minimum involvement in the governance of the corporation rather than depending on complex rules and more direct government regulation that might encourage court cases. It should be recognized that fiduciaries of employee stock ownership trusts are generally permitted too much self-dealing and self-policing and so should be replaced by trustees elected by the workers themselves on a one-person/one-vote basis. As a further safeguard, all ESOPs should have an advisory board of employees from representative salary groups with full access to ESOP records and basic financial information about the firm.

Voting rights. There should be full voting rights on all stock in ESOPs and all other employee-benefit plans (to eliminate the current loophole whereby a company can set up a profit-sharing plan to get around this obligation) involving employee ownership of more than 15 percent of the firm. This rule will allow limited forms of employee ownership to continue. Every 15 percent of employee equity in privately or publicly held companies should entitle worker-owners to choose a member of the board of directors on a one-person/one-vote basis. There should be full pass-through of voting rights on all stock in majority employee-owned companies, no matter what form of employee-benefit plan holds the equity. Specified small businesses where total ownership is being slowly transferred to employees over a limited number of years should be temporarily excused from this requirement.

Reforming Tax Incentives. Adjustments to the ESOP should be encouraged by means of the tax system. Broadly speaking, deduction limits should be increased so that companies can establish more worker equity in any one year, and tax incentives should be greater for companies adopting more complete employee ownership involving more participation and property rights for employees. ESOPs that include larger number of workers, allocate shares more equitably, and pay dividends directly to workers should receive progressive increases in a number of tax benefits.

Other benefit plans involving employee ownership. There should be special incentives for defined-benefit plans that invest a larger but limited percentage of their assets in employer stock. The insignificant differences in employee ownership through stock-bonus plans, profit-sharing plans, and other employee-benefit plans should be acknowledged, and new ceilings should apply to all plans that hold more than 15 percent of their assets in employer stock. Incentive stock-option plans and qualified stock-purchase plans should also be revised further to encourage broader participation of a larger percentage of the workforce, and the incentives for these plans should be progressively graded according to the liberality of their eligibility requirements.

Compensation according to performance. In order to promote a system of flexible compensation, there should be special incentives for ESOPs combined with profit-sharing plans. To speed a shift from ascribed to earned status, special expanded tax incentives should be allowed employee-ownership plans that tie the pay of managers and workers to performance.

Worker buyouts and start-ups through ESOPs. The financial incentives for ESOPs should be redesigned so that they can be used more effectively in start-ups of new companies and in place of debt financing and straight equity financing. In publicly held companies, representative groups of 80 percent of the employees or collective-bargaining units should have the option to set up worker-investment funds that could function as leveraged ESOPs and borrow funds to purchase employer stock without prior agreement of management or the board of directors. The amount of stock purchased should depend solely on decisions by private-sector banks.

A new plan to broaden stock ownership. A stock ownership plan discussed during the Ford administration should be reconsidered, whereby any citizen could get a tax credit of a specified percent toward the purchase price of stock. This tax credit should be increased if stock is held in the employer corporation.

Promoting Labor-Management Cooperation

Federal Support. Labor-management cooperation should figure as a major part of the economic policy of the country. The Department of Labor should begin a more aggressive campaign of public education on this issue aimed at business, labor, and educational organizations. It should be directed to target cooperation as a major policy goal and fund or match-fund demonstration projects in which experienced change agents would help labor and management create models of cooperation in firms of every size, industry, and type, in every region of the country. It should also establish an elite office of change agents who could work with companies facing serious difficulties. Special tax incentives should be designed for business expenditures for these services.

Organized labor. Labor law must be reformed to remove contradictions between labor-management cooperation and the law. It should be recognized that unions are one of the few forms of employee organization and worker participation familiar to American workers, and procedures governing union elections should be liberalized to make it easier to form unions in this new environment.

Employee ownership of government. The federal government should establish a commission to study how the civil service and unionized federal workers can become more involved in improving the efficiency of federal operations. In other words, improving productivity in the federal service industry should be a major goal, and lessons learned from this experiment should be disseminated to the private sector. The government should privatize various parts of the federal government by selling them to the employees. This privatization should invest aggressively in human-resources training and education to create model enterprises of labor-management cooperation. The process could begin with the Federal Housing Administration's insurance program, since the Reagan administration has been pondering its sale to the private sector. In a related area, a presidential task force on economic justice has suggested how employee ownership could be used in foreign policy.[3]

Worker-owned small businesses. The Small Business Administration and the Department of Agriculture should create more focused programs to encourage worker ownership. In the small-business sector, such ownership may further business continuity, which is a serious problem requiring more attention, while, in agriculture, worker-owned enterprises may provide an important alternative for poorly paid workers.

State and Local Action. State and local governments would be logical sources of technical assistance in setting up or converting to employee-owned firms with labor-management cooperation. Many states have passed employee-ownership laws, and the governors and mayors of the nation should meet to discuss the elements of local legislation.

Some existing models. Under the direction of John Simmons, labor expert at the University of Massachusetts at Amherst, a Massachusetts Commission on Employee Ownership and Participation is drawing up a statewide plan for the legislature and the governor. The author is serving on a similar task force in Pennsylvania's Department of Commerce. Another exciting state initiative is an act proposed by Bruce Scott and George Cabot Lodge of the Harvard Business School, filed with the Massachusetts legislature in 1986. The Commonwealth would reward firms that establish an incentive-compensation plan tied to overall firm performance, make a commitment to train and retrain all employees, agree to collaborate with state and federal programs to enhance workforce productivity, and create a fund to promote job creation and long-term opportunity, which would be administered by a board representing all employees. The incentives would be the exemption of incentive compensation from state income taxes and the deductibility from corporate income taxes of employer contributions to the job-creation fund.

The Role of Business. A careful ongoing process of labor-management cooperation should be the goal. Businesses will be challenged to hire and train or to retrain managers and supervisors to be more adaptable and comfortable in corporate cultures that emphasize partnership. This cooperation can effectively make use of ownership and profit sharing.

Reorganization of whole industries. As entire industrial sectors consider the reorganization of work, industry associations should become more active in examining employee-ownership models in their industries, especially if such associations and industry leaders realize that the misuse of these concepts will likely benefit no one in the long run.

Fortune directory companies. The demise of the tax-credit ESOP is more than compensated for by the new tax incentives for employee ownership, which will create substantial opportunities for large publicly held companies to gain competitive advantages through employee ownership and related programs of labor-management cooperation by borrowing capital, refinancing existing plans with cheaper credit through leveraged ESOPs, redesigning their employee-benefit programs, doing stock buybacks and preemptive takeover defenses, and creating workable systems of flexible compensation. The main challenge to these firms will be to find ways of ensuring effective worker representation in both unionized and nonunionized workplaces and turning employee ownership into a foundation for labor-management cooperation.

Demonstration projects. Many Fortune Directory companies have begun to experiment with forms of labor-management cooperation; they should set up demonstration projects in various subsidiaries.

Employee-equity and labor-management cooperation audits. A number of these companies, as shown, also have many varied programs to encourage employee stock ownership, but these usually are not based on a sound concept of incentives, are not coordinated into a meaningful compensation program, exclude many employees, or contain other barriers to success. They should require employee-equity audits and labor-management cooperation audits to assess how they can begin to integrate these ideas effectively into corporate culture.

Human-resource management. Fortune Directory companies that intend to institute progressive human-resource management can explore ways to make ownership and cooperation a more significant part of their corporate cultures.

The Role of Organized Labor. As this book indicates, the depth of the power conflict between American labor and management suggests a continued role for unions, even under employee ownership. The varied uses of employee ownership challenge unions to cultivate the kind of labor relations they have been pressing management to accept for decades. In addition, organized and even unorganized labor in businesses will increasingly prefer leveraged buyouts of both privately and publicly held companies. The union movement must develop a coherent description of its function in a high-trust/low-conflict company with sizable employee ownership or joint cooperation.

The AFL-CIO. The AFL-CIO must finally enter the fray of employee-ownership legislation. Unorganized workers have no spokespeople, and labor can play the role it has played many times before regarding issues such as unemployment compensation and retirement benefits. The federation should initiate a study of current union involvement in employee ownership and systematically collect and disseminate information to the national unions. In-house experts on the subject should be appointed.

Financial backing of worker ownership. Labor as a whole can take important steps to broaden stock ownership. A small percentage of union pension funds can be set aside to be loaned to workers for new start-ups, buyouts of failing firms, or leveraged buyouts of successful firms. The federation should coordinate this new investment banking role of labor on a national level.

Support for local initiative. National unions should provide locals with encouragement and the best technical assistance possible. Each national union should build employee-ownership and worker-participation efforts that will create models of cooperation in its industries. Unions in hard-pressed industries, such as the Amalgamated Clothing and Textile Workers Union and the International Ladies' Garment Workers' Union, may want to evaluate the potential of these concepts more seriously and even use the leverage and job-creation aspects of employee ownership to create new enterprises and jobs for dislocated members.

Union participation in the structure of ownership. Many sizably, majority, or totally employee-owned firms currently lack and will continue to lack important protections, property rights, and governance rights for the employee-owners. In those firms that are unionized, labor should raise issues and propose amendments to ESOP documents. Where unions are not included in the employee ownership, they should consider bargaining, when possible, for inclusion instead of for cost-of-living increases in defined-benefit pension plans.

Organization of worker-owned firms. In nonunionized firms, unions may well begin organizing drives offering various forms of full or associated membership to worker-owners, in which the union will agree to help the employees monitor and negotiate adequate property and governance rights. Many firms with "new-class" workers have no unions; their extremely narrowly conceived employee-ownership plans, often controlling sizable percentages of the company, offer a potential opening to organization.

A FINAL NOTE

Employee ownership has not lived up to its potential as a revolutionary advance in labor-management relations and entrepreneurial revival. As the evidence here has shown, employee ownership leads to greater worker identification and commitment to the company, yet increased motivation and productivity only result from practical labor-management problem solving and work organized in an interesting way. A complete transformation of American business would require simultaneous attention to properly structured employee ownership, joint labor-management involvement and cooperation in strategic decisions, redesign of work tasks to enhance job enrichment, and short-term profit sharing or gainsharing to reward clearly measurable improvements in productivity. Together, these elements can revitalize a company. But, sadly, we have witnessed only partial applications and, as such only limited success.

Whether Congress and Capitol Hill have the courage to provide the intellectual leadership and the legislative expertise to reshape corporate America in the twenty-first century remains to be seen.

Federal Tax Incentives for ESOPs

These specific and often technical aspects of the tax code comprise a set of standards of behavior created by the government to define the relationship between work and ownership in corporations. They are not mere accounting details; as this book shows, issues important to labor-management relations are also determined by these norms. Changes from the new 1986 tax reform law are italicized; employee ownership was one of the few areas actually treated more favorably under this new law. Unless noted, each incentive is an ongoing part of the law and has no provision to expire.

The Basic Ownership Deduction

A company can deduct from its corporate income taxes contributions to an employee stock ownership trust of stock or cash valuing up to 15 to 25 percent of the compensation of participating workers. An ESOP set up in this manner is often referred to as a nonleveraged ESOP. The maximum 25-percent deduction applies when a nonleveraged ESOP is combined with a money-purchase pension plan.

The Ownership-through-Loans Deduction

A company can deduct from its corporate income taxes contributions to an employee stock ownership trust of stock or cash equaling the principal of a loan used to provide employee stock ownership, up to 25 percent of the compensation of participating workers. The company can deduct an unlimited amount of interest over and above its contributions to other types of retirement plans. An ESOP set up in this manner is often referred to as a leveraged ESOP. *If a company chooses to allocate immediately all the shares acquired by a loan to an ESOP, the company can deduct the entire allocation in the year it is made. This new provision is an incentive for companies to use leveraged ESOPs to carry out large stock buybacks in one year. The deductibility of ESOP dividends used to pay off such a loan also facilitates stock buybacks.*

The Investment, or Payroll-Based, Tax Credit

Until 1982, a company could claim an additional percent on its investment tax credits if that percent was contributed to an employee-ownership trust; the company could also claim an additional 1/2 percent if workers contributed an amount equal to this 1/2 percent. From 1982 to 1986, a company could take a tax credit equal to 0.5 percent of the payroll of participating employees for contributions to an ESOP. The cost of setting up and administering such a plan was deductible. The investment tax credit was in addition to the deduction limits noted above. Utilities were especially favored because they were not required to pass along the tax saving to their consumers. An ESOP set up in this manner is often referred to as the TRASOP (Tax Reduction Act Stock Ownership Plan) or PAYSOP

(Payroll-based Stock Ownership Plan). *This tax credit has now been repealed for compensation paid or accrued after December 31, 1986.*

The Carryover of Tax Deductions

A company can carry over unused deductions from any past year as long as its total deduction in any particular year does not exceed 25 percent of the compensation of participating workers. A corporation could make a tax-deductible contribution of its stock to an ESOP one year and carry that loss back three taxpaying years. *After 1987, deduction carryforwards are repealed.*

The Carryover of Tax Credits

In a given year, the investment tax credit can be carried back three taxable years and carried forward fifteen taxable years. A deduction is allowed for any unused tax credits at the end of that fifteen-year period. *While the tax-credit ESOP has been repealed, some carryovers of tax credits are still allowed.*

No Capital-Gains Taxes for Selling Business to Employees

A businessperson who sells his or her business to the employees by means of an ESOP or worker cooperative is excused from capital-gains taxes on the sale if the ESOP or an eligible worker cooperative holds more than 30 percent of the stock, and the seller invests the proceeds of the sale in the stock of another domestic corporation.

The Deduction of Dividends Paid on ESOP Stock

Dividends paid to workers on stock held by an ESOP can be deducted from corporate taxable income if they are paid within 90 days of being contributed to the ESOP. This deduction is in addition to other deductions. *Dividends on unallocated shares are also deductible. Also, dividends paid into workers' ESOP accounts—rather than to the workers directly—are deductible if they are used to repay a loan to buy worker equity. This makes possible larger ESOP loans with faster repayment.*

The Assumption of a Previous Owner's Estate-Tax Liability in the Sale of a Company to the Employees

Part or all of the estate-tax liability from a deceased owners' estate can be assumed by an ESOP or an eligible worker cooperative in return for a transfer of stock from the estate of equal value. The ESOP can be established before or after the death of the deceased.

The Partial Elimination of a Previous Owner's Estate-Tax Liability in Sale of a Company to the Employees

From October 22, 1986, to January 1, 1992, 50 percent of the proceeds from a sale to an ESOP or an eligible worker-owned cooperative can be excluded from the previous owner's gross estate.

Combination Interest Subsidy to ESOPs and Deduction for Lenders Making Loans to ESOPs

A bank, insurance company, or other commercial lender may exclude from its income 50 percent of the interest earned on loans to ESOP companies, if the loans are used to finance employee ownership of company stock. Such lenders usually pass on some of this saving to the ESOP company by reducing the interest rate on the loan. *Mutual funds, too, can qualify for this interest deduction. This is also extended to the refinancing of loans used to acquire employer securities after May 23, 1984. In addition, the interest exclusion is available with respect to a loan to a corporation if, within thirty days, employer securities are transferred to the ESOP in an amount equal to the proceeds of the loan, and the securities are allocated to workers' accounts within one year after the date of the loan. These loans, which can also be used to refinance existing debt, must have a commitment date of no more than seven years, a limit that includes both the original commitment period and the period of any subsequent refinancing.*

A Subsidy to Employee-Owners for Life Insurance on Key Executives or Other Workers

To protect the value of an ESOP's stock against the death of a key person in the company, an ESOP can insure that person's life. The corporation's contribution of the premium for the insurance to the ESOP is tax deductible from corporate income taxes. The corporation can subsequently borrow from the policy the amount it did not recoup on its tax deduction.

Magnified Tax Value of Charitable Contributions

A shareholder of a closely held corporation can make a contribution of stock to a charitable organization and receive the normal income-tax deduction for the current value of the gift. The charitable organization immediately sells the stock to the company's ESOP at the appraised value of the securities, which establishes the value of the stock for the purpose of the deduction. This arrangement may be more valuable to the donor since the stock may have originally cost less than the current appraised value. The donor thus gets a greater deduction in some cases, and estate tax is reduced by the removal of this asset from his or her estate. Additionally, the donor gets cash for the stock from a convenient market—the ESOP. The corporation contributes the funds to the ESOP to purchase the stock from the charity and receives a tax deduction.

Incentive for Terminating Other Employee-Benefit Plans and Establishing ESOPs in Their Place

Through 1988, the excess assets fom terminated employee-benefit plans (such as other defined-benefit and defined-contribution plans) can be rolled over into an ESOP without the usual 10-percent excise tax that the law otherwise imposes on companies removing such assets.

ESOP Exception to Net Operating-Loss Limitations

While the 1986 tax reform act imposes new limitations on the utilization of a corporation's net operating-loss (and certain other tax-credit) carryforwards, following a more-than-50-percent change in ownership within prescribed periods of time, if any transaction(s) results in ESOP ownership of at least 50 percent of the corporation, these limitations will not apply.

ESOP Exception to Pension-Plan Asset Reversion Excise Tax

The new tax reform law imposes a 10-percent excise tax on the reversion of excess assets from overfunded defined-benefit pension plans. Until January 1, 1989, however, excess assets transferred to an ESOP will not be subject to this tax nor will they be considered taxable income for the employer, as long as the excess assets are used by the ESOP either to acquire employer stock or to repay a loan incurred to acquire employer stock, and the ESOP covers at least 50 percent of the pension plan's participants.

Special Tax Waivers for Individuals

The new tax reform act imposed a 10-percent excise tax on taxable distributions made after 1986 from qualified benefit plans to participants up to age 59 1/2, unless the distribution occurs because of death, disability, or early retirement under the plan. Prior to 1990, this excise tax will not apply to any distributions or cash dividends on employer stock passed through to participants. Also, after December 31, 1986, the act eliminates the preferential tax treatment for capital gains but permits a current ESOP participant to elect to include any appreciation in the value of employer stock as part of the taxable amount eligible for special income tax averaging available for certain lump-sum distributions.

General Sources

Congressional Record (September 18, 1986): H7704–5, H7708–9, H7713–20, H7725, H7744, H7823.

Frisch, Robert A. *The Magic of ESOPs and LBOs.* Rockville Centre, N.Y.: Farnsworth Publishing, 1985, pp. 25–68.

Kaplan, Jared, Gregory Brown, and Ronald Ludwig. *Tax Management: ESOPs.* Washington, D.C.: Bureau of National Affairs, 1985, pp. A1–20. (A revised edition of this work, released on July 7, 1987, contains an extensive review of the new tax laws on pages 75–77 and 307–13 and can be ordered by telephone [1-800-372-1033].)

Ludwig, Ronald, and Jack Curtis. *Memorandum to Our ESOP Clients.* San Francisco: Ludwig & Curtis, Inc., October 22, 1986, pp. 3–4.

Corporate Uses for ESOPs by Current Owners, Managers, and Workers

It is common to think of current owners and managers as the initiators of ESOPs because the law gives this authority to the existing officers of a corporation. However, employees or subgroups of employees and/or managers within a company can also initiate an ESOP if management or the current owners agree to transfer ownership in an acquisition or a worker buyout, or they can establish an ESOP as part of collective bargaining.

The use of the following incentives requires that the corporation: (1) have either taxable income during a certain year or the ability to carry its tax deductions backward or forward; (2) limit its deductions for ESOP contributions to 15 to 25 percent of the compensation of participating workers, depending on the type of ESOP; and (3) ensure that the ESOP is used for the exclusive benefit of the employees (although this does not preclude simultaneous corporate uses). As long as a company abides by these and other legal requirements, it can usually use any number of tax advantages and corporate-financing incentives in any combination it desires. The uses apply to both publicly and privately held firms unless a distinction is made.

Increase Short-Term Cash Flow and Working Capital

If a company contributes stock or cash to purchase stock to an ESOP, the deduction of this contribution from corporate taxes will increase working capital and cash flow without any cash expenditure or additional productive effort. For example, banks are increasingly using ESOPs to strengthen their capital positions.

Provide an Alternative to the Fiscal Responsibilities of a Defined-Benefit Plan

A defined-benefit retirement plan commits the employer to making and investing annual contributions to a pension trust sufficient to pay out the plan's promised benefits. These contributions are tax deductible but reduce working capital and cash flow. Companies may oppose increasing benefits in existing defined-benefit plans, or even establishing such plans at all, because of high funding and administration costs and because companies are now liable for up to 30 percent of the net worth of terminated, underfunded pension plans. A company may replace or supplement such a plan by contributing stock or cash to an ESOP, thus creating an employee benefit without reducing cash flow or working capital and incurring uncertain financial commitments and new liabilities. Through 1988, companies can terminate other defined-benefit and defined-contribution plans and use the excess assets to establish employee stock ownership plans without paying the usual 10-percent excise tax on such asset reversions.[1]

Provide an Alternative to the Fiscal Responsibilities of Another Defined-Contribution Plan

In other defined-contribution retirement plans, such as profit-sharing, stock-bonus, and thrift plans, contributions are tax deductible within limits, and employees bear the investment risk of variable market performance of the funds. But these plans are generally restricted to investing 10 percent of their assets in employer securities, except for certain specially designated profit-sharing plans. A company can set up an ESOP instead and avoid the short-term reduction in working capital and cash flow that attends these other plans. Or a company could convert an existing profit-sharing, thrift, or stock-bonus plan to an ESOP, using the terminated plan's assets to purchase stock from the corporation or from stockholders. In this way, the assets of the defined-contribution plan are brought wholly into the company, thus increasing working capital and cash flow.[1]

Raise Capital for the Firm More Cheaply

Instead of borrowing money for corporate use directly from a bank, a company or its ESOP can borrow for the purpose of employee stock ownership. If the ESOP takes out the loan, it then buys company stock, and the company in turn makes contributions to the ESOP equal to the principal and interest payments, which are deductible within certain limits. (Only interest payments are deductible when companies without ESOPs borrow funds.) If the company takes out the loan, it makes cash contributions to the ESOP equal to the installment payments on the loan so that the ESOP can purchase company stock. In this case the principal is deductible. Either way, the company gets new capital at a discount equal to its tax saving. Since banks and other commercial lenders can deduct 50 percent of their profits from interest on loans to ESOPs, they can pass along these tax savings in lower interest rates. An ESOP set up in this manner is called a leveraged ESOP.

Repurchase Stock

Companies are repurchasing stock more and more frequently. A leveraged or nonleveraged ESOP can be used to integrate a variety of employee-ownership goals with potential tax advantages in an innovative repurchase arrangement. To make this easier, when corporations borrow money to buy back their stock and allocate the shares to workers' accounts in the year the loan is made, the law now permits them to deduct the entire allocation in the year it is made, pay back the loan over seven years, and deduct dividends paid on worker stock that are used to help repay the loan. In this case, the company sets up a nonleveraged ESOP to which it contributes within thirty days stock equal in value to the amount of the loan. Further, the 50-percent exclusion for interest paid on securities-acquisitions loans also applies to the refinancing of loans made after May 23, 1984, and used to acquire employer securities.

Buy Out Minority or Majority Shareholders or Sell Whole Companies to Employees

All or part of a company can be sold to the employees using an ESOP. The company contributes to the ESOP cash on hand or borrowed cash. If the firm is closely held, it can buy out holdings of any size through its ESOP, even though the stock is thinly traded. In some situations this eliminates the need for a public-securities offering. If an owner of a private company wishes to leave, retire, or plan for retirement, he or she can sell stock to the ESOP all at once or gradually. If an owner sells 80 percent or more of his or her stock to another corporation, the capital-gains taxes will be deferred until the newly acquired shares are sold. The law now allows this same provision to ESOPs, except that an owner need not sell 80 percent or more of the shares to qualify—the only requirement is that the ESOP own 30 percent or more of the company stock after the sale, regardless of how it acquired that ownership. If the owner dies, liability for estate taxes can be assumed by the ESOP in return for a transfer of stock of equal value from the estate.

Sell a Company Threatened with Shutdown to Its Employees or Divest an Unwanted Division or Subsidiary

A company threatened with shutdown can set up an ESOP, which then borrows funds to purchase the firm. A company plant or subsidiary threatened with shutdown or divestiture can be taken over by the ESOP of a newly formed company created to acquire it. In some cases, companies save certain shutdown penalties, such as severance pay and pension obligations, through this method.

Defend against Takeover or Maximize Internal Control

A company threatened with a hostile takeover or wishing to protect itself from such a takeover can set up an ESOP to shelter its stock from being purchased publicly or privately. This maneuver can be used to attenuate the control of various key stockholders in both publicly traded and closely held firms or to scare off potential raiders.

Carry out Hostile or Friendly Takeovers by Employees

Employees can use a leveraged ESOP to carry out a friendly or hostile takeover of their own company. In some cases, they will be competing with the bids of foreign firms; in others, they may compete with a proposed buyout by management or other corporate or private investors who may or may not be sympathetic to the needs of the employees. When employees are faced with their company being sold to an unfriendly suitor who intends to finance the purchase almost entirely with borrowed money, a partial or complete ESOP buyout can be an effective strategy by labor.

"Give" Workers Stock at No Cost to the Company

From 1983 to 1986, a company could set up a TRASOP or PAYSOP and take a dollar-for-dollar tax credit for contributions to this ESOP up to 0.5 percent of the total compensation of participating workers. Also, with a nonleveraged ESOP, a company can get an immediate tax deduction for contributing stock to an ESOP used for an employee benefit, even though no capital has as yet left the company's coffers. Upon retirement or separation from service, however, the company must redeem that stock with cash, although departing employee-owners in publicly held firms can sell their stock in the open market.

Finance a Leveraged Buyout of a Public Corporation

Management and/or employees who want to take a large public corporation private can set up an ESOP with which to leverage funds sufficient to buy as much of the company as desired. Frequently, leveraged-ESOP buyouts are combined with management buyouts or buyouts by friendly acquirers.

Deduct Employee Dividends from Corporate Income

Dividends paid directly to workers on ESOP stock can be deducted from corporate income for tax purposes, unlike dividends paid on stock held by nonemployees or other employee-benefit plans. Dividends not paid directly to workers, but deposited in their ESOP accounts and used to repay ESOP loans, can also be deducted, which further lightens the burden of leveraging employee ownership.

Trade Stock for Wage or Benefit Concessions

A company can set up and contribute stock or cash to an ESOP in return for wage or benefit concessions. A company can also coordinate the establishment of the ESOP with its borrowing plans so that some funds are borrowed by the ESOP and made available to the firm when the ESOP buys stock, the value of which actually represents wage or benefit concessions. The company thus gets concessions, as well as tax deductions.

Develop a Flexible Compensation System

A company can use its ESOP alone or in combination with profit sharing to develop a system of payment more sensitive to productivity and profitability than flat wages and customary benefits.

Involve Workers in Equity Participation as Part of a Human-Resource Program

A company setting up an ESOP essentially receives a government subsidy to sell equity to its workers. Whether the company uses existing company funds or stock or leveraged funds, it gains a benefit program with a tax deduction; if it contributes stock, it establishes its program without any immediate cash expenditure.

Purchase Life Insurance for Key Executives or Workers

See Appendix A.

Resolve Estate and Estate-Tax Problems

An ESOP can be used to prevent a closely held company from being sold or liquidated to pay estate taxes. A shareholder can have made this provision before his or her death, or the Executor can agree to the option. The amount of stock sold to the employees must equal the federal estate tax assumed by the ESOP. Alternatively, ESOPs can purchase businesses from estates.

Use as a Strategy in Collective Bargaining

Unions can negotiate for an ESOP in exchange for wage and benefit cuts. An ESOP-sponsored voice in the management of the company through voting rights or seats on the board of directors or a shareholder position to negotiate about company policies can be part of the agreement. The deal may also include the right of first refusal to purchase the company as a future negotiating tool with potential buyers; specified rights and protections in the event of a merger, takeover, or consolidation, such as weighted voting rights, successorship rights for the union, or preemptive shareholder rights to prevent dilution of future worker equity; and limits or controls on the creation of subsidiaries and holding companies that could circumvent labor agreements. The union could secure protections in the case of bankruptcy or liquidation, such as special liquidation preferences for worker-owned stock.[2]

Increase the Value and Possibilities of Charitable Contributions

See Appendix A.

Convert Ownership of a Proprietorship or Partnership

A proprietorship or partnership may choose to convert to employee ownership for any of the reasons already noted. The firm can convert to a corporation and then use an ESOP to make ownership available to its employees. This may be an attractive method for a single proprietor who wishes to convert to the corporate form to limit his or her liability and/or raise capital without the separation of ownership and control of the conventional corporation. Members of a partnership may want to extend the partnership to workers lacking sufficient capital to buy in. They may wish to expand the business or acquire other businesses to take advantage of new opportunities or growing demand. They may prefer having employee-owners to the interpersonal and financial uncertainties of finding stockholders for a new closely held corporation or of taking a new company public.

Refinance Existing Debt

A corporation with an existing loan can refinance at a lower interest rate with employee ownership. Essentially, the refinanced loan is made to the ESOP, which uses the proceeds to invest in employer stock. Because banks are allowed to deduct 50 percent of the interest income from refinancing loans taken out after May 23, 1984, and used to acquire employer securities, banks will generally refinance at a lower interest rate.

Finance Acquisition of Another Company

Under present tax law, stock or assets of another company must be purchased with after-tax dollars. If assets are bought, the purchase price is allocated among the various assets such as plant, equipment, inventory, and goodwill. If stock is purchased, there is no such allocation, but additional liabilities are involved. The acquisition can be leveraged using employee ownership. The acquiring company sets up an ESOP, and, if the transaction is leveraged, this ESOP obtains a loan. The subsidiary's stock is purchased by the ESOP, or parent-company stock is exchanged for subsidiary stock. Either a merger of the two firms or the continuation of the acquired company as a subsidiary is possible. Or the assets are acquired, which go to the acquiring company, and company stock is transferred to the ESOP trust to offset payments for the assets—the ESOP trust acts as an intermediary between the parent corporation and the subsidiary.

Notes

1. For the best discussion of the conversion of defined-contribution and defined-benefit plans into ESOPs, see Ronald L. Ludwig, "Conversion of Existing Plans to Employee Stock Ownership Plans," *American University Law Review* 26 (Spring 1977): 632–56.
2. Adapted completely from Randy Barber, *Employee Stock Ownership Plans: Their Uses and Abuses* (Washington, D.C.: Center for Economic Organizing, 1985), pp. 22–24.

General Sources

American Capital Strategies. *American Capital Strategies: An Investment Banking Firm for Labor.* Prospectus. Bethesda, Md.: American Capital Strategies, April 2, 1987, pp. 5–7.

Frisch, Robert A. *The Magic of ESOPs and LBOs.* Rockville Centre, N.Y.: Farnsworth Publishing, 1985.

Jochim, Timothy C. *Employee Stock Ownership and Related Plans: Analysis and Practice.* Westport, Conn.: Quorum Books, 1982.

Kravitz, William N., and Charles Smith. *ESOPs and ESOP Transactions.* New York: Practicing Law Institute, 1985, pp. 9–110.

Selected Background Facts

Table C–1. The Sources of Funds for Nonfarm, Nonfinancial Corporations in Selected Years 1955–1985 (percent).[a]

	1955	1960	1965	1970	1975	1980
Total dollars	$52,660	$48,622	$91,840	$102,344	$156,953	$335,231
Internal	55.9	72.8	63.7	60.4	76.2	5,.5
Retained earnings	22.4	16.5	20.8	7.4	21.7	14.6
Capital-consumption allowance	36.1	54.8	35.4	50.6	59.8	50.1
Iva and cca[b]	-7.1	-4.7	2.7	-4.0	-13.5	-17.1
Foreign earnings	4.5	6.2	4.8	6.4	8.3	8.9
External	44.1	27.2	36.3	39.6%	23.8	43.5
New equity issues	3.3	2.8	[c]	5.6	6.3	3.8
Debt	16.0	22.0	20.0	28.9	13.3	23.3
Other	24.8	2.4	16.1	5.2	4.2	16.3

	1981	1982	1983	1984	1985
Total dollars	$364,155	$309,360	$436,349	$482,597	$449,520
Internal	63.3	75.7	64.3	69.4	79.0
Retained earnings	12.6	3.3	4.3	7.1	5.5
Capital-consumption allowance	52.0	66.9	49.3	47.3	53.1
Iva and cca[b]	-8.1	-1.8	5.0	10.2	15.2
Foreign earnings	6.7	7.2	5.7	4.8	5.2
External	36.7	24.3	35.7	30.6	21.0
New equity issues	-3.1[d]	3.7	6.5	-16.0[d]	-18.9[d]
Debt	28.3	22.6	13.6	36.4	31.8
Other	11.6	-2.1	15.6	10.2	8.2

a. Dollars current in millions, adjusted seasonally but not annually for inflation. All figures based on quarterly estimates, except 1985, which is based on first-quarter estimates only.
b. Iva = inventory valuation adjustment; cca = capital consumption adjustment.
c. Less than 0.05 percent.
d. Indicates firms bought more stock than they issued.

Source: U.S. General Accounting Office, *Employee Stock Ownership Plans: Interim Report on b Survey and Related Economic Trends* (Washinton, D.C.: U.S. General Accounting Office, February 1986), p. 49.

Table C–2.   Fortune 500 Companies Where Internal Employee Funds Are the Largest Stockholder.

Company	Percentage of Outstanding Stock	Type of Plan/Trust
Abbott Laboratories	5.6	Stock Retirement
American Brands	3.6	Profit-Sharing
Armco Steel	14.7	Thrift, ESOP
Ashland Oil	7.1	Thrift/ESOP
Atlantic Richfield	3.1	Thrift and Savings
Bendix	19.7	Savings, Stock Ownership (Salaried)
Bethlehem Steel	7.4	Savings (Salaried)
Blue Bell	10.0	Savings, Profit-Sharing Retirement
Burlington Industries	12.9	Profit-Sharing
Butler Manufacturing	15.9	Profit-Sharing Stock-Purchase
Caterpillar Tractor	7.0	Investment
Celanese	19.8	Stock-Bonus and Investment
Chrysler	11.3	Thrift/Stock Ownership
Cities Service	8.0	Thrift, TRASOP
Combustion Engineering	8.8	Thrift-Investment (Salaried)
Conoco	4.8	Thrift, Investment, ESOP
Crown Zellerbach	7.9	Savings and Stock-Purchase (Salaried)
Cyclops Corp.	9.1	Profit-Sharing Investment
Dayco	27.3	Stock-Purchase and Other Pension Trusts
Dennison Manufacturing	8.4	ESOP, Stock-Savings
Eastman Kodak	2.6	Savings and Investment, Stock-Purchase
Eaton Corp.	3.9	Share-Purchase
Exxon	2.4	Thrift, ESOP
Federal-Mogull	11.6	Savings and Investment (Salaried)
FMC Corp.	9.0	Thrift and Stock-Purchase, TRASOP
General Electric	4.1	Savings and Security

General Motors	12.8	Stock-Purchase, ESOP (Salaried)
Georgia-Pacific	2.6	Stock-Bonus
Gillette	4.7	Savings
B. F. Goodrich	14.7	Stock-Purchase and Savings, TRASOP
Gould	4.4	Saving and Profit-Sharing
Grumman	38.2	Investment, Pension
Hart Shaffner & Marx	5.2	Savings/Investment
Hercules	9.6	Savings
International Harvester	9.7	Savings and Investment ESOP (Salaried)
Johns-Manville	7.1	Thrift Stock-Purchase
McCormick & Co.	14.0	Profit-Sharing
McDonnell Douglas	24.4	Savings
McGraw Edison	18.6	Profit-Sharing
Mobil Oil	5.7	Savings, ESOP
Nabisco	7.6	Stock-Purchase
Nalco Chemical	6.4	Profit-Sharing
National Steel	18.4	Stock-Investment (Salaried)
Northrop	27.3	Savings
Occidental	4.2	Thrift, TRASOP
Olin Corp.	16.3	Incentive Thrift, TRASOP
Owens-Illinois	8.7	Stock-Purchase and Savings
Phillips Petroleum	6.8	Thrift, ESOP
Procter & Gamble	12.7	Profit-Sharing, Stock-Purchase
Rockwell International	25.8	Savings
SCM Corp.	5.2	Savings and Investment
Sherwin Williams	27.3	Stock-Purchase and Investment
Signal Companies	21.0	Savings and Stock-Purchase, TRASOP
Signode Corp.	6.2	Savings and Profit-Sharing
Standard Oil of California	9.8	Stock
Standard Oil (Indiana)	7.5	Savings, ESOP
Tenneco	4.6	Thrift, ESOP
Texaco	4.4	Savings, ESOP
Texas Instruments	9.4	Profit-Sharing

Textron	18.3	Stock/Savings
TRW	10.6	Stock/Savings
Tyler Corp.	15.9	Saving and Investment
Union Carbide	1.9	Savings
Union Oil of California	6.2	Profit-Sharing
Uniroyal	7.4	Savings (Salaried), TRASOP
U.S. Steel	16.7	U.S. Steel and Carnegie Pension Trust, Savings (Salaried)
Universal Leaf Tobacco	8.6	Stock-Purchase Savings and
Westinghouse	5.8	Investment Savings and
Westvaco	10.2	Investment (Salaried)

Source: Corporate Data Exchange, *Fortune 500 Stock Ownership Directory* (New York: Corporate Data Exchange, Inc., 1981).

Table C–3.   Prevalence of Other Plans Providing Company Stock Ownership (percent).

	Status of PAYSOP			
	Have/Are Establishing	*Still Considering*	*No Plan*	*All Companies*
Have Other Company Stock Plans	87.5	73.8	58.2	78.2
Profit-sharing plan investing 10 percent or more in company stock	19.4	9.5	5.1	14.5
Matching savings/thrift plan investing in company stock	48.3	50.0	31.6	44.1
ESOP (other than PAYSOP/TRASOP)	4.7	4.8	2.0	4.0
Nonqualified stock-purchase plan	34.1	21.4	18.4	28.5
Qualified stock-purchase plans (under Code Section 423)	9.9	11.9	12.2	10.8
Other type of company stock plans for a broad group of employees	3.5	2.4	5.1	3.8
No Other Company Stock Plans	12.5	26.2	41.8	21.8
Total Number of Responses	232	42	98	372

Source: Hewitt Associates, *1984 PAYSOP Survey of Fortune Directory Companies* (Lincolnshire, Ill.: Hewitt Associates, 1984).

The Effect of Employee Ownership on Firm Performance

Findings from three very important summaries of ESOPs—Steven Bloom, *Employee Ownership and Firm Performance* (Cambridge: Harvard University Department of Economics, 1986), Michael Quarrey, *Employee Ownership and Corporate Performance* (Oakland, Calif.: National Center for Employee Ownership, 1986), and the 1987 GAO study—are not included here because they are addressed in the text.

ESOPs in U.S Companies

One hundred twenty-eight ESOP companies showed an average annual productivity growth rate 1.52 percentage points higher than that of conventional companies from 1975 to 1979. Unfortunately, the companies were compared to a weighted national average, and no controls were used to check for alternative explanations of the productivity growth.

Source: Thomas R. Marsh and Dale E. McAllister, "ESOP Tables: A Survey of Companies with Employee Stock Ownership Plans," *Journal of Corporation Law* 6, no. 3 (1981): 552–623.

From 1976 to 1978, productivity grew four times faster in seventy-five ESOP firms than in U.S. firms as a whole. Profits increased twice as fast as in all U.S. companies. Again, controls were not used to determine what was responsible for the increases.

Source: Russell Long, "Expanded Ownership—Its Importance to the Free Enterprise System," *Congressional Record* 127, no. 50 (March 27, 1981): n.p.

Seventy percent of ESOP companies surveyed in 1982 reported that their ESOPs tended to improve employees' motivation and productivity. The figure was 72 percent in 1983, 74 percent in 1985, and 76 percent in 1985. The data were based on subjective reports by the managers of ESOP firms, with no actual empirical study to support their opinions.

Sources: ESOP Association, *ESOP Survey: 1982* (Washington, D.C.: ESOP Association of America, 1982), Idem., *ESOP Survey: 1983* (Washington, D.C.: ESOP Association of America, 1983), Idem., *ESOP Survey: 1984* (Washington, D.C.: ESOP Association of America, 1984), Idem., *ESOP Survey: 1985* (Washington, D.C.: ESOP Association of America, 1985).

In case studies of two newspaper companies, ESOPs were found to provide an incentive for improving productivity and the flow of information. Broader comparisons were not made.

Source: Paul C. Taylor, *Employee Stock Ownership: A Microeconomic Analysis* (Ann Arbor, Mich.: University Microfilms International, 1981).

The hypothesis that employee ownership causes employees to work harder at their jobs was only weakly supported by case studies of two individual companies where extensive surveys of employees' attitudes and behaviors were conducted. Some economic-performance data were collected for one of the firms, but the results were inconclusive.

Source: Douglas Kruse, *Employee Ownership and Employee Attitudes: Two Case Studies* (Norwood, Pa.: Norwood Editions, 1984).

Seventy percent of 180 ESOP companies, most closely held with two to three principal stockholders, cited improved employee motivation as a benefit of the plan, but most respondents were unsure of the actual effects. Comments indicated that the ESOP did not create team spirit where none existed previously. Many respondents considered their own financial benefit to be the main advantage. No empirical economic research was conducted.

Source: Graduate School of Management, University of California at Los Angeles, "Summary of the Results of the Survey of Employee Stock Ownership Plans," (UCLA Mimeograph, December 1977).

ESOPs were credited with improving operating profits in a sample of 165 manufacturing companies. The percent of stock owned by employees, the percent of employees with vested interests, and the size of the most recent ESOP contribution were cited to explain the results. Adequate controls were not exercised in the study.

Sources: Randy G. Swad, *ESOPs and Tax Policy: An Empirical Investigation of the Impact of ESOPs on Company Performance* (Baton Rouge: Louisiana State University, 1979); *Idem.*, "Some Empirical Evidence on the Impact of ESOPs on Company Performance," *Oil and Gas Tax Quarterly* 29 (June 1981): 751–58.

The rate of return on equity for fifty-one ESOP firms averaged 2.3 percentage points lower than that of fifty-one comparable non-ESOP firms from 1967 to 1976. The causes were not explored in detail.

Source: D. T. Livingston and J. B. Henry, "The Effect of Employee Ownership Plans on Corporate Profits," *Journal of Risk Insurance* 47 (September 1980): 493–99.

Ten ESOP and non-ESOP firms in the electrical and electronic machinery, equipment, and supplies industry were matched from 1978 to 1981. Productivity in the non-ESOP firms generally equaled or surpassed that of the ESOP firms. The ESOP firms, however, consistently outperformed the non-ESOP firms during 1980 and 1981. Reasons for this were not explored.

Source: Harold Hamilton, *The Effects of Employee Stock Ownership Plans on the Financial Performance of the Electrical and Electronic Machinery, Equipment, and Supplies Industry* (Ann Arbor, Mich.: University Microfilms International, 1983).

Ten ESOP firms were not significantly more profitable than ten matched firms by three measures of profitability (ratios of net profits to net sales, net worth, and net working capital). Reasons for this were not explored.

Source: Corey Rosen and Katherine Klein, "Job-Creating Performance of Employee-Owned Firms," *Monthly Labor Review* 106 (August 1983): 15–19.

Twenty-eight companies sold to the employees by departing owners were studied from the time of the owners' departure until 1984. Sales figures from Dun and Bradstreet's Million Dollar Directory were compared to figures for five comparable companies in Standard and Poor's Index of Corporations. Sales in the ESOP companies grew on average 1.3 times faster than those of comparable non-ESOP companies. The research establishes that companies transferred to employee ownership are not necessarily sinking ships deserted by their captains. The study did not apply appropriate controls.

Source: Alan Cohen, "After the Owner Leaves: Corporate Performance after an ESOP Buys out an Owner," *Employee Ownership* 5, no. 4 (August 1985): 1, 5.

A number of case studies of individual companies have included data on economic performance and documented substantial post-ESOP improvements. In some cases, a disastrous pre-ESOP record was reversed in a modest or startling way.

Sources: John Simmons and William Mares, *Working Together* (New York: Alfred A. Knopf, 1983); Karl Frieden, *Workplace Democracy and Productivity* (Washington, D.C.: National Center for Economic Alternatives, 1980); Michael A. Gurdon, *The Structure of Ownership: Implications for Employee Influence and Organizational Design* (Ann Arbor, Mich.: University Microfilms International, 1979); William Foote Whyte, Tove Helland Hammer, Christopher Meek, Reed Nelson, and Robert N. Stern, *Worker Participation and Ownership: Cooperative Strategies for Strengthening Local Economies* (Ithaca, N.Y.: ILR Press, 1983); Richard J. Long, *The Effects of Formal Employee Participation in Ownership and Decision-making on Perceived and Desired Patterns of Organizational Influence: A Longitudinal Study* (Saskatoon, Canada: University of Saskatchewan, 1981); Richard J. Long, "Job Attitudes and Organizational Performance under Employee Ownership," *Academy of Management Journal* 23 (1980): 726–37; Stewart Perry, *San Francisco Scavengers: Dirty Work and the Pride of Ownership* (Berkeley: University of California Press, 1978).

Two hundred and forty-two employees in seven American firms in different industries were studied to investigate the relationship between adoption of an ESOP and financial performance. Financial performance was measured for the two years preceding and the two years following the adoption of the ESOP. Sales growth, earnings growth, earning to sales ratio, and earnings to total capital ratio did not improve significantly, but employees' personal motivations did. However, the research could not confirm that coworkers encouraged each other to be more productive, although group problem-solving processes did improve in the companies. Neither managerial leadership nor organizational climate changed for the better after the ESOP's adoption, but the researchers found that there was a relationship between changes in managerial leadership and positive changes in peer encouragement and improved group problem-solving processes.

Source: Stephen G. Franklin, *The Impact of Employee Stock Ownership Plans on Individual Motivation, Peer Group Behavior, and Organizational Performance* (Ann Arbor, Mich.: University Microfilms International, 1979).

Ninety-eight employee-owned companies were between 50 and 70 percent more profitable than comparable conventional companies in 1976. The ratio increased with the amount of ownership held by workers, although worker ownership had a negative effect on profitability when equity was skewed toward management. Direct employee ownership increased profits more than employee ownership through an ESOP. Managers believed that employee ownership increased profitability and productivity. Adequate controls were not exercised to trace the cause of the profitability.

Source: Michael Conte and Arnold Tannenbaum, *Employee Ownership* (Ann Arbor, Mich.: Survey Research Center, University of Michigan, 1980).

Majority employee ownership appears to have a positive impact on profitability, although there seems to be no relationship between nonmanagerial employee ownership and profitability. A sample of 156 companies with employee ownership performed at roughly the same level as comparable companies, although the employee-owned firms were 10 percent more likely to stay in business. Thus, this follow-up of the 1980 Conte and Tannenbaum research found no evidence of better performance or growth from 1977 to 1982. The study covered 55 companies from the previous study, as well as 101 new companies. The authors suggested that the earlier study may have been performed in a less recessionary period, which biased the data, and that employee-owned firms were more inclined to accept fewer profits in recessionary years.

Source: Arnold Tannenbaum, Jack R. Lohmann, and Harold B. Cook, *Worker Ownership and the Technological Modernness of Companies. Report to the National Science Foundation* (Ann Arbor, Mich.: University of Michigan Institute for Social Research, 1984).

Thirteen publicly traded companies with 10 percent or more employee ownership in 1984 ranked above two-thirds of comparable nonemployee-owned companies in terms of average profits per dollar of revenues as well as average return on equity. Stock prices in these firms tended to follow industry norms. Adequate controls were not exercised in this study.

Source: Ira Wagner and Corey Rosen, "Employee Ownership: Its Effects on Corporate Performance," *Employee Relations Today*, Spring 1985: n.p.

Other Forms of Employee Ownership in U.S.
Companies

Sixty-one percent of companies with stock-purchase plans reported that their plans improved productivity. Seventy-three percent of companies with profit sharing reported the same. The data were based on managers' own obsevations, with no corroborating empirical study.

Source: William C. Freund and Eugene Epstein, *People and Productivity* (Homewood, Ill.: Dow Jones-Irwin, 1984).

In a study of data on labor productivity in individual producer cooperatives, Derek Jones found output per worker to be greater than in comparable conventional firms in some cases and lower in others. The successful cooperatives were profitable over substantial periods of time (more than ten years). The data suggest that cooperative performance can equal or surpass that of conventional firms, although information on capitalization was not included.

Sources: Derek C. Jones, "U.S. Producer Cooperatives: The Record to Date," *Industrial Relations* 8, no. 2 (Fall 1979): 342–56; *Idem.*, "The Economics and Industrial Relations of Producer Cooperatives in the U.S., 1791–1939," *Economic Analysis and Workers' Management* 12 (1977): 295–316.

Studying tax audits of U.S. plywood cooperatives as part of an Internal Revenue Service inquiry, Katrina Berman found that their output per worker was 30 percent higher than in comparable conventional plywood firms. Berman, however, examined only the most successful cooperatives, which were not representative of the norm, and did not try to establish the reasons for the increases.

Source: Katrina V. Berman, *Worker-Owned Plywood Companies* (Pullman, Wash.: Washington State University Press, 1967).

A study of high-performance and low-performance plywood cooperatives—defined by the average financial distribution per member in a five-year period and the change in book value of a member's share in the same period—confirmed that the variation among cooperatives was due to differences in participation, the ratio of worker-owners to all owners, the ratio of worker-owners to all employees, and average total capital. Output per worker was found to be marginally higher in cooperatives than in comparable plywood companies. Adequate controls were not applied.

Source: Carl J. Bellas, *Industrial Democracy and the Worker-Owned Firm: A Study of Twenty-One Plywood Companies in the Pacific Northwest* (New York: Praeger, 1972).

A survey of 364 electronic and computer companies in 1985 indicated that those sharing ownership with employees grew two to four times faster than companies where employees did not own stock. If the companies offered stock to managers alone, the growth rate was 50 percent lower than if the companies did not offer stock at all. Those encouraging broadened stock ownership and participation grow 275 percent faster than those limiting stock to management. Adequate controls were not used in the survey.

Source: Matthew Trachman, *Employee Ownership and Corporate Growth in High Technology Companies: Report to the National Venture Capital Association* (Oakland, Calif.: National Center for Employee Ownership, 1985).

Employee Ownership in Foreign Companies

Profit sharing, worker participation, and worker ownership in Italian producer cooperatives have tended to improve productivity, or at least not to diminish it. These cooperatives experienced much higher rates of profit than conventional firms. It is not possible to assess the reasons for this, although the study explored possible explanations somewhat more carefully than did others.

Source: Alberto Zevi, "The Performance of Italian Producer Cooperatives," in *Participatory and Self-Managed Firms: Evaluating Economic Performance*, ed. Derek C. Jones and Jan Svejnar (Lexington, Mass.: Lexington Books,1982), pp. 239–52.

A study of the organizational structure and productivity of British producer cooperatives from 1948 to 1968 indicated that worker ownership seldom affected productivity one way or the other. When worker participation in the enterprise was low, worker ownership could actually reduce productivity. Derek Jones found that incentives contributed to productivity in small producer cooperatives but were ineffective in larger enterprises, with or without participation in management. Worker ownership in which a high proportion of workers were also owners combined with a great degree of participation in management did enhance productivity. These conclusions support a study of West German cooperative firms by J. Cable and F. Fitzroy.

Sources: Derek C. Jones, "British Producer Cooperatives: 1948–1968: Productivity and Organizational Structure," in *Participatory and Self-Managed Firms: Evaluating Economic Performance*, ed. Derek C. Jones and Jan Svejnar (Lexington, Mass.: Lexington Books,1982), pp. 175–98; J. Cable and F. Fitzroy, "Productivity, Efficiency, Incentives, and Employee Participation: Some Preliminary Results from West Germany," Kyklos 33, no. 1 (1980a): 100–121; *Idem.*, "Cooperation and Productivity: Some Evidence from West German Experience," *Economic Analysis and Workers' Management* 14 (1980b): 163–80.

Researchers studying the economic records of enterprises employing a total of over 50,000 workers in Israel's approximately 300 kibbutz communities have documented higher productivity and profitability in both industry and agriculture for several decades. None of the studies applied adequate controls to explain the major causes. However, there are indications that the kibbutz movement's high rate of saving and capital investment, aggressive investment in human capital, and the role of the kibbutz federation in obtaining credit and aiding firms with technical assistance were major factors. The impressive data were culled during the movement's period of high growth and expansion; subsequent research indicates a significant narrowing in the margin of the kibbutz's superior performance over Israeli industry. There is some evidence that more participative kibbutz factories without hired labor are more successful.

Sources: Haim Barkai, *Growth Patterns in the Kibbutz Economy* (New York: North Holland,1977); Y. Don, "Industrialization in Advanced Rural Communities: The Israeli Kibbutz," *Sociologia Ruralis* 17 (1977): 1–12; Elihu Kanovsky, *The Economy of the Israeli Kibbutz: A Study of Kibbutz Productivity and Profitability and the Position of the Kibbutzim in the Economy of Israel* (Cambridge: Harvard University Center for Middle Eastern Affairs, 1966); Seymour Melman, *Managerial versus Cooperative Decision-making in Israel*, Studies in Comparative International Development, vol. 6 (Beverly Hills, Calif.: Sage Publications, 1971); Y. Don, "The Economic Performance of the Israeli Kibbutz" (unpublished manuscript, Bar-Ilan University, Ramat Gan, Israel,1986); Uri Leviatan and Menachem Rosner, *Work and Organization in Kibbutz Industry* (Norwood, Pa.: Norwood Editions, 1982); Menachem Rosner, *Democracy, Equality, and Change: The Kibbutz and Social Theory* (Norwood, Pa.: Norwood Editions, 1982).

Based on the economic records, researchers discovered higher productivity and profitability in Mondragon's worker cooperatives in the Basque Autonomous Region of Spain, in which over 16,000 workers participate, than in conventional firms. The measures of productivity were sales per person, value added divided by factors of production, value added per person, and value added per fixed assets; the measures of profitability were pure surplus as a percentage of total sales and pure surplus divided by the cooperatives' own resources. The cooperatives' profitability generally measured high, but their superiority to Spanish industry in this area seems to be decreasing. They performed better than the 500 biggest Spanish industries by most measures of productivity. These results are explained by Mondragon's high rate of capital accumulation and investment, its capital intensivity relative to Spanish industry, its emphasis on human capital, flexible wages, the importance of the ownership stake to individual workers, the role of a sheltering organization providing banking and technical assistance, and strong labor-management cooperation. Researchers also cite low turnover and "local area identity," which reinforces a spirit of cooperation, as contributing factors. The scholars have insufficiently evaluated the relative importance of economic and sociological factors.

Sources: Henk Thomas and Chris Logan, *Mondragon: An Economic Analysis* (London: Allen & Unwin, 1982); Keith Bradley and Alan Gelb, *Worker Capitalism: The New Industrial Relations* (Cambridge, Mass.: MIT Press, 1983); Idem., *Cooperation at Work: The Mondragon Experience* (London: Heinemann Educational Books, 1984).

Richard Long studied the Byers Transport Company of Canada, the second largest freight carrier in the Province of Alberta, after an employee purchase of the company. Comparing gross revenues and net profit, customer freight-damage claims, and loss per pounds loaded before and after the buyout, he found that performance did increase somewhat. He also discovered that ownership increased commitment to the organization, while participation was related to enhanced satisfaction and motivation. In research on a Canadian electronics firm, he concluded that employee ownership improves employee attitudes only if workers have an opportunity to participate in decisions.

Sources: Richard J. Long, *The Effect of Employee Ownership on Job Attitudes and Organizational Performance: An Exploratory Study* (Ann Arbor, Mich.: University Microfilms International, 1977); Idem., "The Effects of Employee Ownership on Organizational Identification, Employee Job Attitudes, and Organizational Performance: A Tentative Framework and Empirical Findings," *Human Relations* 31 (1978a): 29–48; Idem., "The Relative Effects of Share Ownership vs. Control on Job Attitudes in an Employee-Owned Company," *Human Relations* 31 (1978a): 753–63; Idem., "Worker Ownership and Job Attitudes: A Field Study," *Industrial Relations* 21 (Spring 1982): 196–215.

Research on Labor-
Management Cooperation
Under Employee Ownership

Type of Company: Non-ESOP Canadian trucking company.

Origins of Employee Ownership: Worker purchase of a spun-off subsidiary of a unionized firm.

Research Findings: One hundred percent of the managers and 65 percent of the workers were shareholders at the outset. After two years, 42 percent of the workers were shareholders, and total shareholding fell from 73 to 52 percent of the workforce. The stock was owned directly, and workers elected the board of directors. In an attitude survey, 50 percent of the workers said that participation at the company, departmental, and job levels had either stayed the same or decreased during the two years of employee ownership. The average worker had some say in job decisions and little or no say at the organizational or departmental level. Management felt it had a great deal of say in job and departmental decisions and some in organizational decisions. Share ownership appeared to make no difference to motivation, job satisfaction, or effort, but it did result in greater commitment to the company. An employee's perceived participation, however, did have a significant effect on job satisfaction, motivation, and effort. Workers most wanted participation at the job level, then at the departmental level, and, finally, at the company level, where lay the greatest discrepancy between desired participation and the degree of participation they felt they enjoyed. Union and nonunion members both believed that the union was compatible with worker ownership, which did not change their views toward the union.

Sources: Richard J. Long, "The Effects of Employee Ownership on Organizational Identification, Employee Job Attitudes, and Organizational Performance: A Tentative Framework and Empirical Findings," *Human Relations* 31 (1978a): 29–48; *Idem.*, "The Relative Effects of Share Ownership vs. Control on Job Attitudes in an Employee-Owned Company," *Human Relations* 31 (1978a): 753–63; *Idem.*, "Employee Ownership and Attitudes toward the Union," *Relations Industrielles* 33 (1978b); 237–54; *Idem.*, "Desires for and Patterns of Worker Participation in Decision Making after Conversion to Employee Ownership," *Academy of Management Journal* 22 (1979): 611–17.

Type of Company: Non-ESOP Canadian electronics firm.

Origins of Employee Ownership: Conversion for the purposes of capital expansion and independence from the owning university.

Research Findings: The ownership plan distributed one-third of the shares to 83 percent of the eligible employees, who elected one-third of the nine-member board. An attitude survey found that motivation among nonmanagers and their identification and integration with the company did not change with employee ownership, although workers who felt they had more involvement reported increased motivation, which suggests that participation had supplemented and enhanced the effects of the ownership. A further study showed a steady decline in motivation, integration with the company, and satisfaction, stemming from a deterioration of labor relations because of frustration over lack of participation in management. Worker-owners felt they had some additional influence in company decisions—probably as a result of electing three board representatives—but patterns of participation were generally identical before and after the buyout.

Source: Richard J. Long, "Worker Ownership and Job Attitudes: A Field Study," *Industrial Relations* 21 (Spring 1982): 196–215.

Type of Company: Non-ESOP knitting mill.

Origins of Employee Ownership: Worker purchase of subsidiary.

Research Findings: Thirty percent of the employees were shareholders, owning 70 percent of the stock and with voting rights and one representative on a seven-person board. A survey indicated that employee turnover and waste decreased. Motivation did not differ notably between worker-owners and nonowner workers, but shareowners had greater satisfaction and identification with and commitment to the company than nonshareholders. The researcher suggested that perhaps favorable work norms originating with the worker-owners had become generalized throughout the company. A related study found that managers and employees felt they had comparable influence over decisionmaking.

Sources: Michael A. Gurdon, *The Structure of Ownership: Implications for Employee Influence and Organizational Design* (Ann Arbor, Mich.: University Microfilms International, 1979); Tove Helland Hammer and Robert N. Stern, "Employee Ownership: Implications for the Organizational Distribution of Power," *Academy of Management Journal* 23 (1980): 78–100.

Type of Company: ESOP unionized furniture manufacturer.

Origins of Employee Ownership: Worker buyout of a subsidiary from a conglomerate threatening shutdown.

Research Findings: At the time of the employee buyout, the firm had begun to decline after its purchase by a conglomerate that had decided to restrict its sales to the United States, despite a record of international successes. Surveys found that shareownership did not create a desire for participation, and that owners and nonowners largely agreed on the distribution of power and the degree of participation they perceived they had. Shareowners desired less personal influence over decisions and preferred to delegate more to management. Management petitioned to decertify the union, but both clerical and office workers opposed this move, feeling that the union had an important role in the employee-owned firm.

Sources: Tove Helland Hammer, Jacqueline C. Landau, and Robert N. Stern, "Absenteeism When Workers Have a Voice: The Case of Employee Ownership," *Journal of Applied Psychology* 66 (1981): 561–73; Tove Helland Hammer and Robert N. Stern, "Employee Ownership: Implications for the Organizational Distribution of Power," *Academy of Management Journal* 23 (1980): 78–100; Donna Sockell, *The Union's Role under Employee Ownership: Stability or Change?* (Ann Arbor, Mich.: University Microfilms International, 1982); Robert N. Stern, K. Haydn Wood, and Tove Helland Hammer, *Employee Ownership in Plant Shutdowns: Prospects for Employment Stability* (Kalamazoo, Mich.: W. E. Upjohn Institute for Employment Research, 1979); Tove Helland Hammer, Robert N. Stern, and Michael A. Gurdon, "Workers' Ownership and Attitudes towards Participation," in *Workplace Democracy and Social Change,* ed. Frank Lindenfeld and Joyce Rothschild-Whitt (Boston: Porter Sargent, 1982), pp. 87–108.

Type of Company: South Bend Lathe ESOP.

Origins of Employee Ownership: Worker purchase of successful subsidiary.

Research Findings: As part of a survey of sixty-eight majority employee-owned ESOPs, researchers interviewed fifty-one managers and employees out of a workforce of 500, eighteen months after the 100-percent buyout of South Bend Lathe, in which most employees participated. Increased motivation, more labor-management cooperation, and improvements in the quality and quantity of work were reported, but 65 percent of those interviewed felt that ownership had not changed their participation in decisions affecting them. Two years after the buyout, the firm suffered a major strike because of serious distrust between labor and management and lack of employee involvement in the company. In the related survey of managers in sixty-eight ESOPs, 36 percent reported workers on the board and 51 percent of the managers reported that workers had some input in major decisions. Managers were more likely to describe workers' job attitudes as positive when workers had no board representation. Managers consistently extolled employee ownership but did not include worker influence as one of its components.

Source: Survey Research Center, University of Michigan, *Employee Ownership* (Ann Arbor, Mich.: Survey Research Center, University of Michigan, 1978).

Type of Company: San Franscisco non-ESOP refuse collection cooperatives.

Origins of Employee Ownership: Not applicable. Ongoing successful firms.

Research Findings: Worker-owners were compared to hired workers in the same coopera-tives and similar workers in municipal and private enterprises. Worker-owners were more satisfied and committed to the firm and reported a better work environment. How-ever, they did less work than comparable workers in other firms because of their ten-dency to assign more difficult tasks to hired nonowner workers.

Source: Stewart Perry, *San Francisco Scavengers: Dirty Work and the Pride of Ownership* (Berkeley: Univer-sity of California Press, 1978).

Type of Company: Non-ESOP plywood cooperative.

Origins of Employee Ownership: Not applicable. Ongoing successful firm.

Research Findings: Sixty-five employees out of a workforce of 160 were nonowners. Worker-members were more committed to the company than were workers in conven-tional plywood companies, and this commitment was closely tied to the amount of per-ceived participation. The cooperative had less turnover and fewer grievances than comparable firms, but absenteeism, tardiness, and accidents were the same. The coopera-tive had not established group norms favoring production, and worker-owners saw the reward system as more contingent on performance than did nonowner workers.

Source: Susan R. Rhodes, *The Relationship between Worker Ownership and Control in Organizations and Work Attitudes and Behavior* (Ann Arbor, Mich.: University Microfilms International, 1978).

Type of Company: Plywood cooperatives.

Origins of Employee Ownership: Not applicable. Ongoing successful firms.

Research Findings: Actual as opposed to theoretical participation was measured in terms of the percentage of worker-owners on the board of directors, the number of board meetings and general meetings held, and the degree to which minutes were communicated effec-tively to worker-owners. The researcher found that feelings of participation came from actual involvement. High-performance and low-performance cooperatives, measured by hourly income, were compared. High performance was explained by the degree of partici-pation, the ratio of worker-owners to all owners, average total capital, and the ratio of worker-owners to the total workforce.

Source: Carl J. Bellas, *Industrial Democracy and the Worker-Owned Firm: A Study of Twenty-One Plywood Companies in the Pacific Northwest* (New York: Praeger, 1972).

Type of Company: Unionized ESOP valve-manufacturing firm.

Origins of Employee Ownership: Ongoing successful firm bought by employees from a foundation.

Research Findings: Attitude surveys within the firm were compared to a national sample from the Quality of Employment Survey in order to establish a baseline. Six managers owned 48 percent of the stock with voting rights, and all other employees owned the remaining 52 percent without voting rights. Employees were not appreciably more motivated than workers in the comparison group. Twenty-three percent of employees said they had influence in job decisions, and 3 percent said they influenced departmental decisions—but 91.1 percent felt that worker ownership had given them no new say in decisionmaking. Of managers, 65.1 percent wanted more involvement in job-level decisions, and 76.2 percent wanted more say in departmental decisions. Fifty-three percent of the shopfloor employees desired more participation in job-level decisions; 75 percent wanted to participate more in departmental decisions. The company had a bitter strike a few years before the research was conducted. The vast majority of the employees—85.3 percent—felt that workers and management did not share the same goals, and 88.3 percent believed that management would not treat them fairly without a union; 51.4 percent perceived an increased need for union involvement in the company. Management, however, thought that employees had responded positively to ownership. Employees liked the financial benefits of the ESOP, but complained that they received too little information about it. Those workers who had increased say in decisions reported greater identification with the company; the mere fact of employee ownership did not affect this identification. Employees reported lower job satisfaction than the national sample. Evidence indicates that this was because employees had expected—unjustifiably, as it turned out—to share in the company's profits, receive more information about the company, and gain a friendlier atmosphere and more say as a result of employee ownership.

Source: Douglas Kruse, *Employee Ownership and Employee Attitudes: Two Case Studies* (Norwood, Pa.: Norwood Editions,1984).

Type of Company: Nonunionized retail-store chain ESOP.

Origins of Employee Ownership: Several thousand employees used leveraging to buy 100 percent of the ongoing successful company from retiring owners.

Research Findings: An attitude survey was compared to a national sample from the Quality of Employment Survey. The ESOP does not have full voting rights and is governed by board-appointed trustees. Managers reported that employees were more motivated by the ESOP than did the employees themselves. However, older workers closer to retirement, differing significantly from younger workers, did begin to put more effort into their work than was required. The firm's economic performance relative to comparable firms improved somewhat after the adoption of the ESOP, especially in the reduction in shoplifting and waste. The company has a relatively open style of management, and employees and managers generally agree that employees are consulted about various job decisions, although managers see this more than do employees. Nevertheless, about 88 percent of the workers reported that the ESOP made no difference in participation. But only one-third to one-half desired more say in decisions about work tasks, working conditions, pay, and fringe benefits. In the main, then, employees did not express more of a desire for participation with the ESOP, although older employees did report more willingness to participate in decisions on safety and the organization of work. Seventy-nine percent said that the ESOP made no difference to their job satisfaction, and 65.4 percent reported that it made no difference to their pride in being an employee. Employees reported similar job satisfaction and interest in changing jobs as the national sample.

Source: Douglas Kruse, *Employee Ownership and Employee Attitudes: Two Case Studies* (Norwood, Pa.: Norwood Editions, 1984).

Type of Company: Twenty-one cases of employee ownership and participation in the steel industry up to March 1986.

Origins of Employee Ownership: Some companies have undergone complete worker buyouts, such as Weirton Steel and Ironton Steel. Others have used partial equity as part of a restructuring of the company, such as McLouth, Johnstown, and Continental. The 1980 master wage agreement in steel specifically authorized ESOPs "in addition to or in substitution for other provisions," and the United Steel Workers of America became experts on the subject. USX, National, and Inland Steel do not have employee-ownership arrangements, but USX and National have each spun off at least one employee-owned plant.

Research Findings: Each study evaluates the changes in the roles of the government, labor, and management, and in firm structure that accompanied the adoption of employee ownership. The overall study shows that most of the new employee ownership is based on short-term agreements and does not involve extensive plans to reorganize firm structure through substantially greater labor-management cooperation. The White Pine Copper Mine is the only case where government, labor, and management all have representatives on a tripartite board. The structure of the ownership varies widely, some firms have minority ownership, some majority, and stock arrangements differ as well. Most of the twenty-one firms have labor-management participation teams at the shopfloor level. Three companies have some kind of joint labor-management board at the plant level. Four companies have union representation on the company board. In a few years Weirton and Copper Range workers will elect the majority of board members.

Source: Adam Blumenthal, *Interest and Equity: Uses of Employee Ownership and Participation in the Restructuring of the U.S. Steel Industry* (Cambridge: Harvard University Committee on Degrees in Social Studies, 1986).

Type of Company: Several ESOP buyouts. The firms include AL Tech Specialty Steel (Allegheny Ludlum Industries), Atlas Chain Company (Renold, Ltd.), Bates Fabric Company (BMC Inc.), Hyatt-Clark Industries (General Motors), Mohawk Valley Community Corporation (Sperry Rand), Okonite Company (LTV), Pacific Fiberboard (Fiberboard Corporation), Rath Packing Company (Rath Packing), Rich–Sea-Pak (W. R. Grace and Company), the Saratoga Knitting Mill (Cluett Peabody), and South Bend Lathe (Amsted Industries).

Origins of Employee Ownership: Federally assisted worker buyouts of companies that were threatened with shutdown or were spun off by a larger corporate parent. Not all the firms were failing; some simply did not fit into the strategic plans of their parent firms. Most were organized as ESOPs, and many received federal loans and loan guarantees. In some cases, the employee ownership was a transitional strategy and was not maintained.

Research Findings: Most of the companies stayed in business; some actually prospered. In each instance, the evaluation discusses the parent corporation's decision to close or divest and its role in the buyout. The first stage after a buyout is typified by general euphoria—workers are glad to have held on to their jobs. They have made no specific demands for greater participation, but have vague expectations that management will treat them differently in an employee-owned company. The second stage is generally marked by the failure of employee ownership to lead to substantial labor-management cooperation in most of the firms. There was substantial conflict between the international and the local unions in a number of cases. There were also indications that unions had not quite figured out their roles under employee ownership. Management also found it difficult to develop effective programs of cooperative problem solving after so many years of confrontation.

Source: William Foote Whyte, Charles Craypo, et al., *Evaluation Research on Federally-Assisted Worker Buyouts* (Washington, D.C.: U.S. Department of Commerce, Economic Development Administration Research and Policy Unit, 1987).

Type of Company: A common freight carrier, a manufacturer of bedspreads, and a manufacturer of high-quality wooden furniture with ESOPs in which unions play a role. The unions involved are the Teamsters (IBT), the Electrical Workers (IUE), and the Amalgamated Clothing and Textile Workers (ACTWU).

Origins of Employee Ownership: One-hundred-percent employee buyouts of parts of publicly held firms.

Research Findings: Employee ownership had no consistent effects on employee attitudes and behaviors related to the unions, apart from a decrease in strike willingness. The amount of stock ownership had no effect on these results. Expectations about labor relations and workers' views of their possible options when dissatisfied were not affected. All three firms made little attempt to change labor-management relations, which might explain why employee ownership had so little impact in these areas. Managers at all three firms had no consensus that employee ownership made unions unnecessary. In none of the companies were employees encouraged to settle problems themselves or with the aid of other nonmanagerial employees. Supervisors seemed to prefer more informal approaches to problem solving, but there is no proof that employee ownership was responsible for this. Management's bargaining posture also underwent no change under employee ownership. Employee ownership did not appear to affect the methods chosen by stewards to resolve problems. It had no effect on eight contract negotiations, contract administration, and overall union/management relations. Employee ownership simply did not raise employees' consciousnesses about issues outside of narrow work concerns or lead to interest in issues within management's domain. This appears to be because union leaders can reap no benefits for themselves through involvement in decisions outside their limited sphere of influence. Finally, employee ownership does nothing to increase management's motivation to accept union input.

Source: Donna Sockell, *The Union's Role under Employee Ownership: Stability or Change?* (Ann Arbor, Mich.: University Microfilms International, 1982).

Type of Company: Thirty-seven ESOP companies with a total of 2,804 employees. Companies had an average of 514 employees. Just over half of the workers were mainly in manufacturing, with the other half divided almost equally between the professional service and the retail or wholesale sectors.

Origins of Employee Ownership: Nine of the ESOPs were installed for philosophical reasons, eight were intended as additional employee benefits, seven were set up to supply a market for the stock of company founders and other shareholders, four were to provide incentives for improved employee performance, four were used for financing or as tax mechanisms, four were the outcome of corporate divestitures, and one involved a worker buyout of failing firm.

Research Findings: The average ESOP owned 43.33 percent of company stock, with the smallest owning 1 percent and five owning 100 percent. Twenty-four of the companies did not offer full voting rights on the ESOP stock. Generally, employees broadly endorsed the concept of ownership and its financial benefits, but saw no relationship between employee ownership in their companies and greater labor-management cooperation, work effort, job satisfaction, or participation in decisions. Workers desired more influence in every level of company decisionmaking—from social events to broader company policy—although they tended to want more influence over issues closest to their work sites, such as social events, working conditions, job performance, and so forth. The discrepancy between actual and desired influence was greater regarding personnel decisions, selection of supervisors and management, and company policy. Management overestimated worker influence at all levels of the company, but especially at levels beyond the work site. The primary focus of study was the relationship between positive employee attitudes (ESOP satisfaction, organizational commitment, job satisfaction, and intention to stay with the company) and characteristics of the ESOP. The amount of the annual company contribution to the ESOP was the major factor that significantly predicted positive attitudes. Management's employee-ownership philosophy showed a similar effect. The size of the company, the reason for establishing the ESOP, its public or private status, the presence of a union, voting rights, and the sharing of financial information with employees did not influence employee attitudes. However, there is a strong correlation between enlightened employee-ownership philosophies on the part of management and companies that have voting rights, extensive efforts to educate employees about the ESOP, the sharing of financial information, and various forms of worker participation, which makes it difficult to isolate single reasons for change. Positive managerial behavior involving acting differently toward employees was key. The details of worker participation are more complex: Formal participation groups are not strongly related to positive employee attitudes, while worker perception that they have influence is. Again, the companies offering voting rights tended to be the more participative firms, so it is hard to trace the exact causes of improved worker attitudes.

Sources: Corey Rosen, Katherine Klein, and Karen Young, *Employee Ownership in America: The Equity Solution* (Lexington, Mass.: Lexington Books, 1986); Michael Quarrey, Joseph Raphael Blasi, and Corey Rosen, *Taking Stock: Employee Ownership at Work* (Cambridge, Mass.: Ballinger Publishing, 1986).

Type of Company: Potential ESOPs in steel.

Origins of Employee Ownership: Not applicable. Study exploring how employees of two locals of the United Steelworkers of America would respond to and structure an ESOP in their plants if given the choice. Local 2499 in Williamsport, Pennsylvania, of the Wire Rope Division of Bethlehem Steel Corporation, had been threatened with closure; Local 2600 in Bethlehem, Pennsylvania, of the same company, was successful.

Research Findings: Seventy-six out of the 150 workers in the Bethlehem local and 27 out of the 150 in the Williamsport local were surveyed. They were asked to choose among six scenarios involving varying degrees of urgency for change and different types of concessions, stock voting rights, and board representation. Employees of both plants showed the strongest support—73 percent—for scenario 1, where the ESOP was necessary to save the plant. They preferred a structure with majority board representation and full voting rights on ESOP shares and accepted wage concessions of $20 a week. Scenario 2 was the second most acceptable option, involving the same ESOP structure and wage concessions as scenario 1, without its plant conditions. Indeed, in all cases, employees accepted the wage concessions, but did not support scenarios without voting rights and majority board representation (13 percent—scenario 3) or with pension-benefit concessions, even with full voting rights and majority board representation (19 percent—scenario 4). A sizable group of workers were satisfied with full voting rights and minority board representation (34 percent—scenario 5) or with majority board representation and the right to elect ESOP trustees who would vote the stock (43 percent—scenario 6). There were no significant differences in the responses from the two plants. Employees with high job satisfaction were less likely to support scenario 2, presumably worried that the ESOP would change their situations for the worse. Seniority did not influence employees' openness to pension-benefit concessions in scenario 4. Workers supporting scenario 1, in which the ESOP was intended to save the plant, tended to be younger and have pro-ESOP ideologies, lower job satisfaction, and little interest in relocating. Ideology most consistently accounted for differences in employees' attitudes toward voting rights and was a major factor in workers' willingness to reduce employee control in scenarios 4 and 5. Employees who were satisfied with management's abilities were likely to support scenario 6, which involved the least amount of worker control. The cost of the concession plan, the financial security of the firm, and job satisfaction were not very significant in most cases. The study concluded that control issues and the structure of the financial package, represented here by choice between wage and pension concessions, most influenced the workers' preferences.

Source: Wendy Coleman, *Attitudes of Unionized Workers to ESOP Structure in Prospective Worker Buyouts* (Cambridge: Harvard University Department of Economics, 1984).

Type of Company: Community employee-owned furniture company and knitting mill.

Origins of Employee Ownership: Transformed from conglomerate ownership by public companies to worker ownership.

Research Findings: The amount of stock owned by a worker had only a weak effect on job-related attitudes, slightly increasing the feeling of ownership, perception of self-benefit, and sense of commitment to the organization. It had no relationship to satisfaction or alienation. Compared to nonowner employees, employee-owners were more committed to the organization and less alienated, but both groups had similar feelings of control and self-benefit. Employee-owners of the textile mill reported greater control, but analysis reveals that 40 percent of the owners in the mill were managers, as opposed to 20 percent in the furniture manufacturer. In general, while the job attitudes of owners differed somewhat from nonowners', both groups felt that management retained the most control and reaped the most benefits from the ownership. These perceptions did not change with the sex, age, tenure, or education of the employees. However, production workers who were owners reported less alienation. White-collar nonmanagerial employees had a greater sense of ownership than blue-collar workers, but had lower job satisfaction. Generally identifying with management, they had expected more involvement in the firm as a result of their ownership and had been disappointed by the actual situation. When all employees were divided according to hierarchical position—production workers, office workers, middle managers, and top managers—and compared in terms of their job attitudes, the results resembled what one would find in a traditional firm. Top management felt a greater sense of ownership, control, satisfaction, and organizational commitment. The production workers reported low education and lack of control, but were not alienated from their work. Middle managers, uneasily placed midway labor and management, must carry out the wishes of top management, yet exercise authority over former coworkers with similar backgrounds. They had lower organizational commitment than top managers, less political alienation than production workers, but more work alienation than office workers. Ownership has only a limited ability to break down traditional occupational or class barriers, and more attention must be given to the distribution of the benefits and control of ownership if that ability is to be extended.

Source: Tove Helland Hammer, Robert N. Stern, and Michael A. Gurdon, "Workers' Ownership and Attitudes towards Participation," in *Workplace Democracy and Social Change*, ed. Frank Lindenfeld and Joyce Rothschild-Whitt (Boston: Porter Sargent, 1982), pp. 87–108.

Type of Company: ESOP in a privately held Boston bank.

Origins of Employee Ownership: Minority worker ownership to forestall a management crisis, deal with problems of capitalization, and encourage employee ownership.

Research Findings: The research is based on interviews and an attitude survey of the bank, which is 46.5 percent controlled by its leveraged ESOP with an additional 23.5 percent held individually by the president and four directors. Management saw the ESOP as an opportunity to reward and retain employees, but mainly set it up for financial reasons and in their own interests. Employees did not vote their stock or participate in decisions, although good supervisory relations and an open-door policy predominated. The results of the study indicated that the ESOP did not give employees a strong sense of ownership, although they did feel more committed to the bank's success. Workers reported that the ESOP was "far away, like a pension." The higher the income of the respondent, the greater the sense of ownership. Dostart said that the allocation of ESOP stock by salary explained this greater incentive effect among managers. Generally, nonmanagerial employees perceived little connection between the ESOP and their work effort. There was no indication that the organization of work had been altered. Workers did not feel a high degree of job freedom or job variety. Task significance, job freedom, job variety, and role overload were higher among men, who were mainly in management, than among women, who were usually tellers. Despite high organizational commitment to the bank, employees were moderately interested in changing jobs at some point. The bank's commitment to minority worker ownership explained employee loyalty, rather than the ESOP itself. Forty-four percent of the employees did not feel that owning stock made them want to stay with the bank. Those who disagreed tended to be managers with higher stock allocations. Employees did not report that ownership increased their influence at any level, and there was a substantial gap between perceived and desired influence among nonmanagers. Managers and nonmanagers disagreed about where employees should have influence. Deregulation, favorable rulings by the Federal Reserve Board on ESOPs in banks, and the need to develop human-resource management more aggressively in the competitive banking industry are all likely to increase the use of ESOPs in banking.

Source: Steven Dostart, *The Use of ESOPs in the Banking Industry: Participation or Manipulation?* (Cambridge: Harvard University Department of Social Studies, March 1986).

Type of Company: ESOP unionized furniture manufacturer.

Origins of Employee Ownership: Former subsidiary of a large conglomerate that changed to community employee ownership.

Research Findings: All employees owned 34 percent of the stock. Of this, 65 percent was owned by 149 rank-and-file employees who were organized by two unions, and 35 percent was owned by 29 managers. The study, which covered 112 workers, including 87 shareholders, was intended to establish whether absenteeism decreased because of the switch to employee ownership. (Voluntary absenteeism is believed to vary according to job satisfaction and other work-related conditions, e.g., reward systems, group norms, commitment, economic conditions, personal work ethics.) The amount of ownership did not affect absenteeism among worker-owners. But stockholders were voluntarily absent less frequently than nonstockholders. However, although voluntary absenteeism among worker-owners declined, this was offset by an increase in their involuntary absenteeism, as employees began to call in with reasons for their absence when before they had not bothered to do so. Why did employee ownership only affect the kind of absenteeism, not the volume? The authors concluded that, before the adoption of the ESOP, the union and the voice mechanism may not have been sufficiently strong to make it worthwhile to come to work. With the ESOP, workers felt a need to account for absence from their own company. If this was the case, the utility of employee ownership will not lie in automatically reducing absenteeism but in the opportunities it offers for increased communication as a means to effect improvements.

Source: Tove Helland Hammer, Jacqueline C. Landau, and Robert N. Stern, "Absenteeism When Workers Have a Voice: The Case of Employee Ownership," *Journal of Applied Psychology* 66 (1981): 561–73.

NOTES

Introduction

1. George C. Lodge, The New American Ideology (New York: Alfred A. Knopf, 1975). Regarding management status and authority, see George Lodge, Janice McCormick, and Shoshana Zuboff, "Sources and Patterns of Management Authority," in Readings in Human Resource Management, ed. Michael Beer and Bert Spector (New York: Free Press, 1985), pp. 92–100 (originally published as Harvard Business School Note 9–484–039).

Chapter 1: The Birth of the ESOP

1. Robert Levering, Milton Moskowitz, and Michael Katz, The Hundred Best Companies to Work for in America (New York: New American Library, 1985), pp. 136–39.
2. Ibid., pp. 139–41.
3. William C. Freund and Eugene Epstein, People and Productivity (Homewood, Ill.: Dow Jones-Irwin, 1984), pp. 3–4.
4. Levering, Moskowitz, and Katz, The Hundred Best Companies, pp. 110–15.
5. Gay Sands Miller and Laurie P. Cohen, "Avis, Inc., Is Sold for Fifth Time in Four Years," Wall Street Journal, September 29, 1987, p. 3; Larry Reibstein, "Charter Medical Gets Proposal for Buyout," Wall Street Journal, September 29, 1987, p. 4; Alex Kotlowitz and Ed Bean, "Spate of Corporate Buyouts by ESOPs Raises Questions of Benefits to Workers," Wall Street Journal, September 30, 1987, p. 14.
6. Keck, Mahin & Cate, ESOPs: Uses, Applications and Special Tax Characteristics (Chicago: Keck, Mahin & Cate, 1986), p. 1.
7. Based on telescoping the 1986 March estimate by the U.S. General Accounting Office. See U.S. General Accounting Office, Employee Stock Ownership Plans: Interim Report on a Survey and Related Economic Trends, Federal Reserve Board's Flow of Funds Section (Washington, D.C.: U.S. General Accounting Office, February 1986), p. 1.
8. Both quotations are from the Center for Economic and Social Justice, Citations and Quotes on Expanded Ownership (Washington, D.C.: Center for Economic and Social Justice, n.d.).
9. The Hart findings are quoted in Jeremy Rifkin, Own Your Own Job (New York: Bantam Books, 1977), and J. F. Zipp, P. Luebke, and R. Landermann, "The Social Bases for Support of Workplace Democracy," Perspectives 27: 395–425. The Gallup findings are quoted in Russell Long, "Employee Stock Ownership: A New Approach to Productivity," Congressional Record 129, no. 63 (May 10, 1983a): n.p.
10. Freund and Epstein, People and Productivity.
11. See Appendix C, Table C–1.

12. See Louis Kelso and Mortimer Adler, *The Capitalist Manifesto* (New York: Random House, 1958). See also Stuart M. Speiser, *A Piece Of The Action* (New York: Van Nostrand Reinhold, 1977), especially Chapter 5, for an excellent discussion of the weaknesses of Kelso's broader theory.

13. U.S. Congressional Research Service, *Designing a Retirement System for Federal Workers Covered by Social Security* (Washington, D.C.: Committee on Post Office and Civil Service, U.S. House of Representatives, 1984).

14. Ray Schmitt, *Private Pension Plans: Which Way Are They Headed?* (Washington, D.C.: Library of Congress, U.S. Congressional Research Service, April 15, 1985), p. 13; Profit Sharing Research Foundation, *Cumulative Growth in Number of Qualified Deferred Profit Sharing Plans and Pensions in the U.S. 1939 through 1984* (Evanston, Ill.: Profit Sharing Research Foundation, 1984); U.S. Congress, House Committee on Ways and Means, *Retirement Income Security in the U.S.* (Washington, D.C.: Government Printing Office, 1986), pp. 532–36.

15. Schmitt, *Private Pension Plans*, p. 9.

16. U.S. Congressional Research Service, *Designing a Retirement System*, p. 52.

17. Martin Weitzman, *The Share Economy* (Cambridge: Harvard University Press, 1984).

18. Richard A. Ippolito and Walter W. Koludrubetz, *The Handbook of Pension Statistics* (Chicago: Commerce Clearing House, 1986).

19. *Pensions and Investments Age 6*, no. 3 (April 1986): 5.

20. U.S. Department of Labor, Bureau of Labor Statistics, *Employee Benefits in Medium and Large Firms, 1986*, Bulletin 2262 (Washington, D.C.: U.S. Department of Labor, Bureau of Labor Statistics, July 1986); Hewitt Associates, *Salaried Employee Benefits Provided by Major U.S. Employers in 1985* (Lincolnshire, Ill.: Hewitt Associates, 1986); Hewitt Associates, *Salaried Employee Benefits Provided by Major U.S. Employers: A Comparison Study, 1979 through 1984* (Lincolnshire, Ill.: Hewitt Associates, 1985a); Hewitt Associates, *1984 PAYSOP Survey of Fortune Directory Companies* (Lincolnshire, Ill.: Hewitt Associates, 1984); Employee Benefit Research Institute (EBRI), "1985/1986 Estimates Show More Pension Plans," *Employee Benefit Notes 7* (September 1986): 5–7.

21. Hewitt Associates and Profit Sharing Council of America, *1985 Profit Sharing Survey* (Chicago: Profit Sharing Council of America, 1985), p. 35; Freund and Epstein, *People and Productivity*, p. 158; U.S. Department of Labor, *Employee Benefits*, p. 75; Schmitt, *Private Pension Plans*, pp. 25, 29.

22. U.S. Congressional Research Service, *Designing a Retirement System*, p. 42; Ippolito and Kolodrubetz, *Handbook of Pension Statistics*, pp. 68–69; U.S. Department of Labor, *Employee Benefits*, p. 75.

23. Hewitt Associates, "Update on 401(k) Plans," *On Employee Benefits*, March 1985: 5–6.

24. Profit Sharing Research Foundation, *Cumulative Growth in Number of Qualified Deferred Profit Sharing Plans*, n.p.; U.S. Department of Labor, *Employee Benefits*, p. 75.

25. Hewitt Associates, *1984 PAYSOP Survey*, p. 15.

26. Mitchell Meyer, *Profile of Employee Benefits, 1981 Edition* (New York: The Conference Board, Inc., 1981) pp. 33–34; Freund and Epstein, *People and Productivity*, pp. 75–76,158; New York Stock Exchange, *Shareownership 1983* (New York: New York Stock Exchange, April 1984), p. 28; New York Stock Exchange, *Direct Ownership Employee Stock Purchase Plans* (New York: New York Stock Exchange, September 1984), pp. 4–12.

27. Quote is from U.S. Congress, House Committee on Ways and Means, *Report on the 1981 Tax Act* (Washington, D.C.: U.S. Government Printing Office, 1981), Part F, "Stock Options etc.," p. 158. Regarding state support for incentive stock options,

see Section 83 of the Internal Revenue Code. The new tax bill will reduce the role of stock options. For a recent update, see Amanda Bennett, "Down but Not Out: Stock Options Will Have a Role after Tax Change," *Wall Street Journal*, September 19, 1986, p. 25.

28. Howard Aldrich and Robert N. Stern, "Resource Mobilization and the Creation of U.S. Producer Cooperatives, 1835–1935," *Economic and Industrial Democracy* 4 (1983): 375.

29. For discussion of other estimates, Joyce Rothschild and Raymond Russell, "Alternatives To Bureaucracy: Democratic Participation in the Economy," *Annual Review of Sociology* 12 (1986): 307–28.

30. Peter Drucker, *The Unseen Revolution* (New York: Harper & Row, 1976).

31. Schmitt, *Private Pension Plans*, p. 36.

32. U.S. General Accounting Office, *Employee Stock Ownership Plans: Interim Report*, p. 39.

33. U.S. Congress, Joint Economic Committee, Democratic Staff, and James D. Smith, *The Concentration of Wealth in the U.S.: Trends in the Distribution of Wealth among American Families* (Washington, D.C.: U.S. Congress, Joint Economic Committee, July 1986), p. 24.

34. New York Stock Exchange, *Direct Ownership Employee Stock Purchase Plans*.

35. *Ibid.*

36. Robert Dahl, *An Introduction to Economic Democracy* (Berkeley: University of California Press, 1985).

37. Peter S. Fisher, "Corporate Tax Incentives: The American Version of Industrial Policy," *Journal of Economic Issues* 19, no. 1 (March 1983):1–19; U.S. Congress, *Joint Economic Committee*, Democratic Staff, and Smith, *The Concentration of Wealth in the U.S.*

38. Jeffrey R. Gates, *ESOP Legislation—Past and Future* (Lincolnshire, Ill.: Hewitt Associates, February 21, 1980), pp. 1–5.

39. Major hearings and studies are: U.S. Congress, Joint Economic Committee, *Hearings on Employee Stock Ownership Plans* (Washington, D.C.: U.S. Government Printing Office, 1976), "December 11, 1975" (Part 1) and "December 12, 1975" (Part 2); U.S. Congress, Senate Finance Committee, *Employee Stock Ownership Plans and General Stock Ownership Trusts* (Washington, D.C.: U.S. Government Printing Office, 1978a); U.S. Congress, Senate Select Committee on Small Business. *Hearings, S. 388, The Small Business Employee Ownership Act, February 27, 1979* (Washington, D.C.: U.S. Government Printing Office, 1979); U.S. Congress, House Small Business Subcommittee on Access to Equity Capital and Business Opportunities, *Hearings, H.R. 3056, Small Business Employee Ownership Act, May 8 and 15, 1979* (Washington, D.C.: U.S. Government Printing Office, 1979); U.S. Congress, Joint Economic Committee Staff, *Broadening the Ownership of New Capital: ESOPs and Other Alternatives* (Washington, D.C.: U.S. Government Printing Office, 1976); and U.S. Congress, Senate Select Committee on Small Business Staff, *The Role of the Federal Government and Employee Ownership of Business* (Washington, D.C.: U.S. Government Printing Office, 1979).

40. Russell Long, "Floor Statement of Senator Long on S. 2767," *Congressional Record* 119, no. 194 (December 11, 1973): n.p.

41. Speiser, *A Piece of the Action*, pp. 191–207. The Rail Reorganization Act of 1974, Public Law 93–236, involved the following hearings and statements: U.S. Congress, House Commerce Committee, *House Report 93–744, H.R. 9142, December 20, 1973* (Washington, D.C.: U.S. Government Printing Office, 1973), pp. 3, 14, 22, 46; U.S. Congress, Senate Commerce Committee, *Report on S. 2767, December 6, 1973* (Washington, D.C.: U.S. Government Printing Office, 1973), pp. 20, 27, 30; statements by

Senators Hatfield, Javits, Long, and Hartke, *Congressional Record* (December 11, 1973): S22527–28, S22533–34, S22547–52; statements by Senators Long and Hartke, *Congressional Record* (December 21, 1973): S23784–85, statement by Senator Hatfield, *Congressional Record* (February 26, 1975): S2625–27; statement by Louis Kelso, U.S. Congress, Senate Commerce Surface Transportation Subcommittee, *Hearings, S. 1031, Northeastern Railroad Transportation Crisis, February 28 and March 2, 1973* (Washington, D.C.: U.S. Government Printing Office, 1973), pp. 89–149; statement by Norman G. Kurland, U.S. Congress, Senate Commerce Surface Transportation Subcommittee, *Hearings, S. 2188 and H.R. 9142, Northeastern and Midwestern Railroad Transportation Crisis, November 16, 1973* (Washington, D.C.: U.S. Government Printing Office, 1973), pp. 908–11.

42.   U.S. Congress, House Committee on Ways and Means, *Tax Proposals Affecting Private Pension Plans, May 16, 1972* (Washington, D.C.: U.S. Government Printing Office, 1973), pp. 647–720. U.S. Congress, Joint Economic Committee, *Hearings on Employee Stock Ownership Plans* (Part 1), pp. 423–88, contains background material: "Should Congress Prohibit ESOP Financing?" a memorandum by Kelso debating the Treasury Department's opposition to initial ESOP laws, pp. 478–80; Kelso's letter to the Chief Counsel of the Ways and Means Committee, pp. 481–88; and a further bill, *S. 1370*, introduced by Senators Fannin, Hansen, and Dominick on March 27, 1973, which proposed a further tax deduction for ESOPs, deductibility of ESOP dividends, the ability of ESOPs to receive donations of employer stock as if they were charitable organizations, and other provisions, pp. 472–76. Speiser, *A Piece of the Action*, pp. 230–38, 251–58, reviews the post–1974 hearings in more detail and discusses the Joint Economic Committee report by Robert Hamrin.

43.   Jared Kaplan, Gregory Brown, and Ronald Ludwig, *Tax Management: ESOPs* (Washington, D.C.: Bureau of National Affairs, 1985), p. A4.

44.   William Frenzel, "Introduction of the Accelerated Capital Formation Act of 1975, " *Congressional Record* 121, no. 1 (January 14, 1975): n.p.

45.   U.S. Congress, Joint Economic Committee, *Hearings on Employee Stock Ownership Plans* (Part 1).

46.   *Ibid*. (Part 1), pp. 86, 521–39.

47.   *Ibid*. (Part 2), pp. 1–6, 35–38, 52.

48.   Russell Long, *Employee Ownership: A Political History* (Cambridge: Study Group on Worker Ownership and Participation in Business at Harvard University, 1983b), p. 7.

49.   On the Kostmayer initiatives, see William Foote Whyte and Joseph R. Blasi, "From Research to Legislation on Employee Ownership," *Economic and Industrial Democracy* 1 (1980): 395–415; Peter H. Kostmayer, Stanley Lundine, and Matthew McHugh, "The Voluntary Job Preservation and Community Stabilization Act," *Congressional Record* 27 (March 1, 1978): n.p. The Small Business Employee Ownership Act was introduced on February 28, 1979, by Congressmen Kostmayer and Baldus and became law on June 12, 1980, as Title V of the Small Business Development Act of 1980. Hearings: U.S Congress, House Banking, Finance, and Urban Affairs Subcommittee on Economic Stabilization, *Employee Stock Ownership Plans, February 27, 1979* (Washington, D.C.: U.S. Government Printing Office, 1979); U.S. Congress, House Small Business Subcommittee on Access To Equity Capital and Business Opportunities, *H.R. 3056*.

50.   See U.S Congress, Senate Committee on Banking, Housing and Urban Affairs, *Hearings, Chrysler Corporation Loan Guarantee Act* (Washington, D.C.: U.S. Government Printing Office, 1979).

51.   Regarding the new deduction limits and the rollover, see Kaplan, Brown, and Ludwig, *Tax Management*, pp. A13–A14, A16.

52. See U.S. Congress, Joint Economic Committee, *Hearings on Employee Stock Owner-ship Plans* (Part 1), pp. 86–93, 472–77.
53. Russell Long, "Expanded Ownership—Its Importance to the Free Enterprise System," *Congressional Record* 127, n. 50 (March 27, 1981): 2. See also Long's major summative statement on ESOPs: Russell Long, "S. 1162—Expanded Ownership Act of 1981," *Congressional Record* 127, no. 72 (May 12, 1981): S4779–96.
54. Long, "Expanded Ownership," p. 9.
55. U.S. Congress, House Small Business Subcommittee on Access to Equity Capital and Business Opportunities, *H.R. 3056*, pp. 138–42.
56. Long, "S. 1162—Expanded Ownership Act," p. S4787.
57. U.S. General Accounting Office, *Employee Stock Ownership Plans: Interim Report*, p. 49.
58. Long, "Floor Statement," n.p.
59. *Ibid.*
60. *Ibid.*
61. U.S. Congress, Joint Economic Committee, *Hearings on Employee Stock Ownership Plans* (Part 1), p. 367. See also William Jones, "Rail Act to Spur Worker Owners," *Washington Post*, January 2, 1974.
62. U.S. Congress, Joint Economic Committee, *Hearings on Employee Stock Ownership Plans* (Part 1), pp. 49, 96.
63. U.S. Congress, Senate Finance Committee, *Employee Stock Ownership Plans*, p. 164.
64. Long, *Employee Ownership*, p. 17.
65. U.S. Congress, Joint Economic Committee, *Hearings on Employee Stock Ownership Plans* (Part 1), pp. 3–6.
66. U.S. Congress, Joint Economic Committee, *Hearings on Employee Stock Ownership Plans* (Part 1), pp. 5, 74, 97, 207, 361–63, 523; Saul Gellerman/Consulting, Inc., *Analysis of the Probable Motivational Effects of Employee Stock Ownership Plans on Railways in Reorganization*, document dated April 25, 1977, Transportation Library, Northwestern University, Chicago, Illinois.
67. U.S. Comptroller General, *Employee Stock Ownership Plans: Who Benefits Most in Closely-Held Companies?* (Washington, D.C.: U.S. General Accounting Office, 1980), pp. 3, 37–42; U.S. Congress, Joint Economic Committee Staff, *Broadening the Ownership of New Capital*, p. 54.
68. Long, "Expanded Ownership"; Survey Research Center, University of Michigan, *Employee Ownership* (Ann Arbor, Mich.: Survey Research Center, University of Michigan,1978).
69. See Speiser, *A Piece of the Action*, pp. 154–55, 161–63, 223–30, about the failure of attempts at the University of Pennsylvania, Wharton School, and at Harvard University to complete sound econometric studies on the ESOP.
70. Long, "Expanded Ownership," p. 10; U.S Congress, Joint Economic Committee, *Hearings on Employee Stock Ownership Plans* (Part 1), p. 372.
71. Long, "Expanded Ownership," p. 3.
72. Russell Long, "An Ownership Approach to Productivity," *Congressional Record* 127, no. 115 (July 28, 1981), p. 1.
73. Kaplan, Brown, and Ludwig, *Tax Management*, p. A14.
74. Social science research and literature on democratic participation in the economy have been reviewed in an excellent article by Joyce Rothschild and Raymond Russell ("Alternatives To Bureaucracy: Democratic Participation in the Economy," *Annual Review of Sociology* 12 [1986]: 307–28). Blasi has reviewed the major research literature on organizational behavior in employee-owned companies (*Employee Ownership through ESOPs: Implications for the Public Corporation* [Scarsdale, N.Y.: Work in America Institute, 1987]). In one of the first radical proposals to academic

economists, Martin Weitzman of MIT recommended tying the wages of workers to the economic performance of firms (*The Share Economy* [Cambridge: Harvard University Press, 1984]).

Corey Rosen, Katherine Klein, and Karen Young have reported on the results of intensive study of employee attitudes in fifty ESOP companies and suggested how to make the concept work better (*Employee Ownership in America: The Equity Solution* [Lexington, Mass.: Lexington Books, 1986]). Timothy C. Jochim has described the background, functioning, and implementation of the ESOP with a helpful review of the regulations and necessary forms (*Employee Stock Ownership and Related Plans: Analysis and Practice* [Westport, Conn.: Quorum Books, 1982]). William Foote Whyte, Tove Helland Hammer, Christopher Meek, Reed Nelson, and Robert Stern have explored the uses of employee ownership for economic development (*Worker Participation and Ownership: Cooperative Strategies for Strengthening Local Economies* [Ithaca, N.Y.: ILR Press, 1983]). Raymond Russell has analyzed a variety of problems and settings in worker ownership (*Sharing Ownership in the Workplace* [Albany, N.Y.: SUNY Press, 1985]). Keith Bradley and Alan Gelb have compared the British and American experiences with worker buyouts and discussed a new form of worker capitalism (*Worker Capitalism: The New Industrial Relations* [Cambridge, Mass.: MIT Press, 1983]).

Michael Quarrey, Joseph Blasi, and Corey Rosen selected and presented actual cases of generally promising and progressive firms that have substantial employee ownership and participation (*Taking Stock: Employee Ownership at Work* [Cambridge, Mass.: Ballinger Publishing, 1986]). Stewart Perry has contributed an excellent case study of worker-owned refuse collection firms in San Francisco (*San Francisco Scavengers: Dirty Work and the Pride of Ownership* [Berkeley: University of California Press, 1978]). Daniel Zwerdling has compared a number of national and international examples of workplace democracy (*Democracy at Work: A Guide to Workplace Ownership, Participation and Self-Management Experiments in the U.S. and Europe* [New York: Harper & Row, 1978]). John Simmons and William Mares have also presented such cases to illustrate how employee ownership and participation can improve productivity and foster more cooperative labor-management relations (*Working Together* [New York: Alfred A. Knopf, 1983]). Douglas Kruse studied two "worst-case" ESOPs (*Employee Ownership and Employee Attitudes: Two Case Studies* [Norwood, Pa.: Norwood Editions, 1984]). Christopher Eaton Gunn examined a number of cases in light of the necessary conditions for workers' self-management (*Workers' Self-Management in the United States* [Ithaca, N.Y.: Cornell University Press, 1984]), and Frank Lindenfeld and Joyce Rothschild-Whitt have provided a more general overview of the relationship between workplace democracy and social change (*Workplace Democracy and Social Change* [Boston: Porter Sargent, 1982]).

Other books have been primarily concerned with garnering policy support. Louis Kelso and Mortimer Adler first popularized the idea of broadened ownership in *The Capitalist Manifesto* (New York: Random House, 1958). Louis Kelso and Patricia Hetter argue that broadened ownership should be extended from business enterprises to cover every kind of economic enterprise in our society (*Democracy and Economic Power: Extending the ESOP Revolution* [Cambridge, Mass.: Ballinger Books, 1986]). Stuart M. Speiser provides a detailed history of the ESOP policy debate up to 1977 (*A Piece Of The Action* [New York: Van Nostrand Reinhold, 1977]).

Other authors have focused on how-to books. Robert A. Frisch walks the reader through setting up an ESOP (*The Magic of ESOPs and LBOs* [Rockville Centre, N.Y.: Farnsworth Publishing, 1985]). The definitive legal guides to date are *Tax Management: ESOPs*, by Jared Kaplan, Gregory Brown, and Ronald Ludwig (Washington, D.C.: Bureau of National Affairs, 1985; rev. ed., 1987), *ESOPs and ESOP Transac-*

tions, by William N. Kravitz and Charles Smith (New York: Practicing Law Institute, 1985), and a recent book by Harry Weyher and Hiram Knott that discusses a number of legal cases (*ESOP: The Employee Stock Ownership Plan* [Chicago: Commerce Clearing House, 1985]). Useful newsletters, such as the monthly *Employee Ownership* of the National Center for Employee Ownership in Oakland, California, trace the development of the phenomenon and provide the best up-to-date information on employee ownership.

75. Personal communication from one of the top ESOP lawyers in the country, April 1986.

76. John Hoerr, "ESOPs: Revolution or Ripoff?" *Business Week,* April 15, 1985.

Chapter 2: The ESOP's Moving Parts

Note: This chapter has been updated on the basis of the new 1986 tax reform law. The Internal Revenue Service of the Department of the Treasury, the National Labor Relations Board (as relates to ESOPs with organized labor participation), and the Bureau of Labor-Management Services of the Department of Labor all propose, update, and promulgate regulations and rulings, which must be reviewed as they appear. U.S. Law is organized by the U.S. Code. IRS material is in Title 26 and ERISA material in Title 29—Labor of that code. The reader should be able to analyze any ESOP after studying this chapter and referring to the two recommended legal sources: the September 18, 1986, *Congressional Record,* which summarizes present and new law (pages 7704–5, 7708–9, 7713–20, 7725, 7744, 7823) and is referred to in this chapter as "*Congressional Record* 1986," and *Tax Management: ESOPs,* by Jared Kaplan, Gregory Brown, and Ronald Ludwig (Washington, D.C.: Bureau of National Affairs, 1985). A new edition of *Tax Management,* released on July 7, 1987, contains a review of regulatory changes and new developments in ESOP tax law (pp. 75–77) and a detailed analysis of pre–1986 ESOP law and ESOPs after the 1986 tax reform act (pp. 307–13). This new edition can be ordered by calling 1 (800) 372–1033. All references here are to the 1985 edition.

1. Based on an address by Michael Kearney, UAW union president, Harvard University Trade Union Program, March 1987, and on a personal communication.

2. Douglas Kruse, *Employee Ownership and Employee Attitudes: Two Case Studies* (Norwood, Pa.: Norwood Editions, 1984).

3. Sam Wessinger, "American Recreation Centers: A Case Study," *Employee Ownership* 5, no. 5 (October 1985): 3.

4. Randy Barber, *Employee Stock Ownership Plans: Their Uses and Abuses* (Washington, D.C.: Center for Economic Organizing, 1985), pp. 25–28.

5. Leon Lipson and Stanton Wheeler, eds., *Law and the Social Sciences* (New York: Russell Sage Foundation, 1986).

6. In 1975, the Senate considered a proposal to help large firms with huge losses, such as Pan Am, Lockheed, and Chrysler. The idea was to allow firms to average their profits and losses over a longer period of time. Senator Long unsuccessfully proposed that the first time a corporation used this approach it would have to put 25 percent of the tax saving into an ESOP, with the exception that the automobile industry could put 12 1/2 percent in an ESOP and the balance in a supplemental unemployment-benefits plan (Russell Long, *Congressional Record* [March 18, 1985]: 7231, 8861). Steps were taken to make sure that the Small Business Administration encouraged employee ownership or made it preferable when the government helped companies affected by foreign competition.

7. Internal Revenue Code 401; Kaplan, Brown, and Ludwig, *Tax Management,* pp. A1–7, A10–15; *Congressional Record* 1986: 7744–46.

8.   See American Capital Strategies, *American Capital Strategies: An Investment Banking Firm for Labor*, prospectus (Bethesda, Md.: American Capital Strategies, Inc., 1987).

9.   Lawyers have devised a way around the obligations of the leveraged ESOP. Instead of the ESOT borrowing the money from the lender and the company guaranteeing this loan, the company itself borrows the money and simply makes annual contributions to the ESOP that match its loan-principal payments. This is called a company-financed leveraged ESOP. See Kaplan, Brown, and Ludwig, *Tax Management*, p. A23; Timothy C. Jochim, *Employee Stock Ownership and Related Plans: Analysis and Practice* (Westport, Conn.: Quorum Books, 1982), pp. 33–35, 44–47.

10. Corey Rosen, Katherine Klein, and Karen Young, *Employee Ownership in America: The Equity Solution* (Lexington, Mass.: Lexington Books, 1986), pp. 101–38.

11. Hewitt Associates, *1984 PAYSOP Survey of Fortune Directory Companies* (Lincolnshire, Ill.: Hewitt Associates, 1984), pp. 6, 8.

12. Thomas R. Marsh and Dale E. McAllister, "ESOP Tables: A Survey of Companies with Employee Stock Ownership Plans," *Journal of Corporation Law* 6, no. 3 (1981): 595.

13. Rosen, Klein, and Young, *Employee Ownership*, pp. 86–87.

14. Internal Revenue Code 410 and 411; Kaplan, Brown, and Ludwig, *Tax Management*, pp. A7–9; *Congressional Record* 1986: 7704–6.

15. If a plan meets this special added nondiscrimination test, in addition to the other tests described in the text, company contributions to the ESOP used to pay interest on the loan for the worker stock and forfeitures of stock originally acquired by leveraging may be disregarded in computing the yearly allocation to a worker's account (Kaplan, Brown, and Ludwig, *Tax Management*, pp. A12–13).

16. In a leveraged ESOP, the employer has some incentive to include more employees because the employer's tax deduction and the size of the loan will increase proportionately with the total compensation of participating employees.

17. Marsh and McAllister, *ESOP Tables*.

18. The U.S. General Accounting Office data in Table 2–2 is based on 1983 IRS tapes. The data in Table 2–3, based on 1984 IRS tapes, are for ESOPs of all kinds with 100 or more employees. They include plans with ESOP features that the GAO generally excluded from their calculations. Larger firms that generally used tax-credit ESOPs tended to make the exclusions more pronounced. Thus, when the average number of workers excluded was computed for each particular company and then averaged, rather than the total number for all firms as shown in Table 2–3, 18.8 percent of employees are excluded because of minimum age or years of service, 9.6 percent because they are union or foreign workers, and 6.9 percent because they are ineligible. The average firm included 62. 7 percent of its employees. This alternate way of figuring suggests that the government could increase employee participation in ESOPs by changing the coverage requirements for minimum age and years of service in a way that would not inconvenience the operations of businesses. To some extent, the new tax law has done this. Two other factors distort these data: (1) Some firms have more than one ESOP, one for the collective-bargaining unit and another for other employees; and (2) some of these firms are part of large controlled groups of companies whose greater employment base seems to exaggerate the exclusion.

19. Personal communication from an anonymous source.

20. Defined in Internal Revenue Code 401(a)(4): An employee is considered highly compensated if compensation exceeds twice the normal dollar limitation for defined-contribution plan allocations under Internal Revenue Code 415(c)(l)(A), as adjusted for cost of living increases (Internal Revenue Code 414(c)(6)(B)(iii). See *Congressional Record* 1986: 7714–15 for a review.

21. See Internal Revenue Code, Section 415; Kaplan, Brown, and Ludwig, *Tax Manage-ment*, pp. A3–4, A13–14; *Congressional Record* 1986: 7744–46.

22. *Congressional Record* 1986: 7714–15. The law clarifies further issues such as the defi-nition of an officer, exceptions to employees included in the top-paid group, and the treatment of family members and former employees.

23. Recently Harvard Business School professor Rosabeth Moss Kanter has raised seri-ous questions about this attitude in "The Attack on Pay," *Harvard Business Review*, no. 2 (March/April 1987): 60–67.

24. Kaplan, Brown, and Ludwig, *Tax Management*, p. A3.

25. See PACE of Philadelphia, *Design of a Worker Cooperative Worker Education Program: The O & O Project as a Case Study* (Philadelphia: Philadelphia Association for Cooper-ative Enterprise, Inc., 1983). The author appreciates the assistance of William Steiker, ESOP counsel of PACE, in preparing this section. For alternative IRS-approved allocation formulas, see *Idem., Garrett Road Supermarket, Inc. ESOP* (Phila-delphia: Philadelphia Association for Cooperative Enterprise, Inc., October 17, 1986), and *Idem., Atlas Chain Co. ESOP* (Philadelphia: Philadelphia Association for Cooperative Enterprise, Inc., July 1, 1983). Generally, alternative allocation formu-las must be individually designed for each company to ensure that they do not discriminate because of special features of a firm's workforce. Allocation according to hours worked will largely eliminate a primary barrier to equitable division of ownership.

26. The Tax Equity and Fiscal Responsibility Act of 1982 defined a top-heavy plan in Internal Revenue Code 416; *Congressional Record* 1986: H7713.

27. Barber, *Employee Stock Ownership Plans*, p. 4.

28. Not to be confused with when the worker gets the stock or the cash for the stock, which usually happens at retirement. Internal Revenue Code, Section 411; Kaplan, Brown, and Ludwig, *Tax Management*, pp. A5, A9.

29. Marsh and McAllister, *ESOP Tables*, p. 595 (Table 9); ESOP Association, *ESOP Sur-vey: 1986* (Washington, D.C.: ESOP Association of America, 1986a), pp. 50–51.

30. For a review of vesting law and ESOPs, see *Congressional Record* 1986: H7708–9.

31. *Congressional Record* 1986: H7744 45. Companies must begin to distribute a worker's shares if he or she decides to leave the job, even though this triggers a 10-percent penalty tax on early withdrawals unless the distribution is paid in an annuity or rolled over into an IRA. In the case of ESOPs, this ruling is applicable only after January 1, 1990. Stock acquired under a leveraged ESOP is an exception. See Inter-nal Revenue Code, Section 409.

32. Kaplan, Brown, and Ludwig, *Tax Management*, pp. A5, A11, A23–24; Harry Weyher and Hiram Knott, *ESOP: The Employee Stock Ownership Plan* (Chicago: Commerce Clearing House, 1985), pp. 201–32.

33. ESOP Association, *ESOP Survey: 1985* (Washington, D.C.: ESOP Association of America, 1985a), pp. 36–37.

34. U.S. Congress, Joint Committee on Taxation, *General Explanation of the Tax Reform Act of 1976* (Washington, D.C.: U.S. Government Printing Office, December 29, 1976), p. 173.

35. *Congressional Record* 1986: H7744–45; Marsh and McAllister, *ESOP Tables*, pp. 596–97.

36. ESOP Association, *ESOP Survey: 1985*, pp. 42–45.

37. See *Congressional Record* 1986: H7744–46.

38. Kaplan, Brown, and Ludwig, *Tax Management*, pp. A3–4; Internal Revenue Code, Section 409(e); *Congressional Record* 1986: H7744–46.

39. In the Internal Revenue Code, Section 409(e)(3), the new tax law specifies these major corporate issues.

40. U.S. General Accounting Office, *Employee Stock Ownership Plans: Interim Report on a Survey and Related Economic Trends* (Washington, D.C.: U.S. General Accounting Office, February 1986), pp. 11,19.
41. ESOP Association, *ESOP Survey: 1986*, pp. 42–43.
42. David Ellerman and P. Pitegoff, *The Democratic ESOP* (Somerville, Mass.: Industrial Cooperative Association, 1986).
43. U.S. General Accounting Office, *Employee Stock Ownership Plans: Interim Report*, pp. 36–37.
44. ESOP Association, *ESOP Survey: 1982* (Washington, D.C.: ESOP Association of America, 1982), pp. 32–33.
45. *Ibid.*, p. 33.
46. ESOP Association, *ESOP Survey: 1986*, pp. 30–31.
47. U.S. Congress, Joint Committee on Taxation Staff, *General Explanation of the Revenue Act of 1978* (Washington, D.C.: U.S. Government Printing Office, March 12, 1979), p. 87.
48. Barber, *Employee Stock Ownership Plans*, pp. 3, 23–24.

Chapter 3: Capital Formation and Corporate Finance

1. ESOP Association, *Profile: Old Stone Corporation* (Washington, D.C.: ESOP Association of America, July 1985b).
2. J. Curtis, Jr. and A. Jeans, "The Financially Troubled Company: What About Its Qualified Employee Benefit Plans?" *Journal of Pension Planning and Compliance* 11 (Summer 1985): 121–34; "Unions Step Up the Battle with Pan Am," *Business Week*, July 27, 1987.
3. Andrew H. Malcolm, "Chicago's Largest Bookstore Chain Is Being Turned over to Employees," *New York Times*, June 22, 1986, p. 22.
4. American Capital Strategies, *American Capital Strategies: An Investment Banking Firm for Labor*, prospectus (Bethesda, Md.: American Capital Strategies, Inc., 1987).
5. For brevity, all financial tables are not shown here. Detailed financial tables covering ten-year spans for the various scenarios discussed in this chapter can be found in Timothy C. Jochim, *Employee Stock Ownership and Related Plans: Analysis and Practice* (Westport, Conn.: Quorum Books, 1982), pp. 31–61; 95–126. Those here are based on a useful technique from Hewitt Associates, *ESOPs: An Analytical Report* (Deerfield, Ill.: Hewitt Associates, 1976). Different company numbers can show that the leveraged ESOP increases or decreases net income compared to debt financing. The author's statement that the leveraged ESOP increases net income refers to the general effect of the leveraged ESOP: it shelters taxes more than the debt-financed model and therefore will lead to excess earnings and more rapid accumulation of assets. New laws change these models' estimates, too.
6. U.S. General Accounting Office, *Employee Stock Ownership Plans: Benefits and Costs of ESOP Tax Incentives for Broadening Stock Ownership* (Washington, D.C.: U.S. General Accounting Office, December 1986), p. 22. For a discussion of stock distribution, see Jared Kaplan, Gregory Brown, and Ronald Ludwig, *Tax Management: ESOPs* (Washington, D.C.: Bureau of National Affairs, 1985), p. A23.
7. A nonleveraged ESOP may be a better method to cash out a major shareholder than a leveraged ESOP because the purchase involves only an internal transferral of equity—the company contributes cash to the ESOP, which then purchases shares from a principal stockholder.
8. Jochim (*Employee Stock Ownership*, p. 100) notes that even publicly traded companies may have problems marketing securities because of infrequent sales and low vol-

ume. The Internal Revenue Service has defined circumstances under which it will issue an advance ruling that the sale of stock to the ESOP trust by a controlling shareholder is not a dividend distribution (Revenue Ruling 77–30).

9. ESOP Association, *ESOP Survey: 1985* (Washington, D.C.: ESOP Association of America, 1985a); *Idem., ESOP Survey: 1986* (Washington, D.C.: ESOP Association of America, 1986a). The association's 1986 survey indicated that 81 percent of ESOPs acquired existing stock.

10. A number of earlier Internal Revenue Rulings allowed this mechanism. For example, see Rev. Rul. 53–46, 1953–1 C.B. 287 and Rev. Rul. 71–311, 1971–2 C.B. 205.

11. On deducting dividend payments, see Kaplan, Brown, and Ludwig, *Tax Management*, p. A15. The American Institute of Certified Public Accountants has ruled that the company's obligation for credit in a leveraged ESOP is recorded as a liability that reduces shareholder equity.

12. Bumgarner discusses an example where an employee earns $20,000 per year, with annual 6-percent pay increases, in a company making ESOP contributions equal to 10.07 percent of pay, where stock values increase 11.53 percent per year. Stock values increase more than two-and-one-half times during the next ten years. In a nonleveraged ESOP the value of the employee's account would increase 2,000 percent, to $43,404. In the leveraged ESOP the account's value would increase 3,366 percent in the same period, to $71,148. See Robert R. Bumgarner, *ESOP Repurchase Liability* (Honolulu: American Trust Company of Hawaii, 1986), p. 2; Robert W. Smiley, Jr., "How to Plan for an ESOP's Repurchase Liability," in *Pension and Profit Sharing Service* (Englewood Cliffs, N.J.: Prentice-Hall, February 27, 1987), pp. 1215–29.

13. The comparisons do not take into account the fact that leveraged ESOPs may be able to get a loan at a lower interest rate because of Section 543 of the new 1984 Tax Reform Act (Internal Revenue Code 133) allowing commercial lenders to deduct 50 percent of their income on loans to ESOPs from their taxable income.

14. U.S. General Accounting Office, *Employee Stock Ownership Plans: Benefits and Costs*, p. 50; National Center for Employee Ownership, *Attitudes and Practices of Bankers towards ESOPs* (Oakland, Calif.: National Center for Employee Ownership, December 1985).

15. The source of this analysis is Kaplan, Brown, and Ludwig, *Tax Management*, pp. A26–27. When new shares are issued to the ESOP by the employer, an increase in shareholders' equity is reported only as the debt that financed that increase is reduced. When outstanding shares—as opposed to unissued shares—are acquired by the ESOP, shareholders' equity should be similarly reduced by the offsetting debits until the debt is repaid. The liability recorded by the employer is reduced as the ESOP makes payments on the debt. Also, the employer charges the amount contributed or committed to be contributed to an ESOP for a given year to the expenses for that year, whether or not such contributions are used concurrently to reduce the debt guaranteed by the employer.

16. An employer can get tax deductions by contributing to any eligible individual account plan and then amending it to have more than 10 percent of its assets in company stock. If the value of the stock rises significantly over the course of the repayments, the company can easily reduce the number of shares contributed to the plan to make sure that previously existing shareholders get the new value. Because workers get their stock gradually as the company contributes it to the trust, dilution is spread over a longer period. The employer is not locked into making specific contributions since it has not guaranteed the ESOP loan. This approach has a few limitations. It cannot be used in a shareholder bailout where a loan is necessary to purchase the securities. Deductible contributions are lower than for lever-

aged ESOPs. This discussion of the alternate method is based on Kaplan, Brown, and Ludwig, *Tax Management*, p. A23.

17. U.S. General Accounting Office, *Employee Stock Ownership Plans: Interim Report on a Survey and Related Economic Trends* (Washington, D.C.: U.S. General Accounting Office, February 1986).

18. The employer corporation creates a subsidiary corporation, which in turn sets up a leveraged ESOP. The leveraged ESOP borrows funds from a lender subject to the parent corporation's guarantee (or perhaps a guarantee by the new company). The leveraged ESOP can purchase the stock of the newly formed company, which then uses the funds to purchase its assets from the parent corporation. Or the leveraged ESOP can acquire the assets from the parent company, which it puts into the subsidiary in exchange for the stock of the newly formed corporation. The new corporation makes annual contributions to the leveraged ESOP to amortize the loan. Occasionally, other sources of capital are used for the purchase price: direct investments by workers and/or key managers, reductions in compensation or staffing and organizational changes that improve the new company's ability to repay the loan, a note from the parent corporation itself, the conversion of an existing benefit plan, partnership with an outside investor, or a combination of these. The new company has made a capital acquisition with pretax dollars. If the parent company is publicly traded, the stock is purchased on a public market subject to certain limitations (Kaplan, Brown, and Ludwig, *Tax Management*, p. A21). For further details, see Jochim, *Employee Stock Ownership*, pp. 97–100. His financial comparison of alternative acquisition scenarios further illustrates the ESOP's comparative advantage in transfers of ownership: In comparison to a conventional acquisition, the tax benefits increase working capital and increase the ESOP-acquired company's ability to meet its debt burden.

19. There is a growing legal literature on whether the use of an ESOP as a takeover defense conflicts with the exclusive benefit of the employee participants. Indeed, courts have stopped such uses and heard claims by raiders that employee ownership is simply a cover for management entrenchment. In other cases, the court has questioned how a trustee of an employee-investment plan can balance a suitor's offers for worker equity with the interests of the employee participants. An excellent treatment of this instance of the conflict between the corporate-finance and the employee-benefit uses of ESOPs can be found in Weyher and Knott, *ESOP: The Employee Stock Ownership Plan*, pp. 16–21; 233–65. See also Kravitz and Smith, *ESOPs and ESOP Transactions*; Margaret McLean, "Employee Stock Ownership Plans and Corporate Takeovers: Restraints on the Use of ESOPs by Corporate Officers and Directors to Avert Hostile Takeover," *Pepperdine Law Review* 10 (1983): 731–66; Alvin D. Lurie, "The ESOP as Stockholder: Whose Business Is It Anyway?" *Journal of Pension Planning and Compliance* 11 (Summer 1985): 115–34; Gretel Weatherly, "Special Report/ESOPs: The Latest Weapon in Corporate Takeover Wars," *Benefits News Analysis* 7 (May 1985): 11–19; Norman P. Goldberg, *The Fiduciary Issues in the Use of Employee Benefit Plans in Takeovers and Leveraged Buyouts* (Washington, D.C.: U.S. Department of Labor, Pension Benefits Welfare Administration, January 1986); John Hoerr, "ESOPs: Revolution or Ripoff?" *Business Week*, April 15, 1985; Lawrence J. Tell, "ESOP or MESOP: A Good Idea Is Being Put to Dubious Use," *Barron's*, March 18,1985: 8–9; 22.

20. Based on a review of news articles from 1983 to 1986 gathered by a clipping service sponsored by the National Center for Employee Ownership.

21. U.S. General Accounting Office, *Employee Stock Ownership Plans: Benefits and Costs*, p. 20.

22. ESOP Association, *ESOP Survey: 1985*, p. 24.

23. U.S. General Accounting Office, *Employee Stock Ownership Plans: Benefits and Costs*, pp. 51–52.

24. Kaplan, Brown, and Ludwig, *Tax Management*, p. A21.

25. National Center for Employee Ownership, *Majority Employee-Owned Firms* (Oakland, Calif.: National Center for Employee Ownership, August 1986).

26. Peter S. Fisher, "Corporate Tax Incentives: The American Version of Industrial Policy," *Journal of Economic Issues* 19, no. 1 (March 1983): 1–2.

27. Projecting actual 1975–1982 figures from Appendix C, Table C–1.

28. For defenses of the tax-credit ESOP by Senators Long and Fannin and Congressman Ullman, see *Congressional Record* (March 18,1975): S4223–24, S4246; *Congressional Record* (March 20,1975): S4489, S4492–3, S4549–50; *Congressional Record* (March 26,1975): H2358–59, H2368–69 (House-Senate Conference Explanation), S5245, S5263. It would seem that the strategy was to write ESOPs into most relevant bills. Thus, on January 5,1975, ESOP provisions were signed into law as part of the Trade Act of 1975 (Section 273[f]). For the defense of this provision see Russell Long, "Floor Statement on H.R. 10710," *Congressional Record* (October 3, 1974): S18261–62.

29. Russell Long, *Employee Ownership: A Political History* (Cambridge: Study Group on Worker Ownership and Participation in Business at Harvard University, 1983b), p. 3.

30. Russell Long, "S. 1162—Expanded Ownership Act of 1981," *Congressional Record* 127, no. 72 (May 12, 1981): 9; Russell Long, "An Ownership Approach to Productivity," Congressional Record 127, no. 115 (July 28, 1981): n.p.

31. Stuart Speiser, *A Piece of the Action* (New York: Van Nostrand Reinhold, 1977), pp. 207–12; 258–68.

32. *Ibid.*

33. U.S. Congress, Joint Economic Committee Staff, *Broadening the Ownership of New Capital: ESOPs and Other Alternatives* (Washington, D.C.: U.S. Government Printing Office, 1976).

34. U.S Congress, Senate Finance Committee, *ESOPs and General Stock Ownership Trusts* (Washington, D.C.: U.S. Government Printing Office, 1978a), p. 503.

35. ESOP Association, *ESOP Survey: 1983* (Washington, D.C.: ESOP Association of America, 1983), p. 23; *Idem., ESOP Survey: 1985*, pp. 24–25; and *Idem., ESOP Survey: 1986*, pp. 22–23.

36. Hewitt Associates, *1984 PAYSOP Survey of Fortune Directory Companies* (Lincolnshire, Ill.: Hewitt Associates, 1984). Responding to a separate question, about 27 percent of the Fortune Directory companies said they had no plans to establish a PAYSOP. Of these, about 34 percent said they could not use the additional tax credit, about 29 percent indicated that the benefit per employee was too small, and about 17 percent said they were not publicly traded or that there was no company stock (e.g., mutual insurance companies).

37. U.S. General Accounting Office, *Employee Stock Ownership Plans: Benefits and Costs*, p. 1.

38. For a discussion of the conditions under which employer securities must remain in the plan, see Kaplan, Brown, and Ludwig, *Tax Management*, p. A5.

39. U.S. General Accounting Office, *Employee Stock Ownership Plans: Benefits and Costs*, pp. 26–32.

40. Jane G. Gravelle, "Effects of the 1981 Depreciation Revisions on the Taxation of Income from Business Capital," *National Tax Journal* 35 (March 1982): 1–20.

41. Robert S. McIntyre and Dean C. Tipps, "Exploding the Investment Incentive Myth," *Challenge*, May/June 1985: 47–52.

42. Figures are from the Internal Revenue Service and the Flow of Funds Section of the Federal Reserve Board, quoted in U.S. General Accounting Office, *Employee Stock Ownership Plans: Interim Report*, pp. 45; 49.

43. According to the ESOP Association's *ESOP Survey: 1985*, p. 22, benefit-plan coverage in existing ESOPs is as follows:

	Total	Under 250 Participants	Over 250 Participants	Union Members Included	Publicly Traded
Pension	57	40	17	14	10
	26%	41%	29%	64%	42%
Profit-sharing	17	9	8	0	5
	11	9	14	0	21
Stock-purchase	13	8	5	0	3
	8	8	8	0	12
401(k)	34	18	16	7	3
	22	19	27	32	12
Other	36	22	13	1	3
	23	23	22	4	12

44. These problems arose when the Conrail ESOP was rejected. See U.S. Congress, Joint Economic Committee, *Hearings on Employee Stock Ownership Plans* (Washington, D.C.: U.S. Government Printing Office, 1976), "December 11, 1975" (Part 1), pp. 49–55, 66–77,77–84, 274–355; "December 12, 1976" (Part 2), pp. 641–796.

45. So far there is little information about the new opportunities for employee ownership in the 1986 tax reform law, and few publications outline the radical way these changes make ESOPs preferable for stock buybacks. Sources at the New York investment bank, Lazard Frere, report that this provision is more frequently being used by large companies in 1987. Ludwig and Curtis, *Memorandum to Our ESOP Clients* (San Francisco: Ludwig & Curtis, October 22, 1986) is one of the best summaries of all the changes relating to ESOPs in the new law.

46. The margin rules refer to Regulations G, T, U, and X of the Federal Reserve Board. Regarding the ESOP exemptions, see U.S. Government Federal Register, 48 *Federal Register* 35074 (August 3, 1983) and 50 *Federal Register* 26354 (June 26, 1985), as well as U.S. Federal Reserve Board, Federal Reserve Board Staff Opinion, March 12, 1985. A detailed discussion appears in Weyher and Knott, *ESOP: The Employee Stock Ownership Plan*, pp. 184–88.

47. See Joseph Raphael Blasi, *Employee Ownership through ESOPs: Implications for the Public Corporation* (Scarsdale, N.Y.: Work in America Institute, 1987).

48. U.S. Congress, Senate Committee on Government Operations, *Disclosure On Corporate Ownership* (Washington, D.C.: U.S. Government Printing Office, 1974), n.p.; 1981 data is from Appendix C, Table C–2.

49. Thomas R. Marsh and Dale E. McAllister, "ESOP Tables: A Survey of Companies with Employee Stock Ownership Plans," *Journal of Corporation Law* 6, no. 3 (1981): 552–623.

50. Michael Quarrey, Joseph Raphael Blasi, and Corey Rosen, *Taking Stock: Employee Ownership at Work* (Cambridge, Mass.: Ballinger Publishing, 1986).

51. See Arlene Hershman, "The Spreading Wave of Stock Buybacks," *Dun's Business Month*, August 1984: 40–46. Evidence on the advantages of such buybacks can also be found in Francis A. Lees, *Repurchasing Common Stock*, Research Bulletin No. 146 (New York: The Conference Board, Inc., 1983.)

52. ESOP Association, *ESOP Survey: 1986*.

53. Zachary Schiller, "Merger Phobia Has Unions Wheeling and Dealing," *Business Week*, March 23, 1987: 118.
54. Estimates based on figures in U.S. General Accounting Office, *Employee Stock Ownership Plans: Benefits and Costs*, pp. 26–32.

Chapter 4: Sharing Wealth though the ESOP

Note: All ESOP tables and numbers are from U.S. General Accounting Office, *Initial Results of a Survey on ESOPs and Information on Related Economic Trends* (Washington, D.C.: U.S. General Accounting Office, September 30, 1985), U.S. General Accounting Office, *Employee Stock Ownership Plans: Interim Report on a Survey and Related Economic Trends* (Washington, D.C.: U.S. General Accounting Office, February 1986), and U.S. General Accounting Office, *Employee Stock Ownership Plans: Benefits and Costs of ESOP Tax Incentives for Broadening Stock Ownership* (Washington, D.C.: U.S. General Accounting Office, December 1986).

1. Wendy Fox, "Boston Advertising Agency Will Be Sold to Employees," *Boston Globe*, November 19, 1985.
2. International Union of Bricklayers and Allied Craftsmen, "Kick-off BAC Co-op," *The Journal*, September 1986: 1.
3. Alex Kotlowitz, "Pilots Offer May Spur Other Unions to Attempt to Purchase Companies," *Wall Street Journal*, April 17, 1987; Judith Valente and Scott Kilman, "Pilots May Seek Partners to Buy Parent of United," *Wall Street Journal*, April 27, 1987, p. 6.
4. "Bank Building Plans to Buy Back Shares; LVI Lowers Its Stake," *Wall Street Journal*, May 5, 1987. See also Laura Landro, "Time Will Buy as Much as 16 Percent of Its Common," *Wall Street Journal*, June 20, 1986.
5. A leverageable ESOP is an ESOP that is permitted to leverage under the terms of the employee stock ownership trust plan documents but has not done so by a given date.
6. U.S. General Accounting Office, *Employee Stock Ownership Plans: Interim Report*. See also ESOP Association, *ESOP Survey: 1985* (Washington, D.C.: ESOP Association, 1985a); Idem., *ESOP Survey: 1986* (Washington, D.C.: ESOP Association, 1986a). On the percentage of ESOPs owning their entire companies, see U.S. General Accounting Office, *Employee Stock Ownership Plans: Benefits and Costs*, p. 30.
7. See National Center for Employee Ownership, "GAO Report Puts Numbers on ESOPs," *Employee Ownership* 7, no. 1 (January/February 1987): 1; Michael Quarrey, *Employee Ownership and Corporate Performance* (Oakland, Calif.: National Center for Employee Ownership, 1986), p. 1. General Accounting Office methods for estimating ESOPs are explained in U.S. General Accounting Office, *Employee Stock Ownership Plans: Benefits and Costs*, pp. 62–66. (Note that these figures do not include employee ownership in profit-sharing plans, which we have attempted to estimate in Chapter 1.) The 7-percent figure is from the same source, pp.12, 36, and is based on a 1983 employed labor force of 102.5 million. The figure of 7,500 is based on the GAO's estimate of 4,800 active ESOPs and similar stock-bonus plans, as well as an estimate by the National Center for Employee Ownership for new ESOP growth in 1986. Because of the insignificance of the tax-credit ESOP, the National Center for Employee Ownership has begun issuing annual estimates of participants in leveraged and nonleveraged ESOPs and ESOP-type stock-bonus plans. They now estimate that there are 8,000 employee-ownership plans of these types with 8 million participating employees in 1987. The GAO has not collected comprehensive information on these ESOP-type stock-bonus plans.
8. Hewitt Associates, *Survey of Tax Reduction Act ESOPs* (Deerfield, Ill : Hewitt Associates, 1977, 1978), p. 7. Steven Bloom, *Employee Ownership and Firm Performance*

(Cambridge: Harvard University Department of Economics, 1986), pp. 176–77, reports on total employees versus participants in tax-credit ESOPs, as do Tables 2–2 and 2–3.

9.   U.S. General Accounting Office, *Employee Stock Ownership Plans: Interim Report*, p. 9; *Ibid.*, *Employee Stock Ownership Plans: Benefits and Costs*, p. 19. See also Table 4–2.

10. U.S. General Accounting Office, *Employee Stock Ownership Plans: Benefits and Costs*, p. 19.

11. For recent discussions by the author and others on the takeover game and employee ownership, see Zachary Schiller, "Merger Phobia Has Unions Wheeling and Dealing," *Business Week*, March 23, 1987: 118; Bruce Nussbaum and Judith Dobrynski, "Corporate Control: Shareholders vs. Managers," *Business Week*, May 18, 1987: 102; and Clemens P. Work, "When Workers Get In the Takeover Game," *U.S. News and World Report*, June 8, 1987: 47; Amy Pershing, "Wall Street Pays Its Union Dues," *Institutional Investor* 21, no. 8 (August 1987): 195–97.

12. For detailed data, see U.S. General Accounting Office, *Employee Stock Ownership Plans: Interim Report*, pp. 15, 19.

13. *Ibid.* The growth of ESOPs, also discernible in the 1983, 1985, and 1986 ESOP Association surveys, was independently confirmed by the author from 1982 to 1986, through review of materials from the National Center for Employee Ownership reporting on companies with sizable, majority, or complete employee ownership supplied by a national clipping service.

14. The author identifies many worker buyouts of failing firms or employee acquisition of generally ongoing units in spinoffs or divestitures in *Employee Ownership Through ESOPs: Implications for the Public Corporation* (Scarsdale, N.Y.: Work in America Institute, 1987).

15. U.S. Congress, Joint Economic Committee, Democratic Staff, and James D. Smith, "The Concentration of Wealth in the U.S.: Trends in the Distribution of Wealth among American Families" (Washington, D.C.: U.S. Congress, Joint Economic Committee, July 1986). This study was recently withdrawn because of some computing errors. The author has turned to revised figures made available by the press spokesperson of the committee during a November 8, 1986, telephone interview and by the Federal Reserve Board in U.S. General Accounting Office, *Employee Stock Ownership Plans: Benefits and Costs*, p. 35.

16. Averages are based on measurements taken in 1958, 1965, 1972, and 1976, which appear in James D. Smith, "The Concentration of Personal Wealth in the United States, 1958–1976," *Review of Income and Wealth*, series 30, no. 4 (December 1984): 422–23, although only 1958 and 1976 figures are reported here for comparison. Note that the Smith figures compute wealth for the top 1/2 percent and 1 percent of individuals while the U.S. Congress, Joint Economic Committee, Democratic Staff and Smith, "The Concentration of Wealth," computes them for the top households.

17. U.S. Congress, Joint Economic Committee Staff, *Broadening the Ownership of New Capital: ESOPs and Other Alternatives* (Washington, D.C.: U.S. Government Printing Office, 1976), p. 7.

18. Marvin Schwartz, *Preliminary Estimates of Personal Wealth, 1982: Composition of Assets* (Washington, D.C.: Internal Revenue Service, 1982).

19. Robert B. Avery, Gregory E. Elliehausen, Glenn B. Canner, and Thomas A. Gustafson, "Survey of Consumer Finances, 1983," *Federal Reserve Bulletin*, September 1984: 679–90; Robert B. Avery, Gregory E. Elliehausen, Glenn B. Canner, Thomas A. Gustafson, and Julia Springer, "Financial Characteristics of High-Income Families," *Federal Reserve Bulletin*, March 1986: 163–77.

20. *Ibid.* The Social Security data was quoted by Senator Russell Long, "An Ownership Approach to Productivity," *Congressional Record* 127, no. 115 (July 28, 1981).

21.   U.S. General Accounting Office, *Initial Results of a Survey on ESOPs*, pp. 18–19, based on University of Michigan data.

22.   Avery et al., "Survey of Consumer Finances," pp. 680–81.

23.   The exchange's figures do not add up to 100 percent; the reason for this is not reported. See New York Stock Exchange, *Direct Ownership Employee Stock Purchase Plans* (New York: New York Stock Exchange, September 1984), p. 1; *Ibid., Shareownership 1983* (New York: New York Stock Exchange, April 1984), p. 28. These findings were generally confirmed in a 1985 shareownership study by the exchange. See also Alexander Cockburn, "Excusing U.S. Capitalism by Denying Its Presence," *The Wall Street Journal*, December 12, 1985, p. 31.

24.   Avery et al., "Survey of Consumer Finances"; Avery et al., "Financial Characteristics," pp. 108–73.

25.   U.S. General Accounting Office, *Employee Stock Ownership Plans: Benefits and Costs*, p. 35.

26.   Computed from numbers in U.S. General Accounting Office, *Employee Stock Ownership Plans: Benefits and Costs*, p. 36. Wealth is defined here as the gross assets in Table 4–2a.

27.   New York Stock Exchange, *Direct Ownership Employee Stock Purchase Plans*, p. 4.

28.   U.S. General Accounting Office, *Employee Stock Ownership Plans: Benefits and Costs*, pp. 19, 31.

29.   Avery et al., *Financial Characteristics*, p. 165. By comparison, 8 percent of family heads in clerical or sales, 2 percent of craftspeople or foremen/women, and 0 percent of operative, labor, or service workers are in the top 2 percent of wealthholders.

30.   By another set of GAO estimates, these nontax-credit ESOPs cost the government only $227 million in the same period—$1.00 of government tax expenditure producing $17.02 of employee ownership. These lower estimates presume that ESOPs entail no extra revenue losses, since in their absence contributions could be made to other types of pension and profit-sharing plans or replaced by wages and salaries, which are subject to most of the same deduction rules. Thus, the GAO concludes, no matter which set of estimates is used, nearly all of the revenue losses and inefficiency are related to the tax-credit ESOP. It appears that government encouragement of employee ownership could, in fact, be efficient and efficacious. For a full discussion of revenue estimates, see U.S. General Accounting Office, *Employee Stock Ownership Plans: Benefits and Costs*, pp. 26–32, 67–70.

31.   U.S. General Accounting Office, *Employee Stock Ownership Plans: Interim Report*, p. 23.

32.   Thirty-five percent of the ESOP Association's member ESOPs did convert profit-sharing plans into ESOPs. On terminated pension plans, wage concessions, and ESOPs, see National Center for Employee Ownership, *Employee Ownership: A Handbook for Unions* (Oakland, Calif.: National Center for Employee Ownership, 1985e), pp. 38–40, 50–55; ESOP Association, *ESOP Survey: 1985*, pp. 12, 19. Regarding Dan River, where benefit concessions hurt employees, see John Hoerr, "ESOPs: Revolution or Ripoff?" *Business Week*, April 15, 1985: 94.

Chapter 5: The Law and Employee Rights

1.   Mino Capossela and Lexa Edsall, "Federal Distillers: A Case Study" (term paper, Harvard University Freshman Seminar Program, January 18, 1986).

2.   Michael A. Hiltzik, "Employee Ownership Is Fraught with Pitfalls," *Cleveland Plain Dealer*, June 1, 1986.

3. Michael J. McCarthy, "Amsted Agrees to Revised Bid by Management," *Wall Street Journal*, January 31, 1986.

4. Ashland, Kentucky, *Independent*, May 5, 1986; Huntington, West Virginia, *Herald-Dispatch*, May 16, 1986; Seth H. Lubove, "Ashland Oil Proposes Stock Buyback, Other Steps to Enhance Value of Shares," *Wall Street Journal*, April 3, 1986.

5. Louisville, Kentucky, *Courier-Journal*, March 26, 1986.

6. Robert A. Frisch, *The Magic of ESOPs and LBOs* (Rockville Centre, N.Y.: Farnsworth Publishing Co.,1985) is an extreme example of this favoritism.

7. National Center for Employee Ownership, "How Consultants View Employee Ownership," *Employee Ownership* 4, no. 1 (March 1984): 1.

8. U.S. Comptroller General, *Employee Stock Ownership Plans: Who Benefits Most in Closely-Held Companies?* (Washington, D.C.: U.S. General Accounting Office, 1980).

9. Alison Leigh Cowan, "A Game of Musical Chairs in Avondale's Boardroom," *Business Week*, October 20, 1986: 52.

10. Based on Timothy C. Jochim, *Employee Stock Ownership and Related Plans: Analysis and Practice* (Westport, Conn.: Quorum Books,1982), pp. 184–85. See Internal Revenue Code 402(a); Harry Weyher and Hiram Knott, *ESOP: The Employee Stock Ownership Plan* (Chicago: Commerce Clearing House,1985), pp. 201–32.

11. For a copy of the act, see U.S. Congress, Joint Economic Committee Staff, *Broadening the Ownership of New Capital: ESOPs and Other Alternatives* (Washington, D.C.: U.S. Government Printing Office,1976), pp. 60–62.

12. *Ibid.*

13. Frisch, *The Magic of ESOPs and LBOs*, p. 35.

14. Copper Range Company, *Copper Range Company Employee Stock Ownership Plan* (Upper Peninsula, Mich.: Copper Range Company, 1985), pp. 56–57.

15. Jared Kaplan, Gregory Brown, and Ronald Ludwig, *Tax Management: ESOPs* (Washington, D.C.: Bureau of National Affairs, 1985), p. A28; SEC Release No. 33–6281 (1/15/81).

16. ERISA, Title 1, Section 2(a). See Kaplan, Brown, and Ludwig, *Tax Management*, p. A18. For a review of the restrictions and exemptions related to ESOPs, see Internal Revenue Code, Sections 404 (the prudent-man rule), 406 (the rule against transactions with a party in interest), 407 (the diversification rule), and 408 (exempting the ESOP from prohibited transactions). Exemptions are contained in ERISA 407(d)(6)(a); ERISA 407(b); ERISA 408(e), Labor Regulation2550.408e, and ERISA 3(18); ERISA 408(b)(3) and Internal Revenue Code 4975(d)(3); and Labor Regulations 2550.408b–3 a–j and IRS Regulations 54.4975–7(b) 1–11. See also William N. Kravitz and Charles Smith, *ESOPs and ESOP Transactions* (New York: Practicing Law Institute, 1985), pp. 410–11.

17. Generally, fiduciaries are not only trustees but also persons controlling the disposition of the trust assets, rendering investment advice to the plan for a fee, exercising discretionary authority in plan administration, or so named by the plan instrument. For a review of ERISA cases involving plan investments in employer securities, see Ronald S. Rizzo and Robert P. Hardy, *Fiduciary Concerns in Stock Ownership Transactions* (Los Angeles: Jones, Davy, Reavis, and Pogue, October 6, 1986).

18. Norman P. Goldberg, *The Fiduciary Issues in the Use of Employee Benefit Plans in Takeovers and Leveraged Buyouts* (Washington, D.C.: U.S. Department of Labor, Pension Benefits Welfare Administration, Fiduciary Litigation Division, January 1986), p. 17.

19. D. Bret Carlson, "ESOP and Universal Capitalism," *Tax Law Review* 31 (1976): 289–315.

20. See House Committee on Ways and Means, *Conference Report Accompanying H.R. 2, ERISA, No. 93–1280* (Washington, D.C.: U.S. Government Printing Office, August

12, 1974), pp. 63–66, 172, 176, 191–92, 308, 312–15, 317, especially page 313. See also U.S. Comptroller General, *Employee Stock Ownership Plans*, pp. 8–19, 29–30.

21. David Ellerman, *Worker Ownership: Economic Democracy or Worker Capitalism?* (Somerville, Mass.: Industrial Cooperative Association, 1986). For a review of scholarly views on ESOPs and securities law, see Timothy Tomlinson, "Securities Regulation of ESOPs: A Comparison of SEC Policy and Congressional Intent," *Stanford Law Review* 31 (November 1978): 121–64; John K. Drisdale, "ESOPs and Securities Laws," *Baylor Law Review* 32 (1980): 19–49; and Zane O. Gresham, "ESOPs: Obligations of the Sponsor and Protection of Beneficiaries under the Federal Securities Laws," *American University Law Review* 26 (1977): 569–92.

22. The Hyatt-Clark case is discussed in Michael Quarrey, Joseph Raphael Blasi, and Corey Rosen, *Taking Stock: Employee Ownership at Work* (Cambridge, Mass.: Ballinger Publishing, 1986), while the ESOP at South Bend Lathe, Inc., is covered in William Foote Whyte, Charles Craypo, et al., *Evaluation Research on Federally-Assisted Worker Buyouts* (Washington, D.C.: U.S. Department of Commerce, Economic Development Administration Research and Policy Unit, 1987).

23. See William J. Kilberg and John J. Canary, Jr., *Position Paper: A Legal Commentary on Behalf of Kelso & Company Regarding ERISA Regulation of ESOP Participation in Multi-Investor Leveraged Buyouts Presented to Assistant Secretary for Pension and Welfare Benefit Programs, U.S. Department of Labor* (Washington, D.C.: Gibson, Dunn & Crutcher, October 7, 1987). The position paper discusses many other technical aspects of ESOP-leveraged buyouts that are necessary to make them economically feasible, which I do not challenge. My point is that the Department of Labor and court rulings on these issues should be guided by a recognition that employees are real investors using real capital credit in ESOPs as well as being the people who operate the company, and as such they should be involved in managing their investment.

24. In one particularly specious bit of reasoning furthered by this analysis, investment bankers argue that in a multi-investor LBO using employee ownership, company management should pay less for its stock because it may be nonvoting and therefore appraised for less by valuation consultants. This argument overlooks the fact that management will often control all the voting rights in the ESOP in any case by not passing them through to the workers and by appointing an ESOP trustee favorable to its own interests.

25. Stephen Schlossberg and Steven Fetter, *U.S. Labor Laws and the Future of Labor-Management Cooperation* (Washington, D.C.: U.S. Department of Labor, 1986); *Ibid., First Interim Report* (Washington, D.C.: U.S. Department of Labor, 1987).

26. Kaplan, Brown, and Ludwig, *Tax Management*, pp. 27–28.

27. U.S. Comptroller General, *Employee Stock Ownership Plans*, p. 24.

28. *Ibid.*; Joseph Raphael Blasi, *Employee Ownership through ESOPs: Implications for the Public Organization* (Scarsdale, N.Y.: Work in America Institute, 1987).

29. Goldberg, *Fiduciary Issues in the Use of Employee Benefit Plans*, p. 4. Full discussion of the case is in Norlin Corporation *v.* Rooney, Pace, Inc., at 744 F. 2D 255 (1984).

30. Norman P. Goldberg, "From the Enforcement Point of View," in *ESOPs and ESOP Transactions*, ed. Kravitz and Smith, pp. 445–46; Goldberg, *Fiduciary Issues in the Use of Employee Benefit Plans*, p. 17. The author wishes to thank an anonymous lawyer who provided a brief on this important case.

31. The Labor Department ruling letter on Blue Bell is contained in an unpaginated appendix to Goldberg, *Fiduciary Issues in the Use of Employee Benefit Plans*.

32. *Ibid.*, pp. 9–17.

33. "ESOP Watchdogs Are Writing New Rules," *Business Week*, October 21, 1985.

34. See James S. Zukin and Richard S. Braun, *ERISA Advisory Council Papers* (Los Angeles: Houlihan, Lokey, Howard & Zukin, 1986). The main idea is that investors are

entitled to claim a percentage of future firm earnings based on their percentages of ownership. See American Capital Strategies, A $75-Million ESOP Leveraged Buyout Fund and ESOP Leveraged Buyout Presentation (Bethesda, Md.: American Capital Strategies, 1987).

35.   Personal communication, July 1987.

36.   U.S. Comptroller General, Employee Stock Ownership Plans, includes evidence showing that the Department of Labor and the IRS cannot effectively police employee ownership.

37.   Alan Lebowitz, U.S Department of Labor, Office of Pension and Welfare Benefits Program, January 30, 1985, correspondence with the Securities and Exchange Commission regarding Phillips Petroleum Company's preliminary proxy materials and their proposed ESOP. A solution to these problems would be to have employees select the trustees of the ESOP. Thomas R. Marsh and Dale E. McAllister report in "ESOP Tables: A Survey of Companies with Employee Stock Ownership Plans," Journal of Corporation Law 6, no. 3 (1981): 592, that a survey of 229 leveraged and nonleveraged ESOP companies shows that the board of directors chooses the trustees in 90 percent of the cases, the employees in 3 percent of the cases, both in 3 percent of the cases, while 4 percent use another arrangement.

38.   Internal Revenue Code, Sections 401(a)(4) and 401(a)(5).

39.   Joseph E. Bachelder, Employee Stock Ownership Plans (New York: Practicing Law Institute, 1979), p. 25.

40.   U.S. Congress, Senate Finance Committee, Hearings, Employee Stock Ownership Plans and General Stock Ownership Trusts (Washington, D.C.: U.S. Government Printing Office, 1978b), pp. 148–49; Hewitt Associates, 1984 PAYSOP Survey of Fortune Directory Companies (Lincolnshire, Ill.: Hewitt Associates, 1984), p. 7; U.S. Comptroller General, Employee Stock Ownership Plans, p. 23.

41.   U.S. General Accounting Office, Employee Stock Ownership Plans: Interim Report on a Survey and Related Economic Trends (Washington, D.C.: U.S. General Accounting Office, February 1986), pp. 34–35. This is the major and fundamental flaw in the GAO analysis of ESOPs.

42.   I am indebted to Andrew Strom for these insights. See Andrew Strom, Ownership and Control in the U.S. Private Pension System (Cambridge, Mass.: Harvard University Committee on Social Studies, May 18, 1986). See also Dennis Logue, Legislative Influence on Corporate Pension Plans (Washington, D.C.: American Enterprise Institute, 1979), pp. 31, 34; William Greenough and Francis King, Pension Plans and Public Policy (New York: Columbia University Press, 1976); John Brooks, Conflicts of Interest: Corporate Pension Fund Asset Management (New York: The Twentieth Century Fund, 1977); Randy Barber and Jeremy Rifkin, The North Will Rise Again: Pensions, Politics and Power in the 1980's (Boston: Beacon Press, 1978); and AFL-CIO, Industrial Union Department, Pensions: A Study of Benefit Fund Investment Policies (Washington, D.C.: AFL-CIO, Industrial Union Department, 1980).

43.   U.S. Congress, Senate Finance Committee, Report, Tax Reduction Act of 1975 (Washington, D.C.: U.S. Government Printing Office, March 17, 1975), p. 58.

44.   "Reports" and "General Explanations" are binding interpretations of public laws and thus important texts for analyzing the meaning of the curt legalese in which the law itself is expressed. The evolution of these texts is very revealing. See U.S. Congress, Senate Finance Committee, Report, Tax Reduction Act of 1975, p. 58. Substantially the same wording is repeated in the official reports on the Tax Reform Act of 1976 and the Revenue Act of 1978. See U.S. Congress, Joint Committee on Taxation, General Explanation of the Tax Reform Act of 1976 (Washington, D.C.: U.S. Government Printing Office, December 29, 1976), p. 168; Ibid., General Explanation of the Revenue Act of 1978 (Washington, D.C.: U.S. Government Printing Office, March 12,

1979), p. 85. In 1981 a definite change in language occurs. This may be explained by the controversy raised by the U.S. Comptroller General's criticism of a lack of employee rights in ESOPs. All of the sudden the phrase "without the surrender of any other rights on the part of such employees" (1975) or "without requiring . . . the surrender of any rights on the part of employees" (1976 and 1978) is removed from the definition of the ESOP in 1981, 1984, and 1986. See U.S. Congress, Senate Finance Committee, *Summary of the Economic Recovery Tax Act of 1981* (Washington, D.C.: U.S. Government Printing Office, June 25, 1981), p. 25; U.S. Congress, Joint Committee on Taxation, General Explanation of the Revenue Provisions of the Deficit Reduction Act of 1984 (Washington, D. C.: U.S. Government Printing Office, December 31, 1984), p. 873. Despite the fact that in 1986, as part of the tax reform package, Congress rejected Senator Long's statement of congressional policy that would give primacy to the corporate-finance uses over the employee-benefit goal of ESOPs, the House-Senate report's language de-emphasizes employee rights and benefits: "An employee stock ownership plan (ESOP) is a qualified stock-bonus plan and a money-purchase pension plan which may be utilized as a technique of corporate finance and under which an employer's stock is held for the benefit of the employees." Suddenly, the original concept of broad-based ownership that encourages a "common interest in the firm" and motivation is reduced to something that workers are "under"—the incidental nature of employee ownership to corporate finance is starting to be stressed (*Congressional Record* [September 18, 1986]: H7744). Note that the concept of "beneficial ownership" is not used in ERISA's treatment of ESOPs or in Treasury regulations, but Senate Finance Committee staffers added it to much of the report. It seems to arise when congresspeople wish again to emphasize the passive aspect of the ESOP. Thus, the 1984 tax act report notes that an ESOP is where the "stock is held for the benefit of employees." Some critics of this shift have suggested that various ESOP consultants whose self-interest is more served by the new version of employee ownership actually may have had a hand in drafting this language.

45. See U.S. Congress, Joint Economic Committee, *Hearings on Employee Stock Ownership Plans* (Washington, D.C.: U.S. Government Printing Office, 1976), "December 11, 1975" (Part 1) and "December 12, 1975" (Part 2); U.S. Congress, Senate Finance Committee, *ESOPs and General Stock Ownership Trusts* (Washington, D.C.: U.S. Government Printing Office, 1978a); and U.S. Congress, Senate Finance Committee, *Hearings, Employee Stock Ownership Plans*.

46. For the proposed ESOP regulations, see the draft published jointly by the U.S. Department of Labor and U.S. Department of Treasury, Internal Revenue Service, on July 30, 1976, in 41 *Federal Register* 31, 833 (1976). For a detailed discussion, see R. Scot Faley and Richard L. Sussman, "The Tax Aspects of ESOPs: The IRS's Proposed Regulations," *American University Law Review* 26 (1977): 593–631; Robert S. Paulock and Paul Lieberman, "Employee Stock Ownership Trusts: The Final Regulations," *Tax Advisor*, May 1978: 260–69.

47. For Congress's response to the proposed regulations, see U.S. Congress, Joint Committee on Taxation, *General Explanation of the Tax Reform Act of 1976*, pp. 172–75. The actual final regulations were issued on September 2, 1977, in 42 *Federal Register* 44, 384 (1977).

48. See U.S. Department of Treasury, *Treasury 2: The President's Tax Proposals for Fairness, Growth, and Simplicity* (Washington, D.C.: U.S. Government Printing Office, May 1985).

49. U.S. Congress, Joint Committee on Taxation Staff, *Tax Reform Proposals: Tax Treatment of Employee Stock Ownership Plans* (ESOPs) (Washington, D.C.: U.S. Government Printing Office, September 20, 1985), pp. 20–27.

50.   *Congressional Record* (September 18, 1986): H7744–46.
51.   There is a technical explanation of the importance of this amendment. In 1978, Presidential Reorganization Plan #4 passed the Congress, giving the Department of Labor full authority to oversee issues related to the definition of exclusive benefit of employees and the responsibility of fiduciaries. Before then, this function had been shared by Labor and Treasury. Until 1978, proponents of limited property rights could count on the earlier statement of congressional intent in the Internal Revenue Code to check Treasury's ability to reduce the importance of corporate finance in ESOPs in favor of worker rights. After the presidential order, Long could no longer control Labor since the tax bill does not have direct authority over ERISA. The next strategy was to make a general amendment to the body of U.S. law, the U.S. Code, as an indirect way of bringing ERISA and Labor under control. This failed at the eleventh hour; few people ever realized the implications of this defeat.

Chapter 6: The Responsibilities of Capitalism

1.   John D. Williams, "Buyouts Made with ESOPs Are Criticized," *Wall Street Journal*, February 21, 1984, p. 35.
2.   Steven Dostart, *The Use of ESOPs in the Banking Industry: Participation or Manipulation?* (Cambridge: Harvard University Committee on Social Studies, March 1986).
3.   Eileen McCarthy and Corey Rosen, *Employee Ownership in the Grocery Industry* (Oakland, Calif.: National Center for Employee Ownership, May 1987).
4.   Copper Range Company, *Copper Range Company Employee Stock Ownership Plan* (Upper Peninsula, Mich.: Copper Range Company, 1985).
5.   Cathy Ivancic and Corey Rosen. *Voting and Participation in Employee Ownership Firms* (Oakland, Calif.: National Center for Employee Ownership, 1986).
6.   U.S. Congress, Joint Committee on Taxation, *General Explanation of the Tax Reform Act of 1976* (Washington, D.C.: U.S. Government Printing Office, December 29, 1976), p. 174.
7.   U.S. Congress, Joint Committee on Taxation Staff, *General Explanation of the Revenue Act of 1978* (Washington, D.C.: U.S. Government Printing Office, March 12, 1979), p. 87.
8.   National Center for Employee Ownership, "Banks and Loans to ESOPs: An NCEO Survey," *Employee Ownership* 5, no. 6 (December 1985d): 1; 4; 6.
9.   U.S. Congress, Joint Economic Committee Staff, *Broadening the Ownership of New Capital: ESOPs and Other Alternatives* (Washington, D.C.: U.S. Government Printing Office, 1976), pp. 52–55. Kelso has both supported and opposed voting rights: See U.S. Congress, Joint Economic Committee, *Hearings on Employee Stock Ownership Plans* (Washington, D.C.: U.S. Government Printing Office, 1976), "December 12, 1976" (Part 2), pp. 175–203, especially pages 201–3 on voting rights; and U.S. Congress, Joint Economic Committee Staff, *Broadening the Ownership of New Capital*, p. 53, note 9.
10.   U.S. Congress, Joint Committee on Taxation Staff, *Tax Reform Proposals: Tax Treatment of Employee Stock Ownership Plans* (ESOPs) (Washington, D.C.: U.S. Government Printing Office, September 20, 1985), pp. 17, 23–27.
11.   U.S. Comptroller General, *Employee Stock Ownership Plans: Who Benefits Most in Closely-Held Companies?* (Washington, D.C.: U.S. General Accounting Office, 1980), pp. 37–42; U.S. Congress, Joint Economic Committee Staff, *Broadening the Ownership of New Capital*, pp. 31–32, 34.
12.   ESOP Association, *ESOP Survey: 1986* (Washington, D.C.: ESOP Association of America, 1986), pp. 42–43.

13. Luis Granados, "Employee Stock Ownership Plans: An Analysis of Current Reform Proposals," *Journal of Law Reform* 14 (Fall 1980): 31–39.

14. Corey Rosen, Katherine Klein, and Karen Young, *Employee Ownership in America: The Equity Solution* (Lexington, Mass.: Lexington Books, 1986).

15. Granados, "Employee Stock Ownership Plans," p. 33.

16. ESOP Association, *ESOP Survey: 1983* (Washington, D.C.: ESOP Association of America, 1983), pp. 34–35; *Ibid., ESOP Survey: 1982* (Washington, D.C.: ESOP Association of America, 1982), pp. 34–35.

17. ESOP Association, *ESOP Survey: 1982*, pp. 34–35. See also U.S. General Accounting Office, *Employee Stock Ownership Plans: Interim Report on a Survey and Related Economic Trends* (Washington, D.C.: U.S. General Accounting Office, February 1986), p. 11, Table 2.

18. Michael Quarrey, Joseph Raphael Blasi, and Corey Rosen, *Taking Stock: Employee Ownership at Work* (Cambridge, Mass.: Ballinger Publishing, 1986).

19. See Jeffrey R. Gates, *Overview of ESOP Amendments in the Tax Reform Act of 1986* (Washington, D.C.: Senate Finance Committee, 1986).

20. U.S. General Accounting Office, *Employee Stock Ownership Plans: Benefits and Costs of ESOP Tax Incentives for Broadening Stock Ownership* (Washington, D.C.: U.S. General Accounting Office, December 1986), pp. 39–40.

21. U.S. Comptroller General, *Employee Stock Ownership Plans*, p. 26.

22. Milton Friedman, "The Social Responsibility of Business Is to Increase Its Profits," *New York Times Sunday Magazine*, September 13, 1970.

23. Carl Icahn, "What Ails Corporate America—And What Should Be Done," *Business Week*, October 27, 1986: 101. For an outrageous example of management entrenchment in employee ownership, see "A Saga of Shareholder Neglect: Whose Interests Was This Management Protecting?" *Barron's*, May 4, 1987.

24. A. A. Berle and Gardiner Means, *The Corporation and Private Property* (New York: Macmillan, 1932).

25. Nicholas Wolfson, *The Modern Corporation: Free Markets vs. Regulation* (New York: The Free Press, 1984), pp. 15, 23.

26. Regarding ESOPs in takeovers, see Michael G. Galloway, "Employee Stock Ownership Plans and Other Defenses to Hostile Tender Offers," *Washburn Law Journal* 21 (1982): 580–606; Robert A. Profusek and Jeffrey S. Leavitt, "Dealing with Employee Benefit Plans: Part 1, Roles in Hostile Takeovers; Part 2, Points to Negotiate in Friendly Transactions," *Mergers and Acquisitions* 18 (Winter 1984): 44–51; R. M. Horwood, "The ABCs of ESOP LBOs—Past, Present, and Future," *Journal of Corporate Taxation* 13 (Autumn 1986): 233–63.

27. I am indebted to Douglas Kruse for a research memorandum on this subject.

28. F. Hodge O'Neal, *Close Corporations: Law and Practice*, vol. 1 (Chicago: Callaghan & Company, 1958), pp. 5, 13.

29. I am indebted to Noam S. Cohen for his research in this area. See Noam S. Cohen, *How Illusory Property Rights Further the Success of People Express and Mondragon* (Cambridge: Harvard University Freshman Seminar Program, January 21, 1986); J. Roland Pennock, ed., *Property* (New York: New York University Press, 1980); Richard Schlatter, *Private Property* (London: Unwin Brothers Ltd., 1951); Alvin D. Lurie, "The ESOP as Stockholder: Whose Business Is It Anyway?" *Journal of Pension Planning and Compliance* 11 (Summer 1985): 115–34.

30. Karl E. Klare, "Judicial Deradicalization of the Wagner Act and the Origins of Modern Legal Consciousness, 1937–1941," *Minnesota Law Review*, 1978: 266–339; Karl E. Klare, "Labor Law as Ideology: Toward A New Historiography of Collective Bargaining Law," *Industrial Relations Law Journal*, 1981: 450–82.

31. These additional protections were discussed recently in "Beyond Unions," *Business Week*, July 8, 1985: 2.

32. For example, the conversion of profit-sharing or pension plans to ESOPs happens in 35 percent and 7 percent of all ESOP companies, but it is almost twice as frequent in companies that are not unionized. Such conversions can constitute an abuse of employees' security and rights, so it is notable that they occur more where they are not subject to collective bargaining. ESOP Association, *ESOP Survey: 1985* (Washington, D.C.: ESOP Association of America, 1985), pp. 12–13, 19–23, 26–27.

33. See Thomas R. Marsh and Dale E. McAllister, "ESOP Tables: A Survey of Companies with Employee Stock Ownership Plans," *Journal of Corporation Law* 6, no. 3 (1981): 600; ESOP Association, *ESOP Survey: 1985*, p. 49; Bobbie McCrackin and Sandra Davis, "Employee Stock Ownership Plans: Economic Boon for the Southeast," *Economic Review of the Federal Reserve Board of Atlanta*, October 1983: 20–33; National Center for Employee Ownership, *Employee Ownership: A Handbook for Unions* (Oakland, Calif.: National Center for Employee Ownership, 1985e).

34. Discussed in National Center for Employee Ownership, *Employee Ownership: A Handbook for Unions*, pp. 62–66. See also James D. Hutchinson, "Employee Stock Ownership Plans: A New Tool in the Collective Bargaining Inventory," *American University Law Review* 26 (1977): 536–68; and Deborah Groban Olson, "Union Experiences with Worker Ownership: Legal and Practical Issues Raised by ESOPs, TRASOPs, Stock Purchases and Cooperatives," *Wisconsin Law Review*, 1982, no. 5: 785 (this excellent article is required reading on problems of conflict of interest under the NLRA, unions' problems of fair representation, and conflicts of interest under the Landrum-Griffin act and antitrust laws).

35. Olson, "Union Experiences," p. 786.

36. *Ibid.*, pp. 787–88.

37. *Ibid.*, pp. 800–808.

38. *Ibid.*, p. 782, n. 280.

39. *Ibid.*, pp. 780–91. Quote is on p. 781, n. 279. See Olson's article for extensive citations of the NLRB cases.

40. Stephen Schlossberg and Steven Fetter, U.S. *Labor Laws and the Future of Labor-Management Cooperation: First Interim Report* (Washington, D.C.: U.S. Department of Labor, 1987). Several important contributions on this problem exist; see Donna Sockell, "The Legality of Employee Participation Programs in Unionized Firms," *Industrial and Labor Relations Review* 37 (1984): 541–55; Katie Miller and Lisa Schur, "Quality of Worklife Programs: An Analysis of Legal Issues and Case Materials (unpublished manuscript, Northeastern University School of Law, Boston, Massachusetts, 1986).

41. This section draws heavily on Gerald E. Frug, "The Ideology of Bureaucracy in American Law," *Harvard Law Review* 97, no. 6 (April 1984): 1277–1388. Full citations for authors referred to here can be found in Frug's article.

42. Personal communication from anonymous source, March 1984.

43. Quarrey, Blasi, and Rosen, *Taking Stock*.

44. Williams, "Buyouts Made with ESOPs," p. 35.

45. Michael Brody, "Helping Workers to Work Smarter," *Fortune*, June 8, 1987: 87.

Chapter 7: Labor-Management Cooperation

1. Eileen McCarthy and Corey Rosen, *Employee Ownership in the Grocery Industry* (Oakland, Calif.: National Center for Employee Ownership, May 1987), pp. 25–28.

2.   Steven Prokesch, "Labor Policy Aids Miller Furniture," *New York Times*, August 14, 1986; Robert Levering, Milton Moskowitz, and Michael Katz, *The Hundred Best Companies to Work for in America* (New York: New American Library, 1985), pp. 223–26.

3.   Deborah Groban Olson, *Republic Container: Case Study* (Detroit, Mich.: Michigan Employee Ownership Center, 1985).

4.   Levering, Moskowitz, and Katz, *The Hundred Best Companies*, pp. 295–99.

5.   John Hoerr, "The New Industrial Relations," *Business Week*, May 11, 1981: 2.

6.   See Russell Long, "Expanded Ownership—Its Importance to the Free Enterprise System," *Congressional Record* 127, no. 50 (March 27, 1981): n.p.; *Ibid.*, "S. 1162—Expanded Ownership Act of 1981," *Congressional Record* 127, no. 72 (May 12, 1981): n.p.; *Ibid.*, "An Ownership Approach to Productivity," *Congressional Record* 127, no. 115 (July 28, 1981): n.p.; *Ibid.*, "Employee Stock Ownership: A New Approach to Productivity," *Congressional Record* 129, no. 63 (May 10, 1983a); n.p.

7.   See Keith Bradley and Alan Gelb, *Worker Capitalism: The New Industrial Relations* (Cambridge, Mass.: MIT Press, 1983).

8.   See Rosabeth Moss Kanter, *Men and Women of the Corporation* (New York: Basic Books, 1983).

9.   Lecture notes from course given by John Dunlop at Harvard University during the fall semester of 1985.

10. Edward Cohen-Rosenthal, "Orienting Labor-Management Cooperation toward Revenue and Growth," *National Productivity Review*, Autumn 1985: 385–86.

11. New York Stock Exchange, *People and Productivity: A Challenge to Corporate America* (New York: New York Stock Exchange, 1982).

12. Bradley and Gelb, *Worker Capitalism*; Henk Thomas and Chris Logan, *Mondragon: An Economic Analysis* (London: George Allen & Unwin, 1982); Joseph Raphael Blasi, Perry Mehrling, and William Foote Whyte, "Environmental Influences in the Growth of Worker Ownership and Control," in Frank Heller et al., *The International Yearbook of Organizational Democracy* (Sussex, England: John Wiley & Sons, 1984), pp. 289–313; William Foote Whyte and Kathleen King Whyte, *The Making of Mondragon* (Ithaca, N.Y.: ILR Press, forthcoming in 1988).

13. Menachem Rosner, *Democracy, Equality, and Change: The Kibbutz and Social Theory* (Norwood, Pa.: Norwood Editions, 1982), pp. 61–80.

14. Additional kibbutz data drawn from Joseph Raphael Blasi, *The Communal Experience of the Kibbutz* (New Brunswick, N.J.: Transaction Books, 1986).

15. See Rosner, *Democracy, Equality, and Change*; A. S. Tannenbaum, B. Karcic, M. Rosner, M. Vianello and G. Weiser, *Hierarchy in Organizations* (San Francisco: Jossey-Bass, 1974).

16. Corey Rosen, Katherine Klein, and Karen Young, *Employee Ownership in America: The Equity Solution* (Lexington, Mass.: Lexington Books, 1986), pp. 112, 116, 127.

17. Corey Rosen, National Center for Employee Ownership, 1986 interview with author.

18. ESOP Association, *ESOP Survey: 1983* (Washington, D.C.: ESOP Association of America, 1983), pp. 48–51.

19. Michael Quarrey, Joseph Raphael Blasi, and Corey Rosen, *Taking Stock: Employee Ownership at Work* (Cambridge, Mass.: Ballinger Publishing, 1986).

20. These characteristics emerged in the National Center for Employee Ownership's study, *Employee Ownership in America: The Equity Solution*, as the best predictors of positive employee attitudes towards employee ownership. A number of these companies have been studied more closely by the center, and they are covered in *Taking Stock*. Nevertheless, extensive scientific study of this class of firms to examine labor-management cooperation and its impact on firm operations has not yet occurred.

21. Karen Young, *Beyond Taxes: Managing an Employee Ownership Company* (Oakland, Calif.: National Center for Employee Ownership, 1987).

22. This research, conducted mainly by scholars and students at Cornell and Harvard Universities and at the National Center for Employee Ownership, covers only a small number of firms, with the exception of the large study by the National Center for Employee Ownership. Many of these firms do not have ESOPs; indeed, most are the result of worker buyouts, which, as noted, represent a small percentage of ESOPs. Unionized firms are inordinately represented. Most of the studies have not tried to relate worker and management attitudes and behavior to economic performance. They have not looked closely at the structure of the employee ownership.

23. The Weirton case is largely drawn from Joseph Raphael Blasi, *Employee Ownership through ESOPs: Implications for the Public Corporation* (Scarsdale, N.Y.: Work in America Institute, 1987).

24. "Wage Concession Vote Expected in 2 Months," Steubenville, Ohio, *Herald-Star*, August 5, 1982, p. 1.

25. "Making Money—and History—at Weirton," *Business Week*, November 12, 1984: 138.

26. Interview with senior manager, November 1986.

27. Edward Lawler, *Pay and Organizational Effectiveness: A Psychological View* (New York: McGraw-Hill, 1971); Edward Lawler, "Reward Systems," in *Improving Life at Work*, ed. R. J. Hackman and J. R. Suttle (Santa Monica: Goodyear, 1977), pp. 163–226; and Edward Lawler, *Motivation in Work Organizations* (Belmont, Calif.: Brooks/Cole Publishing, 1973). The view of equity presented in this chapter draws heavily on M. J. Wallace and C. H. Fay, *Compensation Theory and Practice* (Boston: Kent Publishing, 1983); E. Walster, W. Walster, and E. Berscheid, *Equity: Theory and Research* (Boston: Allyn & Bacon, 1978); and Victor H. Vroom, *Work and Motivation* (New York: John Wiley & Sons, 1967). Powerful evidence that the incentive structure of most ESOPs prevents cooperation is found in Morton Deutsch's exhaustive review of research, *Distributive Justice: A Social Psychological Perspective* (New Haven: Yale University Press, 1985).

Chapter 8: Economic Performance

1. ESOP Association, *ESOP Profile: Katz Communications* (Washington, D.C.: ESOP Association of America, n.d.).

2. ESOP Association, *ESOP Profile: Brooks Camera* (Washington, D.C.: ESOP Association of America, n.d.).

3. ESOP Association, *ESOP Profile: Comsonics* (Washington, D.C.: ESOP Association of America, n.d.).

4. Science Applications International Corporation, *1987 Annual Report: Science Applications International Corporation* (San Diego, Calif.: Science Applications International Corporation, 1987); J. R. Beyster, *Managing An Employee Owned Company* (La Jolla, Calif.: Foundation for Enterprise Development, March 1987); *Idem., Principles and Practices of SAIC* (San Diego, Calif.: Science Applications International Corporation, n.d.).

5. All documents with Kelso's responses are in U.S. Congress, Joint Economic Committee, *Hearings on Employee Stock Ownership Plans* (Washington, D.C.: U.S. Government Printing Office, 1976), "December 11, 1975" (Part 1) and "December 12, 1975" (Part 2).

6. This conclusion was reached by Towers, Perrin, Foster and Crosby, Triad Financial Reports, and E. F. Hutton, in *Ibid*. (Part 1), pp. 49–73, and by Julius Allen, *The Kelso*

Plan (Washington, D.C.: Library of Congress, Congressional Research Service, October 24, 1974), pp. 73–76. All of these disadvantages have been minimized by the new ESOP tax incentives since 1976.

7.   See Steven Bloom, *Employee Ownership and Firm Performance* (Cambridge: Harvard University Department of Economics, 1986), pp. 93–110, for the references in economic literature.

8.   Hans Brems, in U.S. Congress, Joint Economic Committee, *Hearings on Employee Stock Ownership Plans* (Part 1), pp. 521–38, 552–67; Paul A. Samuelson, "Thoughts on Profit-sharing," *Zeitschrift für die Gesamte Staatswissenschaft Special Issue on Profit-sharing*, 1977. Also in U.S. Congress, Joint Economic Committee, *Hearings on Employee Stock Ownership Plans* (Part 1), see testimony of Georgetown University economics professor, Gerard M. Brannon, pp. 539–46, and Harvard University economics professor, Richard Musgrave, pp. 6–8.

9.   Senator Russell Long, "Expanded Ownership—Its Importance to the Free Enterprise System," *Congressional Record* 127, no. 50 (March 27, 1981): n.p.

10. I am indebted to Douglas Kruse for a memorandum on labor productivity, on which this section is based.

11. Statement of Senator Russell Long in U.S. Congress, Senate Select Committee on Small Business, *S. 388, Hearings on the Small Business Employee Ownership Act, February 27, 1979* (Washington, D.C.: U.S. Government Printing Office, 1979), pp. 128–35. Senator Long's remarks were followed by wholehearted agreement by Senator S. I. Hayakawa (R-Calif.) and other senators. See also Long, "Expanded Ownership"; *Idem.*, "The Success of Employee Stock Ownership," *Congressional Record* 127, no. 57 (April 7, 1981); *Idem.*, "Employee Ownership and Productivity," *Congressional Record* 127, no. 187 (December 15, 1981); *Idem.*, "Employee Stock Ownership: A New Approach to Productivity," *Congressional Record* 129, no. 63 (May 10, 1983a).

12. Bloom, *Employee Ownership*, pp. 116–24, 129–213, 247–58.

13. U.S. General Accounting Office, *ESOPs: Little Evidence of Effects of Corporate Performance* (Washington, D.C: U.S. General Accounting Office, October 1987), GAO-PEMD–88–1.

14. Michael Quarrey, *Employee Ownership and Corporate Performance* (Oakland, Calif.: National Center for Employee Ownership, October 1986).

15. Alfred Steinherr, "The Labor-Managed Economy: A Survey of the Economics Literature," *Annals of Public and Cooperative Economy* 49, no. 2(April–June 1978): 129–61. See also Erik G. Furubotn, *The Economics of Industrial Democracy: An Analysis of Labor Participation in the Management of Business Firms* (College Station, Tex.: Center for Education and Research in Free Enterprise, Texas A & M University, 1979); *Idem.*, "The Long-run Analysis of the Labor-Managed Firm," *American Economic Review* 66, no. 1 (March 1976): 104–24; *Idem.*, "Co-determination and the Efficient Partitioning of Ownership Rights in the Firm," *Journal of Institutional and Theoretical Economics* 137, no. 4 (December 1981): 702–9; Jaroslav Vanek, *The General Theory of Labor-Managed Market Economies* (Ithaca, N.Y.: Cornell University Press, 1970); Jaroslav Vanek, *The Participatory Economy: An Evolutionary Hypothesis and a Strategy for Development* (Ithaca, N.Y.: Cornell University Press, 1971); and Derek C. Jones and Jan Svejnar, *Participatory and Self-Managed Firms: Evaluating Economic Performance* (Lexington, Mass.: Lexington Books, 1982). Jones and Svejnar also edit a new series on this topic, *Advances in the Economic Analysis of Participatory and Labor-Managed Firms*, (Greenwich, Conn.: JAI Press); the first volume appeared in 1985.

16. Timothy C. Jochim, *Employee Stock Ownership and Related Plans: Analysis and Practice* (Westport, Conn.: Quorum Books,1982), pp. 36–53, gives balance sheets for these scenarios. Depending on what kinds of ESOPs are used in the research sample and how long the ESOPs have been in existence when data is taken, profitability studies

will always be biased because of the tax subsidy. In addition, all of these computations are inaccurate in light of new ESOP tax incentives since 1982.

17. Most of the ESOPs examined in Quarrey, Blasi, and Rosen, *Taking Stock*, had profit-sharing plans.

18. ESOP Association, *ESOP Survey: 1985* (Washington, D.C.: ESOP Association of America, 1985), pp. 30–31.

19. U.S. Congress, Joint Economic Committee, *Hearings on Employee Stock Ownership Plans* (Part 1), p. 202.

20. *Ibid.* (Part 2), p. 692.

21. Corey Rosen, Katherine Klein, and Karen Young, *Employee Ownership in America: The Equity Solution* (Lexington, Mass.: Lexington Books,1986).

22. These findings are not very different from historical studies of employee stock ownership. See Robert Stern and Philip Comstock, *Employee Stock Ownership Plans: Benefits For Whom?* (Ithaca, N.Y.: ILR Press, 1978); Robert F. Foerster and Else H. Dietel, *Employee Stock Ownership in the United States* (Princeton, N.J.: Princeton University Press, 1926); National Industrial Conference Board, *Employee Stock Purchase Plans in the United States* (New York: National Industrial Conference Board, 1928); Eleanor Davis, *Employee Stock Ownership and the Depression* (Ann Arbor, Mich.: Edwards Brothers, 1933).

23. Recently, the U.S. Congressional Budget Office enumerated the extent of this policy in two studies, *Federal Support of U.S. Business* (Washington, D.C.: U.S. Government Printing Office, January 1984) and *Federal Financial Support for High-Technology Industries* (Washington, D.C.: U.S. Government Printing Office, June 1985).

24. Internal Revenue Service, *Statistics of Income and Corporation Income Tax Returns* (Washington, D.C.: U.S. Government Printing Office, 1978–1982).

25. This section relies substantially on Marc Levinson, "The Shaky Case for Aiding Investment," *Dun's Business Month*, March 1986: 22–24; Alan Murray, "Investment Incentives Lose Political Appeal, House Tax Bill Shows," *Wall Street Journal*, December 11, 1985, p. 1; Robert S. McIntyre and Dean C. Tipps, "Exploding the Investment Incentive Myth," *Challenge*, May/June 1985: 47–52.

26. McIntyre and Tipps, "Exploding the Investment Incentive Myth," pp. 47–48.

27. Robert Heilbroner and Lester Thurow, *Economics Explained* (New York: Simon & Schuster, 1982), p. 74.

Chapter 9: Conclusion and Policy Recommendations

1. The author has prepared a detailed financial and human-resource strategy for carrying out such restructures, which offers the publicly held firm the option of remaining public or going completely private. See Joseph Raphael Blasi, "Flexible Compensation and Restructuring the Publicly Held Corporation" (unpublished paper, California Polytechnic School of Business, San Luis Obispo, California, Fall 1987).

2. Personal communication to the author, January 1987.

3. Presidental Task Force on Economic Justice, *High Road to Economic Justice: U.S. Encouragement of Employee Stock Ownership in Central America and the Caribbean* (Washington, D.C.: Center for Economic and Social Justice, October 1986).

Index

ABOUT THE AUTHOR

Joseph Raphael Blasi is perhaps the most widely quoted commentator on employee ownership. His ideas have been widely discussed in the *Wall Street Journal*, *Business Week*, *Newsweek*, and *Time* as well as on CNN's *Money Line*. He is a Professor at the Institute of Management and Labor Relations, Rutgers University in New Brunswick, New Jersey. Blasi taught for many years at Harvard University and wrote this book while a visiting researcher at the Harvard Business School. He has been an adviser to many large corporations, labor unions, employee buyout groups, and governmental bodies, including Polaroid and Avis.